AF265823

Combining the wisdom of the Bible with a clear, strategic, step-by-step guide to how our brains work, Maureen Chiana has written a book that has the potential to change your life. This powerful tool will challenge and free you to become the person you were created to be.

- **Vivien Johnson,** Finance Director, Innovation Software Ltd

Some books inform, others inspire, but few truly transform. This devotional, structured uniquely into twelve sections for each month of the year, promises not just inspiration but a journey of growth, renewal, and self-discovery. As I read through the outline, I was struck by the profound potential of this work. My first thought? Can't I just do this all in one month? Why do I have to wait for month 7 to learn how to let go of the past, when my transformation beckons now?

Unlike any devotional I've encountered, this one does not just include scripture reading paired with exercises. It is a fusion of spirituality, practicality, and science. Through the lens of neuroscience, it delves into how our brains work and—remarkably—how we can train them. The concept of neuroplasticity is woven throughout, offering practical strategies to rewire the mind, much like exercising to build muscles. This enables us to break free from limits and unlock our true potential.

What sets this devotional apart is its practical application. The daily exercises are not just routines; they are action steps that bring faith to life. From the anecdotes of real-life challenges and triumphs to the science-backed insights on brain health, every page brims with wisdom and encouragement.

The book's central message is anchored in trusting God as our Shepherd. As Maureen beautifully explains, "Like sheep, we don't always know the way to go, but the Shepherd does." By staying rooted in God, we are equipped to flourish. With faith as our foundation, we can rewire our brains to embrace growth, adaptability, and resilience.

Some of the most eye-opening lessons revolve around neuroscience. I learned that stepping into uncertainty helps our brains form new neural pathways, fostering resilience and adaptability. Conversely, negative self-talk activates fear centres in the brain, limiting our potential. But through faith, neuroplasticity, and neurogenesis (the creation of new neurons), we can build resilience, improve health, and transform our minds.

The book likens life to a road trip: Our vehicle (life circumstances, families, etc.) may be given beforehand, but our route is shaped by our choices. Decisions determine destiny, and intentional living helps us align with our divine purpose. Ephesians 5:15 urges us to "be very careful how you live," a reminder that life's transformation requires focus, discipline, and action.

I also loved the insights on kindness. Acts of kindness are not just good for the soul; they stimulate neurotransmitters like serotonin and dopamine, releasing

"feel-good" hormones that reduce stress, enhance mood, and
improve overall well-being. These moments of kindness reflect the beauty of faith
in action.

Each day's reading left me nodding in agreement, sometimes pausing to reread
the overflowing nuggets of wisdom. This devotional challenges readers to stretch
their boundaries, live with intention and rehearse their future selves. By doing
so, our brains adapt, making the journey of transformation not just possible but
exhilarating.

This book is for those who hunger for deeper fulfilment and purpose. It calls us to
multiply the talents God has entrusted to us, shift boundaries, and align our lives
with His higher plan. It isn't just a book; it's a roadmap for spiritual, mental, and
emotional transformation.

As I embark on this journey in the new year, I am filled with excitement for the
new dimensions of life and faith that await me. If you're ready to grow, adapt, and
thrive, this devotional, like none other, should be your guide.

- **Chidi Onyemelukwe**

REWIRE YOUR BRAIN

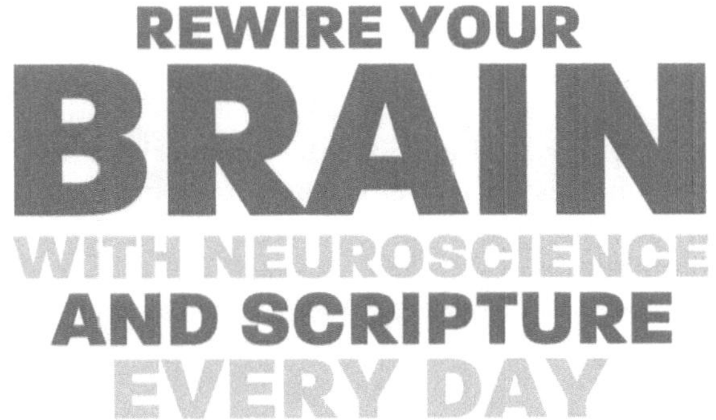

WITH NEUROSCIENCE AND SCRIPTURE EVERY DAY

by

Maureen C. Chiana

Reclaim Your Identity, Master Your Emotions and Unlock Success Daily

The Mindsight Academy
Publishing

Copyright © 2024 Maureen C. Chiana MSc. All rights reserved.

No part of this publication may be reproduced, distributed, or transmitted in any form or by any means, including photocopying, recording, or other electronic or mechanical methods, without the prior written permission of the publisher, except in the case of brief quotations used in critical reviews or articles, which must provide proper attribution to the author.

For permissions, enquiries, or additional resources, please contact: The Mindsight Academy - enquiries@themindsightacademy.com

Scripture Acknowledgment
Scripture quotations are taken from the following versions unless otherwise indicated:

New International Version (NIV): Scripture quotations taken from the Holy Bible, New International Version®. NIV®. Copyright © 1973, 1978, 1984, 2011 by Biblica, Inc.® Used by permission. All rights reserved worldwide.
King James Version (KJV): Public domain.
New King James Version (NKJV): Scripture taken from the New King James Version®. Copyright © 1982 by Thomas Nelson. Used by permission. All rights reserved.
English Standard Version (ESV): Scripture quotations are from The Holy Bible, English Standard Version® (ESV®), copyright © 2001 by Crossway, a publishing ministry of Good News Publishers. Used by permission. All rights reserved.
The Passion Translation (TPT): Scripture quotations from The Passion Translation®. Copyright © 2017, 2018 by BroadStreet Publishing® Group, LLC. Used by permission. All rights reserved. ThePassionTranslation.com.

Published by The Mindsight Academy Publishing, United Kingdom

ISBNs:
Paperback: 978-1-0683170-0-2
Hardcover: 978-1-0683170-1-9
eBook: 978-1-0683170-2-6

First Edition: 2024

Cover and interior design by Chidubem Lawrence Aniemenam, Creative Mind.

Disclaimer

This book is designed to provide educational and inspirational content on the subjects discussed. It is not intended as a substitute for professional advice in medical, psychological, legal, financial, or other fields. Readers should seek professional guidance for their specific needs. The author and publisher assume no liability for actions taken based on the content of this book.

To protect privacy, names, personal details, and situations in any stories or examples used in this book have been adapted or fictionalised, unless otherwise noted.

You can learn more about how Maureen Chinyere transforms lives by combining neuroscience, emotional intelligence, and scripture at www.themindsightacademy.com.

Visit Maureen's bio page at -
https://www.themindsightacademy.com/pages/about-maureen.

You can connect with Maureen on:
◊ LinkedIn @maureenchiana and
◊ Facebook at https://www.facebook.com/maureen.chiana

For information about special discounts for bulk purchases, please contact:
maureen@themindsightacademy.com

To Almighty God,
The author and finisher of my faith,
The source of every good gift,
The One who has walked with me through valleys and lifted me to soar on wings like eagles.
This book is a testament to Your unending grace, love, and faithfulness.
May every word in these pages glorify You and inspire others to draw closer to You.
With all my heart, I dedicate this work to You, Lord.

To my beloved mum, Hannah Amuma Ekwueme,
Who brought me up to know and love God. Your unwavering faith and deep love for God were a guiding light in my life. You not only taught me how much God loves me but also inspired me to develop a personal relationship with Him. Through your life, you demonstrated the power of faith and love in action.
Mum, your legacy of faith lives on in me, and this book is a reflection of the seeds you planted in my heart. I honour and cherish the profound impact you've had on my journey with God.

With gratitude and love,
Maureen Chinyere

ACKNOWLEDGMENTS

This devotional guide is a testimony to God's unfailing love and faithfulness. Without Him, none of this would have been possible. Every word, every thought, and every insight comes from His grace, and I pray that this book draws you closer to Him, the ultimate source of wisdom, strength, and transformation. Thank You, Lord, for guiding and walking with me through every step of this journey, for holding me up when I felt weary, and for inspiring me to share what You have placed on my heart.

To my beloved husband, Dede: You have been my unwavering rock and my greatest cheerleader. Your steadfast support, boundless patience, and unshakable belief in my calling have given me the strength and courage to keep moving forward. I am deeply grateful for you. To my children, Peter and David, thank you for your unwavering love and support, even as I poured myself into this work. You continue to be my greatest blessings and a source of endless joy and pride. I pray that this guide inspires you to embrace your own journeys with the same passion and faith that you inspire in me every day.

To my dear family and friends—too many to name—you are such a vital part of my journey. Thank you for your prayers, encouragement, and constant reminders of God's goodness. Your love and friendship have been a gift, and your belief in me has lifted me in more ways than you'll ever know. You have been a reflection of God's grace, and I am forever grateful for each one of you.

To the women of **The Mindsight Women's Network**, thank you for trusting me to walk alongside you on your journey of faith and growth. Your stories, your courage, and your commitment to becoming all God has called you to be have deeply inspired me. This guide was written with you in mind, and I pray it blesses you as much as you have blessed me.

To everyone who has spoken into my life, whether through a kind word, a prayer, or a moment of wisdom, thank you. Your contributions have woven into the fabric of this book, and I am forever grateful. A heartfelt thank you to my incredible graphics designer, Dubem, for your exceptional talent and patience throughout this journey—I truly appreciate your dedication and creativity.

Finally, to you, the reader, thank you for allowing me to share this journey with you. My prayer is that this guide helps you draw closer to God, discover His purpose for your life, and live each day in His abundance and grace. May you soar higher in His strength and rest in His peace.

With love and gratitude,

Maureen

FOREWORD

Maureen and I have been friends for over 50 years, and I am thrilled to have been chosen to write this foreword.

Over the years, I have witnessed Maureen's growth as she has evolved into the mature, wise, and God-fearing woman she is today. She is an example of the good seed that fell onto good soil in the parable of the Sower. She has thrived under harsh climate conditions to bear much fruit, proving once again how deeply rooted she is in Almighty God. She exemplifies the quote, "All things work out for the good of those who love God and who are called according to His purpose." This book is one of the many "fruits" she has produced by His Grace. The book is an act of obedience to Our Father and will honour Him, as the truth and knowledge shared here will certainly bring healing and growth to the many who read it.

Maureen is an established entrepreneur whose vast and varied career and experience span the scientific, medical, education, and IT sectors.

Her professional steps and career choices were indeed ordered by God the Father. Each challenge, opportunity, success, or setback was a necessary stepping stone in a journey culminating in this book.

This book is not your typical self-help book. These types of books can identify and recognize your issues but don't really offer any practical or convincing tools to promote sustainable change. And if, as a Christian, you have found yourself constantly trying to start a new project, open a new business or even adopt better eating habits, then this book is certainly for you.

You may also have committed these plans to prayer, yet you still have not made any significant progress, or you may find yourself pushing them off to "tomorrow." If that is you (like "me"), then this daily guide is the solution. In fact, consider it part of your answered prayer!

Maureen's approach will literally transform you from day to day as you work through the guide. Maureen provides real physiological and scientific reasons supported by scripture that may potentially be holding you back from fulfilling your God-ordained mandate.

Each daily entry offers a holistic approach to addressing the vast array of issues that prevent us from moving forward with our plans.

She skillfully navigates the scientific reasons for current mindsets, which often result in self-sabotage, and intersperses corresponding reference scripture to support her prognosis.

She identifies the "why" and then prescribes the treatment- a multi-dimensional application to address the physiological, mental and spiritual components of the issue. The goal is to reset and rewire our minds for success. You will be amazed to learn that the process of forming new habits is underpinned by the formation of new neuro pathways in the brain! The most fascinating part is that the "science" is supported by scripture, too, and as you go through your daily readings, you will see where Maureen makes the connection for you.

You will find yourself eagerly looking forward to your next daily offering, building on the knowledge, tools, and techniques you have already gained from prior daily readings. You will realize your strengths and capabilities, thus gaining confidence. You will move forward to embrace your mandate and recognize that you are indeed limitless!

Grace Ume
Author of Embrace With His Grace: *A Personal Testimony on How to Deal with the Good, the Bad, and the Ugly in Life*

CONTENTS

PART ONE

THE FOUNDATION OF POSITIVE THINKING

PART TWO

RENEW AND REWIRE – THE PATH TO MENTAL MASTERY

PART THREE

UNLOCKING THE POWER OF YOUR BRAIN

PART FOUR

BECOME LIMITLESS

PART FIVE

SELF DISCOVERY

PART SIX

EMOTIONAL INTELLIGENCE UNLOCKED

PART SEVEN

LETTING GO OF THE PAST

PART EIGHT

TURN YOUR DREAMS INTO REALITY

PART NINE

ELEVATING YOUR RELATIONSHIPS

PART TEN

NEUROLEADERSHIP: UNLOCKING CAREER AND BUSINESS SUCCESS

PART ELEVEN

LIVING A FULFILLED AND PURPOSEFUL LIFE

PART TWELVE

REFLECT, RECHARGE, AND MOVE FORWARD

CONCLUSION

SOURCES

FURTHER READING OR RESOURCES

INTRODUCTION

You Are Not Stuck, and I Am Proof

"Your past is only a chapter, not the whole story. True transformation begins the moment you renew your mind and embrace the limitless potential within you—a gift from God to fulfil His purpose." — Maureen Chinyere Chiana

"Chinyere," my Nigerian Igbo name, means "God's gift." I believe, with all my heart, that I am a gift from God to this world—called to help people unlock their limitless potential and live in alignment with His purpose. I have experienced firsthand the power of transformation, and I am here to help you step into that same freedom.

Have you ever felt stuck—like no matter how hard you try, you just can't break free from cycles of frustration, doubt, or unfulfilled dreams? Perhaps you start projects with excitement but lose momentum, struggle with imposter syndrome, or question your worth. Maybe you feel disconnected from your purpose, constantly wondering what's next and unsure how to move forward.

If any of this resonates with you, pause for a moment and reflect: What's one area in your life where you feel stuck? Hold onto that thought, because together, we're going to unravel it. Let me assure you that you are not stuck and that you are not alone. This book will guide you to renew your mind, embrace your God-given potential, and step boldly into the life of freedom and purpose you were created for.

My journey is a testament to resilience, transformation, and unwavering faith. In 2010, I developed severe sciatica and back pain due to two prolapsed discs. I was scheduled for surgery, but I made a bold decision to put my faith in God and put the concept of neuroplasticity into practice for my healing. Over time, I not only avoided surgery, but I also experienced complete recovery and have had no back issues since. However, I've learned to pay close attention to my body, ensuring I don't overdo things and maintaining regular exercise to stay healthy. This experience cemented my belief in the power of God's word and the mind's ability to heal.

I began my entrepreneurial career by founding Evania Hair & Beauty, a pioneering Afro hair and beauty salon in Kent. It gained widespread recognition for its innovation and excellence, featured on platforms like the BBC and ITV. Yet, after four years, I was faced with the painful decision to close the business. This loss was compounded just three months later when I lost my mother, my anchor and greatest supporter. The grief was overwhelming. I felt as though my world had fallen apart, and I struggled with feelings of failure and despair.

One day, as I poured out my heartbreak to God, something caught my attention on a Christian TV channel. Dr. Caroline Leaf was talking about a question that changed everything for me: "Who switched off your brain?" Intrigued, I listened closely as she explained the profound connection between the brain and behaviour. That moment sparked a transformative journey of discovery.

I immersed myself in the study of neuroscience, learning about the brain's incredible ability to heal, adapt, and grow—a concept called neuroplasticity. This was a revelation: Science confirmed what scripture had been saying all along: We have the power to renew our minds (Romans 12:2) and rewire our thoughts to create new, God-ordained possibilities.

With this new understanding, I did not only begin healing but also found my purpose. In 2009, I began speaking globally, sharing the transformative principles of neuroscience, emotional intelligence (EQ), and scripture. I have since had the privilege of speaking in countries across the world, working with corporate leaders, entrepreneurs, churches and faith-filled women to help them achieve extraordinary results.

In 2015, I ventured back into business, founding what is now The Mindsight Academy, where I combine neuroscience, emotional intelligence and leadership training with neurocoaching to help professionals elevate their decision-making, emotional intelligence, and performance. By integrating the brain-mind-body connection, my work empowers leaders and entrepreneurs to break mental barriers, build resilience, and thrive. I've had the honour of supporting top organisations such as NHS UK,University of Kent, UK, Johnson & Johnson, and Siemens Healthineers, bringing these principles to life in corporate environments.

In 2023, I launched The Mindsight Women's Network (MWN), a nurturing community where faith, neuroscience, and emotional intelligence merge to empower women. MWN is more than a network; it is a sanctuary where women are equipped to break barriers, overcome obstacles, and embrace their God-given purpose with courage and conviction. Through mentorship, neurocoaching, workshops, and collaborative initiatives, MWN fosters a ripple effect of positive change as women learn to thrive in their homes, businesses, communities, and workplaces.

The lessons I've learned along this journey are the foundation of this book. Within these pages, you'll find tools and insights to help you break free from limiting beliefs, understand and harness your emotions, and live a life of limitless possibilities. This book combines neuroscience, emotional intelligence, and scripture to guide you through a journey of transformation.

Repetition is key to rewiring the brain. As you revisit concepts and apply them in your daily life, your neural pathways will strengthen, enabling real and lasting change. This guide's daily structure is designed to encourage that process, so even if some ideas are repeated, remember that repetition is an essential part of the transformation.

Each day includes practical exercises, reflective questions, and actionable tips to help you apply what you learn. These are more than just activities—they are opportunities to integrate new patterns of thinking and behaving into your life. Commit to practicing these exercises intentionally; they will deepen your understanding and help you move closer to the freedom and purpose God has for you.

To protect privacy, names, details, and situations in the stories and examples shared throughout this book have been adapted or fictionalized unless otherwise noted. These stories are designed to illustrate key principles while respecting the confidentiality of the individuals involved.

It's also important to acknowledge that neuroscience is a continually evolving field. As new discoveries emerge, our understanding deepens, and the possibilities for transformation expand. This book reflects the knowledge and insights available at the time of writing, grounded in scripture, science, and personal experience.

Finally, I'm excited to share that an accompanying workbook to this guide will be available soon. It will provide additional exercises and resources to support you on your journey of transformation. Stay connected with me through The Mindsight Academy website for updates and more tools to help you soar higher.

I want you to know that you are not defined by your past, failures, or circumstances. God has created you with the ability to renew your mind, and in doing so, you can transform your life.

This is your opportunity to rise above the limits that have held you back and to soar higher—living a life of freedom, purpose, and abundance.

Let's take this journey together.

Maureen

PART ONE

THE FOUNDATION OF POSITIVE THINKING

PART 1 INTRODUCTION

In this first part, you'll focus on building a strong mindset through positive thinking.

Over the next 30 days, you'll learn how your thoughts influence your emotions, behaviours, and overall outlook on life.
Simple, practical steps—like practising gratitude, reframing challenges, and embracing self-compassion—will help you create lasting change.

Drawing from scripture and science, this section guides you in transforming your thought patterns, helping you cultivate resilience, confidence, and a more joyful, purposeful life.

Day 1: The Power of Thoughts

"Thoughts are energy, and you can make your world or break your world by your thinking."—Susan Taylor

Understanding how your thoughts impact your behaviour and actions will transform your life. Your thoughts determine your reality, influencing your emotions, behaviour, and perspectives. Proverbs 23:7 (NKJV) says, *"For as he thinks in his heart, so is he,"* highlighting that our thoughts determine who we become and how we experience things.

Imagine how empowering it would be to begin your day with a powerful affirmation, such as, *"I am fully capable and incredibly strong."* This simple statement can uplift your spirit and positively impact your life.

My client Mary often doubted her abilities at work, which caused her to feel overwhelmed and stressed. However, as she actively practised positive thinking and consistently reaffirmed her identity in Christ, her confidence gradually grew. She also started acknowledging and embracing her own strengths. Through a shift in mindset, she improved her performance and overcame obstacles, leading to recognition for her work. This shows the transformative power positive thinking can have in our lives.

Our brain's ability to rewire by focusing on positive thoughts and fostering a more optimistic and successful outlook on life is life-changing. Embracing our identity in Christ empowers us to live victoriously. Aligning our thoughts with the truth of God enables us to experience personal transformation, affirming that our thoughts shape our reality.

Practical Tips:
◊ Start a thought journal.
◊ Each day, write down your recurring thoughts.
◊ Identify which are empowering and which are limiting.
◊ Replace negative thoughts with positive ones, like *"I am learning and growing."*

Revisit these positive statements regularly.

DAY 2: THE CREATIVE POWER OF THOUGHT

"Thought is the first level of creation. If you don't like what you've just created, choose again." – Neale Donald Walsch

Our thoughts are powerful tools in shaping our reality. As Neale Donald Walsch highlights, every creation begins with a thought. In Genesis 1:3 (NIV), *"And God said, 'Let there be light,' and there was light,"* we see that God's words brought creation into existence. Likewise, our thoughts and words have the power to create our personal world.

When we focus on positive, constructive thoughts, we align ourselves with God's creative process, helping to bring the life we desire into reality.

Imagine starting your day with thoughts centred on what you want to create rather than what you fear. By consciously choosing positive thoughts that align with the outcomes you desire, you engage in a process of deliberate creation, much like how God created the universe with intention.

Practical Tips:
- ◊ Begin each day with a moment of reflection.
- ◊ Identify the thoughts you want to guide your day and write them down.
- ◊ If a negative thought arises, recognise it and replace it with a thought that aligns with the reality you wish to create.

Reflective Questions:
- » What thoughts are you allowing to shape your reality today?
- » How can you focus your thoughts on creating your desired life?
- » How does recognising your thoughts as the first step in creation change your approach to challenges?

By understanding that your thoughts are the foundation of your reality, you can harness them to create a life that reflects your highest aspirations and aligns with God's will for you.

DAY 3: EMBRACE POSSIBILITIES

"To change your life, you must first change your thinking." – Unknown

Genuine change starts with your mindset. Romans 12:2 (NIV) reminds us: "Do not conform to the pattern of this world, but be transformed by the renewing of your mind." This transformation begins with how we approach life's circumstances and possibilities.

Take Sarah, for example, who faced career setbacks. Instead of giving in to frustration, she changed her perspective, asking, *"What can I learn from this?"* This slight shift helped her discover new strengths and resilience, ultimately resulting in her achieving great career success.

When you focus on possibilities, something unique happens in your brain. Your brain is flexible and can change — a concept known as *neuroplasticity.* When you intentionally focus on new opportunities, your brain cells form new connections, helping you think more positively and be solution-focused. This rewiring creates a habit of seeing possibilities instead of obstacles, and over time, it makes you more open to growth and change.

Take a moment to imagine yourself in a challenging situation, like the demanding task of efficiently managing a bustling household or successfully tackling a complex assignment at your workplace. Instead of feeling overwhelmed, view these as opportunities to develop new skills or strengthen relationships. This mindset shift doesn't only reduce stress, but it also allows you to find more meaningful outcomes.

Practical Tips:
- ◊ Every morning, list three new possibilities for your day.
- ◊ Take small steps to pursue them. For instance, if you want to improve a skill, allocate time to practice.
- ◊ Reflect on your progress daily and celebrate your small wins.

By shifting your thinking to embrace new possibilities, you actively train your brain to thrive, unlocking a world of growth and potential.

DAY 4: THE BEGINNER'S MINDSET

"You can learn new things at any time in your life if you're willing to be a beginner." –
Barbara Sher

Embracing a beginner's mindset lets you stay curious, open to new experiences,
and ready to learn. This mindset drives personal and professional growth.

Consider Carol, who had suffered significant losses and ill health, leading her to
retire early from a job she loved. Feeling lost and unsure about her future, she
decided to learn to paint at the age of 55. Although initially afraid of failing, she
embraced the learning process with enthusiasm. Over time, her skills improved,
and she found a new passion that enriched her life. Her willingness to be a
beginner allowed her to discover a hidden talent that brought her immense joy and
a sense of fulfilment she had longed for.

Adopting a beginner's mindset can help you approach tasks with a fresh
perspective in everyday life. Whether you're learning a new technology at work
or trying a new recipe at home, being open to learning can enhance your creativity
and problem-solving abilities.

Practical Tips:

◊ Try something new today. It could be a new hobby, a different route to work, or
learning a new skill.
◊ Embrace the experience and enjoy learning.
◊ Then, take a moment to reflect on how this new experience makes you feel and
what you have learned from it.
◊ Reflection is a powerful tool for personal growth, and it can help you understand the value of a beginner's mindset in your life.

Reflective Questions:

» What new skill or activity have you been hesitant to try?
» How can adopting a beginner's mindset benefit your personal or professional
life?

What steps can you take today to embrace new learning opportunities?

Day 5: Reframe Your Challenges

"You cannot control your circumstances, but you can control your responses to those circumstances." - Lou Holtz

Life is full of challenges, but how we respond to them determines our growth and success. James 1:2-4 (NIV) encourages us, *"Consider it pure joy, my brothers and sisters, whenever you face trials of many kinds, because you know that the testing of your faith produces perseverance."* This scripture highlights that challenges can be growth opportunities that strengthen our character.

Imagine you face a sudden job loss. Initially, this might feel like a devastating setback. By reframing the situation, you can transform it into an opportunity to explore alternative career paths, develop new skills, and possibly even discover a job that aligns more with your passions and talents.

Consider Rachel, who was diagnosed with a chronic illness. Instead of succumbing to despair, she educated herself about her condition and advocated for her health. This proactive approach improved the quality of her life and also serves as an inspiration to others facing similar challenges.

Practical Tips:

◊ The next time you face a challenge, take a moment to reframe it.
◊ Ask yourself, *"What can I learn from this?"* and *"How can this situation help me grow?"*

Write down your thoughts and develop a plan of action to turn the challenge into an opportunity.

Day 6: The Importance of Gratitude

"Gratitude turns what we have into enough." – Anonymous

Gratitude is a powerful practice that can transform your perspective and life experience. 1 Thessalonians 5:18 (NIV) says, *"Give thanks in all circumstances, for this is God's will for you in Christ Jesus."*

Gratitude helps us focus on the positive aspects of our lives and acknowledge God's faithfulness even during difficult times.

It's as simple as starting each day with gratitude for the simple things—the warmth of the sun, the comfort of your home, and the love of your family. This slight shift in mindset can significantly improve mood, stress levels, and overall happiness. Scientific studies have shown that practising gratitude can enhance mental well-being and foster a positive outlook on life, empowering you to take control of your well-being.

Consider Laura, who started a daily gratitude practice during a challenging period in her life. Every evening, she wrote down three things she was grateful for. Over time, this practice helped her shift her focus from her problems to the blessings in her life, significantly improving her mental and emotional well-being.

Practical Tips:

◊ Start a gratitude journal.
◊ Each day, write down at least three things you are grateful for.
◊ Reflect on these entries regularly to cultivate a habit of gratitude.
◊ Share your gratitude with others by expressing appreciation for their kindness and support.

Reflective Questions:

» What are the three things you are grateful for today?
» How can practising gratitude shift your focus from problems to blessings?
» In what ways can you express gratitude to others?

Embracing gratitude aligns with God's will and opens our hearts to His blessings. It helps us to see beyond our struggles and recognise His provision and love in every circumstance.

Day 7: The Power of Positive Affirmations

"Affirmations are our mental vitamins, providing the supplementary positive thoughts we need to balance the barrage of negative events and thoughts we experience daily." – Tia Walker

Positive affirmations are powerful tools that can help reprogram your subconscious mind and promote a positive mindset. Philippians 4:8 (NIV) advises, *"Finally, brothers and sisters, whatever is true, whatever is noble, whatever is right, whatever is pure, whatever is lovely, whatever is admirable—if anything is excellent or praiseworthy—think about such things."* Focusing on positive thoughts can cultivate a healthier and more optimistic mindset.

Picture yourself preparing for a big presentation at work. Instead of allowing negative self-talk to undermine your confidence, use statements like *"I am well-prepared and confident"* or *"I have the skills and knowledge to succeed."* These positive statements can help reduce anxiety and boost your self-esteem.

My client Karen, who once struggled with low self-esteem. Through neurocoaching, she began using daily positive statements such as "I am worthy of love and respect" and "I am capable of achieving my goals."
These simple yet powerful affirmations gradually rewired her brain, transforming her narrative from feeling unworthy to recognising her true value.

This transformation helped her gain an 80% pay increase, showing how changing her mindset boosted her confidence and life satisfaction. Karen's story highlights the power of positive affirmations, offering hope to anyone looking to improve their mindset and self-esteem.

Practical Tips:

◊ Choose a few positive statements that resonate with you. Repeat them daily, preferably in front of a mirror.

◊ For example, you can say, *"I am strong and capable,"* or *"I am deserving of love and happiness."*

◊ Write these statements on sticky notes and place them in visible areas to reinforce positive thinking throughout the day.

Reflective Questions:

» What positive statements can you incorporate into your daily routine?
» How can focusing on positive thoughts improve your self-esteem and outlook on life?
» How will you consistently remind yourself of these positive daily affirmations?

Day 8: Embrace Self-Compassion

"Talk to yourself like you would to someone you love." – Brené Brown

Self-compassion involves treating yourself with the same kindness, care, and understanding you would offer to a good friend. Psalm 139:14 (NIV) reminds us, *"I praise you because I am fearfully and wonderfully made; your works are wonderful, I know that full well."* Recognising our inherent worth and treating ourselves with compassion is crucial for our mental and emotional well-being.

Imagine you made a mistake at work. Instead of condemning yourself, practice self-compassion by acknowledging your mistakes and understanding that everyone makes mistakes. Use kind and supportive language towards yourself, and focus on what you can learn from the experience.

Consider the story of Emily, who struggled with perfectionism. She constantly berated herself for not meeting her high standards. Emily had a habit of focusing on every minor mistake, which left her feeling stressed and inadequate. However, through a dedicated practice of self-compassion, she started to treat herself with the same kindness she extended to her friends. She began writing compassionate letters to herself, acknowledging her efforts and embracing her imperfections. This shift allowed Emily to see herself more positively, reducing her stress and increasing her resilience. Her performance improved, as she was no longer paralysed by the fear of making mistakes.

Practical Tips:

◊ Practice self-compassion by writing a compassionate letter to yourself.
◊ Reflect on a recent challenge or mistake, and write as if you were comforting a friend. Use kind and understanding words, and remind yourself that it's okay to be imperfect.
◊ Re-read this letter whenever you need a boost of self-compassion.

Reflective Questions:

» How do you typically respond to your mistakes?
» What steps can you take to practice more self-compassion?
» How might treating yourself with kindness change your approach to challenges?

Day 9: Setting Intentions

"Therefore I tell you, whatever you ask for in prayer, believe that you have received it, and it will be yours." - Mark 11:24 (NIV)

Setting clear intentions helps focus your energy and efforts on achieving specific goals. Intentions align your actions with your desires, paving the way for manifestation.
Assume you feel stuck in your career. Setting the intention to find a job that aligns with your passions and values will give you the clarity to identify opportunities, network effectively, and ultimately secure a fulfilling position. This clarity can help transform your career path and bring satisfaction and purpose to your work.

Setting intentions is not wishful thinking; it's about creating a focused action plan. When you set a clear intention, you define a specific outcome and prepare your mind to work towards it. This aligns with the biblical principle of faith and action, as described in Mark 11:24.

Imagine wanting to improve your physical health. By setting a clear intention, such as *"I intend to exercise three times a week and eat more nutritious foods to improve my health,"* - you create a roadmap for your actions.
This focused approach increases your chances of achieving your health goals.

Practical Tips:

◊ **Identify Your Intentions:** Start by identifying what you truly want. Write your intentions in a journal. Be specific about what you aim to achieve.

◊ **Visualisation:** Visualise the successful achievement of your intention. Spend a few minutes each day imagining reaching your goals.

◊ **Affirmative Statements:** Create positive statements that reinforce your intentions. For example, "I intend to find a job that fulfils me and aligns with my values."

◊ **Action Plan:** Break down your intention into actionable steps. What do you need to do each day to move closer to achieving your goal?

Reflective Questions:

» What are your current intentions, and how do they align with your goals?
» How can setting clear intentions help you achieve your desires?
» What steps can you take today to set and follow through on a powerful intention?

Day 10: Overcoming Fear

"Do not fear, for I am with you; do not be dismayed, for I am your God." – Isaiah 41:10 (NIV)

Fear is a natural emotion that can paralyse us if left unchecked. Isaiah 41:10 reassures us we are not alone and that God is with us, providing strength and courage. We can overcome obstacles and grow stronger in faith and resilience by confronting our fears.

Fear can manifest in many forms, such as fear of failure, rejection, or the unknown. These fears can prevent you from pursuing opportunities and achieving your divine potential. Neuroscience studies have shown that fear activates the amygdala, the brain's fear centre, which triggers the fight-or-flight response. While this response is essential for survival, chronic fear can hinder your growth and well-being.

Overcoming Fear: Imagine you have a fear of public speaking. This fear might prevent you from sharing your ideas or pursuing opportunities that require speaking in front of others. You can build confidence and reduce anxiety over time by acknowledging and gradually facing this fear—perhaps by starting with small group presentations.

My Personal Story: I was afraid to start my neuroleadership training and neurocoaching business after I had to close my previous business. The fear of failure and financial instability was overwhelming. However, I drew closer to God, immersed myself in the Word, and leveraged my knowledge of how the brain works. This spiritual and scientific approach provided the encouragement and guidance I needed. I learned to listen to God and His promises and chose to focus on what He said I could do, embracing the concept of being limitless. I overcame my fears and launched my business, gradually transforming fear into a source of strength and growth.

Practical Tips:

◊ Identify one fear that is holding you back.
◊ Break it down into smaller, manageable steps, and gradually face each step. For example, if you fear public speaking, start by speaking in front of a small, supportive group.
◊ Celebrate each milestone to build confidence and momentum.

Reflective Questions:

» What fear is currently holding you back?
» What actions can you take to break this fear into smaller, manageable steps?
» How can confronting this fear strengthen your faith and resilience?

Day 11: The Role of Faith

"Faith is taking the first step even when you don't see the whole staircase." – Martin Luther King Jr.

Faith involves trusting in a higher power and believing in the unseen. Hebrews 11:1 (NIV) defines faith as *"confidence in what we hope for and assurance about what we do not see."* This trust in God can reduce anxiety and provide a profound sense of peace and purpose, especially during uncertain times.

Faith can serve as a powerful anchor during life's storms. Faith and our belief in God positively impact the brain, enhancing mental resilience and overall well-being by activating areas involved in emotional regulation and stress relief.

Imagine embarking on a new career path without knowing exactly how it will turn out. With faith, you can trust that every step you take will bring you closer to your goal, even if the entire journey seems uncertain and unclear.

When I started my first business—a hair and beauty salon—I knew it was God's will but felt scared because of my lack of experience. Despite the fear and *"what if"* questions, I stepped out in faith, sought advice, researched, studied scripture, prayed, and took business training. I learned to listen to God, focus on His promises, and adopt a limitless mindset, turning my fear into strength and growth.

Practical Tips:

◊ Reflect on an area where you need to exercise more faith.
◊ Write down your hopes and aspirations, and pray or meditate on them daily.
◊ Trust that each step you take is guided and that you are being led towards your desired goal.
◊ Keep a journal of your journey to track how your faith grows and guides you through challenges.

Reflective Questions:

» How does faith affect your daily decisions and actions?
» What steps can you take to deepen your faith in uncertain areas of your life?
» How can you remind yourself of God's promises and faithfulness in your daily routine?

Embracing faith enables you to navigate uncertainties with confidence and peace, knowing that it will lead you to your desired goal.

Day 12: Embracing Change

"Change is the only constant in life." – Heraclitus

Life is full of changes, and learning to embrace them is crucial for growth. Ecclesiastes 3:1 (NIV) reminds us, *"There is a time for everything and a season for every activity under the heavens."* Change can bring new opportunities and experiences that enrich our lives.

Embracing change is essential for personal and professional development. Our brains naturally seek stability, but personal and professional development often requires stepping out of our comfort zones. Neuroplasticity allows our brains to adapt to new experiences and challenges, forming new neural (brain) connections that enhance our cognitive and emotional capacities.

Embracing change helps your brain learn and adapt better. This allows you to handle new situations with more ease. By accepting change, you boost your brain's flexibility, making it easier to overcome challenges and thrive in different environments.

John came to me when his company was undergoing a restructuring, and he was anxious about the impending change. Through neurocoaching, I helped him understand and reframe the negative narrative about the change. This helped calm his emotional brain, enabling him to think clearly and explore new opportunities. John applied for a senior role in a different department, secured the position, and is now thriving.

Practical Tips:

◊ Identify a recent change in your life and list the potential opportunities it presents.
◊ Focus on the positives and how you can grow from this change.
◊ Embrace the unknown by staying open to new experiences and learning from them.

Reflective Questions:

» What recent changes have you experienced, and how have they impacted your life?
» How can you shift your perspective to see change as an opportunity for growth?
» What steps can you take today to embrace and adapt to changes in your life?

By embracing change, you open yourself to new opportunities and experiences, fostering personal growth and resilience.

Day 13: The Gift of Patience

"Patience is the companion of wisdom." – Saint Augustine

Patience isn't just about waiting but about how we grow in the process.
Picture a seed you plant: you provide for it, but it takes time to sprout. Our lives mirror this process. During waiting times, we can learn, grow, and develop, just as a seed develops roots before it can sprout. Even in waiting, growth is happening.

Practising patience activates the prefrontal cortex in our brain, which plays a crucial role in managing impulses and regulating emotions. This reduces stress and enables thoughtful responses rather than impulsive reactions. Developing patience allows us to handle uncertainty with greater calm and resilience.

Trusting in God's timing is essential for spiritual growth. Proverbs 3:5-6 (NIV) says, *"Trust in the Lord with all your heart and lean not on your own understanding; in all your ways submit to Him, and He will make your paths straight."*
While waiting, you build character, gain wisdom, and strengthen your faith, knowing that God's timing is perfect.

Practical Tips:

◊ **Embrace Stillness:** Use quiet moments for reflection and prayer.
◊ **Practice Mindfulness:** View waiting as an opportunity for growth and self-discovery.
◊ **Affirm Trust:** Remember God's promises to stay patient and be at peace.

Reflective Questions:

» How do you manage your emotions during waiting periods?
» How have past waiting experiences contributed to your personal growth?
» In what ways can embracing patience enhance your well-being and faith?

Exercise: Identify something that you are currently waiting on in your life. Reflect on how embracing patience and trusting in God's timing can transform this experience.

Day 14: The Importance of Rest

"Come to me, all you who are weary and burdened, and I will give you rest." – Matthew 11:28 (NIV)

Rest is essential for our physical, mental, and spiritual well-being. Psalm 23:2-3 (NIV) says, *"He makes me lie down in green pastures, he leads me beside quiet waters, he refreshes my soul."* Taking time to rest and rejuvenate helps us to restore our energy and focus.

Imagine running a marathon without taking any breaks. Eventually, you would become exhausted and unable to continue.
Likewise, continuous work without rest leads to burnout and decreased productivity. Our brain needs regular breaks to function optimally. Studies in neuroscience highlight how rest can improve cognitive function and emotional regulation, enabling us to perform better in all aspects of life.

One key sign of the importance of resting was that God worked for six days and rested on the seventh. Since He made humans on the sixth day, humanity's first day of existence was a day of rest.
God is sharing a powerful truth here—our journey begins from a place of rest. It's a paradox, but we are always meant to work from a place of rest. Rest is the foundation of everything we are created to do.

Work from a place of rest, not rest from work!

Practical Tips:

- ◊ Schedule regular rest periods in your day, such as short breaks during work or a day off each week.
- ◊ Use this time to do activities that rejuvenate you, such as reading, walking, or spending time in nature.
- ◊ Prioritise sleep by establishing a consistent bedtime routine.

Reflective Questions:

- » How do you currently incorporate rest into your daily routine?
- » What activities help you feel rejuvenated and rested?
- » How can you make rest and self-care a regular part of your schedule?

By prioritising rest, you will improve your overall well-being, enhance productivity, and maintain a balanced and fulfilling life.

DAY 15: THE POWER OF WORDS

"The tongue has the power of life and death, and those who love it will eat its fruit."
– Proverbs 18:21 (NIV)

Our words hold immense power to build up or tear down. Ephesians 4:29 advises, *"Do not let any unwholesome talk come out of your mouths, but only what is helpful for building others up according to their needs, that it may benefit those who listen."* By choosing our words carefully, we can create positive and uplifting interactions. In everyday life, our words can significantly affect our relationships and well-being.

Neuroscience has shown positive language can enhance brain function and improve mental health. Positive words activate brain regions responsible for motivation and decision-making, such as the prefrontal cortex, promoting cognitive functions like problem-solving and planning. Conversely, negative or hostile language can activate the amygdala, the brain's centre for fear and stress responses, which can hinder cognitive processing and decision-making by flooding the brain with stress hormones like cortisol.
Understanding this helps us recognise the importance of choosing our words carefully. By cultivating the habit of using positive language, you enhance your mental well-being and create a supportive and constructive environment for those around you.

Consider Remi, a mother who struggled with her children's behaviour. She decided to focus on using positive, affirming language, praising their efforts and strengths. Over time, she noticed a significant improvement in their confidence and behaviour. Remi created a supportive home environment by intentionally choosing encouraging words, fostering her children's self-esteem and resilience.

Practical Tips:

◊ Pay attention to your words today.
◊ Aim to speak positively and avoid negative or harsh language.
◊ Practice gratitude and compliments in your interactions.
◊ Reflect on how your words affected your mood and relationships.

Reflective Questions:

» How do your words impact those around you?
» What steps can you take to ensure your language is positive and uplifting?
» How does speaking positively affect your own well-being and mindset?

By consciously choosing positive words, you can build stronger relationships and create a more supportive environment for yourself and others.

DAY 16: EMBRACING FORGIVENESS

"Forgive, and you will be forgiven." – Luke 6:37 (NIV)

Forgiveness is a powerful act that releases us from the burden of resentment and anger. Colossians 3:13 (NIV) encourages us to *"Bear with each other and forgive one another if any of you has a grievance against someone. Forgive as the Lord forgave you."* Forgiveness fosters healing and peace.

Allowing a grudge to persist against someone who has wronged you can lead to an emotional tension that extends beyond its original source, affecting various aspects of your life, such as relationships, mood, and overall well-being. This unresolved resentment can foster negativity, increase stress, and hinder your ability to move forward. Releasing a grudge frees you from the emotional weight, allowing you to experience inner peace, healthier connections with others, and a more positive outlook on life.

Letting go of grudges promotes mental and emotional well-being, bringing clarity and balance into your daily life. Chronic stress from unforgiveness can lead to issues such as high blood pressure, weakened immune function, and depression. By choosing to forgive, you release these negative emotions, allowing your brain to deactivate its stress response and promote a state of calm and well-being. This paves the way for a more positive and productive relationship and significantly improves your health.

Practical Tips:

◊ Think of someone you need to forgive.

◊ Write an email or text expressing your feelings and your decision to forgive, even if you don't send it.

◊ Practice releasing negative emotions through prayer and meditation, and focus on the healing that forgiveness brings.

Reflective Questions:

» How does holding onto grudges affect your mental and physical health?

» What steps can you take to practice forgiveness daily?

» How can releasing negative emotions through forgiveness improve your relationships and overall well-being?

By embracing forgiveness, you can experience emotional freedom, improve your mental health, and foster healthier relationships.

Day 17: The Gift of Giving

"It is more blessed to give than to receive." – Acts 20:35 (NIV)

Giving enriches both the giver and the receiver. 2 Corinthians 9:7 (NIV) reminds us, *"Each of you should give what you have decided in your heart to give, not reluctantly or under compulsion, for God loves a cheerful giver."*
Generosity fosters a sense of community and enhances well-being.

When you give, your brain releases *"feel-good"* neurotransmitters like dopamine, serotonin, and oxytocin. These chemicals boost your mood, creating a sense of satisfaction and happiness. These positive experiences enhance neuroplasticity, the brain's ability to form new neural connections, making generosity a habit that can improve mental health and emotional resilience.

Imagine volunteering at a local shelter. The act of giving your time and resources not only helps those in need but also brings you a sense of fulfilment and purpose. This sense of purpose can enhance your overall well-being, creating a positive feedback loop of giving and receiving.

Linda, who dedicated her weekends to mentoring young girls, found that this generosity brought her joy and improved her interpersonal skills. These enhanced skills allowed her to build stronger relationships with her colleagues at work, enabling a more collaborative and supportive team dynamic at work.

Practical Tips:

◊ Find a way to give back today.
◊ It could be through volunteering, donating to a cause you care about, or helping a needy neighbour.
◊ Reflect on how the act of giving makes you feel and how it impacts others.

Reflective Questions:

» How do you feel after giving to others?
» How can you incorporate acts of giving into your daily routine?
» How can you use the positive feelings from giving to create a habit of generosity?

Giving enhances mental well-being, strengthens relationships, and contributes positively to the community, creating a ripple effect of kindness and connection. Your acts of giving benefit you and strengthen the bonds with those around you, making you feel more connected and valued.

Day 18: The Importance of Humility

"Humility is the fear of the Lord; its wages are riches and honor and life." – Proverbs 22:4 (NIV)

Humility is about recognising that you don't have all the answers and remaining open to other perspectives. This openness enhances the brain's ability to form new neural (brain) connections and adapt to new information. Philippians 2:3-4 advises, *"Do nothing out of selfish ambition or vain conceit. Rather, in humility, value others above yourselves...."*

Practising humility requires acknowledging that our successes are not solely our own but are shaped by God's grace and the contributions of others. This mindset helps us avoid the pitfalls of pride, which can isolate us and hinder personal growth. Humility activates brain regions associated with empathy and social connection, such as the prefrontal cortex, strengthening pathways for collaboration and respect.

When I led a large team of staff in a college, I expressed my desire to learn from them and encouraged honest feedback. By recognising God's grace in my leadership and avoiding pride, I praised team members when deserved, building trust and fostering a culture of humility. This approach created an environment where everyone felt valued, leading to a high-performing team with excellent results.

Practical Tips:

◊ Practice humility by acknowledging the strengths and contributions of others.
◊ Focus on supporting and uplifting those around you rather than only self-promotion.
◊ Reflect on how humility enhances your relationships and fosters a collaborative environment.

Reflective Questions:

» How can you practice humility in your daily interactions?
» What are some ways you can acknowledge and appreciate the strengths of others?
» How does practising humility impact your personal and professional relationships?

By embracing humility, you acknowledge the role of God's grace in your life and open your mind to continuous learning, building stronger, more respectful relationships and fostering a positive and collaborative environment.

Day 19: Embracing Joy for Resilience and Strength

"The joy of the Lord is your strength." – Nehemiah 8:10 (NIV)

Joy is a profound sense of well-being rooted in trusting and knowing God. Psalm 16:11 (NIV) says, *"You make known to me the path of life; you will fill me with joy in your presence, with eternal pleasures at your right hand."* Joy provides strength and resilience during challenging times.

When you face a difficult situation with a joyful heart, you engage neural (brain) pathways that calm the emotional brain, particularly the amygdala. This allows your prefrontal cortex, responsible for decision-making and problem-solving, to function optimally. Positive emotions stimulate the release of neurotransmitters like dopamine and serotonin, which enhance mood and motivation. These chemicals help regulate your stress response, improve focus, and foster resilience.

By cultivating joy, you create a brain environment that drives better thoughts, actions, and behaviours, reinforcing a positive feedback loop for emotional and cognitive health. Joy doesn't mean ignoring difficulties but finding strength and hope in God's presence and promises. This shift in perspective helps you navigate challenges with a sense of calm and purpose, ultimately leading to more constructive outcomes.

Consider the example of Chioma, who faced many personal challenges but maintained her joy through her faith. Her intentional, positive mindset gave her the strength to overcome adversity and kept her resilient. Chioma's brain was better equipped to handle stress and make wise decisions by focusing on God's promises and the joy He provides. This approach enabled her to navigate difficulties with grace, ultimately allowing her to overcome and thrive, leading to a more fulfilling and balanced life.

Practical Tips:

◊ Cultivate joy by spending time on activities that uplift your spirit, such as prayer, worship, listening to music, or nature walks.
◊ Reflect on the blessings in your life and express gratitude for them.
◊ Share your joy with others through acts of kindness and encouragement.

Reflective Questions:

» How do you currently respond to challenging situations?
» What activities or practices help you cultivate joy in your life?
» How can you incorporate more moments of joy into your daily routine?

Embrace joy to blend science and scripture, building resilience and creating a positive impact on yourself and others.

Day 20: Cultivating Resilience

"We are hard pressed on every side, but not crushed; perplexed, but not in despair."
– 2 Corinthians 4:8 (NIV)

Resilience is the ability to bounce back from difficulties and challenges. James 1:2-4 teaches that facing trials produces perseverance, helping us grow stronger in faith and character. This aligns with how resilience works in life: it's about maintaining hope, adapting to new situations, and growing through challenges.

Just like muscles stretch during exercise, our brains strengthen when we overcome challenges. While stress triggers cortisol, practising resilience can lower cortisol levels and boost positive neurotransmitters like dopamine, which enhance our mood and motivation.

Resilience is cultivated by practising gratitude, optimism, and flexibility in thought.

Practical Tips:

◊ Reflect on a recent challenge and identify ways you demonstrated resilience.
◊ Write down what helped you cope and grow through the experience.
◊ Practice resilience-building activities, such as setting small goals, seeking support, and maintaining a positive outlook.

Reflective Questions:

» How have you demonstrated resilience in the past?
» What strategies can you use to build resilience in your current challenges?
» How does maintaining a positive outlook impact your ability to overcome difficulties?

By cultivating resilience, you can navigate life's challenges with strength and grace, ultimately growing stronger and more capable. Embrace resilience-building practices and watch your ability to bounce back and thrive improve.

DAY 21: OVERCOME NEGATIVE THOUGHTS

"You must learn a new way to think before you can master a new way to be." – Marianne Williamson

Negative thoughts are like invisible barriers, limiting our ability to achieve the life we desire. They cloud our judgment, drain our energy, and hold us back from embracing our full potential. However, with intentional effort and the right strategies, we can break free from these limiting patterns and cultivate a more positive mindset. We now know that our brains are highly adaptable, so even if we consistently have negative thoughts that have become deeply ingrained habits, we can rewire our brains by consciously forming new, positive thought patterns. As Marianne Williamson's quote suggests, by doing so, we don't only change how we think but also how we live.

One effective approach to overcoming negative thoughts is **cognitive restructuring**. This involves identifying negative thoughts as they arise, challenging their validity, and replacing them with more balanced, empowering truths based on God's word and promises. For instance, if you think, *"I always fail,"* counter it with, *"I am learning and growing with each experience,"* and *"I can do ALL things through Christ who strengthens me."* Another powerful strategy is visualisation. Spend a few minutes each day visualising yourself successfully navigating situations that usually trigger negative thoughts. By repeatedly imagining positive outcomes, you can train your brain to focus on possibilities rather than limitations.

Incorporate mindfulness practices like prayer and reflection to centre your mind on God and let go of negative thoughts, allowing His words and peace to guide your thinking. This will help you observe them without judgment, reducing their power over you. To reinforce a positive mental state, engage in activities that promote positive emotions, such as gratitude journaling or spending time with uplifting people.

Practical Exercise:

◊ Today, identify one recurring negative thought.
◊ Write it down, then challenge it by writing a positive, empowering alternative.
◊ Repeat this new thought throughout the day whenever the negative one arises.

Reflective Questions:

» What negative thoughts do you frequently have, and how have they shaped your actions?
» How can you begin to challenge and reframe these thoughts to align with your desired outcomes?

Day 22: Embracing Vulnerability

"Vulnerability sounds like truth and feels like courage. Truth and courage aren't always comfortable, but they're never weakness." – Brené Brown

Embracing vulnerability means being open and honest about our feelings and experiences, even when it's uncomfortable. It's about showing up as our true selves and finding strength in that honesty. The Bible reminds us in 2 Corinthians 12:9-10 (NIV), *"But he said to me, 'My grace is sufficient for you, for my power is made perfect in weakness. Therefore, I will boast all the more gladly about my weaknesses so that Christ's power may rest on me."*

When you allow yourself to be vulnerable, you show courage, not weakness. This authenticity opens the door to personal growth and deeper self-reflection. By acknowledging your weaknesses, you create space for God's strength to shine through you. Vulnerability is an act of trust — in yourself first, in others and in God's ability to work through your honesty.

From a scientific perspective, expressing vulnerability helps reduce stress and anxiety by allowing our brains to process and release pent-up emotions. It also triggers the release of oxytocin, the "bonding hormone," which strengthens relationships by fostering trust and connection.

Consider the impact of being open about your struggles with a trusted friend or family member. This honesty strengthens your relationships and provides emotional relief and a sense of empowerment as you receive the support you need.

Practical Tips:

◊ Find a trusted person to share a personal struggle with.
◊ Be sincere about your feelings and experiences and reflect on how this act of vulnerability strengthens your relationship and empowers you.

Reflective Questions:

» How does embracing vulnerability impact your relationships?
» What personal struggles can you share with a trusted individual?
» How does being open and honest about your experiences help you feel more supported?

By embracing vulnerability, you invite God's strength into your life, deepen your connections, and empower yourself to grow and thrive.

Day 23: The Power of Hope

"May the God of hope fill you with all joy and peace as you trust in him, so that you may overflow with hope by the power of the Holy Spirit." – Romans 15:13 (NIV)

Hope is a powerful force that provides strength and motivation, even in difficult times. Jeremiah 29:11 (NIV) assures us, *"For I know the plans I have for you, declares the Lord, plans to prosper you and not to harm you, plans to give you hope and a future."*

When you approach difficulties with hope, you activate your brain's reward system, releasing endorphins and enkephalins, which reduce pain and enhance well-being. This positive outlook triggers changes in the brain, fostering resilience and improving immune function.

Think of someone dealing with a severe illness. Despite the uncertainty, their hope in God's plan gives them the strength to fight and the peace to endure the journey. This hopeful outlook inspires those around them and aids in their recovery. Hope creates a positive feedback loop, where a positive mindset leads to better health outcomes, reinforcing hope.

By fostering hope, you improve both your mental and physical health, strengthen your ability to bounce back and develop a more positive and proactive mindset when facing life's challenges. Hope helps you set and pursue goals, even in challenging situations.

Practical Tips:

◊ Cultivate hope by focusing on positive outcomes and trusting in God's plan.
◊ Write down your hopes and dreams, pray and meditate on them daily, and reflect on past experiences where hope helped you overcome challenges.

Reflective Questions:

» How does hope influence your ability to face challenges?
» What are some hopes and dreams you have for your future?
» How can you cultivate a mindset of hope in your daily life?

By embracing hope, you can harness its power to navigate life's difficulties and foster a resilient and optimistic outlook.

Day 24: Developing Self-Discipline

"No discipline seems pleasant at the time, but painful. Later on, however, it produces a harvest of righteousness and peace for those who have been trained by it." – Hebrews 12:11 (NIV)

Self-discipline, often underestimated, is a key tool for achieving our goals and living by our values. Proverbs 25:28 compares a person without self-control to a city with broken walls, highlighting the instability that comes without discipline. Developing self-discipline not only helps us stay focused on what truly matters but also brings many benefits.

Neuroscience reveals that self-discipline plays a crucial role in strengthening the prefrontal cortex, the part of the brain responsible for decision-making and impulse control. By practising self-discipline, we enhance our decision-making abilities and also boost dopamine levels, reinforcing positive behaviour.
For example, sticking to a workout plan, even when it's tempting to skip, improves physical health and brings long-term satisfaction.

Practical Tips:

◊ Identify an area where you need to develop self-discipline.
◊ Set specific, achievable goals and create a plan to reach them.
◊ Hold yourself accountable by tracking your progress and rewarding yourself for milestones achieved.

For example, to improve your financial situation, create a budget and stick to it, celebrating minor victories.

Reflective Questions:

» What areas of your life require more self-discipline?
» How can you create a plan to develop self-discipline in these areas?
» What strategies can you use to stay motivated and accountable?

By developing self-discipline, you can direct your life based on your values and goals. This creates a more meaningful and intentional life where your decisions shape your future. Self-discipline helps you stay focused instead of being driven by immediate desires or distractions. It ensures that your actions lead you toward the life you want. It empowers you to control your destiny, making each step more purposeful and fulfilling.

DAY 25: NURTURING RELATIONSHIPS

"Above all, love each other deeply, because love covers over a multitude of sins." – 1 Peter 4:8 (NIV)

Love, trust, and mutual respect form the foundation of healthy relationships. Ephesians 4:2-3 (NIV) advises, *"Be completely humble and gentle; be patient, bearing with one another in love. Make every effort to keep the unity of the Spirit through the bond of peace."*

Strong social connections enhance mental and emotional well-being. Oxytocin, known as the *"love hormone,"* is released during positive social interactions, fostering trust and bonding.
The prefrontal cortex helps regulate emotions and make rational decisions, while the amygdala processes emotions such as fear and pleasure. Balancing the interactions between these brain regions helps manage emotions effectively, which is essential for nurturing healthy relationships.

It is important to prioritise and invest time and effort in nurturing your relationships as part of your daily routine. You can achieve this by dedicating quality time to your loved ones, expressing gratitude for their presence, and approaching conflicts with kindness and understanding.
Nurturing relationships leads to a support system that enhances resilience, reduces stress, and promotes overall well-being. Positive relationships contribute to emotional stability and a sense of belonging.

Practical Tips:

◊ Choose a relationship to focus on today.

◊ Plan an act of kindness, a heartfelt conversation, or a shared activity to nurture this relationship.

◊ Reflect on how these actions strengthen your connection and bring you closer.

Exercise:

◊ Show appreciation to someone important in your life—whether it's a colleague, family member, child, or spouse.

◊ Write them a brief, heartfelt note acknowledging their positive impact and highlighting qualities you admire.

◊ This act of gratitude will strengthen your bond and deepen your connection, enhancing mutual respect and emotional well-being.

Reflective Questions:

» Which relationships in your life need more nurturing?

» How can you show appreciation and love to those around you?

» What actions can you take today to strengthen a specific relationship?

Day 26: The Practice of Mindfulness

"Be still, and know that I am God." – Psalm 46:10 (NIV)

Mindfulness is about being fully present and intentional in each moment. It's an invitation to slow down, release anxiety, and find peace in God's presence, as Philippians 4:6-7 encourages us to do. Rather than constantly talking at God, mindfulness invites us to be still, listen, and be attentive to His guidance.

Practising mindfulness—focusing on your breathing, observing your thoughts without judgment, and centring yourself in the present enables you to create a mental environment that reduces stress and enhances overall well-being. This stillness allows your mind to reset, increasing mental clarity and deepening your spiritual connection with God.

Neuroscience shows that mindfulness also boosts dopamine levels in the brain, a neurotransmitter associated with pleasure, motivation, and creativity. When you practice mindfulness, you calm your mind and stimulate your brain's creativity centres, making it easier to think clearly and solve problems more effectively. This boost in dopamine can inspire innovative ideas and creative solutions, whether at work or in your personal life.

Try taking intentional pauses during a busy day to breathe deeply and centre your thoughts on the present. This will not only calm your mind but also create a space for you to hear God's guidance, fostering a deeper relationship with Him. This practice helps you stay grounded in a fast-paced world, reduce overwhelm, and improve your emotional health.

Practical Tips:

◊ Take five minutes daily to practice mindful breathing.
◊ Sit comfortably, close your eyes, and focus on your slow, deep breaths.
◊ If your mind wanders, gently return your attention to your breathing.
◊ Notice how this practice reduces stress and sharpens mental clarity.

Reflective Questions:

» How often do you feel distracted or overwhelmed by stress?
» What steps can you take to incorporate mindfulness into your daily routine?
» How does practising mindfulness impact your overall well-being, creativity, and spiritual connection?

Day 27: Embracing Authenticity

"To thine own self be true." – William Shakespeare

Authenticity involves being true to ourselves and our values. Psalm 139:14 (NIV) reminds us, *"I praise you because I am fearfully and wonderfully made; your works are wonderful, I know that full well."* Embracing our true selves allows us to live more fulfilling and meaningful lives.

Authenticity means living in alignment with your true self, expressing your genuine thoughts and feelings, and acting according to your values. It requires self-awareness and courage, as it often involves being vulnerable and open with yourself and others.
It's about being aware of your thoughts, mindset, and values and ensuring they align with who you want to be now rather than being influenced by preconditioned beliefs from childhood or past experiences. This fosters self-respect and genuine connections with others.

Many people struggle with people-pleasing, often hiding their true selves to gain approval. This can lead to a lack of fulfilment and genuine connections. Embracing authenticity helps you break free from this pattern and live a more meaningful life.

Embracing authenticity boosts self-confidence, nurtures genuine relationships, and leads to a more fulfilling life. It allows you to live in alignment with whom God says you are, staying true to yourself and your values, which brings inner peace and deep satisfaction.

Practical Tips:

◊ Identify one area of your life where you feel you are not being authentic.
◊ Write down your genuine thoughts and feelings about this.
◊ Then, create a plan to start expressing your true self in this area, whether it's in your relationships, work, or personal pursuits.
◊ Practice this consistently and observe the positive changes in your life.

Reflective Questions:

» In what areas of your life do you feel you are not being authentic?
» How can you start expressing your true self more openly?
» What steps can you take to align your actions with your values?

DAY 28: TRUSTING BEYOND WHAT YOU SEE

"Now faith is confidence in what we hope for and assurance about what we do not see."
– Hebrews 11:1 (NIV)

Faith is more than just belief; it's a guiding force that helps us navigate uncertainty and find strength during difficult times. Proverbs 3:5-6 (NIV) reminds us to, *"Trust in the Lord with all your heart and lean not on your own understanding; in all your ways submit to him, and he will make your paths straight."*
This verse captures the essence of faith—trusting God's plan, even when the outcome is unclear.

Faith involves believing that God is working everything for your good, even when you can't see how. This trust allows you to find peace amid turmoil, knowing that God is leading you toward the best possible outcome. Faith isn't just about waiting for things to improve; it's about living with the confidence that God's plan is unfolding perfectly, even if you don't fully understand it yet. When faced with challenges, faith helps you see them as opportunities for growth and deeper trust in God rather than as obstacles.

Maintaining faith can be difficult, especially when circumstances shake your confidence. However, trusting in God can help your brain manage these emotions better. Faith activates the prefrontal cortex, which helps manage emotional impulses from the limbic system. This allows you to pause, reflect, and respond calmly instead of reacting impulsively. Over time, as you consistently choose actions grounded in faith, the brain strengthens these pathways until they become second nature, helping you take actions rooted in faith.

Practical Tips:

◊ Identify a specific challenge you're facing and reflect on how faith can guide you through it.
◊ Write down your hopes and aspirations about this, and spend time each day in prayer or meditation, trusting that God is guiding your steps.
◊ Commit to this practice daily, and observe how your faith grows stronger and more resilient.

Reflective Questions:

» In what areas of your life do you struggle to maintain faith?
» How can you strengthen your trust in God's plan?
» What steps can you take to deepen your faith in challenging situations?

By consistently practising faith, you're wiring and rewiring your brain to respond with trust instead of fear.

Day 29: The Role of Self-Care

"Do you not know that your bodies are temples of the Holy Spirit, who is in you, whom you have received from God?" – 1 Corinthians 6:19 (NIV)

Self-care is essential for our physical, mental, and spiritual well-being, helping us restore energy and focus. It involves taking intentional steps to care for your body, mind, and spirit by recognising your needs and making choices that promote overall well-being.
This can include physical activities like exercise and healthy eating and mental and spiritual activities like prayer, meditation, and spending time in nature.

It's easy to forget about self-care when life gets busy or stressful. However, taking regular time for yourself helps improve your health, lower stress levels, and boost productivity. By recharging, you can handle daily tasks more effectively with renewed focus and energy.

Research shows that activities like exercise and meditation enhance brain function and reduce stress by promoting the release of positive neurotransmitters such as serotonin and dopamine, improving mood, cognitive function, and overall mental health.

Practical Tips:

◊ Identify one self-care activity you enjoy, such as reading, walking, or spending time in nature, and commit to practising it regularly for one month.
◊ Track how it impacts your mood, energy levels, and overall well-being.
◊ Then, adjust your routine to include this activity regularly, along with other rejuvenating practices like short breaks during work, spa days, or establishing a consistent bedtime routine to ensure you stay refreshed and well-rested.

Reflective Questions:

» What self-care activities bring you the most joy and relaxation?
» How can you incorporate these activities into your daily routine?
» What obstacles prevent you from practising self-care, and how can you overcome them?

Day 30: Building Unshakeable Confidence

"With confidence, you have won before you have started." – Marcus Garvey

Confidence isn't just a feeling—it's the key to positive thinking and success. It's the belief that you can overcome challenges and keep progressing. Confidence acts as a strong foundation for your mindset, and without it, your positive thinking ability can be a struggle.
People are not necessarily born with confidence, but they can develop it as a skill. Neuroscience shows that when you achieve something, your brain releases dopamine, the "feel-good" chemical, which encourages you to keep going. This reinforcement helps you take on bigger challenges with even more confidence.

Emotional intelligence also plays a crucial role in building confidence. When you're aware of your emotions and how they impact your actions, you can manage self-doubt and foster self-assurance. As Philippians 4:13 (NKJV) says, *"I can do all things through Christ who strengthens me,"* reminding us that confidence, when grounded in faith, becomes unshakable.
To build confidence, start with small goals that you can achieve. Each success strengthens your belief in your abilities.

Visualisation can also help. By regularly picturing yourself succeeding, you train your brain to respond with confidence when those situations arise.

Think of a young professional nervous about public speaking. By starting with small presentations and gradually facing larger audiences, they built their confidence. What once made them anxious became an opportunity to shine. Confidence grows with practice and success. It's a muscle you can build, and with faith and emotional awareness, it becomes a powerful force that propels you through life's challenges.

Practical Exercise:

◊ Identify an area where you lack confidence.
◊ Set a small, achievable goal related to this area, and take a concrete step toward accomplishing it today.
◊ Reflect on your progress and use it to build greater confidence in the future.

Reflective Questions:

» In which areas of your life do you feel the least confident, and how does this impact your thoughts and actions?
» What small, practical steps can you take today to begin building your confidence in those areas?

PART TWO

RENEW AND REWIRE – THE PATH TO MENTAL MASTERY

PART 2 INTRODUCTION

Welcome to Part 2 of your journey, where we explore the power of the mind and how to reshape it for growth and success. Think of your brain as moldable clay—ready to be shaped by your thoughts, habits, and actions. This is where neuroplasticity comes in—the brain's ability to adapt and rewire based on what you focus on daily.

In this section, you'll discover how your thoughts shape your reality, how new habits create fresh pathways in your brain, and how to overcome negative thinking. Each day is designed to help you break free from limiting beliefs and embrace a mindset of endless possibilities.

Science shows that positive thinking, combined with self-reflection, can physically change the brain. Like training a muscle, cultivating positivity and letting go of negative patterns can train your mind for success.

We'll explore practical strategies like emotional regulation, building focus, and how rest and nutrition support brain health.
Tying these insights to biblical truths, we'll see how scripture rewires your mind and aligns your actions with God's purpose. Proverbs 23:7 says, *"As he thinks in his heart, so is he."* By renewing your mind, you open the door to becoming the person God created you to be.

Get ready to challenge yourself, embrace change, and step into the fullness of life through mental mastery.

Day 31: Understanding Neuroplasticity

"The brain is like a muscle. When it's in use we feel very good. Understanding is joyous."
– Carl Sagan

Neuroplasticity is the brain's incredible ability to reorganise itself by forming new connections between its neurons (brain cells). Neurons are the building blocks of the brain, sending signals throughout your nervous system to help you think, move, and experience emotions. The human brain has about 80 billion neurons, and each neuron connects with thousands of others, creating a vast, complex network of trillions of connections. As you experience new things, your brain strengthens or forms new connections, allowing you to learn and adapt.

Think of neuroplasticity like a construction project. Every time you learn a new skill—like learning a language, mastering a hobby, or even adjusting to new job tasks—your brain is busy building and reinforcing the pathways needed to support that activity. Over time, these connections become stronger, making the task easier. This process enables you to adapt to new experiences and recover from setbacks, demonstrating how flexible and capable your brain is.

Romans 12:2 (NIV) encourages us to *"be transformed by the renewing of your mind."* This beautifully aligns with the idea of neuroplasticity, as adopting new thoughts, habits, and behaviours literally rewires our brain. It reminds us that positive transformation is not just spiritual but neurological, offering us the ability to grow and change over a lifetime.

Starting something new, like learning a skill or navigating a career change, can initially feel tough. But with consistent practice, your brain forms the pathways needed to make these tasks easier. Neuroplasticity ensures that the more you challenge yourself, the more your brain grows and adapts.

Practical Tips:

◊ **Learn Something New:** Spend 15 minutes daily on a new skill, whether related to work, leadership, or personal growth.
◊ **Challenge Your Brain:** Engage in activities that push your thinking, such as problem-solving or learning new technologies.

Reflective Questions:

» How have you adapted to new experiences in the past?
» What skill would you like to develop next?
» What are some ways that you can consistently challenge your brain?

DAY 32: BUILDING NEW NEURAL PATHWAYS

"Every time you learn something new, you stretch your mind and make your life a little bit bigger." – Unknown

Building new neural pathways is like creating fresh trails in your brain. Every time you learn something new or take on a challenge, your brain forms new connections between neurons—these are called synapses. The more you practice a new skill or habit, the stronger these connections become, making the task easier and more automatic.

Think of your brain as a city with roads. When you first learn something, it's like paving a new road. Initially feeling rough and slow-going, it becomes a smooth, well-travelled motorway or highway with repetition. This process helps you master new skills and makes them a natural part of your life.

Romans 12:2 encourages us to renew our minds, which aligns perfectly with building new neural pathways. By engaging in new and challenging activities, you grow not only cognitively but also spiritually. This renewal helps you discern God's will and grow personally and professionally.

Imagine you're learning a new project management tool at work. Initially, it might feel overwhelming. However, as you practice using the tool daily, you become more comfortable and efficient with it. Repeated practice strengthens the neural network associated with this skill, making it less challenging.

Practical Tips:

◊ **Daily Practice:** Spend 15 minutes daily on a new skill or activity that challenges your brain.
◊ **Stay Consistent:** A few minutes daily can make a big difference.
◊ **Try New Things:** Keep your brain active by exploring different activities, like picking up a new hobby or learning a language.
◊ **Track Progress:** Watch how regular practice helps you improve over time.

Reflective Questions:

» What new skills have you recently gained that helped your professional life?
» How did consistent practice help you master these skills?
» What new activity can you start today to challenge your brain and enhance your growth?

DAY 33: OVERCOMING NEGATIVE THOUGHT PATTERNS

"Whether you think you can, or you think you can't – you're right." – Henry Ford

Negative thought patterns can feel like wearing foggy glasses, clouding your ability to see opportunities clearly and dragging down your mood. These thoughts—rooted in fear, doubt, or self-criticism—can become so automatic that they shape how you view yourself and the world around you. However, the power of neuroplasticity, which allows your brain to reorganise and form new connections, enables you to change these negative patterns into positive ones.

Neuroscientific studies show that the brain is highly adaptable. Dr. Jeffrey Schwartz, a leading researcher in neuroplasticity, found that consciously focusing on new, positive thought patterns can weaken old, negative neural pathways and build stronger, healthier ones. Essentially, the more you focus on positive thoughts, the more they become automatic, shifting your brain's default mode away from negativity.

Imagine an artist who believes they are not talented. If they constantly think, *"I'm not creative,"* they reinforce that belief, limiting their potential. But by choosing to replace that thought with something positive, like *"I have unique creative skills,"* they open doors for new ideas, creativity, and growth.
Proverbs 23:7 (NKJV) perfectly captures this: *"For as he thinks in his heart, so is he."* When you think positively about yourself, you can start to see yourself and your circumstances in a more hopeful light.

Dr Daniel Amen refers to these harmful thought patterns as **ANTs—Automatic Negative Thoughts**—that creep in uninvited. Research supports that eliminating ANTs and replacing them with positive affirmations can actually rewire your brain for positivity. A study published in Psychological Science shows positive affirmations reduce stress, boost problem-solving abilities, and improve overall mental health.

Practical Tips:

◊ **Meditative Affirmations:** Each morning, identify one negative thought (ANT) and replace it with a positive affirmation such as, *"I am fearfully and wonderfully made"* (Psalm 139:14 - NIV).

◊ **Thought Journal:** Write down your negative thoughts. Next to each one, write a positive counter-thought. This helps challenge and change ingrained patterns.

◊ **Gratitude Practice:** Write three positive things that happened each day. Gratitude rewires your brain to focus on the good.

You can rewire your brain for a more positive outlook by actively identifying and changing negative thought patterns.

DAY 34: MIND OVER MATTER – THE POWER OF MENTAL AGILITY

"The measure of intelligence is the ability to change." – Albert Einstein

Scripture Inspiration: *"Be renewed in the spirit of your mind."* — Ephesians 4:23 (NKJV)

Imagine your brain as a gymnast, flipping and twisting to adapt to new routines and challenges. This ability to switch gears is called cognitive flexibility—or mental agility. Just like a gymnast needs physical agility, your brain needs this mental skill to adapt to new situations, solve problems, and think creatively.

Cognitive flexibility is like having a mental 'Swiss Army' knife handy for every situation. Whether switching tasks at work, handling a last-minute change, or improvising in the kitchen, you're using this agility skill. It's what helps you navigate life's surprises smoothly without getting stuck.

Life can feel overwhelming without cognitive flexibility, like trying to run in shoes that don't fit. But with it, you can shift from one task to another, adapt quickly, and keep moving forward with ease, providing a sense of relief and comfort.
Imagine you're working on an important project when suddenly your boss asks for help with something urgent. Without mental agility, this might feel overwhelming. But with it, you smoothly transition, complete the new task, and return to your project without missing a beat—that's the power of cognitive flexibility.

Practical Tips:
- ◊ **Puzzles and Games:** Challenge your brain with activities like Sudoku or crosswords. These games train your brain to think differently and adapt quickly.
- ◊ **Learn Something New:** Take up a new hobby or skill, such as learning a language. This will keep your mind sharp and adaptable.
- ◊ **Mindfulness Practice:** Practice mindfulness meditation. It helps your brain stay focused and flexible by bringing awareness to the present moment.

Weekly Challenge: Try something new this week, like taking a different route to work or a new hobby. Notice how your brain adjusts and reflects on how you handle these changes, fostering a sense of accomplishment and motivation.

By embracing cognitive flexibility, you're equipping your mind to adapt, solve problems creatively, and handle challenges gracefully, instilling a sense of empowerment and confidence.

Day 35: Thriving Through Adversity

"Strength grows in the moments when you think you can't go on but keep going anyway."
– Unknown

Scripture Inspiration: *"Consider it pure joy, my brothers and sisters, whenever you face trials of many kinds, because you know that the testing of your faith produces perseverance."* — James 1:2-3 (NIV)

Resilience is the ability to bounce back from life's challenges and maintain a positive mindset. Just like a muscle, it can be strengthened through practice. The more you face and overcome adversity, the better you become at handling future difficulties.

Think of resilience as a tree bending in the wind. While it sways under pressure, it doesn't break, and over time, it grows stronger. Every challenge you face is like a gust of wind—it tests your strength but also helps you grow.

In James 1:2-3, we are encouraged to find joy in trials because they build perseverance. This aligns perfectly with resilience. When you view life's challenges as opportunities for growth, you build both spiritual and emotional strength, becoming better equipped to face whatever comes your way. Everyday setbacks—whether job loss, personal disappointment, or unexpected change—are part of life. Resilience doesn't mean avoiding these challenges but learning to adapt, find new opportunities, and come back stronger.

Practical Tips:
- ◊ **Positive Thinking:** Focus on what you can control and learn from setbacks. This helps keep you grounded and optimistic.
- ◊ **Set Small Goals:** Break down big challenges into smaller, achievable goals to build confidence and maintain motivation.
- ◊ **Lean on Support:** When facing tough times, don't hesitate to lean on friends, family, or mentors. A strong support system is key to resilience.

Resilience Practice: Think about a recent setback. Reflect on what you learned and how it helped you grow. Write down how this experience can build your resilience for future challenges.

Reflection Questions:
- » How do you usually respond to setbacks?
- » What strategies can help you strengthen your resilience?
- » How can you apply these strategies to current challenges?

DAY 36: AWARENESS AND TRANSFORMATION

"Until you make the unconscious conscious, it will direct your life and you will call it fate."
— C.G. Jung

Carl Jung's quote highlights how many challenges, behaviours, and patterns stem from unconscious beliefs formed through past experiences and assumptions we've never questioned. These hidden influences shape our thoughts and actions without us even realising it, making life feel like it's happening to us—like we're at the mercy of fate or luck.

Think of it like driving a car with blind spots. If you're unaware of those blind spots, you could drift into danger without understanding why. Similarly, if you're unaware of the thoughts driving your actions, you'll keep repeating the same struggles without realising you have the power to change them.
A study by researchers at the University of California shows that bringing these unconscious beliefs to the surface reduces anxiety and improves decision-making. When you become aware of what's hidden beneath, you unlock the potential to change your life.

Imagine someone who keeps ending up in jobs where they feel undervalued. They might unknowingly carry a belief from childhood that they're *"not good enough,"* and that belief influences their choices. But once they recognise it, they can challenge it, leading to more empowering career decisions that align with their true worth.
Harvard psychologist Dr. Daniel Wegner's research found that trying to suppress unwanted thoughts only makes them come back stronger. Instead of pushing those thoughts away, explore them with curiosity to change old patterns.

Practical Steps for Today:

◊ **Identify Your Reactions:** Pay attention to your automatic responses in moments of frustration or fear. Ask yourself, "What belief is behind this?"

◊ **Challenge Your Thoughts:** Is this belief helping or holding you back? Consider if it's time to change the story you're telling yourself.

◊ **Journaling:** Write about moments that trigger strong emotions in you. What underlying beliefs might be at play?

Reflective Questions:

» What recurring situations in your life might be influenced by unconscious beliefs?
» How will you challenge and change these beliefs?

DAY 37: THE POWER OF THOUGHTS IN SHAPING REALITY

"Your life is a reflection of your thoughts. If you change your thinking, you change your life." – Brian Tracy

Our minds are like filters through which we interpret the world. How we think about situations shapes how we perceive and respond to them. If your thoughts are positive, you tend to see opportunities, solutions, and reasons to be grateful. However, if you fill your thoughts with negativity or fear, everything can seem overwhelming, and even minor challenges may feel insurmountable. Take, for example, someone who faces a difficult work project. If they think, *"This is too hard; I'll never get it done,"* that belief will limit their effort and creativity. But if they think, *"This is a challenge I can handle,"* they're more likely to stay motivated, find solutions, and succeed. This shift in mindset can drastically change how you approach tasks, impacting your confidence and performance. Research by Dr. Martin Seligman, known for his work in positive psychology, shows that optimism boosts mental health and improves resilience and problem-solving skills.

Isaiah 26:3 (NIV) captures this well: *"You will keep in perfect peace those whose minds are steadfast because they trust in you."*
A steadfast mind focused on trust and positivity can bring peace and stability, allowing you to navigate life with greater clarity and assurance. The way you think about your circumstances affects how you feel and how you act. When you believe in positive outcomes, your actions follow suit, increasing your chances of success.

Practical Tips:

◊ **Visualisation:** Spend time daily visualising success. Imagine yourself overcoming obstacles and achieving your goals.

◊ **Affirmations:** Reinforce positive beliefs with daily affirmations like "I am capable of handling challenges."

Reflective Questions:

» How have your thoughts shaped your reality in the past?
» What negative beliefs are currently holding you back?
» How can you use your mind to create a more positive reality?

Exercise: Identify a challenge you're facing. Write your negative beliefs about it, then rewrite them into positive, empowering statements. Reflect on how this shift might change your approach and outcome.

You can start directing your thoughts toward a more fulfilling life by recognising how your mind shapes your reality.

Day 38: The Role of Nutrition in Brain Health

"Let food be thy medicine and medicine be thy food."— Hippocrates

Imagine your brain as a high-performance engine. Just as an engine needs clean, premium fuel to run smoothly, your brain requires the right nutrients to function at its best. The food you eat directly affects your brain's performance, influencing your memory, focus, mood, and long-term cognitive health.

Research shows that a diet rich in omega-3 fatty acids (found in fish like salmon), antioxidants (from berries), and vitamins (from leafy greens) can help your brain grow and adapt. These nutrients support neuroplasticity, which is your brain's ability to form new connections and recover from damage. David Robson discusses in "The Expectation Effect" how our beliefs and mindset impact our body's response to food. If you expect healthy food to energise and fuel you, you're more likely to experience those benefits. On the flip side, filling your diet with processed foods, sugary snacks, and unhealthy fats is like dumping dirty fuel into an engine— leading to mental sluggishness and even long-term cognitive decline.

Our bodies, described in 1 Corinthians 6:19-20 as temples, deserve to be treated with care and respect. By choosing brain-nourishing foods, you support your cognitive abilities and honour the body God has gifted you. Being mindful of what you eat—knowing how different foods affect your mood and energy—allows you to make informed decisions that benefit both your mind and body. Consider someone who always feels mentally foggy and tired. By switching from a diet of sugary snacks to one filled with whole foods, they will experience clearer thinking, sustained energy, and more productivity.

Practical Tips:
- ◊ **Track and Observe:** This week, pay attention to how your diet affects your mental clarity, energy, and focus.
- ◊ **Enhance Nutrition:** Incorporate more brain-boosting foods like fatty fish, leafy greens, nuts, and berries into your meals.
- ◊ **Plan for Success:** Create a weekly meal plan with brain-healthy foods and observe how they affect your focus and mood.

Reflection Questions:
- » How does your current diet impact your mental clarity and energy?
- » What brain-healthy foods can you add to your meals starting today?
- » How can you change your diet to improve brain health in the long run?

Day 39: Exercises to Strengthen Memory

"Memory is the treasure house of the mind wherein the monuments thereof are kept and preserved."— Thomas Fuller

Memory is like a muscle—regular exercise strengthens it, keeping it sharp and responsive. Just as physical workouts keep your body fit, memory exercises challenge your brain, enhancing cognitive function and slowing cognitive decline, especially as you age. Your brain possesses a remarkable ability to grow new neurons and form new connections throughout life, so engaging in activities such as memorisation, recall exercises, and mnemonic devices can significantly improve memory retention and retrieval.

It's natural to experience changes in memory and cognitive function as we age. However, this doesn't mean decline is inevitable. By consistently challenging your brain, you can keep your memory strong and your mind agile. Think of these exercises as mental workouts that help maintain your cognitive health, similar to how physical exercises sustain your physical well-being.

An elderly person who takes on the challenge of learning a new language will find their memory improving, their focus sharpening, and their mind becoming more agile. This mental workout will boost their overall quality of life and keep their brain active and engaged.

Practical Tips:

◊ **Daily Memory Exercise:** Choose a memory exercise, such as memorising a short poem, a list of words, or important dates. Practice recalling this information daily to strengthen your memory.

◊ **Use Mnemonics:** Incorporate mnemonic techniques such as acronyms or visualisations to make remembering information easier and more effective.

◊ **Track Progress:** Spend 15 minutes daily on memory exercises and observe improvements in your recall abilities. Reflect on how these exercises help you manage daily tasks more efficiently.

Reflection Questions:

» What memory challenges do you encounter in your daily life?
» How can you integrate memory exercises into your daily routine?
» What strategies could help you enhance your memory retention?

Day 40: Develop Focus and Concentration

"Concentration is the secret of strength." — Ralph Waldo Emerson

Focus and concentration are like muscles that strengthen with consistent practice. Consistent practice is required to build focus and concentration, similar to how regular training strengthens physical muscles. The prefrontal cortex, the part of the brain responsible for decision-making and attention, plays a crucial role in maintaining focus. Engaging in activities that challenge this part of the brain enhances your ability to stay on task and improve productivity.

Colossians 3:2 (NIV) encourages us to *"set your minds on things above, not on earthly things."* This scripture reminds us to prioritise what truly matters and direct our focus toward higher goals. By applying this principle, we can train our minds to concentrate on tasks that align with our purpose and filter out distractions that distract us from what's important.

Imagine focus as a spotlight that illuminates only what is necessary, leaving the rest in darkness. When your focus is sharp, you can complete tasks more efficiently, reduce errors, and achieve higher-quality outcomes. Whether working on a project, studying for an exam, or managing daily tasks, improving focus enhances productivity and satisfaction.

Practical Tips:

◊ **Time Blocking:** Schedule your day using time blocks, dedicating specific periods to focused work followed by short breaks.
◊ **Minimise Interruptions:** Create a distraction-free environment by turning off notifications and finding a quiet space.
◊ **Practice Mindfulness:** Use mindfulness techniques to return your attention when distractions arise.
◊ **Practice Focus:** Try the Pomodoro Technique: set a timer for 25 minutes and work on a task without distractions. Afterwards, take a 5-minute break and repeat. Notice how this method improves your focus and productivity.

Reflection Questions:

» What distractions commonly affect your focus?
» How can you create a more focused work environment?
» What strategies will help you enhance your concentration?

Strengthening focus and concentration empowers you to tackle tasks with clarity and efficiency, aligning your efforts with higher purposes and minimising distractions.

Day 41: The Impact of Physical Exercise on the Brain

"Exercise is the most transformative thing that you can do for your brain." - Wendy Suzuki

Scripture Inspiration: *"Do you not know that your bodies are temples of the Holy Spirit, who is in you, whom you have received from God? You are not your own."*- 1 Corinthians 6:19 (NIV)

Physical exercise is like fertiliser for your brain. It nourishes it by increasing blood flow, delivering essential nutrients and oxygen, and promoting the growth of neurons. Just as a well-tended garden flourishes, your brain thrives when you regularly engage in physical activity. Exercise enhances cognitive functions like memory, attention, and problem-solving, making your mind sharper and more resilient.

1 Corinthians 6:19 reminds us that our bodies are temples of the Holy Spirit. Taking care of our physical health through exercise honours this divine gift, creating a healthy environment for both our bodies and brains. When we exercise, we strengthen our muscles and build stronger neural connections, which support mental clarity and emotional balance.

At over 50, I decided to learn how to swim. Initially, my brain resisted the challenge—struggling to float felt daunting, and progress seemed slow. But I persevered, and over time, I went from being unable to float to swimming comfortably. This journey was a powerful reminder that no matter our age, we can create new neural pathways and continue to grow. My experience proves that making positive changes is always possible, transforming both body and mind.

Practical Tips:

◊ **Regular Exercise:** Incorporate physical activity into your daily routine with simple exercises like walking, jogging, or cycling.

◊ **Exercise Variety:** Keep your routine engaging by mixing different activities and stimulating different brain areas.

◊ **Daily Commitment:** Begin with 10-15 minutes of activity daily, and gradually increase. Track your progress and note changes in mood, energy, and focus.

Reflection Questions:

» How does physical exercise affect your mood and cognitive function?
» What physical activities do you enjoy and can be easily incorporated into your routine?

Regular exercise strengthens your brain and honours your body as a temple, empowering you to unlock your potential and live with greater purpose.

Day 42: Mastering Emotional Regulation

"Feelings are much like waves; we can't stop them from coming, but we can choose which ones to surf." – Jonatan Mårtensson

Emotional regulation is all about managing your emotions in a healthy, constructive way. Since our thoughts and emotions are closely intertwined, what we think directly influences how we feel. For example, telling yourself, *"I'm not good enough for this,"* can trigger feelings of anxiety and stress. This happens because the amygdala, your brain's emotional centre, reacts to negative thoughts by activating the fight-flight-freeze response, releasing stress hormones into your body.

However, the good news is that by practising emotional regulation, you can calm this automatic response and activate your prefrontal cortex—the part of the brain responsible for reasoning and decision-making. For instance, imagine you are a manager dealing with a tight deadline. Without emotional regulation, stress might cause you to lash out at your team or make hasty decisions. But by using techniques like deep breathing, you can calm your amygdala and allow your prefrontal cortex to take control, enabling you to handle the situation with focus and clarity. Research shows that practices like mindfulness and changing the way you think about situations (cognitive reappraisal) can help calm the brain's emotional centre, the amygdala, and improve your ability to manage emotions [Harvard Health Publishing, 2020]. Emotional regulation enhances your mental well-being and positively impacts your relationships and professional success.

Practical Tips:

◊ **Deep Breathing:** When stressed, inhale for four counts, hold for four, and exhale for four. This reduces the immediate stress response.

◊ **Stay Present:** Focus on the current moment to keep your emotions grounded and reduce negative thoughts.

◊ **Reframe Negative Thoughts:** Replace negative thoughts with a more balanced perspective.

Reflective Questions:

» How do you currently manage stress and regulate your emotions?
» What techniques can you use to improve your emotional control?
» How can emotional regulation improve your relationships and overall well-being?

By mastering emotional regulation, you'll respond more thoughtfully and improve your mental health and relationships.

Day 43: The Importance of Sleep for Brain Function

"Sleep is that golden chain that ties health and our bodies together." – Thomas Dekker

Sleep is like your brain's nightly housekeeping service. It sweeps away the day's mental clutter and tidies up memories; think of sleep as the brain's night shift—a crucial time when the "clean-up crew" comes in to organise files, sweep out toxins, and repair any damage from the day. Just like a factory needs downtime to maintain its machines, your brain needs sleep to function optimally. Without enough rest, it's like working on a cluttered desk—it's harder to find things, make decisions, and stay focused.

The Critical Role of Sleep:
During sleep, your brain consolidates memories, strengthens neural connections, and clears out harmful waste products. This process, known as "consolidation," is essential for learning and memory. Chronic sleep deprivation, especially less than five hours a night, can lead to cognitive decline, impacting your ability to think clearly and increasing health risks.

Imagine operating heavy machinery without a proper night's sleep—risky, right? The same goes for your brain. Whether you're tackling a big project at work or simply managing daily tasks, quality sleep is essential. Struggling with brain fog or irritability? These are often signs that your brain's "maintenance crew" didn't get enough time on the job.

Practical Tips:

◊ **Set a Regular Sleep Routine:** Go to bed and wake up at the same time daily, helping regulate your body's internal clock.
◊ **Create a Relaxing Environment:** Keep your bedroom cool, dark, and quiet. Avoid screens or stimulating activities before bed.
◊ **Monitor Your Sleep:** Track your sleep patterns with a sleep diary to identify areas for improvement.

Reflective Questions:

» How does your current sleep routine impact your cognitive function and mood?
» What changes can you make to improve your sleep quality?
» How can you prioritise sleep to support your brain health?

Prioritising sleep is like giving your brain the necessary maintenance to operate at full capacity. Embrace a regular sleep routine, and watch your mental clarity and overall well-being improve.

Day 44: Rewiring for Positive Thinking

"Positive thinking will let you do everything better than negative thinking will."
– Zig Ziglar

Imagine your brain as a garden. Every thought you have is like a seed. Positive thoughts are the flowers that bring beauty and joy, while negative thoughts are the weeds that can take over if left unchecked. By nurturing the flowers and diligently removing the weeds, you have the power to create a garden that not only flourishes but also brings immense happiness. Positive thinking is about planting and nurturing those flowers, even when life tries to sow weeds.

Rewiring Your Brain for Positivity:
Positive thinking is like exercising a muscle—the more you practice, the stronger it gets. When you focus on the good, your brain forms and strengthens neural connections that support optimism and resilience; over time, this helps you manage stress better, stay emotionally stable, and bounce back from challenges more easily.

Start your day with positive declarations like watering the flowers in your mental garden. For example, saying, "I am capable and strong," sets a positive tone, just like sunshine helps flowers bloom. Practising gratitude is like adding fertiliser, enriching the soil of your mind so positivity can grow stronger. When you regularly focus on the positive, you train your brain to look for opportunities and joy rather than get bogged down by negativity and what you lack.

Practical Tips:
- ◊ **Daily Gratitude:** Write down three things you're thankful for each day—think of it as planting seeds of joy.
- ◊ **Positive Declarations:** Start your morning by repeating positive affirmations to give your brain a shot of sunshine.
- ◊ **Gratitude Journal:** Keep a journal where you note the positive things in your life. Regularly revisiting these entries is like revisiting your garden, appreciating how it's growing.

Reflective Questions:
- » How do negative thoughts act like weeds in your mental garden?
- » What positive "flowers" can you focus on to shift your mindset?
- » How can you make planting positivity a daily habit?

By focusing on positive thinking, you can cultivate a beautiful mental garden, leading to better mental health.

DAY 45: UNLEASHING YOUR GOD-GIVEN CREATIVITY

"Creativity is intelligence having fun." – Albert Einstein

Scripture Inspiration: *"So God created mankind in his own image, in the image of God he created them; male and female he created them."* — Genesis 1:27 (NIV)

Creativity is a divine gift, reflecting the image of God, who created the heavens and the earth. Just as God created the world, we can create, innovate, and bring new ideas to life. Engaging in creative activities is an expression of this divine nature and a powerful way to enhance brain function, boost mood, and improve problem-solving skills.

Think of creativity as a playground for your brain. When you engage in creative tasks, like painting, writing, or brainstorming, your brain releases dopamine—a "feel-good" neurotransmitter that enhances motivation and reinforces positive behaviour. This dopamine boost makes you feel good and encourages the formation of new neural pathways, improving cognitive flexibility and problem-solving abilities.

Whether you're solving a problem at work or finding new ways to connect with your family, creativity plays a crucial role. Feeling stuck or uninspired? That's when engaging in creative activities can help you see things from a new perspective, sparking innovation and fresh ideas.

Practical Tips:
- ◊ **Explore Creativity:** Dedicate time to creative activities that excite you, whether painting, writing, or playing music.
- ◊ **Brainstorm Often:** Engage in brainstorming sessions to generate new ideas, especially when facing challenges.
- ◊ **Creativity Challenge:** Pick a creative activity to focus on each week. Track your progress and reflect on how it enhances your problem-solving skills and overall well-being.

Reflective Questions:
- » How can you incorporate creativity into your daily life?
- » What creative activities bring you joy and help you think outside the box?
- » How does engaging in creative pursuits affect your mood and problem-solving skills?

By embracing your God-given creativity, you align with your divine purpose, improve your brain's flexibility, and discover new ways to overcome challenges.

Day 46: Mastering Problem-Solving Skills

"Every problem is a gift—without problems, we would not grow." – Tony Robbins

Enhancing problem-solving skills is about developing cognitive flexibility, critical thinking, and creativity. These skills allow you to approach challenges confidently and find effective solutions, contributing to personal growth and resilience. Problem-solving involves more than just fixing issues; it's about analysing problems, generating solutions, and choosing the best course of action. This process activates the prefrontal cortex (PFC), the part of the brain responsible for complex thinking and decision-making. Strengthening your problem-solving skills enhances cognitive function and emotional regulation.

Imagine being at work and a crucial piece of equipment stops working. Instead of panicking, you calmly assess the situation, brainstorm solutions, and implement the most effective one. This approach will help resolve the issue quickly and build your confidence for future challenges. Think of planning a family vacation. You research destinations, compare costs, and create an itinerary that maximises enjoyment while staying within budget. This problem-solving process reduces stress and leads to a more fulfilling experience. Dopamine, the brain's "reward" chemical, plays a key role in problem-solving. Successfully solving a problem releases dopamine, reinforcing positive behaviour and sharpening cognitive abilities, making you more prepared for future challenges.

Enhancing problem-solving skills helps you tackle challenges, make better decisions, and achieve positive outcomes. It fosters cognitive flexibility, enabling you to adapt to new situations and think creatively. Overcoming obstacles builds confidence and strengthens resilience.

Practical Tips:

◊ **Break It Down:** Simplify the problem by dividing it into manageable parts.
◊ **Think Critically:** Challenge assumptions and consider different perspectives.
◊ **Regular Practice:** Apply problem-solving techniques to an ongoing issue in your life, reflecting on the outcome and how it improves future decisions.

Reflective Questions:

» How do you currently handle problem-solving in your life?
» What strategies can you use to enhance your problem-solving abilities?

Embrace these techniques, and watch your confidence and resilience grow.

DAY 47: THE POWER OF VISUALISATION

"Visualisation is daydreaming with a purpose." – Bo Bennett

Visualisation is a powerful mental tool that involves creating vivid images in your mind to practice or achieve goals. Visualising success strengthens the neural pathways associated with positive outcomes, boosting both your performance and confidence.

Think of visualisation as a mental rehearsal. Just like athletes picture themselves winning a race, you can use visualisation to prepare for any challenge. This technique activates the same neural circuits used during the actual task, making your brain more efficient and improving your ability to perform under pressure. Neuroscience shows that mental imagery helps build new neural connections, reinforcing your skills and intentions.

Visualisation can be applied to many areas of life, such as preparing for a big presentation, improving at a sport, or setting personal goals. For instance, if you're gearing up for an important work meeting, visualise yourself speaking confidently and effectively communicating your points. This mental practice will help reduce anxiety and enhance your actual performance.

In Jeremiah 1:11-12 (NIV), the Lord asks, *"What do you see, Jeremiah?"* And when Jeremiah describes his vision, God affirms, *"You have seen correctly, for I am watching to see that my word is fulfilled."* This passage highlights the power of vision and perception. It reminds us that what we focus on in our mind's eye manifests in reality through faith and action. Visualisation boosts confidence, reduces anxiety, and enhances performance by mentally rehearsing success. It helps you set clear intentions and stay motivated toward achieving your goals.

Practical Tips:

◊ **Mental Rehearsal:** Regularly visualise yourself achieving a specific goal, vividly picturing the details and emotions associated with success.
◊ **Positive Imagery:** Use visualisation to boost confidence by imagining the best possible outcomes and the steps to get there.
◊ **Daily Practice:** Dedicate a few minutes daily to visualise your goals, creating a clear and positive mental image of success.

Reflective Questions:

» How do you currently use visualisation in your life?
» What goals can you visualise to enhance your confidence and performance?

By embracing visualisation techniques, you can enhance your performance and achieve your goals more effectively. Embrace positive visualisation, and see your confidence and success improve.

DAY 48: THE POWER OF REPETITION

"Success is the sum of small efforts, repeated day in and day out." – Robert Collier

Repetition is a powerful tool for shaping and rewiring your brain. Practising a new skill or behaviour strengthens the neural pathways that make these actions more automatic and natural. Imagine repetition as carving a path through a dense forest; the more you walk the path, the clearer and easier it becomes to navigate. This concept, known as neuroplasticity, allows the brain to adapt and grow in response to repeated experiences. The more you practice a new skill, the more your brain reinforces the neural connections associated with it, gradually making it second nature. Carol Dweck's growth mindset theory emphasises that consistent practice strengthens and reinforces the brain's learning pathways.

Galatians 6:9 (NIV) says, *"Let us not become weary in doing good, for at the proper time we will reap a harvest if we do not give up."* This verse highlights the importance of perseverance and repetition in achieving long-term success. As you persist in your practice, you build the skill and emotional resilience as your brain releases dopamine—a neurotransmitter associated with pleasure and reward—each time you succeed. Whether you're trying to adopt a new habit, such as regular exercise, or learning a new skill, like playing an instrument, repetition is vital. Your brain may initially resist the change, but the behaviour becomes ingrained with consistent effort, making it feel more natural and automatic over time.

Practical Tips:

◊ **Consistent Practice:** Choose a skill or habit you want to develop and commit to practising it daily. Dedicate specific times each day or week to ensure consistency.

◊ **Track Progress:** Keep a journal or use an app to log your practice sessions, noting improvements and milestones. Celebrating minor victories will keep you motivated.

◊ **Daily Exercise:** Select a new skill or habit to focus on and commit to practising it consistently for at least 21 days (though 60-90 days are preferable). Track your progress, noting how repetition makes the behaviour or skill effortless.

Reflective Questions:

» What new skill or habit are you working on?
» How can you incorporate consistent practice into your routine?

What benefits have you noticed from repeated practice?

By using repetition, you can rewire your brain and incorporate new skills and habits into your daily life.

Day 49: Cultivating Lasting Healthy Habits

"We are what we repeatedly do. Excellence, then, is not an act, but a habit." – Aristotle

Healthy habits are crucial for sustaining physical, mental, and emotional well-being. These habits are the foundation for a fulfilling life, enabling you to achieve your goals and maintain overall health. Developing healthy habits requires consistency, commitment, and a positive mindset.

Neuroscience shows that habit formation strengthens neural pathways, making behaviours more automatic and natural over time. This process, known as neuroplasticity, allows the brain to adapt and reorganise itself through repeated actions. For instance, regular physical activity improves fitness and enhances brain function by increasing blood flow and promoting the growth of new neurons. Renowned behaviour scientist Dr BJ Fogg emphasises the importance of starting small when building new habits. He suggests that tiny, incremental changes are more sustainable and less overwhelming, ultimately leading to more significant long-term improvements. This aligns with the idea that small, consistent efforts can produce substantial positive changes over time.

Proverbs 13:4 (ESV) says, *"The soul of the sluggard craves and gets nothing, while the soul of the diligent is richly supplied."* This verse highlights the value of diligence and consistency in cultivating habits that lead to a fruitful and fulfilling life.

Healthy habits can enhance physical health, improve mental well-being, and support overall life satisfaction. Incorporating regular exercise, balanced nutrition, sufficient sleep, and mindfulness practices into daily routines is crucial for maintaining optimal brain health and overall well-being.

Practical Tips:

◊ **Start Small:** Make manageable changes to build healthy habits. For example, if you want to eat healthier, incorporate one additional serving of vegetables into your meals each day.

◊ **Be Consistent:** Incorporate healthy habits into your daily routine. Set reminders and track your progress.

◊ **Exercise and Daily Reflection:** Use a habit tracker to monitor your progress in developing healthy habits. Choose a few essential habits to focus on and track your consistency each day.

Reflection Questions:

» What healthy habits do you want to develop and maintain?
» How can you incorporate small changes into your routine to build these habits?
» What benefits have you noticed from practising healthy habits?

Day 50: Managing Stress

"It's not the load that breaks you down, it's the way you carry it." – Lou Holtz

Stress is a natural part of life, but it can become harmful when it overwhelms our ability to cope. If the release of cortisol caused by stress remains elevated for a prolonged period, it can harm the brain and overall health. Brain training helps lower cortisol and builds mental resilience. For instance, mindfulness meditation can alter brain structures related to attention, emotion regulation, and self-awareness.

Philippians 4:6-7 (NIV) encourages us: *"Do not be anxious about anything, but in every situation, by prayer and petition, with thanksgiving, present your requests to God."* This verse does not only provide spiritual comfort but also profoundly impacts the brain. Praying and being grateful can activate the anterior cingulate cortex in the brain, reducing anxiety and promoting calmness. Additionally, the act of prayer can lower cortisol levels and release dopamine, enhancing mood and reinforcing a positive outlook.

Picture yourself in a challenging situation at work, like a big presentation. Instead of letting anxiety take over, you take a moment to practice mindfulness, refocusing your attention on the present and reframing limiting narratives. Later, you spend a few minutes in prayer, presenting your concerns to God and expressing gratitude for the opportunity. This combination helps calm your mind, lowers stress levels, and enhances your focus, allowing you to perform better.

Practical Tips:

◊ **Meditation:** Set aside 10-15 minutes daily to sit quietly, focus on your breathing, and bring your attention to the present moment.

◊ **Cognitive-Behavioural Exercises:** Challenge negative thoughts and reframe them into positive or neutral perspectives.

◊ **Prayer:** Include prayer in your daily routine, expressing gratitude and seeking guidance for managing stress and challenges.

Reflective Questions:

» How do you currently manage stress in your daily life?
» What techniques can you use to improve your stress management?
» How does reducing stress impact your overall well-being and mental resilience?

Incorporating mindfulness, cognitive-behavioural techniques, and prayer into your routine can reduce stress and improve your mental resilience. Embrace these practices, and watch your ability to handle stress and challenges improve.

Day 51: Mastering Decision-Making Skills

"In any moment of decision, the best thing you can do is the right thing. The worst thing you can do is nothing." – Theodore Roosevelt

Mastering decision-making skills is crucial for navigating life's complexities, from choosing a career path to resolving conflicts. Good decision-making leads to better outcomes, greater satisfaction, and a more fulfilling life.

Neuroscience shows that decision-making engages the prefrontal cortex, which is responsible for planning, reasoning, and problem-solving. Structured decision-making strengthens these neural pathways, making informed choices more natural over time.
Emotions also play a crucial role. Being aware of and managing your emotions helps you stay calm and focused, guiding you toward decisions aligned with your core values.

Proverbs 3:5-6 (NIV) advises, *"Trust in the Lord with all your heart and lean not on your own understanding; in all your ways submit to him, and he will make your paths straight."* This verse highlights the importance of seeking divine guidance, combining our faith in God with thoughtful analysis. Effective decision-making requires clear criteria, diverse perspectives, and a balance between speed and thoroughness. A structured approach—defining the decision, listing options, evaluating pros and cons, and considering outcomes—can help avoid negative emotional biases and lead to better decisions. Incorporating diverse perspectives ensures all aspects are considered, enhancing decision quality.

Imagine facing a tough decision between two job offers. To navigate clearly, define the decision, list options, weigh the pros and cons, and ask for advice. Prayer will also provide peace and guidance, helping you make a God-confident choice.

Practical Tips:

◊ **Define the Decision:** Understand what needs to be decided.
◊ **List Options:** Identify all possible choices.
◊ **Evaluate Options:** Weigh the pros and cons of each.
◊ **Consider Outcomes:** Assess the short-term and long-term effects.
◊ **Seek Advice:** Consult with trusted individuals if needed.
◊ **Decide:** Choose the best option based on your evaluation.
◊ **Review the Decision:** Reflect on the process and learn for future decisions.

Reflective Questions:

» How do you currently approach decision-making?
» How does prayer influence your decisions and outcomes?

DAY 52: THE POWER OF CONNECTION FOR A HEALTHIER MIND

"No man is an island entire of itself." – John Donne

Humans are like trees in a forest. Just as trees share nutrients and support each other's growth through interconnected root systems, we thrive on connections with others. We are naturally wired for social interaction, and our mental and emotional well-being depends on positive relationships.

Engaging in social activities activates brain areas linked to reward and pleasure, like a tree soaking up sunlight. When we interact with others, our brain's reward system stimulates the release of dopamine, which uplifts our mood and motivates us to seek more connection. A strong social network also helps manage stress, acting as a buffer against life's storms, similar to how trees protect each other from strong winds.

Ecclesiastes 4:9-10 (NIV) says, *"Two are better than one because they have a good return for their labour: If either of them falls down, one can help the other up."* We are designed to live in a community, and our brains flourish when we have strong, supportive relationships. Imagine a situation where you're having a tough day at work. Imagine your stress as a heavy backpack. When you reach out to a friend or colleague, it's like sharing the load—suddenly, that heavy backpack feels much lighter. Isolation, on the other hand, is like walking through the forest alone with that heavy pack, making the journey much harder.

Practical Tips:

- ◊ **Reach Out Regularly:** Like trees need sunlight, we need regular social interaction. Make time to connect with friends or family, even just for a quick chat.
- ◊ **Join a Group:** Find your "forest"—a community group, hobby club, or volunteer organisation where you can build meaningful connections.
- ◊ **Deepen Conversations:** Move beyond small talk; share your thoughts and listen actively to others, strengthening the roots of your relationships.

Reflective Questions:

» How do your social connections help lighten your emotional load?
» What steps can you take to strengthen your "root system" of relationships?

How can you make social engagement a natural part of your daily routine?

Nurture your social connections to build relationships and cultivate a healthy, resilient brain. Embrace your community, and watch how these connections help you grow.

DAY 53: BREAKING FREE FROM LIMITING THOUGHTS

"We see the world not as it is but as we are." - Anaïs Nin

Limiting thoughts are like invisible chains that hold you back from reaching your full potential. These thoughts, shaped by past experiences, fears, or negative self-beliefs, distort your perception of yourself and the world. Breaking free from these mental restraints is essential to truly thrive.

Your thoughts shape your reality. If you constantly believe that you're not good enough or that success is out of reach, these beliefs can become self-fulfilling prophecies. In "Rewire Your Brain," Dr. John Arden highlights that our brains are wired to adapt and change. You can rewire your brain to support a more positive and empowered mindset by challenging and replacing limiting beliefs.

Imagine your mind as a hot-air balloon. Limiting thoughts are the sandbags weighing you down. By identifying and releasing these mental weights, you allow yourself to rise, unlocking your true potential.

Romans 12:2 encourages us to renew our minds and transform ourselves. This aligns with the concept of neuroplasticity, the brain's ability to rewire itself. Just as you can change your thought patterns to foster positive beliefs, you are called to renew your mind according to God's truth.

When faced with a challenging project at work, if your first thought is, *"I'm not capable of this,"* recognise it as a limiting thought. Replace it with, *"I have the skills to succeed,"* and observe your confidence and approach shift.

Practical Tips:
- ◊ **Identify the Chains:** Recognise limiting thoughts as they arise. Write them down to expose them.
- ◊ **Replace with Truth:** Counter each limiting thought with a positive statement or a scripture.
- ◊ **Practice Gratitude:** Focus on your strengths and accomplishments to reinforce a positive mindset.

Reflective Questions:
- » What limiting thoughts have been holding you back?
- » How can you replace these thoughts with empowering beliefs?
- » How will breaking free from these thoughts change your approach to challenges?

DAY 54: OVERCOMING A LIMITING MONEY MINDSET

"Your mindset is your wealth." - Unknown

If you're constantly thinking, *"I'll never have enough"* or *"Money is so hard to get,"* it's like putting up roadblocks on your journey to financial freedom. These thoughts become self-fulfilling prophecies, limiting your ability to see opportunities and take action. Shifting from a scarcity mindset to one of abundance is key to breaking free from these mental chains.

Imagine your mind as a garden. If you keep planting seeds of doubt and fear about money, that's all you'll grow—thorns that choke out any chance of prosperity. But when you plant seeds of belief in abundance, rooted in trust in God's provision, you cultivate a garden full of opportunities and financial growth.

Philippians 4:19 reminds us, *"And my God will meet all your needs according to the riches of his glory in Christ Jesus."*
This verse is like a nourishing rain, reminding us that God's provision is limitless. Trusting in God's promises about money and repeating them to yourself daily can help rewire your brain, replacing thoughts of lack with assurance of abundance. Over time, this mental shift opens the door to financial freedom—the freedom to thrive, take risks, and seize opportunities without being paralysed by fear of lack.

Practical Tips:

◊ **Daily Affirmations:** Start your day by repeating positive affirmations about money and abundance. Say things like, *"I am worthy of wealth,"* or *"God provides for all my needs."*

◊ **Visualise Abundance:** Picture yourself living in financial freedom, enjoying the fruits of your labour, and using your resources to bless others.

◊ **Trust and Take Action:** Remember, faith without works is dead. Trust God's promises and take practical steps toward your financial goals.

Reflective Questions:

» How do your current thoughts about money affect your financial decisions?
» What changes can you make to shift from a scarcity mindset to one of abundance?
» How can trust in God's provision change your financial outlook?

Nurturing a mindset of abundance can help you break free from the limitations that hold you back and step into a life of financial freedom. Embrace this new mindset, and watch opportunities bloom in your life.

Day 55: The Power of Self-Reflection

"The unexamined life is not worth living." – Socrates

Self-reflection is like holding up a mirror to your inner world. It allows you to examine your thoughts, feelings, and actions, offering insights that promote personal growth and wiser decisions. Taking just a few moments each day to pause and reflect can make a big difference in how you understand yourself and navigate life.

Just imagine your mind being a garden. Without regular tending, weeds of negative thoughts and unchecked emotions can take over. Self-reflection is the gardener's tool—it helps you pull out those weeds, plant seeds of understanding, and cultivate a space where positive thoughts and intentional actions can flourish.

When you practice self-reflection through activities like journaling or quiet contemplation, you engage the prefrontal cortex—the part of your brain responsible for complex decision-making and emotional regulation. This mental "exercise" strengthens your ability to process experiences and emotions, leading to greater self-awareness and emotional intelligence.

2 Corinthians 13:5 (NIV) tells us to *"examine yourselves to see whether you are in the faith; test yourselves."* This verse reminds us to regularly assess whether our actions and thoughts align with our values and beliefs, promoting spiritual and personal growth.
Consider a time when you made a hasty decision that you regretted. Reflecting on your motivations and emotions could have provided the clarity needed to make a better choice. Self-reflection helps you understand the "why" behind your actions, guiding you toward more thoughtful and intentional decisions.

Practical Tips:

◊ **Journaling:** Spend a few minutes each day writing about your thoughts, feelings, and actions. This practice helps clarify your experiences and uncover patterns.
◊ **Quiet Contemplation:** Find a peaceful moment in your day to sit quietly and reflect on what you've learned and how you can grow.
◊ **Daily Reflection:** Dedicate time each evening to review your day. What went well? What could have been better? How did your emotions influence your actions?

Reflective Questions:

» How often do you take time to reflect on your thoughts and actions?
» What insights have you gained from self-reflection?
» How can you incorporate regular self-reflection into your routine?

Day 56: Embracing a Growth Mindset

"In a growth mindset, challenges are exciting rather than threatening." – Carol Dweck

A growth mindset is the belief that one can develop one's abilities and intelligence through effort and practice. Unlike a fixed mindset, where talents are seen as fixed, a growth mindset views challenges as opportunities to learn and grow. This shift in perspective enhances resilience, learning, and overall success, transforming life's obstacles into exciting opportunities.

Understanding a Growth Mindset:
In a recent coaching session, my client shared she felt she could never be a leader because she wasn't a "born leader." This belief reflects a fixed mindset, where leadership is seen as an innate talent rather than a skill to be developed. I encouraged her to view leadership as a muscle that can be strengthened with practice. Just as lifting weights builds physical strength, embracing challenges strengthens your brain. Through neuroplasticity, your brain forms and strengthens connections as you learn and grow. With a growth mindset, setbacks become opportunities for improvement, not barriers to success.

James 1:2-4 (NIV) tells us, *"Consider it pure joy, my brothers and sisters, whenever you face trials of many kinds because you know that the testing of your faith produces perseverance."* This scripture encourages us to view challenges as opportunities for growth, perfectly aligning with a growth mindset. When faced with a setback, try to see it as a chance to learn and improve. For example, if a presentation at work doesn't go as planned, reflect on what you can learn and how you can do better next time. This mindset enhances your skills and also builds your resilience.

Practical Tips:
- ◊ **Positive Reframing:** When encountering challenges, shift your thoughts from negative to positive. Ask, *"What can I learn from this?"*
- ◊ **Learn from Mistakes:** View mistakes as lessons. Reflect on what you can improve.
- ◊ **Daily Reflection:** Spend a few moments each day reflecting on your challenges and how you handled them.

Reflective Questions:
- » How do you typically react to challenges?
- » What steps can you take to shift from a fixed to a growth mindset?
- » How can a growth mindset improve your learning and success?

By embracing a growth mindset, you can turn challenges into stepping stones for personal growth and success.

Day 57: Igniting the Spark of Lifelong Learning

"Education is not the filling of a pail, but the lighting of a fire." – William Butler Yeats

Lifelong learning is about staying curious and continuously seeking knowledge and new experiences. It's not just about formal education; it's about keeping your brain engaged and growing throughout life. The books you don't read, the skills you don't learn, and the experiences you avoid can't help you grow. Lifelong learning keeps your mind sharp, your skills up to date, and your life exciting.

When you learn something new, your brain forms new neural (brain) connections. This is called neuroplasticity, the brain's ability to adapt and reorganise itself. Engaging in new learning keeps your brain flexible and open to change. This can even help delay mental decline as you age.

Proverbs 18:15 (NIV) says, *"The heart of the discerning acquires knowledge, for the ears of the wise seek it out."* This verse reminds us that wisdom and learning go hand in hand. Just like a book that stays on the shelf can't share its knowledge, a life without learning misses out on countless growth opportunities. Every new experience you embrace adds value and richness to your life.

Feeling stuck or in a rut? Learning something new can reignite your passion and energy. Whether it's taking up a new hobby, reading a book, or signing up for a course, each step towards learning helps you grow.

Practical Tips:

◊ **Stay Curious:** Explore new interests or hobbies. Set small learning goals to keep you motivated.
◊ **Create a Learning Routine:** Dedicate regular time—daily or weekly—to focus on learning. Whether it's reading or trying a new skill, make it a habit.
◊ **Track and Reflect:** Monitor your progress and think about how learning improves your life.

Reflective Questions:

» How are you engaging in lifelong learning right now?
» What new areas could you explore to expand your knowledge?
» How can you make lifelong learning a regular part of your routine?

Embrace lifelong learning, and see how it fuels your mind, heart, and life with endless possibilities. Keep learning, and watch your world grow.

Day 58: Rest as a Key to Renewal

"Night and day, whether he sleeps or gets up, the seed sprouts and grows, though he does not know how." – Mark 4:27

Rest is more than just taking a break; it's essential for growth and renewal. As a seed grows underground while the farmer sleeps, your mind and body need rest to thrive. Without enough rest, your ability to think, create, and make decisions weakens.
Rest works like a reset button for your brain. During sleep, your brain processes information, strengthens memories and clears out toxins that build up throughout the day. This recovery time is vital for your cognitive function, memory, and emotional balance.

Research shows that deep sleep strengthens brain connections, improving memory and problem-solving skills. Conversely, lack of rest can lead to mental fatigue, poor decision-making, and increased stress.

In Mark 4:27, Jesus talks about how the seed grows even when the farmer rests. This powerful reminder that sometimes growth happens when we step back and let things unfold highlights the biblical principle of rest and renewal, aligning with the Sabbath—a day set aside for rest, reflection, and worship.

Making rest a priority is vital for long-term success. Whether through sleep, short breaks, or time for reflection and prayer, rest helps recharge your mind and body. Resting allows you to function better and achieve more in the long run.

Practical Tips:

◊ **Prioritise Sleep:** Aim for 7-8 hours of sleep each night to give your brain and body the rest they need.
◊ **Take Breaks:** Include short breaks during your day to relax and refresh your focus.
◊ **Embrace Sabbath:** Dedicate one day each week for rest and spiritual renewal to recharge your mind and soul.

Reflective Questions:

» How do you incorporate rest into your daily routine?
» What changes can you make to improve your rest?
How does rest affect your productivity and overall well-being?

By making rest a priority, you're nurturing your future growth and success. Embrace the power of rest, and see how it renews your mind, body, and spirit.

Day 59: Rewiring Your Mind with God's Word

"The Bible isn't just a book; it's the most powerful tool you'll ever use to transform your mind."

Think of your mind as a home. Every thought you allow inside is like decorating a room. If you fill it with worry, doubt, and negativity, it becomes cluttered, chaotic, and stressful. But when you choose to furnish it with God's promises, words of faith, and hope, it becomes a peaceful, beautiful space that brings joy and clarity.

God's Word is not just inspirational—it's transformative. Neuroscience tells us that our brains can change through consistent thoughts and habits. This means you're actively rewiring your brain when you regularly meditate on scripture and fill your mind with truth. It strengthens the neural pathways that lead to peace, joy, and emotional stability.

Think of it like renovating a house. The more you invest time in replacing the old, worn-out areas of your thinking with God's promises, the more your mind becomes a place of calm and strength. Proverbs 23:7 says, *"For as he thinks in his heart, so is he."* What you think about shapes who you become. By meditating on God's Word, you're equipping yourself to handle life's challenges with confidence and grace. Spending time in God's Word rewires your brain for emotional mastery and spiritual growth. Start each day by reading a passage of Scripture and reflect on how it speaks to your life. Throughout the day, let God's promises guide your decisions and actions.

Practical Tips:

◊ **Verse of the Week:** Choose one Scripture to focus on each week. Repeat it throughout the day and reflect on how it applies to your life.

◊ **Daily Devotion:** Make a daily routine of reading and reflecting on the Bible. Let God's wisdom sink deep into your heart and mind.

◊ **Live It:** Apply what you read. Whether it's through showing love, offering for-giveness, or trusting God's timing, let His Word shape your actions.

Reflective Questions:

» How has spending time in God's Word changed your thoughts and emotions?
» What steps can you take to make Scripture meditation a daily habit?
» How can you apply God's Word to overcome challenges in your life?

Feeding your mind with Scripture rewires your brain for peace, joy, and resilience. Embrace it and see your life transform.

DAY 60: CHANGE YOUR BRAIN, CHANGE YOUR LIFE

"The only way to make sense out of change is to plunge into it, move with it, and join the dance." – Alan Watts

As we conclude Part 2 of your journey, it's time to celebrate the incredible power of neuroplasticity—your brain's ability to adapt, change, and grow.
Over the last 30 days, you've taken steps to rewire your brain for greater cognitive function, emotional resilience, and overall well-being. This journey isn't just a chapter; it's the beginning of a lifelong dance with growth and change.

You've explored neuroplasticity and practised techniques like gratitude, visualisation, and mindfulness. Each exercise was like taking a new step in a dance that strengthens your brain, allowing you to adapt and thrive.

Neuroscience teaches us that the brain remains adaptable throughout life, forming new neural pathways with each new experience. Proverbs 4:7 (NIV) says, *"The beginning of wisdom is this: Get wisdom. Though it cost all you have, get understanding."* This wisdom aligns with continuous growth, urging us to embrace lifelong learning.

Practical Tips:

◊ **Reflect Regularly:** Set time aside each week to reflect on your progress and identify areas for growth. Journaling can be an effective tool for this.

◊ **Stay Curious:** Embrace new learning opportunities, whether a new hobby, a course, or reading. Keep your mind active and challenged.

◊ **Integrate Practices:** Continue using techniques like mindfulness and visualisation to maintain and build on your progress.

◊ **Weekly Reflection:** Spend time each week reflecting on your journey and setting new goals. Consider what has worked well and what can be improved. Write down your thoughts and plan actionable steps for the coming week.

Reflective Questions:

How has your understanding of neuroplasticity changed over the past 30 days?

» What practices have been most beneficial for your brain health and overall well-being?

» How can you continue challenging your brain and embracing lifelong learning?

By summarising your journey and committing to continuous growth, you can harness the power of neuroplasticity for a limitless future. Embrace the dance of change and watch as your mind and life expand and thrive.

PART THREE

UNLOCKING THE POWER OF YOUR BRAIN

PART 3 INTRODUCTION

This section explores how you can tap into the full potential of your brain. By understanding how your brain works, you'll discover practical ways to improve your thinking, manage your emotions, and transform your mindset.

As you go through each day, you'll gain tools to help you rewire your brain for growth, resilience, and a deeper connection with God.

Get ready to unlock the limitless possibilities within you.

Day 61: Understanding the Brain's Structure

"The human brain is the most complex organ in the body and is the seat of intelligence, interpreter of the senses, initiator of body movement, and controller of behaviour."—Dr. John Henley

The human brain is a divine masterpiece, designed with such complexity that it controls every thought, emotion, and action. As Psalm 139:14 (NIV) reminds us, *"I praise you because I am fearfully and wonderfully made; your works are wonderful, I know that full well."* Our brain is a reflection of this wonderful design, intricately woven to function in miraculous ways.

Think of your brain as the ultimate command centre.

The **brain's cerebrum** is the CEO, making decisions, solving problems, and directing actions. Beneath it, the **cerebellum** acts like a seasoned coach, fine-tuning your movements and keeping you balanced, whether walking down the street or catching a ball. The **brainstem** is the life support team, quietly keeping your heart beating and lungs breathing. Deep inside, the **limbic system** is like your personal memory and emotion library, storing the stories of your life and guiding your feelings.

Imagine you're cooking a meal. Your cerebrum decides the recipe, the cerebellum ensures your hands chop and stir with precision, the brainstem keeps your heart and lungs steady, and the limbic system might bring a wave of nostalgia as you prepare a dish from your childhood. Each part of your brain plays a crucial role in even the simplest tasks. Understanding this structure is fascinating and empowering. It helps us understand why activities like exercise, deep breathing, and learning new skills are vital; they keep different parts of our brain and body healthy and strong.

Practical Tips:

◊ **Visualise:** Draw a simple diagram of the brain. Label its key parts and think about how they're involved in your daily life.
◊ **Engage:** To keep these areas active, try new activities that challenge your brain—like learning a new hobby or practising mindfulness.

Reflective Questions:

» How does understanding your brain's design change how you care for it?
» What new habits can you start to help support your brain's health?

By appreciating the brain's intricate design, you unlock the potential to nurture and grow the incredible power within you, guiding your journey to limitless living.

Day 62: The Role of Neurotransmitters

"Neurotransmitters are the brain's chemical messengers, essential for communication within the nervous system." – Dr. Eric Kandel

Neurotransmitters are like the brain's postal service, delivering vital messages that impact everything—from your mood to how you sleep and deal with stress. As Proverbs 23:7 (KJV) says, *"For as he thinks in his heart, so is he."*
These chemical messengers buzzing around in our brains deeply influence how we think and feel.

Picture your brain as a busy city. Neurons (brain cells) are the residents, and neurotransmitters are the messengers rushing between them, delivering critical information. **Dopamine** is your brain's "feel-good" messenger, giving you that rush of pleasure when you accomplish something. **Serotonin** is your calm and steady friend, helping you feel peaceful after a good night's rest. **Gamma-Aminobutyric Acid (GABA)** steps in when things get too chaotic, helping to calm your nerves, while **glutamate** keeps your brain sharp and ready to learn.

Think about the last time you felt really proud after completing a task—maybe finishing a project at work or hitting a fitness goal. That warm, satisfied feeling? That's dopamine giving you a high five. Or how about the sense of peace you feel after a relaxing walk? That's serotonin, making sure you stay calm and balanced. But when these messengers aren't working well, it can feel like the city is in chaos, leading to mood swings, stress, and trouble sleeping. By understanding how neurotransmitters work, you can take steps to keep these messengers in check. Eating a balanced diet rich in omega-3s (like those found in salmon and walnuts), staying active with regular exercise, cultivating self-awareness, and practising mindfulness can all help keep your brain healthy and thriving.

Journaling:

» Track your thoughts, mood, diet, and activities for a week. Observe how different foods, exercises, and experiences influence your thoughts and feelings.
» Use these insights to make minor adjustments that enhance your overall well-being.

Reflective Question:
How do your daily habits affect your mood and energy?

Understanding neurotransmitters helps you manage your emotions and make intentional choices.

DAY 63: REWIRING YOUR BRAIN WITH POSITIVE HABITS

"Change your thoughts, and you change your world." – Norman Vincent Peale

Neuroplasticity gives your brain the remarkable ability to reshape itself, but it's the daily habits you develop that determine that transformation. Think of your brain as soft clay—every thought and action moulds and shapes it. The habits you choose to form are the tools that carve out new, more positive pathways in your brain.

Imagine your brain as a network of paths. The thoughts and habits you repeat most often become well-trodden trails, easy to follow but hard to change. But with intention, you can forge new trails, leading to healthier, more positive thinking patterns. Whenever you choose to focus on gratitude, talk to God, or approach a challenge with a growth mindset, you create new, stronger pathways.

Scripture guides us in Philippians 4:8 to focus on whatever is true, noble, and praiseworthy. By consistently directing your thoughts and actions toward these virtues, you actively obey and physically rewire your brain to align with Romans 12:2's call to "be transformed by the renewing of your mind."

Building positive habits, like starting your day in prayer or ending it with gratitude, improves your day. It also reshapes your brain, making it easier to think positively and respond with grace. Over time, these habits become ingrained, providing a strong foundation for your mental, emotional, and spiritual well-being.

Habit Builder: Select one positive habit to focus on this week. Track your progress daily, noting how it influences your thoughts and emotions. Reflect on the changes as this habit becomes a routine part of your life.

Practical Tips:

◊ **Focus on One Habit:** Choose a positive habit to establish this week, such as daily gratitude or talking to God each morning.

◊ **Be Consistent:** Regularly practice your chosen habit to strengthen the new pathways in your brain.

Reflective Questions:

» Which habit would most positively impact your life?
» How can you incorporate this habit into your daily routine?
» How have your past habits shaped your current mindset?

By intentionally forming positive habits, you improve your daily life and actively reshape your brain to support a more positive, fulfilling future.

Day 64: Finding Balance in Your Body's Response

"The greatest weapon against stress is our ability to choose one thought over another." – William James

Our bodies are equipped with two powerful nervous systems, the sympathetic and parasympathetic nervous systems. These systems work together to help us respond to life's challenges. Think of them as the gas and brake pedals in a car.

The **sympathetic nervous system** is like the gas pedal, kicking in when action is needed. It revs you up during stressful situations, whether you're dealing with a tight deadline or reacting quickly to danger. This is your body's *'fight, flight, or freeze'* mode, giving you the energy and focus to tackle immediate challenges. But just like a car can't run on full throttle forever, your body needs time to slow down and recover. That's where the **parasympathetic system**, the brake, comes in. Once the stress has passed, it helps you relax, rest, and recharge by slowing your heart rate, calming your mind, and bringing your body back to a state of peace.

For example, after a demanding day at work, during which your sympathetic system has been working overtime, you might finally sit down, take a deep breath, and spend time in prayer. This activates your parasympathetic system, signalling to your body that it's safe to relax and unwind.

Philippians 4:6-7 (NIV) reminds us, *"Do not be anxious about anything, but in every situation, by prayer and petition, with thanksgiving, present your requests to God."* By turning to God in times of stress, we invite peace into our hearts, activating the parasympathetic system and restoring balance in our lives.

Practical Tips:

◊ **Deep Breathing:** When feeling overwhelmed, take slow, deep breaths, followed by a quiet prayer, to release your worries and calm your body.
◊ **Daily Relaxation:** Take 10 minutes each day to relax, breathe, and reflect for inner peace and balance.

Reflective Questions:

» How do you usually respond to stress?
» What daily practices can help you find more calm and peace?
» How can you use your faith to support balance in your body's responses?

Understanding and balancing these systems will help you to manage stress better and live a more peaceful, centred life.

Day 65: The Power of Expectations Over Genes

"The only limits to the possibilities in your life tomorrow are the buts you use today." – Les Brown

There's a widespread belief that our genes dictate our health, intelligence, and potential. However, science and scripture reveal that our expectations and beliefs can shape our reality more than our genes ever could.

The Power of the Mind Over the Body
Proverbs 23:7 (KJV) teaches, *"As a man thinks in his heart, so is he."*
This wisdom goes beyond the spiritual realm—it's supported by neuroscience. When we expect positive outcomes, we can reshape our brain through neuroplasticity. Our thoughts and beliefs create new neural (brain) pathways, reinforcing behaviours and attitudes that align with those beliefs. This power of positive thinking can fill us with hope and optimism for the future.
David Robson's 'The Expectation Effect' demonstrates how mindset can overcome genetic limitations. In one study, participants who believed they were genetically prone to obesity gained more weight than those who did not, even though their genetic risk was identical. This shows that our expectations often determine our experiences more than our DNA.

How Expectations and Emotional Mastery Work Together
Managing our emotions is key to ensuring that our expectations manifest positively in our lives. If we don't manage our emotions, which are commonly triggered by the **amygdala**, the brain's emotional core, fear and doubt can seize control. This leads us to react out of fear or anxiety. But by practising emotional regulation through faith and positive thinking, we allow our **prefrontal cortex (PFC)**, the brain's centre for reasoning and planning, to guide us toward more constructive actions.

Mark 11:24 reminds us, *"Whatever you ask for in prayer, believe that you have received it, and it will be yours."* This scripture highlights the power of faith-driven expectations. When combined with emotional mastery, it becomes a powerful tool for success. By focusing on God's promises and controlling our emotions, we open ourselves to new opportunities and align our actions with His will.

Reflective Questions:
  » Are your expectations driven by faith or by fear?
  » How can you manage your emotions better to support positive outcomes?

By aligning your thoughts with faith and mastering your emotions, you can rewire your brain for success—beyond what your genes might suggest.

Day 66: Understanding the Brain, Mind, and Mindset

"You have power over your mind, not outside events. Realise this, and you will find strength." – Marcus Aurelius

Although the terms brain, mind, and mindset are often used interchangeably, they each represent different aspects of who we are and how we think. Understanding the links and differences between them will help you unlock and maximise your full potential.

The brain is the physical organ in your skull, comprising around 86 billion neurons. These neurons communicate through trillions of connections, enabling you to think, feel, and move. It's the control centre of your body, responsible for processing information, storing memories, and regulating functions. Think of it as your body's hardware—tangible and scientifically observable.

The mind is more abstract, where thoughts, emotions, and memories arise from the brain's activity. While the brain is the physical structure, the mind is like the software running on this hardware. It interprets the world, forms beliefs, and generates thoughts that shape reality. The mind gives meaning to the information your brain processes.

Mindset is your beliefs, values, expectations and behaviour patterns, influencing how you approach life. It's shaped by your thoughts, experiences, and the meaning you assign to them. A fixed mindset might lead you to believe your abilities are set in stone, while a growth mindset encourages you to see challenges as opportunities for learning and growth. Mindset is the lens through which you view and interact with the world.

Mindset Reflection: Reflect on a recent challenge. How did your mindset shape your response? Write down one belief you'd like to change and reframe it to support a growth mindset.

Practical Tips:

◊ **Mindful Awareness:** Notice the thoughts and beliefs shaping your mindset. Are they empowering or limiting?

◊ **Growth Mindset:** Embrace challenges as opportunities for growth, reminding yourself that your abilities can develop.

Reflective Questions:

» How does your mindset influence your actions?
» What beliefs might be holding you back?
» How can you shift toward a growth-oriented mindset?

This guide will explore various mindsets, helping you understand how they shape your thoughts, actions, and growth.

Day 67: Conscious vs. Subconscious Mind

"You can't change what you don't confront. Awareness is the first step to transformation."
– Unknown

Think of your mind as a grand orchestra: the conscious brain is the conductor, while the subconscious is the hidden musician. Together, they create the symphony of your life. Let's explore how these two parts interact and how you can harness their power for growth.

Conscious Brain: The Active Director
Your conscious brain is the maestro, actively engaging in decision-making and planning. It's where you set goals and make deliberate choices. For example, when you decide to start a new business, your conscious mind plans the steps and considers the options.

Subconscious Brain: The Hidden Composer
The subconscious brain works behind the scenes, managing automatic responses, habits, and deep-seated beliefs. It processes information rapidly, influencing about 90% of your behaviour based on past experiences and emotions.

Speed of Processing
The subconscious processes information at lightning speed, handling millions of bits per second. In contrast, the conscious brain processes around 40-50 bits per second. This speed difference explains why some actions happen automatically, like pulling your hand away from a hot stove.

Shaping the Subconscious
Early experiences and repeated patterns shape your subconscious. Proverbs 4:23 (NIV) highlights this: *"Above all else, guard your heart, for everything you do flows from it."* Your subconscious influences your actions based on these deep-seated patterns.

Overcoming Limiting Patterns
Negative beliefs or past traumas can keep you stuck. Recognising and reprogramming these patterns is crucial for growth and success. For example, a past failure might create a fear of new challenges.

Harnessing the Power

> **Self-Awareness:** Reflect on your thoughts to uncover subconscious patterns.
> **Positive Affirmations:** Replace negative beliefs with empowering ones.
> **Visualisation:** Visualise your goals to make them feel achievable.
> **Mindfulness and Meditation:** Practice mindfulness to stay present and use meditation to align your subconscious with your goals.

Reflective Questions

» How do your subconscious beliefs shape your decisions?
» What can you do to align your subconscious with your goals?

Day 68: The Vagus Nerve: Your Brain's Secret Ally

"The body is the servant of the mind." – James Allen

The **vagus nerve** is like a superhighway connecting your brain to your body, influencing everything from your heart rate to digestion and even your mood. But it's more than just a communication pathway; it plays a crucial role in unlocking your brain's power through neuroplasticity and emotional regulation.

This nerve is part of the parasympathetic nervous system, which helps your body relax and recover from stress. When you take deep breaths, stretch, or even hug someone, you activate this nerve, sending calming signals to your brain. This relaxation response is essential not just for managing stress but also for enhancing brain function. When your vagus nerve is stimulated, it helps your brain create new neural connections more easily—the process known as neuroplasticity.

The more relaxed and focused you are, the better your brain can learn, adapt, and grow. By regularly stimulating the vagus nerve—through activities like deep breathing or meditation—you create an environment in your brain that's more conducive to learning and emotional balance.
Psalm 46:10 (NIV) encourages us to *"Be still, and know that I am God."* This stillness, achieved through practices that stimulate the vagus nerve, allows your brain to function at its best, enhancing your mental and physical well-being.

Practical Tips:

◊ **Stimulate the Vagus Nerve:** Spend 10 minutes daily on deep breathing, stretching, or a firm hug to enhance mental calm and brain function.
◊ **Mindful Relaxation:** Practice daily reflection or prayer to support relaxation and promote brain growth.

Reflective Questions:

» How does stress affect your ability to focus and learn?
» What daily practices could you incorporate to stimulate your vagus nerve and enhance your brain's capabilities?
» How can you create an environment that supports neuroplasticity in your everyday life?

By understanding and harnessing the power of the vagus nerve, you can unlock greater potential in your brain, enhancing your ability to think clearly, learn effectively, and grow continuously.

Day 69: The Power of Non-Sleep Deep Rest (NSDR)

"Sometimes the most productive thing you can do is relax." – Mark Black

In our fast-paced world, finding time to truly rest can seem impossible. That's where **Non-Sleep Deep Rest (NSDR)** comes in—a simple and powerful way to recharge without needing actual sleep. Think of NSDR as a quick mental reset, like hitting the pause button on a busy day. It allows your mind and body to rest deeply while you're still awake, helping you stay sharp and focused.

NSDR works like a power nap, but without falling asleep. By relaxing deeply for just 10-15 minutes, you can lower stress, boost focus, and improve your mood. It's perfect when you need to recharge but don't have time for a nap. What makes NSDR special is that it helps your brain support neurogenesis—the creation of new neurons. This means you're not just resting; you're helping your brain grow and adapt, which boosts learning and mental health.

Psalm 23:2 (NIV) says, *"He makes me lie down in green pastures, he leads me beside quiet waters, he refreshes my soul."* NSDR is like your own personal "green pasture"—a space of calm and renewal, even in the middle of a hectic day.

Practical Tips:
- ◊ **Daily NSDR:** Dedicate 10-15 minutes each day to NSDR. Find a quiet spot, close your eyes, and focus on your breath. Let your body relax deeply while staying awake.
- ◊ **Mini-Breaks:** Take short breaks throughout your day. Close your eyes, breathe deeply, and disconnect from any distractions, allowing your brain a quick refresh.

Reflective Questions:
- » How often do you allow yourself real rest during the day?
- » How could regular NSDR practice improve your focus and mood?
- » What small changes can you make to add more restful moments into your routine?

By adding NSDR to your day, you give your brain the rest it needs to stay focused, calm, and ready to handle whatever life throws your way.

Day 70: Unlocking the Power of Neurogenesis

"The brain is a muscle that can move the world." – Stephen King

Your brain is an incredible, ever-changing organ that constantly adapts to the world around you. One of the most exciting ways it does this is through neurogenesis—the creation of new neurons.
For years, it was believed that brain cell growth, or neurogenesis, only occurred during childhood. However, research now shows that the brain can continue to grow and adapt throughout life. This ongoing growth is particularly vital in the hippocampus, a region responsible for memory and learning.

Think of your brain as a garden. Neurogenesis is like planting new seeds that grow into strong, healthy plants, enriching the entire garden. These new neurons help you learn new things, remember better, and adapt to changes in your life. The great news is that you have the power to help your brain grow these new neurons through simple, everyday choices.

Think how you care for a garden: you water it, give it sunlight, and pull out the weeds. Similarly, you can nurture your brain by exercising regularly, trying new activities, and eating brain-healthy foods like blueberries and nuts. Just like tending to a garden, these actions encourage your brain to flourish and stay vibrant.

Psalm 139:14 (NIV) beautifully captures this idea: *"I praise you because I am fearfully and wonderfully made; your works are wonderful; I know that full well."* This verse reminds us of the incredible design of our bodies, including our brain's ability to renew and grow. Neurogenesis is part of this wonderful design, allowing us to keep learning, growing, and improving throughout our lives.

Practical Tips:
- ◊ **Get Moving:** To encourage neurogenesis, engage in regular physical activity, such as walking or dancing, for at least 30 minutes a day.
- ◊ **Try Something New:** Challenge your brain by learning a new skill, starting a hobby, or solving puzzles.
- ◊ **Eat Smart:** Add brain-boosting foods like blueberries, nuts, and leafy greens to your meals.

By embracing the power of neurogenesis, you're not just keeping your brain healthy—you're making sure it stays sharp, ready, and resilient, no matter what life brings your way.

Day 71: Inherited Genes and Epigenetics

"It is not in the stars to hold our destiny but in ourselves." – William Shakespeare

Our genes, inherited from our parents, shape many aspects of our health. But while we can't change the genes we inherit, our lifestyle choices can influence how they are expressed—a concept known as epigenetics.

Take the story of my mother [Hannah]. All her siblings had diabetes, and she could have easily assumed she was destined to develop it, too. But my mother was determined to avoid it. She consistently affirmed that she would not have diabetes, and this belief drove her to adopt a healthy, prayerful lifestyle and diet, stay active, and maintain a positive mindset. Remarkably, she passed away with no trace of diabetes. I believe she likely inherited the gene, but her choices determined whether that gene would be activated.

This is what epigenetics is all about. While our genes provide a blueprint, our daily habits—like diet, exercise, and stress management—can turn specific genes on or off, significantly impacting our health.
Psalm 18:32 (NIV) reminds us, *"It is God who arms me with strength and keeps my way secure."* This scripture speaks to the power we have, with God's help, to make choices that secure our health and future despite our genetic predispositions.

Practical Tips:

- ◊ **Healthy Habits:** Focus on one health area, such as diet or exercise, and make a small, positive change today to positively influence your genes.
- ◊ **Positive Affirmations:** Daily affirmations strengthen your commitment to staying healthy.
- ◊ **Reduce Stress:** Practice meditation, prayer, or deep breathing to lower stress and support healthy gene expression.

Reflective Questions:

- » How does your family's health history influence your lifestyle choices?
- » What small changes can you make to impact your genetic expression positively?
- » How can you use positive affirmations to support your health goals?

By embracing the power of epigenetics, you can take control of your health, making choices that positively shape your life and potentially impact future generations.

Day 72: Fuelling Your Brain with Nutrition

"The food you eat can be either the safest and most powerful form of medicine or the slowest form of poison." – Ann Wigmore

Imagine your brain as the engine of a sleek sports car. It's powerful and capable but needs the right fuel to run smoothly. The food you eat is that fuel. If you give your brain low-quality fuel, it sputters and struggles. But with the right nutrients, it hums along smoothly, keeping you sharp and focused.

Your brain is constantly buzzing with activity, like a busy city with roads full of cars. To keep these roads clear and efficient, your brain needs specific nutrients. Omega-3 fatty acids—found in foods like salmon, walnuts, and flaxseeds—act like premium fuel, keeping your brain cells strong and connected. Antioxidants in berries, nuts, and dark chocolate protect your brain from damage like traffic lights preventing accidents. And vitamins and minerals—like B vitamins, vitamin D, and magnesium—are the maintenance crew, keeping everything running smoothly, from your memory to your mood.

But let's face it: life is busy. It's easy to grab fast food or snacks that fill you up but don't nourish your brain. Over time, this low-grade fuel can leave your brain feeling sluggish and foggy, like a car that needs a tune-up.

1 Corinthians 10:31 (NIV) says, *"So whether you eat or drink or whatever you do, do it all for the glory of God."* This reminds us that our food choices are about more than just satisfying hunger—they're about honouring the incredible brain and body God has given us. By choosing brain-healthy foods, you're fueling your body and mind to perform at their best.

Practical Tips:

◊ **Food Fuel Check:** Keep a food diary for a week. Notice how different foods make you feel mentally and physically.

◊ Choose one area where you can switch to more brain-friendly options and observe how it improves your focus.

◊ **Stay Hydrated:** Water is essential for keeping your brain running smoothly—drink plenty throughout the day.

◊ **Plan Your Meals:** Prepare meals with brain-friendly foods, like getting your car ready for a road trip—better fuel leads to better performance.

Reflective Questions:

» How does your current diet support your brain health?

» What small changes can you make to add more brain-boosting foods to your meals?

» How can viewing your diet as a way to honour God inspire better food choices?

Day 73: The Impact of Exercise on Brain Health

"Exercise is the single best thing you can do for your brain in terms of mood, memory, and learning." – Dr. John Ratey

Exercise isn't just about keeping your body in shape; it's also one of the most powerful tools for boosting your brain health. Regular physical activity can significantly improve mood, sharpen memory, and enhance cognitive abilities. Think of exercise as a natural, all-in-one brain booster.

When you exercise, your heart pumps more blood, increasing oxygen and nutrient delivery to your brain. This process is like giving your brain a refreshing drink of water, making it function more efficiently. Additionally, exercise promotes neurogenesis, the creation of new neurons, particularly in the hippocampus—the area of the brain responsible for memory and learning. This means that by moving your body, you're also helping your brain grow stronger and more capable.

Exercise also plays a crucial role in regulating mood. Physical activity increases the production of neurotransmitters like serotonin and endorphins, often referred to as the "feel-good" chemicals. These natural mood enhancers help reduce feelings of anxiety and depression, leaving you feeling happier and more relaxed.
1 Corinthians 6:19-20 reminds us that our bodies are temples of the Holy Spirit and should be honoured. This scripture encourages us to view exercise as a way to care for and respect the body and mind God has given us.

Practical Tips:

◊ **Find What You Love:** To make exercise fun and sustainable, choose activities you enjoy, such as dancing or walking.
◊ **Make It a Habit:** Schedule 30 minutes of exercise most days and treat it as a non-negotiable part of your day.
◊ **Plan and Track:** Create a weekly exercise plan that includes aerobic, strength, and flexibility exercises. Track how these workouts affect your mood and mental clarity.

Reflective Questions:

» How does regular exercise affect your mood and mental sharpness?
» What physical activities do you enjoy, and how can you incorporate them into your routine?
» How can you prioritise exercise to enhance your brain health and overall well-being?

DAY 74: EXERCISE AND MENTAL HEALTH

"Exercise not only changes your body, it changes your mind, your attitude, and your mood." – Unknown

Think of your mind as a room. Over time, stress and anxiety can clutter it, leaving you feeling overwhelmed. Exercise is like opening the windows and letting in fresh air, clearing out the mental clutter, and making your mind feel refreshed.

When you engage in physical activity—whether it's a jog, dance class, swimming or pilates—your brain releases endorphins, those "feel-good" chemicals that lift your mood. Exercise also reduces stress hormones like cortisol, which can make you feel tense. By moving your body, you're not just staying fit—you're giving your mind a much-needed reset.

Imagine coming home after a stressful day. Your mind feels like a messy room, with thoughts scattered everywhere. Instead of sinking into the chaos, you take a 20-minute walk. With each step, your thoughts become clearer, and by the time you return, your mind feels more organised and peaceful.
Even when you're feeling low, a quick stretch or a short walk can make a big difference. Just as a little daily tidying keeps a room in order, regular exercise maintains mental well-being.

Practical Tips:

◊ **Mind-Body Connection:** Try activities like swimming or Pilates, which combine movement with mindfulness to help manage stress.

◊ **Start Small:** Start with 10 minutes of movement to declutter your mind.

◊ Get Support: Exercise with a friend or join a group to make it more enjoyable and less like a chore.

Reflective Questions:

» How does exercise help you clear your mental space?
» What types of exercise make you feel most refreshed?
» How can you build a regular exercise routine that feels manageable and enjoyable?

By making exercise a regular part of your life, you strengthen your body, clear out mental clutter, and create a space where your mind can feel at ease.

Day 75: Aligning Your Thoughts with the Holy Spirit

"Set your minds on things above, not on earthly things." – Colossians 3:2 (NIV)

Your thoughts have immense power—they shape your reality and influence how you live. If you think like a material being, you will focus on the physical world's limitations, worries, and pressures. But when you think and believe that you are a spiritual being created in God's image, you unlock access to the boundless power and possibilities that come from living in alignment with the Holy Spirit.

Jesus emphasised the importance of focusing our thoughts on God. In John 15:5 (NIV), He says, *"I am the vine; you are the branches. If you remain in me and I in you, you will bear much fruit; apart from me, you can do nothing."* This connection to Christ is vital. When our thoughts are centred on Him, we rise above the limitations of the material world and experience the fullness of life that God intends for us.

Consider the Prodigal Son, who sought fulfilment in the world's pleasures. He eventually found himself lost and empty. He found restoration only when he returned to his father's house, acknowledging his true identity. Similarly, when we return our thoughts to God's truths, we reconnect with the spiritual abundance that only He can provide.

Practical Tips:

◊ **Daily Meditation:** Reflect on scriptures affirming your spiritual identity each day.
◊ **Shift Your Perspective:** When challenges arise, remind yourself that you are empowered by God's spiritual resources, not confined by material limitations.
◊ **Gratitude and Reflection:** Focus on the spiritual blessings in your life, reinforcing your connection to God. Spend 10 minutes reflecting on an area where you've been focused on material limitations.

Reflective Questions:

» How do your thoughts align with your spiritual identity?
» What steps can you take to deepen your connection to God's truth?
» How might shifting from material concerns to spiritual abundance change your life?

By aligning your thoughts with the Holy Spirit and recognising your true identity in Christ, you can live beyond the limitations of the material world and embrace the abundance and power that God has designed for you.

DAY 76: THE BRAIN-SPIRIT CONNECTION

"For God has not given us a spirit of fear, but of power and of love and of a sound mind." –
2 Timothy 1:7 (KJV)

Your brain is a powerful organ that shapes how you perceive the world and is also deeply connected to your spirit. Aligning your thoughts with God's truth unlocks mental clarity, spiritual awareness, and peace. This connection between the brain and spirit allows you to live a life that transcends the limitations of the material world.

Neuroscience shows us that our thoughts can physically change the brain, a concept we now know as neuroplasticity. When you focus on fear and worry, you strengthen the neural pathways that keep those emotions dominant. However, when you focus on faith, love, and God's promises, you reinforce pathways that lead to peace, strength, power and a sound mind.

Jesus often reminded His followers of the importance of where they placed their thoughts. In Luke 12:25-26, He asked, *"Who of you, by worrying, can add a single hour to your life? Since you cannot do this very little thing, why do you worry about the rest?"* This scripture encourages us to focus our minds on God's power rather than being trapped by the fears of the material world.

Think about how your thoughts shape your daily life. If you constantly worry about what might go wrong, you may find yourself stuck in a cycle of anxiety. But when you choose to trust in God's plan, you free your mind to explore new possibilities, grow, and live a life full of purpose and peace.

Practical Tips:

- ◊ **Focus on Faith:** Replace negative thoughts with scriptures that affirm God's power and love.
- ◊ **Practice Mindfulness:** Take moments throughout your day to centre your thoughts on God's presence and peace.
- ◊ **Reinforce Positive:** Engage in activities like prayer and reading scripture to strengthen the brain-spirit connection.

Reflective Questions:

- » How do your thoughts shape your experience of life?
- » Where do you need to shift your focus from fear to faith?

By aligning your thoughts with God's truth, you empower yourself to live with a sound mind, free from fear and filled with divine peace and strength.

Day 77: The Impact of Stress on Your Brain

"Cast all your anxiety on him because he cares for you." – 1 Peter 5:7 (NIV)

Stress is a normal part of life, but understanding its effects on the brain empowers us to handle it more effectively. When you experience stress, your body activates the 'fight, flight or freeze' response, preparing you to face or escape perceived threats. The hypothalamus signals the adrenal glands, which release adrenaline and cortisol. These hormones increase your heart rate, boost blood pressure, and prime your body for action.

However, chronic stress can have a lasting impact on brain health. The hippocampus, which acts as your brain's RAM—temporarily storing new memories—can shrink under prolonged stress, making it harder to retain information. When traumatic events occur, stress hormones like adrenaline enhance memory consolidation, which is why vivid memories of traumatic events often remain clear for years. Likewise, the prefrontal cortex, crucial for decision-making and self-control, can weaken, causing focus and decision-making issues. The amygdala, which governs emotional responses, becomes overactive, heightening feelings of anxiety and fear.

Imagine being stuck in traffic, running late for an important meeting. As stress hormones surge, you become anxious and frustrated. Frequent exposure to such stressors can lead to chronic mental and physical health issues, affecting your brain's ability to function optimally. Many people experience ongoing stress from work, family, and finances, which can severely damage brain health and emotional stability.

Practical Tips:

- ◊ **Identify Stressors:** Make a list of your primary stress triggers to understand and manage them better.
- ◊ **Build Healthy Habits:** Regular exercise, balanced nutrition, and sufficient sleep equip your body to handle stress more effectively.
- ◊ **Practice Relaxation:** Techniques like deep breathing, meditation, or quiet prayer activate the body's relaxation response.
- ◊ **Manage Time Wisely:** Set realistic goals and priorities to reduce feelings of being overwhelmed.

Reflective Questions:

- » What situations trigger stress in your life?
- » How do you typically respond to stress, and is it effective?
- » What small steps can you take to reduce or better manage stress?

Understanding how stress affects your brain empowers you to take steps that protect your mental health and promote peace.

DAY 78: LIGHTENING YOUR MENTAL LOAD

"It's not the burden that defines you, but the strength you find in how you choose to bear it." – Maureen Chiana

Stress is like carrying a heavy backpack. The more weight you add, the harder it becomes to move forward. If you don't take time to adjust how you carry it, the weight can harm your mind and body. This "wear and tear" from chronic stress is known as **allostatic load**—the toll on your body and brain from constantly adapting to stress.

What is Allostatic Load?
Allostatic load occurs when your body stays in "fight or flight" mode for too long, repeatedly activating stress responses like the release of hormones such as cortisol and adrenaline. While these responses help in short bursts, chronic stress disrupts balance (homeostasis), leading to fatigue, inflammation, and even damage to brain areas like the hippocampus (memory) and prefrontal cortex (decision-making). This can make stress feel heavier and harder to manage.

Reducing stress doesn't mean avoiding challenges altogether—it means building strategies to protect your brain and body from harm.

> **Recognise Stressors:** The first step to managing stress is identifying what's weighing you down. Write down the triggers in your life.
> **Reframe Your Thoughts:** The way you think about stress can either lighten or increase the load. If you're facing a tight deadline, instead of thinking, *"I'll never finish this,"* try, *"I can break this down into smaller tasks."*
> **Incorporate Rest:** Proper recovery is essential to reducing allostatic load. Spend time in prayer or meditation to calm your mind.
> **Healthy Habits:** Exercise, eat well, and sleep enough to help your body manage stress more efficiently.
> **Rely on Support:** Share your burdens with trusted people. They can help you navigate challenges.

Reflective Questions:

» How has stress impacted your body or mind?
» What habits can you build to recover better from stress?
» How can relying on God and reframing your thoughts lighten your mental load?

By recognising the signs of stress and reducing your allostatic load, you can protect your brain, restore balance, and move forward with strength and resilience.

Day 79: Enhancing Brain Function Through Sleep

"The best bridge between despair and hope is a good night's sleep." – E. Joseph Cossman

Sleep is much more than rest—it's when your brain and body rejuvenate, preparing you to tackle the next day with clarity and energy. Quality sleep is essential for enhancing brain function, affecting everything from memory to decision-making and emotional regulation.

There are two types of sleep that we go through in cycles: **Non-REM and REM sleep**. Non-REM sleep consists of three stages and helps with physical restoration. During this time, your body repairs tissues, builds muscle, and strengthens the immune system. REM sleep, which happens after about 90 minutes of sleep, is essential for cognitive functions such as memory consolidation and emotional balance. It's also when the most vivid dreams occur.

The Impact of Sleep on Brain Function:

> **Memory Consolidation:** Sleep acts as a processing tool, organising and strengthening memories. During sleep, your brain sorts and stores what you learned throughout the day in long-term memory.
> **Cognitive Function:** A well-rested brain can think more clearly, make better decisions, and solve problems more effectively. Lack of sleep makes focusing and memory recall difficult.
> **Emotional Regulation:** Good sleep helps balance emotions, reduce stress, and improve mood. After a night of poor sleep, you're more likely to be irritable or overwhelmed.

Imagine having a busy workday of meetings and deadlines. A restless night can make you feel groggy, forgetful, and easily frustrated. In contrast, after a restful night, you wake up refreshed, able to focus and handle challenges with ease.

Practical Tips:

◊ **Stick to a Routine:** Go to bed and wake up at the same time daily, even on weekends. A consistent routine trains your body to sleep better.
◊ **Create a Sleep-Friendly Space:** Keep your bedroom dark, quiet, and cool for optimal sleep conditions.
◊ **Track Your Sleep:** Use a journal or app to note your sleep patterns and make adjustments to improve sleep quality.

Reflective Questions:

» How does your sleep affect your daily productivity and mood?
» What small changes can you make to improve your sleep routine?

Day 80: The Impact of Meditation on the Brain

"The thing about meditation is you become more and more you." – David Lynch

Imagine your brain as an orchestra, where each section represents a type of brain wave. The music is beautiful when everything is in harmony, and your mind feels calm and focused. But when stress takes over, it's like the percussion section drowning out the melody—chaos ensues. Meditation acts as the conductor, bringing balance and restoring peace.

The Role of Brain Waves

Your brain operates through different waves, each playing a unique role in your mental and emotional health:

> **Delta Waves:** Think of these as the *"repair crew."* Delta waves dominate during deep sleep, helping your body heal and recharge. Meditation can help you access this restful state, even during the day, for a quick mental reset.

> **Theta Waves:** These waves fuel creativity and intuition. When you're brainstorming or reflecting deeply, theta waves shine. Meditation taps into this state, opening your mind to fresh ideas and divine inspiration.

> **Alpha Waves:** The soothing rhythm of relaxation and focus. Alpha waves are strongest when you're calm but alert, like during prayer or quiet reflection. Meditation amplifies these waves, helping you stay composed in challenging moments.

> **Beta Waves:** The workhorses of your brain. While essential for focus, too much beta activity leads to overthinking and stress. Meditation quiets these waves, creating mental clarity.

> **Gamma Waves:** The "aha!" waves. These promote insight and spiritual connection. Meditation enhances gamma waves, aligning your mind with God's wisdom.

Consider someone overwhelmed by deadlines and worries. Their "orchestra" is out of tune, with stress (beta waves) dominating. A few minutes of meditating on scripture, like Psalm 46:10, allows the brain to recalibrate, boosting calm (alpha) and creativity (theta). Suddenly, challenges feel more manageable, and peace returns. Romans 12:2 reminds us to *"be transformed by the renewing of your mind."* Meditation rewires your brain, aligning your thoughts with God's promises and bringing clarity and resilience.

Practical Tips

◊ **Start Small:** Spend 5 minutes meditating on scripture or a single promise from God.

◊ **Breathe Deeply:** Visualise your mind as a calm lake, letting God's word settle the ripples.

◊ **Consistency:** Build a daily habit to strengthen your mental "orchestra."

Day 81: Don't Be a Prisoner of Your Mind

"The world without is a reflection of the world within." – Charles F. Haanel

Your mind shapes your reality. In The Master Key System, Charles F. Haanel explains that the outer world (effect) directly reflects our inner thoughts and beliefs (cause). When negative thoughts dominate, they create a cycle of negative outcomes, trapping us in a mental prison. To break free, we must master the law of cause and effect by controlling our thoughts.

Understanding the Power of the Mind:
The mind is the key to success, operating under the law of cause and effect. Our inner thoughts are the cause, and our external circumstances are the effect. Positive thoughts lead to positive outcomes, while negative thoughts create negative effects. As Galatians 6:7 (NIV) states, *"A man reaps what he sows."* The thoughts we cultivate determine the quality of our lives. Neuroscience supports this with neuroplasticity, the brain's ability to rewire itself based on thoughts. Positive thinking strengthens neural pathways that promote resilience and well-being. Negative thinking reinforces pathways that lead to stress and anxiety, creating a cycle of negativity.

Benefits of Mastering Your Thoughts:

> **Control Over Outcomes:** Mastering your thoughts gives you control over the effects they produce.
> **Improved Well-Being:** Positive thinking reduces stress and enhances emotional health.
> **Spiritual Growth:** Aligning thoughts with God's truth allows harmony with divine principles.

Your mind is like a garden. The thoughts you plant are the seeds that grow into your reality. Plant seeds of faith and positivity, and your life will flourish. Plant seeds of doubt and fear, and weeds will take over.

Practical Tips:

◊ **Identify the Causes:** Reflect on thoughts producing negative effects in your life.
◊ **Reframe Your Mindset:** Replace negative thoughts with positive ones aligned with your desired outcomes.
◊ **Cultivate Positivity:** Regularly nurture positive thoughts through meditation, affirmation, and gratitude.

Reflective Questions:

» What negative thoughts are causing unwanted effects?
» How can you start planting positive thoughts?

DAY 82: IS YOUR MINDSET MAKING YOU DRIFT?

"If you don't set your course, you'll find yourself anywhere, unsure of how you got there." – Maureen Chiana

Your mindset is like the steering wheel of a car, guiding your journey and determining your destination. But when your mindset becomes unfocused or negative, it's like losing grip of the wheel—you begin to drift, and before you know it, you're veering off course, risking a potential crash. Understanding how your mindset shapes your direction is essential for staying on the path toward your goals and dreams. Your mindset shapes your decisions and your life's direction. A clear, positive mindset acts like a well-calibrated compass, guiding you toward your goals. However, when doubt, fear, or negativity cloud your mindset, it's like driving through fog, increasing the likelihood of straying from your path. A positive, focused mindset strengthens our neural pathways, like clear road signs on a highway. A negative mindset weakens them, leading to indecision and drifting, like not seeing road signs in a storm.

Benefits of a Clear, Positive Mindset:

> **Focused Direction:** Helps you stay on course, making choices aligned with your goals.
> **Greater Resilience:** Builds your ability to navigate life's unexpected challenges while staying focused on your goals.
> **Purposeful Living:** Encourages intention and purpose, moving closer to your desired goals.

Imagine setting off on a road trip without a map or GPS. Without clear directions, you'd likely wander aimlessly. An unclear mindset works the same way, leaving you drifting through life and making choices that take you off course.

Practical Tips:

◊ **Mindset Check:** Regularly assess whether your mindset aligns with your goals.
◊ **Set Clear Goals:** Define your destination clearly and keep it in focus.
◊ **Stay Anchored:** Use daily affirmations or journaling to keep your mindset focused and positive.

Reflective Questions:

» Is your current mindset helping you stay on course or causing you to drift?
» How can you realign your mindset to stay on the path toward your goals?

Day 83: Learn Like Jesus: Transform Your Mindset

"Take my yoke upon you and learn from me, for I am gentle and humble in heart, and you will find rest for your souls."– Matthew 11:29 (NIV)

Learning is not a one-time event but a lifelong journey. When we integrate *Christology* into our approach, we gain knowledge, wisdom, and transformation. Jesus, the greatest teacher, showed us how to learn in a way that changes our minds and hearts. Following His example can make your learning more effective and meaningful.

Jesus used simple, relatable stories to explain deep truths, making His lessons memorable and impactful. He asked questions that made people think and encouraged them to seek understanding. His teaching wasn't just about knowledge—it was about transformation. We can apply these same principles to our learning today.

Key Techniques to Learn Like Jesus:

> **Engage Actively:** Don't just passively take in information. Ask questions, dig deeper, and connect scripture to your life—just like Jesus did with His followers.
> **Use Stories and Analogies:** Jesus often used parables to make complex ideas simple and relatable. Find stories or analogies that help you grasp and remember your learning.
> **Teach to Learn:** One of the best ways to solidify what you've learned is to teach it to someone else. Jesus sent His disciples out to teach, knowing it would reinforce their understanding.
> **Reflect and Apply:** After learning something new, take a moment to reflect on how it applies to your life. Jesus' teachings were always practical—designed to be lived out, not just understood.

Reflective Questions:

» How can you make your learning more like Jesus' teaching?
» What stories or analogies help you understand better?
» How can you apply what you've learned to transform your life?

By learning like Jesus, you can deepen your understanding, retain knowledge more effectively, and transform your mindset in alignment with God's purpose.

Day 84: The Brain-Immune Connection

"The body achieves what the mind believes." – Anonymous

Your brain and immune system are like close teammates, constantly communicating to keep you healthy. This relationship, known as the brain-immune axis, shows how your mental and physical well-being are deeply intertwined. Understanding this connection can empower you to care better for both your mind and body.

Your brain, the control tower of your body, sends signals to your immune system, which acts as your defence team. The immune system is made up of various cells and organs, all working together to protect you from infections and illnesses. When your brain is under stress or filled with negative thoughts, it releases cortisol, a stress hormone. While cortisol is helpful in short bursts, chronic stress leads to high cortisol levels over a prolonged period that can suppress your immune system, making it less effective at fighting illness.

On the other hand, when your mind is calm and positive, it encourages the production of chemicals that strengthen your immune system, helping it protect you more effectively.

Imagine your immune system as a group of soldiers ready to defend your body. Your brain, the commander, is the one who leads and guides them. If the commander is stressed out and overwhelmed, the soldiers become less coordinated and less effective at their jobs. But if the commander is calm and positive, the soldiers are well-coordinated and ready to fight, keeping you safe and healthy. This analogy vividly illustrates how crucial it is to maintain a healthy mindset to keep your body's defences strong.

Practical Tips:

- ◊ **Stress Relief:** Deep breathing, meditation, or prayer can relieve stress and strengthen your immune system.
- ◊ **Stay Uplifted:** Do what makes you happy—spend time with loved ones, enjoy hobbies, or practice gratitude to boost your body's defences.
- ◊ **Healthy Routine:** Maintain a healthy routine by eating well, sleeping well, and exercising regularly to support your brain and immune system.

By recognising the vital link between your brain and immune system, you can take proactive steps to enhance your overall well-being, ensuring that both your mind and body work together to keep you strong and healthy.

Day 85: Managing Expectations and Brain Health

"Hope deferred makes the heart sick, but a longing fulfilled is a tree of life." – Proverbs 13:12 (NIV)

Expectations influence our emotions, mental health, and overall well-being. While having hopes and dreams is natural, unmet expectations can lead to stress and disappointment. Proverbs 13:12 reflects this connection, reminding us that deferred hope can weigh heavily on our hearts and minds.

When expectations aren't met, the brain triggers a stress response, releasing cortisol. Chronic stress from unmet expectations can impair cognitive function and memory. Conversely, managing expectations wisely can reduce stress, improve emotional resilience, and promote better mental health.

How to Manage Expectations:

> **Set Realistic Goals:** Your hopes and dreams should be grounded in the Word of God. Unrealistic expectations can lead to disappointment, while goals rooted in God's promises build confidence and protect your mental and spiritual health.
> **Be Flexible:** Life is unpredictable. Adaptability helps you cope with unexpected outcomes, reducing stress on your brain and spirit.
> **Focus on the Process:** Instead of fixating on the outcome, value the journey and growth it brings. This shift reduces pressure and keeps your brain engaged.

Imagine waiting for a job offer you're confident about. When it doesn't come, disappointment triggers stress. But if you manage expectations by being open-minded, doing your best, and trusting God is in control, you handle the outcome with greater resilience. Remember, God promises to make all things beautiful in His time (Ecclesiastes 3:11).

Practical Tips:

◊ **Assess Your Expectations:** Regularly evaluate if your expectations are grounded in God's Word.
◊ **Embrace Flexibility:** Adjust your expectations as circumstances change, trusting God's plan.
◊ **Celebrate Progress:** Recognise and celebrate the steps you take, even if outcomes differ from your hopes.

Reflective Questions:

» Are your expectations aligned with reality and God's promises?
» How can you adjust your expectations to be more flexible and rooted in faith?
» How can focusing on the journey improve your mental and emotional health?

Day 86: Breaking Free from a Victim Mentality

"You are not a victim. You are a survivor with a story to tell." – Unknown

A victim mentality is like being stuck in quicksand. The more you struggle against life's challenges without changing your mindset, the deeper you sink. This mindset makes you feel powerless, believing that life happens to you rather than for you. Breaking free from this mentality is essential for your mental and spiritual growth.

When you see yourself as a victim, it's easy to blame external factors for your problems, leading to feelings of helplessness and resentment. Over time, this way of thinking can trap your brain in negative thought patterns, reinforcing the belief that you have no control over your circumstances. But just like any other habit, you can change this mindset.

How to Overcome Victim Mentality:

> **Take Responsibility:** The first step is to recognise that you can change your situation. This doesn't mean blaming yourself for everything but acknowledging that your choices and reactions shape your reality. Philippians 4:13 (NIV) reminds us, *"I can do all this through him who gives me strength."* You have the power to make changes.

> **Shift Your Perspective:** Instead of focusing on what's wrong, look for what you can do. Reframe challenges as opportunities to grow stronger. Ask yourself, *"What can I learn from this?"* or *"How can this make me better?"*

> **Practice Gratitude:** Gratitude is like a rope thrown to you when you're sinking. It shifts your focus from what you lack to what you have, lifting you out of negativity. By regularly practising gratitude, you train your brain to see the positives in your life, breaking the cycle of victimhood.

Imagine someone who feels stuck in a job they hate, believing there's no way out. This mindset keeps them in a cycle of frustration and inaction. However, by taking responsibility—perhaps by learning new skills or seeking a different job—they can break free from this mindset and take control of their career.

Reflective Questions:

» Do you often feel powerless or blame others for your circumstances?
» How can you start taking responsibility for your life today?
» What steps can you take to shift from a victim mentality to a victor's mindset?

By breaking free from a victim mentality, you empower yourself to live a life of purpose and strength, moving forward with confidence and trust in God's plan for you.

Day 87: Reset Your Mindset About Money

"The real measure of your wealth is how much you'd be worth if you lost all your money." – Anonymous

Money is a tool, but your mindset determines how you use it. Whether it's a source of stress or a means to achieve your goals, your thoughts about money deeply impact your financial well-being and happiness. By resetting your mindset and aligning your financial choices with your true values, you can create a healthier relationship with money.

Harvard psychologist Dan Gilbert shows that our brains often misjudge what brings us happiness. We believe that more money will make us happy, but after our basic needs are met, we find that additional wealth has less impact on our joy. This misconception can lead to viewing money as the ultimate goal rather than a tool for a fulfilling life.

Resetting Your Money Mindset:

> **See Money as a Tool:** Instead of viewing money as the ultimate goal, recognise it as a tool to fulfil God's purpose. Proverbs 3:9-10 reminds us to honour God with our wealth, seeing it as a resource to be used wisely.

> **Value Over Accumulation:** Shift from accumulating wealth to creating value in your life and others. This approach aligns with biblical stewardship and brings true satisfaction.

> **Practice Gratitude:** Gratitude helps you appreciate what you have, breaking the cycle of constantly wanting more. When you're thankful, you use your resources more wisely.

Imagine someone constantly worried about not having enough money despite having their needs met. This stress can lead to poor financial choices. By shifting their mindset to view money as a tool, they can focus on living with purpose and generosity.

Practical Tips:

◊ **Budget with Purpose:** Create a budget that reflects your values, prioritising needs, giving, and savings.

◊ **Invest in Experiences:** This brings lasting happiness, unlike material things.

◊ **Reframe:** Focus on purpose, not just wealth.

Reflective Questions:

» How do you view money—as a tool or an end goal?
» How can you align your financial decisions with your values and purpose?

Resetting your mindset about money reduces stress and helps you honour God.

Day 88: Breaking Free from Overthinking

"Overthinking is the art of creating problems that weren't even there." – Anonymous

Overthinking is like running on a mental treadmill—exhausting and unproductive. It drains your energy, fuels anxiety, and prevents you from enjoying the present. Breaking free from this cycle is crucial for protecting your mental well-being.

The Overthinking Trap:
When you overthink, your mind gets stuck replaying scenarios and imagining worst-case outcomes. This habit intensifies stress and anxiety as your brain becomes overloaded with negative thoughts. It's like trying to solve a puzzle with missing pieces—frustration builds, but no solution exists.

How to Stop Overthinking:
> **Recognise the Pattern:** The first step to breaking the habit is noticing when you're overthinking.
> **Focus on What You Can Control:** Instead of worrying about things beyond your control, focus on your actions and mindset. Philippians 4:6 reminds us to pray, give thanks, and release anxiety to God.
> **Practice Mindfulness:** Mindfulness keeps you grounded in the present. When you catch yourself overthinking, bring your focus back to the now. Deep breathing or meditation helps reset your thoughts.

Imagine replaying a conversation, worrying about what you said. This keeps you stuck in the past. Recognise the pattern, focus on what you can control (like apologising if needed), and practice mindfulness to regain peace.

Practical Tips:
◊ **Set Time Limits:** Allow yourself a set time to think, then move on.
◊ **Get Active:** Physical activity or a hobby can help redirect your thoughts.
◊ **Write It Down:** Journaling your thoughts helps you process them without ruminating.

Reflective Questions:
» Do you find yourself often overthinking?
» How can you shift focus to the present moment?
» How can trusting God help you release unnecessary worry?

Breaking free from overthinking restores your peace and energy, allowing you to live more fully in the present.

Day 89: Be Fearless and Bold

"The only thing we have to fear is fear itself." – Franklin D. Roosevelt

Fear is a natural emotion that can be a powerful force that prevents us from achieving our desired outcomes. When it controls us, it can prevent us from stepping into opportunities, taking risks, and living boldly. Embracing a fearless mindset is crucial for growth, both personally and professionally.

Fear is rooted in the amygdala, the brain's alarm system. When you encounter something that feels threatening, the amygdala triggers a *fight-or-flight response,* preparing the body to react. While this response is essential for survival, it can also cause you to hesitate or avoid challenges when there is no real danger. Emotional intelligence helps us recognise when fear is guiding our decisions and empowers us to choose courage instead.

The Bible encourages fearlessness. In Joshua 1:9 (NIV), God commands, *"Be strong and courageous. Do not be afraid; do not be discouraged, for the Lord your God will be with you wherever you go."* This scripture reminds us that fearlessness isn't about the absence of fear but about boldly moving forward, knowing that God is with us. Consider someone who dreams of starting their own business but allows fear of failure to hold them back. This fear might stop them from even taking the first step. However, by acknowledging their fear and trusting God's guidance, they can move forward confidently, transforming their dreams into reality.

Practical Tips:

◊ **Acknowledge Fear:** Don't ignore fear—acknowledge it and understand why you feel it. This awareness is the first step to overcoming it.
◊ **Take Small Steps:** Boldness doesn't require giant leaps. Start with small, manageable steps that build your confidence over time.
◊ **Trust in God's Promises:** Remember scriptures that encourage boldness, such as Isaiah 41:10, "Do not fear, for I am with you; do not be dismayed, for I am your God."

Reflective Questions:

» What fears are holding you back from pursuing your goals?
» How can you begin to take small, bold steps toward overcoming these fears?
» How does trusting in God's presence help you act courageously and confidently?

Being fearless and bold opens you up to new possibilities and growth. Remember, boldness is not about never feeling fear—it's about taking action despite it, knowing that with God by your side, there is nothing you cannot face.

Day 90: Understanding Bias

"We don't see things as they are; we see them as we are." – Anaïs Nin

Biases are mental shortcuts our brains use to make sense of the world. While they can help us make quick decisions, they can also lead to distorted thinking and unfair judgments. Understanding how bias operates in both the conscious and subconscious mind is key to overcoming its negative effects.

The Science of Bias:
Our brains are wired to make snap judgments based on past experiences and learned patterns. The subconscious mind, which operates below our awareness, often reinforces biases by filtering information through the lens of our existing beliefs. These subconscious biases also influence the conscious mind, where deliberate thought occurs, even when we think we're being rational.
The brain's pattern recognition system is linked to bias. The amygdala, responsible for processing emotions, responds to stimuli according to previous experiences, resulting in automatic reactions. The prefrontal cortex, responsible for rational thinking, can counteract these biases, but it requires conscious effort and awareness.

Imagine meeting someone for the first time and quickly forming an opinion based on their appearance. This quick judgment comes from subconscious biases. But if you take a moment to recognise these biases and make an effort to get to know the person, you might find that your first impression was wrong.

Practical Tips:
  ◊ **Self-Reflection:** Regularly reflect on your thoughts to identify potential biases.
  ◊ **Seek Diverse Perspectives:** Engage with people from different backgrounds to challenge your perspective.
  ◊ **Practice Mindfulness:** Mindfulness helps you become aware of automatic thoughts, allowing you to challenge biases as they arise.

Reflective Questions:
  » What biases might be influencing your decisions?
  » How can you become more aware of these biases?
  » In what ways can seeking God's wisdom help you make more balanced decisions?

By understanding how bias operates in the conscious and subconscious mind, you can challenge automatic thoughts, leading to more thoughtful, fair, and Christ-centred decisions

PART FOUR

BECOME LIMITLESS

PART 4 INTRODUCTION

This section embarks on an empowering journey to maximise your potential. Each day focuses on equipping you with the mindset, skills, and resilience needed to break free from limitations and embrace new opportunities.

You'll explore how to teach children how to think effectively and critically, develop your emotional intelligence, and embrace disruptive ideas that spark innovation. We'll delve into the transformative power of worship, prayer, and the Holy Spirit, guiding you to build a strong foundation for personal growth.

This part is all about cultivating a mindset that empowers you to overcome challenges and thrive in every aspect of your life. With topics like resilience, focus, and ambition, you'll learn to rewire your brain for success and view obstacles as stepping stones to greatness.

As you journey through these lessons, remember that you are limitless. You can achieve incredible things with faith, determination, and the right tools.

Let's unlock your potential together!

Day 91: I Am Limitless

"The only limits that exist are the ones you place on yourself." – Anonymous

Embracing the belief that **"I am limitless"** can profoundly impact your life. Our brains, through neuroplasticity, can process information in limitless ways, allowing us to reshape our perceived boundaries. For example, if you believe you're not creative, you might avoid tasks that require creativity. However, challenging this belief can unlock new opportunities and abilities.

Think of a child learning to walk. They fall and stumble but persist until they succeed. This persistence mirrors how we can overcome self-imposed limits. Emotional intelligence plays a crucial role by helping us recognise and manage our fears. If public speaking makes you anxious, understanding this fear allows you to take actionable steps to overcome it, like practising or seeking feedback.

Scripture reinforces this limitless mindset. Philippians 4:13 (NIV) says, *"I can do all things through Christ who strengthens me."* This verse reminds us that our potential goes beyond our own strength and is supported by divine power. By aligning our beliefs with our actions, we integrate faith, mindset, and capability.

Success isn't about waiting for luck - with faith and effort, you create your own opportunities and receive God's blessings. It's not about random chance but about intentionally working towards your goals. When you challenge your limitations and act purposefully, you shape your success. A manager who feels restricted in leadership might take on small leadership roles and seek feedback to grow their skills.
If past failures have held you back, view these as learning experiences. This shift in perspective fosters resilience and growth.

Practical Tips:

◊ Write down a limiting belief you have. Develop a step-by-step plan to challenge and change this belief.

◊ Track your progress and celebrate each achievement to reinforce your new, limitless mindset.

Reflective Questions:

» What are three beliefs you hold about your limitations?
» How might these beliefs be preventing you from reaching your goals?

By recognising and overcoming self-imposed limits, you harness your brain's full potential and create opportunities, paving the way for personal and professional growth.

Day 92: Teach Children How To Think

"The highest form of ignorance is when you reject something you don't know anything about." – Wayne Dyer

Teaching children how to think rather than what to think equips them with essential life skills. Imagine guiding a plant by watering it and directing it toward the sunlight. This nurturing approach mirrors how we help children develop effective thinking and critical thinking skills, preparing them to navigate life's challenges independently.
Our brains are highly adaptable, and fostering skills like questioning and problem-solving strengthens cognitive abilities.
Research shows that children who engage in critical thinking from a young age exhibit improved academic performance and emotional intelligence. For example, when children tackle a challenging math problem, breaking it down into manageable steps enhances their problem-solving skills and builds stronger neural connections. According to a study in the Journal of Experimental Psychology, problem-solving techniques lead to better student information retention than memorising facts.

Emotional intelligence is not just a buzzword; it's a vital component of critical thinking. It involves managing one's emotions and understanding others. For instance, when a child encounters difficulty in a science experiment, guiding them to reflect on what went wrong and encouraging them to adapt their approach fosters both emotional resilience and analytical skills. This understanding can help us guide children more effectively. Proverbs 4:7 (NIV) reminds us, *"The beginning of wisdom is this: Get wisdom. Though it cost all you have, get understanding."* The verse highlights the significance of pursuing knowledge and comprehension and emphasises the importance of teaching children critical thinking skills. It's a powerful reminder of the impact we can have on their future.

Practical Tips:

◊ **Encourage Curiosity:** Motivate kids to ask questions and find their own answers.
◊ **Support Exploration:** Help them explore solutions and think critically.
◊ **Use Fun Tools:** Introduce educational games and resources to make learning enjoyable.

Reflective Question:

» How can you support children in developing critical thinking skills?

Teaching children to think empowers them to develop confidence and wisdom, preparing them for future success.

Day 93: Developing Critical Thinking Skills

"The important thing is not to stop questioning. Curiosity has its own reason for existing."
– Albert Einstein

Critical thinking involves thorough information analysis, assessment of evidence, and drawing logical conclusions. **Insightful thinking** refers to those 'aha' moments that provide sudden clarity and understanding, leading to breakthroughs. Both skills are vital for improving problem-solving and decision-making. Practicing critical and insightful thinking activates parts of the brain, such as the prefrontal cortex, which is involved in planning and decision-making, and the anterior cingulate cortex, which helps manage emotions and solve problems. Regular practice strengthens the neural (brain) pathways linked to reasoning and insight, allowing your brain to grow and adapt.

In today's world, where we are bombarded with information, distinguishing truth from misinformation can be tricky. Developing critical and insightful thinking equips you to navigate this complexity, enabling informed decisions. It helps you see challenges as opportunities and approach problems strategically.
For instance, if you are given a work proposal, critical thinking helps assess its feasibility, while insightful thinking might lead to an innovative approach that you hadn't considered before.

Proverbs 2:6 (NIV) says, *"For the Lord gives wisdom; from his mouth come knowledge and understanding."* This verse highlights the importance of seeking wisdom, which aligns with developing critical and insightful thinking. Integrating faith with these skills ensures our reasoning is rooted in divine wisdom.

Practical Tips:

◊ **Question Assumptions:** Examine the assumptions behind your thoughts and decisions.
◊ Perspectives: Look at issues from different points of view.
◊ **Stay Curious:** Foster a habit of continuous learning and curiosity.

Exercise:

> Choose a complex problem to analyse this week.
> Break it down, evaluate the evidence, and consider various perspectives.
> Reflect on your conclusions and seek patterns or connections for an 'aha' moment.

Developing critical and insightful thinking skills enhances your ability to solve problems and make informed decisions.

Day 94: Embrace Disruptive Thinking

"The greatest danger in times of turbulence is not the turbulence; it is to act with yesterday's logic." – Peter Drucker

Disruptive thinking means challenging the status quo and welcoming innovative ideas that can revolutionise your approach to problems. This mindset is crucial for progress, pushing you beyond conventional solutions to achieve remarkable outcomes.

Disruptive thinking activates the brain's creative centres, particularly the prefrontal cortex, which is important for problem-solving and innovation. Breaking away from traditional thought patterns stimulates neural pathways that enhance creativity and adaptability, leading to novel solutions and better responses to change. Often, we stick to familiar methods because they seem safe. Disruptive thinking urges us to question these norms and explore new possibilities. For example, embracing a disruptive idea in your business will lead to more efficient processes or groundbreaking products rather than clinging to outdated practices.

Isaiah 43:19 (NIV) says, *"See, I am doing a new thing! Now it springs up; do you not perceive it?"* This verse calls us to embrace new opportunities and perspectives. It aligns with disruptive thinking by encouraging us to recognise and pursue innovative paths rather than adhering to old routines. Think of disruptive thinking as a storm that clears out the old, creating space for new possibilities. Just like a storm changes the land, disruptive ideas can reshape your thinking and bring about breakthroughs. Embracing such disruptions paves the way for fresh and exciting possibilities.

Practical Tips:

◊ **Question Norms:** Challenge existing practices and explore alternative approaches.

◊ **Encourage Creativity:** Create an environment that welcomes unconventional ideas.

◊ **Be Open to Change:** Welcome new methods and technologies that can help you improve.

Exercise:

>Find a traditional method you use and brainstorm three ways to improve it.

>Reflect on how these changes could impact your outcomes.

>Consider how these ideas enhance your practices, spark innovation, and fuel growth.

Embracing disruptive thinking breaks old habits and unlocks new opportunities.

DAY 95: THRIVE WITH EMOTIONAL INTELLIGENCE

"Emotional intelligence is the key to both personal and professional success." – Unknown

Emotional Intelligence (EQ) is vital to cultivating a limitless mindset. It involves managing one's own emotions and understanding those of others, which helps one turn obstacles into opportunities for growth Mastering EQ transforms challenges into opportunities, empowering you to achieve peak performance and thrive beyond limitations.
Cultivating EQ activates the prefrontal cortex and anterior cingulate cortex, regions critical for emotional regulation and decision-making. Strengthening these areas enables you to handle stress effectively, make informed decisions, and maintain resilience, all supporting a mindset that embraces limitless potential.

2 Timothy 1:7 (ESV) provides insight into this concept: *"For God gave us a spirit not of fear but of power and love and self-control."* This verse highlights how managing emotions—through power, love, and self-control—can propel you towards thriving rather than merely surviving. You unlock your potential to achieve great things by overcoming fear and embracing self-control.

Consider a project with significant challenges. With high EQ, you manage your stress, understand team dynamics, and address obstacles constructively. This approach helps resolve issues and drives you to take bold actions, demonstrating how EQ supports a limitless mindset and peak performance.

Exercise: Emotional Journal: Keep a journal to track and reflect on how your emotions impact your performance. Identify how managing these emotions leads to greater achievements and less limited thinking.

Practical Tips:

◊ **Self-Reflection:** Assess how your emotions influence your decisions and actions. Use this insight to foster growth and resilience.

◊ **Active Listening:** Engage deeply with others to understand their emotions and collaborate effectively.

◊ **Stress Management:** Employ techniques such as mindfulness or exercise to maintain emotional balance and clarity.

Reflective Questions:

» How do your emotional responses affect your approach to challenges and opportunities?

» What strategies can you adopt to enhance your emotional intelligence and overcome limitations?

Day 96: Become a Problem Solver

"Don't only swim where everyone else does. Real discoveries and greatness are found in uncharted waters" – Unknown

Embracing your role as a problem solver can be transformative. By harnessing your cognitive abilities and faith, you can turn challenges into opportunities for growth. Think of problem-solving as a journey. If you're a small business owner seeing a drop in customers, start by identifying the root cause—maybe your marketing needs a refresh. Use your brainpower to brainstorm ideas like enhancing social media engagement or running targeted promotions. Breaking down the problem into manageable parts allows you to tackle it systematically.

Proverbs 3:5-6 (NIV) guides us: *"Trust in the Lord with all your heart and lean not on your own understanding; in all your ways submit to Him, and He will make your paths straight."* This verse reminds us to seek God's guidance while using our intellect and creativity to solve problems. Like the Good Shepherd (John 10:11), who meticulously searches for the lost sheep, we should approach our challenges with faith, thoughtful analysis, and decisive action.

Daily Application: Apply the **SOLVE** method to any challenge. Clearly state the problem, break it into smaller steps, brainstorm all potential solutions, evaluate each option, and then choose and implement the best one. Review the results to see if your approach is working.

Practical Tips:

◊ **State the Problem:** Define the issue clearly.
◊ **Organise:** Break the problem into manageable parts.
◊ **List Solutions:** Brainstorm all possible solutions.
◊ **Value Options:** Weigh the pros and cons of each option.
◊ **Execute and Evaluate:** Implement the best solution and monitor its effectiveness.

Exercise:

> Pick a current challenge in your life or work.
> Use the SOLVE method to understand the problem, generate solutions, and take action.
> Reflect on how this approach helps you handle the issue more effectively.

By embracing problem-solving with faith, creativity, and analytical thinking, you can navigate challenges more effectively and turn obstacles into stepping stones to success.

Day 97: Building Resilience to Become Limitless

"Life doesn't get easier or more forgiving; we get stronger and more resilient." – Steve Maraboli

Resilience is key to embracing a limitless mindset. It's not about escaping challenges but learning to bounce back with grace and strength. By building resilience, you transform obstacles into opportunities for growth.
Resilience is like a muscle that strengthens with use. Every challenge you face—personal or professional—builds this muscle. Your brain adapts through neuroplasticity, and emotional intelligence helps you manage and understand emotions. Picture resilience as a tree that bends but doesn't break in a storm, allowing you to remain flexible and steadfast.

Romans 5:3-4 (NIV) reminds us, *"Not only so, but we also glory in our sufferings because we know that suffering produces perseverance; perseverance, character; and character, hope."* This verse reminds us that enduring hardships can lead to growth and hope. Viewing challenges through this lens enables you to harness them as opportunities for personal development.
Consider an entrepreneur facing a business setback. Instead of giving up, they analyse what went wrong, learn from their mistakes, and adapt their strategy. This resilience helps them survive and thrive, showcasing how overcoming challenges can lead to success.

Practical Tips: The RISE Method

- ◊ **Reflect:** Review past challenges and how you overcame them. Identify your strengths and lessons learned.
- ◊ **Invest in relationships:** Build a support network of family, friends, and mentors who can offer encouragement.
- ◊ **Stay positive:** Maintain an optimistic outlook. Use positive affirmations and remember past successes.
- ◊ **Embrace change:** Accept change as part of life and adapt your plans.

Resilience Journal
Keep a journal to track challenges and your responses. Reflect on what worked, what didn't, and how to improve. Celebrate your progress and growth.

Reflective Questions:

- » How do you handle adversity and setbacks?
- » What steps can you take to enhance your resilience?
- » How can lessons from past challenges improve your future responses?

Building resilience empowers you to transform obstacles into growth opportunities.

Day 98: Enhancing Focus and Attention

"Where your attention goes, your energy flows." – Tony Robbins

Maintaining focus on a single task is increasingly difficult in our distraction-filled world. Yet sharpening our attention can significantly boost productivity and satisfaction. Focusing on one thing at a time—without multitasking—leads to more efficient and effective work.

Focus involves intensely concentrating on one task, which engages the prefrontal cortex, the brain area responsible for decision-making and attention. By practising focused work, we can enhance our brain's ability to concentrate through neuroplasticity, the brain's ability to adapt and grow.

Multitasking is mostly a myth. Our brains are better at quickly switching tasks than doing multiple tasks at once. Juggling too many things can lower efficiency and lead to more mistakes. Instead, practising focus regularly can boost your concentration.

In the Bible, Philippians 4:8 (NIV) offers guidance on focus: *"Finally, brothers and sisters, whatever is true, whatever is noble, whatever is right, whatever is pure, whatever is lovely, whatever is admirable—if anything is excellent or praiseworthy—think about such things."* This verse highlights directing our thoughts toward positive and meaningful things to stay centred and attentive.

Practical Tips:

◊ **Minimise Distractions:** Identify and eliminate common distractions. Turn off notifications, allocate a dedicated workspace, and define set break times.

◊ **Practice Mindfulness:** Mindfulness techniques can help control thoughts and maintain attention, leading to better focus and productivity.

◊ **Focus Training:** Dedicate time daily to practice focusing on a single task. Start with short periods and gradually extend them.

Exercise: Set a timer for 20 minutes and focus on a single task without interruptions. Afterwards, reflect on your progress and feelings, and gradually increase the duration.

Reflective Questions:

» How do you currently handle distractions and maintain focus?
» What methods can you use to improve your focus and attention?
» How might enhanced focus and attention affect your productivity and performance?

Integrating these strategies can enhance your focus, reduce distractions, and improve your overall productivity. Remember, a disciplined mind leads to greater achievement and satisfaction.

Day 99: Unlock Your Memory for Limitless Potential

"Memory is where our life's moments are stored, holding the stories that make us who we are." – Maureen Chiana

Imagine your memory as a powerful library. Each book represents a piece of information you want to remember. Just as a well-organised library allows you to find books easily, effective memory techniques help you access and use information effortlessly.

Memory Techniques:

> **Mnemonic Devices:** Think of mnemonics as bookmarks. For instance, the phrase *"My Very Educated Mother Just Served Us Noodles"* helps you remember the planets, with each word acting as a bookmark for a planet.
> **Visualisation:** Picture your memory as a series of vivid movie scenes. If you need to remember a grocery list, visualise each item appearing in a short, memorable film, such as seeing milk poured into a glass in your kitchen.
> **Spaced Repetition:** Consider this like rehearing a script. Revisit the information at intervals, just as actors practice lines repeatedly to perfect their performance. This reinforces your memory and ensures you remember it long-term.

Scripture offers wisdom on the importance of remembering and understanding. Proverbs 4:7 (KJV) says, *"Wisdom is the principal thing; therefore get wisdom: and with all thy getting get understanding."* Like a well-maintained library of valuable books, enhancing memory helps you better understand and apply wisdom. Jesus also emphasised the power of remembrance. In John 14:26 (NIV), He said, *"But the Advocate, the Holy Spirit, whom the Father will send in my name, will teach you all things and will remind you of everything I have said to you."* Just as the Holy Spirit helps us recall Christ's teachings, memory techniques help us recall important information.

Practical Tips:

◊ **Use Mnemonics:** Create memorable phrases to recall complex information.
◊ **Review Regularly:** Schedule times to revisit and reinforce your learning.

Reflective Questions:

» How do you currently manage your memory?
» Which techniques can you use to enhance your recall?
» How can a stronger memory support your goals?

Boosting your memory unlocks knowledge, possibilities, and valuable insights.

DAY 100: UNLOCK YOUR LEARNING POTENTIAL

"Education is the kindling of a flame, not the filling of a vessel." – Socrates

Effective learning isn't just about soaking up information; it's about actively engaging with it and using strategic methods to truly understand and remember it.

Active Recall: Test yourself on what you've learned. Use tools like flashcards or practice quizzes to pull information from memory rather than just reviewing notes. This active process helps solidify knowledge.

Spaced Repetition: Review information at increasing intervals—like one day, then three days, then a week, and so on. This technique helps transfer information from short-term to long-term memory, making it easier to recall later.

Feynman Technique: Teach what you've learned to someone else. Explaining concepts in simple terms highlights gaps in your understanding and reinforces your own knowledge.

Proverbs 4:7 (NIV) offers wisdom on pursuing knowledge: *"The beginning of wisdom is this: Get wisdom. Though it cost all you have, get understanding."* This verse emphasises the value of actively engaging with and seeking knowledge.

Practical Tips:

◊ **Active Recall:** Incorporate quizzes or flashcards into your study routine.
◊ **Spaced Repetition:** Plan review sessions to revisit information periodically.
◊ **Feynman Technique:** Explain material to a friend or write out an explanation in your own words.

Exercise: Create a study plan that includes these strategies. Identify key topics, schedule review sessions, and use active recall and teaching techniques to deepen your understanding.

Reflective Questions:

» How do you currently learn and retain new information?
» What strategies can you use to improve your learning process?
» How can these techniques enhance your ability to acquire new skills and knowledge?

Applying these strategies can make learning more effective and engaging. Embrace these methods to boost your retention and comprehension, paving the way for academic and professional success.

Day 101: Embracing the Power Within: "I Can Do All Things"

"I can do all things through Christ who strengthens me." – Philippians 4:13 (NKJV)

Philippians 4:13 is a powerful verse often cited for encouragement and empowerment. To fully appreciate its meaning, we must consider the context in which Paul wrote these words. Paul wrote this letter to the Philippians from prison, enduring hardship and uncertainty. Despite his circumstances, he speaks with remarkable contentment and confidence. This verse isn't just about personal achievements; it's about drawing strength and purpose from faith in Christ, regardless of external conditions.

Understanding the Biblical Meaning

> **Strength Through Faith:** Our real strength comes from believing in Jesus Christ, not just from our own abilities. This faith helps us handle any situation with resilience and confidence.

> **Peace in All Circumstances:** Paul's confidence in doing all things stems from his ability to find peace, whether he has plenty or nothing. His trust in Christ allows him to endure and thrive, seeing beyond immediate challenges.

> **Purposeful Empowerment:** This verse reminds us that our skills are meant to fulfil God's purposes. It's about aligning our actions with His will and trusting that He equips us to succeed.

Imagine tackling a big project or challenge. Knowing you have Christ's strength can change how you approach it. It's not just about your own power; it's about trusting in Christ's strength and grace to overcome obstacles and achieve your goals.

Practical Tips:

◊ **Pray for Guidance:** Seek Christ's strength through prayer before tackling challenges.

◊ **Align Your Actions:** Ensure your goals reflect God's guidance and your faith

◊ **Cultivate Resilience:** Rely on Christ's strength to handle difficulties with grace.

Reflective Questions:

» How can relying on Christ's strength change your approach to challenges?
» Where do you need to align your mindset with His empowerment?

With Christ, you can face any challenge and achieve your goals.

Day 102: The Power of the Holy Spirit

"You, however, are not in the realm of the flesh but are in the realm of the Spirit, if indeed the Spirit of God lives in you." – Romans 8:9 (NIV)

God created us with the extraordinary ability to control and transform our minds. The Holy Spirit empowers us to unlock our limitless potential and guides us in this transformative journey.

Empowered Thinking:
God's Design for Our Minds: Romans 12:2 instructs us to *"be transformed by the renewing of your mind."* This resonates with neuroplasticity—the brain's capacity to form new connections and adapt. We can reshape our thought patterns, aligning them with God's purpose.

The Role of the Holy Spirit: The Holy Spirit acts as our divine guide, illuminating our path and offering strength to navigate our thoughts and actions. By embracing the Spirit, we can shift from limited thinking to embracing boundless possibilities, using our God-given mental flexibility to transform our perspectives and overcome challenges.

Transforming Thought Patterns: Through the guidance of the Holy Spirit, we reframe mental barriers into opportunities for growth. This divine relationship helps us break free from self-imposed limits and adopt new, expansive viewpoints, enhancing our capacity for change and growth.

Strength in Challenges
John 14:27 promises, *"Peace I leave with you; my peace I give you."* This divine peace is more than a comforting thought—it is a stabilising force for our emotions. When we face stress or challenges, the peace from the Holy Spirit helps regulate our emotional responses, providing mental clarity and resilience.

By embracing the Holy Spirit's peace, we reduce stress and enhance our focus, improving mental performance. This emotional calm supports our journey to achieving extraordinary results and confidently navigating life's obstacles.

Reflective Questions

> » How can aligning your thoughts with God's will help you manage stress more effectively?
> » In what ways does the Holy Spirit guide you through emotional challenges?
> » How can you utilise the peace of the Holy Spirit to improve your mental clarity and resilience?

Day 103: The Transformative Power of Worship

"Worship is the highest form of gratitude." – Dr. Caroline Leaf

Worship has the ability to transform our mental and emotional landscape, going beyond mere ritual. When we worship, we align ourselves with a higher purpose, inviting God's divine influence that reshapes our minds and hearts.

Dr. Caroline Leaf highlights that worship can reshape our brain's neural pathways, just as exercise strengthens our muscles. Engaging in worship fosters positive emotional states and boosts mental health by releasing endorphins, the brain's natural mood enhancers.

By starting your day with music, prayer, or reflection, you can change your mindset from stress to peace. Worship helps set a positive tone for your day, aligning your thoughts with gratitude and purpose.

Worship triggers biochemical changes in the brain that manage stress and improve emotional intelligence. Psalm 100:4 (NIV) states, *"Enter his gates with thanksgiving and his courts with praise; give thanks to him and praise his name."* Worship is a gateway to experiencing God's presence and peace, reinforcing a positive outlook and emotional resilience.

Practical Tips:

◊ **Start with Gratitude:** Begin each day with a moment of thanks, focusing on positive aspects of your life.
◊ **Integrate Worship:** Listen to worship music or read a devotional during your morning routine.
◊ **Create a Worship Space:** Designate a quiet place for worship and reflection.

Daily Worship Journal: Spend a few minutes each day noting what you're grateful for and how worship influences your mood and thoughts. Reflect on its impact on your interactions and decisions.

Reflective Questions:

» How does worship affect your emotional state and mindset?
» How can you integrate worship into your daily routine to support your well-being?
» How does worship help you manage stress and maintain a positive outlook?

Embrace worship daily to elevate your mindset, boost your emotional resilience, and enrich your overall well-being.

Day 104: Transform Your Reality

"Your outer world reflects your inner world." – Unknown

Our external experiences reflect our inner thoughts and beliefs. When we focus on negativity or limitations, our reality often mirrors those thoughts. Understanding this connection allows us to break free from mental barriers and attract the life we desire.

Our subconscious mind shapes our experiences remarkably, influencing about 90% of our daily actions and reactions. Negative thinking patterns can create self-fulfilling prophecies, while positive thinking opens doors to new opportunities. Neuroscience shows that our thought patterns affect our brain's wiring, which impacts our daily lives.

Imagine someone who constantly worries about financial stability. Their anxiety might cause them to miss opportunities or avoid beneficial decisions, reinforcing their fears. Conversely, maintaining a positive outlook can attract favourable situations and relationships. Quantum Physics suggests that our thoughts emit vibrations that can affect the world around us. These vibrations align with the energy we project, attracting experiences that match our internal state. If we radiate positive thoughts, we attract positive circumstances, and vice versa. This concept links closely to neuroplasticity, where our brain's wiring adapts based on our repeated thoughts and beliefs.

Practical Tips:

◊ **Reframe Limiting Beliefs:** Replace limiting thoughts with positive affirmations.
◊ **Imagine Abundance:** Regularly visualise success and take steps toward it.
◊ **Build Positivity:** Surround yourself with supportive people and uplifting influences.

Exercise: Write down three negative beliefs and counter each with a positive affirmation. Repeat these affirmations daily to reshape your mindset.

Reflective Questions:

» How do your current thoughts shape your experiences and opportunities?
» What negative beliefs might be limiting your potential?
How can shifting your mindset to focus on abundance affect your daily life?

Adopt a mindset of possibility, and your life will reflect abundance and opportunity.

Day 105: Stop Claiming What You Don't Want

"You attract what you are, not what you want. If you want great things, you have to become great first." — Unknown

Think of your words as keys that unlock doors to your reality. When you say *"my stress"* or *"my problems,"* you're essentially handing these issues a VIP pass to your life. Imagine you're at a buffet; if you keep putting unhealthy items on your plate, that's what you'll eat. The same goes for your mind. By claiming what you don't want, you reinforce its hold over you.

Our brains are wired to follow patterns. When we repeatedly use negative language, our neural pathways solidify these thoughts and emotions. It's like walking the same path in the woods; the more you walk it, the more defined it becomes. This mental trail makes it easier to default to negativity. Instead, using positive language creates new, healthier paths in your brain, encouraging a more optimistic mindset.

Emotions are closely tied to self-talk. When you label yourself with negativity, you're setting the stage for your actions and decisions to follow. Imagine if you always thought of yourself as *"bad at maths"*—this belief might make you avoid math-related tasks such as looking at your accounts as a business owner. Changing how you talk about yourself and your challenges influences how you feel and act. Proverbs 18:21 (NIV) reminds us, *"The tongue has the power of life and death, and those who love it will eat its fruit."* This verse shows that our words shape our reality. By focusing on affirmations like *"I am capable"* and *"I am blessed,"* you invite positive change into your life.

Practical Tips:

◊ **Reframe:** Switch from saying "my problems" to "current challenges I'm over-coming."
◊ **Daily Affirmations**: Start your day with affirmations that focus on your strengths and goals.
◊ **Mindful Communication:** Pay attention to your words and consciously choose those that uplift and encourage.

Reflective Questions:

◊ What negative phrases do you often use about yourself or your situation?
◊ How can you reframe these to be more positive and empowering?
◊ What changes do you notice in your mood and actions when you use positive language?

Focusing on positive language can help you embrace the power of your words and transform your reality. This will lead to a brighter, more fulfilling life.

DAY 106: OVERCOMING SHAME

"Shame corrodes the very part of us that believes we are capable of change." — Brené Brown

Shame can feel like a heavy backpack filled with rocks, each representing feelings of failure, inadequacy, or embarrassment. These burdens can weigh you down, making it hard to see your true potential. But shame doesn't define you; it's a challenge you can overcome.

Closing my business in 2006 filled me with a profound sense of shame. The feeling of being ridiculed made me self-conscious, leading me to isolate myself. I avoided social interactions and believed I was a failure, which consumed me. This period was incredibly isolating and disheartening. However, trusting God and learning to rewire my brain to embrace my experiences as valuable lessons helped me rise above those feelings. I now saw my setbacks as stepping stones rather than failures. By shifting my mindset and focusing on my potential, I transformed my approach to life and business. Now, running a fulfilling and successful business, I've learned not to identify as a failure but to view setbacks as integral parts of my growth journey.

Shame activates stress responses in the brain, leading to negative thought patterns and emotional challenges. Neuroplasticity shows that we can rewire our brains to overcome these feelings by intentionally practising positive thinking and self-compassion. Embracing new, healthier thought patterns can break the cycle of shame and help us thrive.

Romans 8:1 (NIV) says, *"There is therefore now no condemnation for those who are in Christ Jesus."* This assures us that shame has no hold on us when we are aligned with Christ. His grace offers us a fresh start and the strength to move beyond our past.

Practical Tips:

◊ Reframe Your Experiences: See setbacks as learning opportunities.
◊ **Practice Self-Compassion:** Be kind to yourself.
◊ **Seek Support:** Seek support from mentors or friends.

Reflective Questions:

» How has shame affected your decisions and actions?
» What strategies can you use to reframe your experiences and embrace growth?
» How can overcoming shame help you achieve your goals and live more fully?

Embrace your journey, fuel success with your experiences, and overcome shame to unlock a fulfilling future.

Day 107: Building Resilience Through Patience

"Patience and perseverance have a magical effect before which difficulties disappear and obstacles vanish." – John Quincy Adams

Patience isn't just about waiting; it's a way to build resilience and mental strength. When you practice patience, you learn to face challenges calmly and with determination. It helps you understand that real progress and success often require time and consistent effort.

Building resilience through patience is like strengthening a muscle. Every time you practice patience in the face of obstacles, you train your brain to handle stress and adversity more effectively. Science shows that practising patience enhances the brain's ability to manage stress and makes you more adaptable. With time, patience strengthens your emotional fortitude, enabling you to persevere in pursuing long-term goals.

Consider an athlete training for a marathon. The process requires weeks or months of preparation, gradual improvements, and setbacks. Patience keeps them moving forward when progress feels slow, and the same patience allows them to reach the finish line.

Spiritually, patience is also an expression of trust in the process. James 1:4 (NKJV) encourages us to *"let patience have its perfect work, that you may be perfect and complete, lacking nothing."* This scripture reminds us that patience refines our character and equips us to handle challenges.

Practical Tips:

◊ **Focus on the Long-Term:** Break large goals into smaller steps, reminding yourself that steady progress is still progress.

◊ **Practice Delayed Gratification:** Remember that the most meaningful achievements often require time and persistence.

◊ **Develop a Growth Mindset:** View setbacks as opportunities to strengthen your resilience.

Reflective Questions:

» How do you usually respond to long-term challenges or setbacks?
» What specific goals could benefit from more patience and perseverance?
» How can patience help you develop resilience in everyday life?

Exercise: Identify a long-term goal that requires patience. Write down three small, manageable actions you can take this week to move closer to that goal and reflect on how practising patience enhances your journey.

Day 108: The Purpose of Prayer

"Prayer is not to inform God, but to reform you." – Anonymous

Prayer is more than asking for help; it's a powerful way to transform your heart and mind. Through prayer, we connect with God, gain clarity, and align ourselves with His purpose. It's a conversation that recharges your spirit and helps you face life's challenges with peace and confidence.

Prayer activates key parts of the brain, like the **limbic system**, which processes emotions, and the **default mode network**, which handles self-reflection and connection. When you pray, your brain releases dopamine and serotonin, chemicals that boost your mood and reduce stress. Studies show regular prayer can lower anxiety and increase emotional resilience.

From a spiritual perspective, Psalm 34:18 tells us, *"The Lord is close to the brokenhearted and saves those who are crushed in spirit."* This reminds us that prayer is a way to experience God's closeness, even during life's hardest moments. Prayer helps us develop emotional intelligence (EQ) by teaching us to pause, reflect, and manage emotions. Instead of reacting to stress or fear, prayer helps you refocus on God's promises and remain calm. This mental and emotional shift allows you to make better decisions and grow stronger in faith.

Practical Tips:

◊ **Set a Time:** Create a daily habit of prayer, even if it's just a few minutes.
◊ **Use Scripture:** Pray using Bible verses that remind you of God's promises.
◊ **Be Still:** Take time to listen, not just speak, and allow God to guide your thoughts.

Reflective Questions:

» How does prayer help you feel more connected to God?
» What emotions do you bring to prayer, and how does it help you process them?
» How can you use prayer to stay calm and focused during challenges?

Action Step:
Dedicate 10 minutes daily to prayer this week. Reflect on a Bible verse, share your concerns with God, and listen for His guidance. Notice how it changes your mindset and helps you face the day with renewed strength.

Prayer transforms not just your spirit but also your thoughts, helping you live with purpose and peace.

Day 109: Epigenetics and Your Life

"Your genes load the gun, but your lifestyle pulls the trigger." – Dr. Mehmet Oz

Epigenetics looks at how our actions and environment affect our genes without changing the DNA itself. These changes are reversible, offering a powerful way to positively impact our health and well-being.

Key Concepts of Epigenetics

> **Gene Expression:** Epigenetics controls which genes are turned on or off, affecting both physical and mental health. Think of it like a light dimmer; our lifestyle can brighten or dim our genetic potential.

> **Environmental Influences:** Things like diet, stress, and toxins can change how our genes behave. For example, long-term stress can trigger changes that might increase the risk of mental health issues.

> **Reversibility:** The great thing about epigenetics is that it's reversible. By adopting healthier habits, we can turn back negative changes. Our choices today can lead to a healthier future.

Practical Implications:

> **Healthy Eating:** What you eat matters. Foods high in antioxidants, like berries and greens, can support positive gene changes. For instance, broccoli has compounds that help prevent cancer.

> **Exercise:** Staying active promotes positive changes in our genes, boosts mental health, and lowers the risk of chronic diseases.

> **Stress Management:** Chronic stress can harm gene expression. Mindfulness and meditation can help manage stress, leading to better mental health.

> **Avoiding Toxins:** Reducing exposure to harmful chemicals, like those in cigarettes, can protect our genes. Choosing natural products and avoiding smoking are essential for health.

Imagine someone with a family history of heart disease. While they may have a genetic predisposition, a healthy lifestyle can significantly lower their risk. Understanding epigenetics helps us manage our health through balanced living.

Reflective Questions:

» In what ways do your daily habits impact your overall health and well-being?
» What positive changes can you make today?
» How can knowing about epigenetics empower your health decisions?

By understanding epigenetics, you can make choices that enhance your well-being and reshape your genetic destiny, aligning with a limitless mindset.

Day 110: Rewiring Your Brain for Success

"Neurons that fire together wire together." – Donald Hebb

Hebb's principle explains how our brain's wiring adapts through repeated experiences and thoughts. Understanding this will help you build positive habits and achieve success. Hebb's principle shows that repeated actions strengthen neural (brain cells) connections, making them more automatic. Consistently practising positive behaviours and thoughts make them more ingrained in your brain, leading to lasting change.

Neuroscience shows that our brain's plasticity allows us to rewire our thought patterns. For example, regular mindfulness practice can build pathways linked to stress reduction. Conversely, persistent negative thinking strengthens pathways that lead to anxiety and self-doubt.

Practical Tips Using the 5 R Step

- >**Recognise:** Identify a negative thought or habit. For example, if you often think, *"I'm not good enough,"* recognise this as a barrier to success.
- >**Reframe:** Replace the negative thought with a positive belief. For example, change *"I'm not good enough"* to *"I am capable and deserving of success."*
- >**Reinforce:** Actively practice the new thought or behaviour. Use affirmations, set reminders, or create habits that support your new belief.
- >**Reflect**: Assess how these changes impact your mindset and behaviour. Observe how the new habits affect your daily life and emotions.
- >**Reward:** Celebrate minor victories. Rewarding yourself for sticking to positive behaviours helps solidify new neural pathways.

Do you struggle with self-doubt? You can boost confidence and create better opportunities by identifying negative self-talk, replacing them with positive affirmations, and reinforcing these beliefs.

Reflective Questions:

- » What negative patterns do you want to change?
- » How can you use the 5 R step to build positive habits?
- » What changes have you noticed from applying these practices?

Practical Exercise:

This week, pick one negative thought or behaviour. Apply the 5 R step: *Recognise, Reframe, Reinforce, Reflect, and Reward*. Track your progress and note the positive changes in your mindset and daily life.

Day 111: Threat in the Brain

"Your brain doesn't react to reality; it reacts to your perception of reality." – Dr. David Rock

Imagine you're in a storm. The dark clouds represent different levels of threat your brain faces: some are distant, some are approaching, and some are right above you. Understanding how your brain navigates these storms will help you manage stress and make better decisions.

Levels of Threat

> **Level 1:** Think of this as a distant storm warning. It's not immediate, like hearing about a hurricane in another state. Your brain notes it but doesn't feel alarmed.
> **Level 2:** This is like the storm approaching your town. Your stress levels rise as you prepare to deal with the situation. Your mind becomes more focused on immediate concerns, which can overwhelm you.
> **Level 3:** This is the full-blown storm hitting your town. Your brain is in panic mode, scrambling to respond with minimal thought. Decisions are made in a rush, often leading to poor outcomes.

When faced with threats, it's crucial to avoid letting your brain escalate to a Level 3 reaction unnecessarily.

Here's how you can manage these mental storms:

> **Raise Certainty:** Create a daily routine to build a sense of stability. Just like finding shelter before a storm, having a structured plan helps you feel more secure.
> **Find Choices:** Empower yourself by identifying small decisions you can control. Creating a plan will increase your sense of control during a storm.
> **Get Connected:** Build a support network to share experiences and reduce stress, like a community weathering a storm together.

Practical Exercise:

◊ This week, focus on one strategy daily.
◊ Observe how it affects your stress levels and decision-making. By applying these techniques, you can weather life's storms with greater resilience and clarity.

Reflective Questions:

» How do you currently perceive and react to different levels of threat?
» Which of the strategies can you use to manage stress better?
» How does understanding your brain's threat levels influence your decisions?

Day 112: Breaking Free from Limitations

"Never be limited by other people's limited imagination." – Mae Jemison

Mae Jemison's words challenge us to expand beyond the constraints others might place on us. Cultivating a limitless mindset means liberating yourself from external limits and embracing your boundless potential. When others project their limitations onto you, it's easy to internalise those constraints. These external voices can inhibit your growth, whether it's doubts about your capabilities or discouragement from pursuing your dreams. This quote encourages you to rise above these imposed limitations and trust in your unique potential. Belief in your abilities can significantly impact your brain's performance. Positive self-belief activates neural pathways related to motivation and perseverance, enhancing problem-solving skills and creativity. When you reject limiting beliefs, you allow your brain to operate at maximum capacity, leading to innovative thinking and problem-solving.

Emotional Intelligence (EQ) helps us recognise and overcome internalised limitations by fostering self-awareness and resilience. Philippians 4:13 (NKJV) reminds us, *"I can do all things through Christ who strengthens me."* This verse highlights that our belief and faith in God's promises strengthens our potential, not being bound by other people's expectations.

Think about yourself—imagine you have a dream that others dismiss as unrealistic. You can transform your idea into a reality by holding onto your vision, setting clear goals, and seeking guidance. Your potential isn't limited by other people's narrow views.

Practical Tips:

◊ **Set Personal Goals**: Identify an area where the opinions of others hinder you, define your goal, and break it down into steps.

◊ **Visualise Success:** Imagine yourself achieving your goals despite external doubts. This mental rehearsal helps build confidence and resilience.

◊ **Seek Inspiration:** Surround yourself with stories and people who've overcome similar challenges to gain motivation and perspective.

Reflective Questions:

» What external limitations have you internalised in your life?
» How can you challenge and overcome these limitations?
» How does your faith or personal conviction help you break free from others' constraints?

Reflect on how breaking free from these limits affects your mindset and progress.

Day 113: Breaking Barriers

"Success is not final, failure is not fatal: It is the courage to continue that counts." – Winston Churchill

Many renowned people faced doubt and scepticism but rose to remarkable success. Their stories remind us that we, too, can overcome obstacles and fulfil our dreams, regardless of other people's doubts. Consider Thomas Edison, who was deemed an impractical dreamer before inventing the practical light bulb. Despite numerous failures and scepticism, his perseverance led to groundbreaking success. Similarly, J.K. Rowling faced multiple rejections for her Harry Potter manuscript and was advised to abandon her writing. Yet, her determination transformed her story into a global sensation, proving that other people's limits do not define our potential.

Our brains react to criticism with stress responses that can inhibit our performance. Criticism triggers the release of cortisol, a stress hormone, which can cloud our thinking and impact performance. However, maintaining a positive mindset and self-belief can boost neurotransmitters like dopamine and serotonin, enhancing motivation and resilience. Research shows that positive self-belief strengthens neural pathways associated with success, helping us manage stress and stay focused. Emotional Intelligence (EQ) helps manage stress and maintain focus. The story of David and Goliath illustrates overcoming doubt with faith and courage. Despite scepticism, David's fearless belief and bravery led him to defeat Goliath, demonstrating that faith and determination can conquer challenges (1 Samuel 17:45-50).

Imagine you're pursuing a new goal but facing criticism. Instead of letting doubts hold you back, concentrate on your vision, accept encouragement from those who believe in you, and see setbacks as chances to learn and grow.

Practical Tips for Success:

◊ **Focus on Your Vision:** Be clear about your goals regardless of external doubts.
◊ **Seek Support:** Connect with coaches, mentors and supporters who believe in your potential.
◊ **Embrace Setbacks:** Use challenges as opportunities to learn and grow.

Reflective Questions:

» What doubts or criticisms have you encountered in pursuing your goals?
» How can you use setbacks as stepping stones to succeed?
» How can you strengthen resilience and positive belief in your journey?

This week, tackle a challenge that has caused you doubt. Focus on your vision, seek support, and learn from any setbacks.

Day 114: Thriving Against the Odds

"And who knows but that you have come to your royal position for such a time as this?"—
Esther 4:14 (NIV)

Esther's story is a powerful example of overcoming significant odds. Despite being an orphan and a Jew in a foreign land, she rose to become Queen of Persia. When a decree threatened her people with annihilation, Esther took a bold risk by approaching King Xerxes without being summoned, which could have cost her life. Her courage and strategic actions led to the king overturning the decree and saving her people.

Our brains react strongly to stress, releasing cortisol that can cloud judgment and make us risk-averse, hindering performance. This stress response often leads to avoiding bold actions. Cultivating resilience, however, can shift this dynamic. When you face challenges with a positive mindset, your brain releases dopamine, improving your stress management and problem-solving abilities. Research shows that believing in your potential helps strengthen neural (brain) connections related to resilience and success, making it easier to tackle obstacles.

Emotional Intelligence (EQ) is crucial for managing stress and focusing on goals. Esther's story shows how courage and faith can turn adversity into triumph. Despite the immense risks, her belief and decisive actions led to a remarkable victory, showing the importance of resilience and faith in achieving success.

Are you facing a significant challenge? Take inspiration from Esther. Embrace your unique position, act courageously, and seek support to overcome obstacles.

Practical Tips:

◊ **Embrace Your Role:** Recognise your unique opportunities, even in challenging situations.
◊ **Act with Courage:** Take bold actions despite your fears and obstacles.
◊ **Seek Support:** Build a network of allies and mentors to reinforce your efforts.

Reflective Questions:

» How can you leverage your unique opportunities in difficult times?
» What fears or challenges are you facing, and how can you confront them courageously?
» How can support from others help you thrive against the odds?

This week, identify a current challenge. Apply Esther's approach: recognise your role, act courageously, and seek support. Reflect on how these actions affect your ability to overcome obstacles and succeed.

Day 115: With Jesus, I Can

"The Lord is my strength and my shield; my heart trusts in him, and he helps me." – Psalm 28:7

Life can throw challenges our way that feel overwhelming. Philippians 4:13 reminds us that we have incredible potential when we lean on Christ's strength. The Holy Spirit helps us tap into this power, guiding us through tough times and helping us grow.
Jesus promised in John 14:26 (NIV), *"But the Helper, the Holy Spirit, whom the Father will send in my name, will teach you all things and remind you of everything I have said to you."* This means we are never alone. The Holy Spirit is here to always offer wisdom and strength.

Our thoughts can shape how we feel and act. Research shows that when we believe in ourselves, we perform better. For example, a study found that students who think positively about their abilities tend to do better on tests. If a student believes they can succeed, they are less likely to feel anxious and more likely to do well.

Ways to Build Positive Thoughts

> **Affirmations:** Start your day with positive statements like, *"I can achieve my goals with Christ's help."*
> **Visualise Success:** Picture yourself succeeding at what you want to do. This will help boost your confidence.
> **Mindfulness:** Pay attention to your thoughts. When you notice negative ones, try to change them into positive ones.
> **Seek Support:** Spend time with people who lift you up and encourage you.

Putting It into Action
If you face a challenging project at work, rely on Christ's strength and the Holy Spirit's guidance. Look at obstacles as opportunities to grow.

Reflective Questions:

» How can you invite Christ's strength into your daily life?
» How does knowing you have divine support change how you handle challenges?

Day 116: Stop Training Yourself to Fail

"For as he thinks in his heart, so is he." – Proverbs 23:7 (KJV)

Proverbs 23:7 reminds us that our thoughts shape our lives. Many people unknowingly train themselves to fail by letting self-doubt and negative beliefs hold them back. This self-sabotage often runs deep in our minds, creating obstacles without us even realising it.

The Power of Mindset
Our beliefs shape how we act. If you constantly doubt yourself or fear failure, you may avoid opportunities or delay important actions. This reinforces negative thoughts, making it more difficult to succeed. Neuroscience shows that repeating negative thoughts strengthens brain pathways tied to doubt, while positive thinking can rewire these pathways, making success more attainable. Research reveals that negative thinking can increase stress and anxiety, reinforcing unhelpful patterns. On the other hand, positive thoughts release dopamine, the brain's "feel-good" chemical, which boosts motivation and helps break the self-sabotaging cycle.

Building emotional intelligence (EQ) helps you identify and manage these patterns. You can redirect triggers and negative thoughts with positive affirmations and goals that focus on success by recognising triggers and negative thoughts. For instance, someone struggling with career growth due to self-doubt can shift their mindset by practising affirmations like *"I am capable"* and setting small, achievable goals. This approach encourages progress and reinforces a positive self-view.

Practical Tips:
- ◊ **Identify Negative Patterns:** Reflect on areas where you might be unintentionally holding yourself back.
- ◊ **Reframe Your Thoughts:** Replace negative self-talk with affirmations and set achievable goals.
- ◊ **Take Positive Actions:** Act on goals that align with success.
- ◊ **Seek Support:** Reach out to a coach or trusted friends for encouragement and guidance.

Reflective Questions:
- » What self-limiting beliefs might be affecting your current goals?
- » How can you reframe these beliefs to support your success?

This week, pick an area where you feel stuck. Use positive affirmations, set clear goals, and take steps toward change. Reflect on how these changes impact your progress and confidence, and experience how a positive mindset shifts your path forward.

Day 117: Finding Light in Darkness

"The Lord is close to the brokenhearted and saves those who are crushed in spirit." – Psalm 34:18 (NIV)

Depression can feel like being lost in a thick fog, where every step feels heavy, and the way forward seems unclear. It's not just sadness—it's an overwhelming sense of emptiness that can make daily tasks feel impossible. But Psalm 34:18 reminds us that God is close to us in these moments, offering comfort and strength when we feel most vulnerable.

From a brain perspective, depression often stems from imbalances in neurotransmitters like serotonin and dopamine, which regulate mood and energy. Dr. Daniel Amen describes depression as a symptom of deeper brain health issues, not a permanent state. This perspective provides hope, as it suggests that with the right steps, we can address these imbalances and move toward healing.

Faith plays a critical role in this journey. Just as God remains near to the brokenhearted, faith in His promises can anchor us during difficult times. By combining practical steps with spiritual guidance, we can rebuild our mental and emotional health.

Depression doesn't define you—it's a season, and seasons change.

Practical Steps:

◊ **Seek Support:** Professional help, such as brain health evaluations or therapy, can provide effective strategies for managing depression.
◊ **Create Positive Habits:** Activities like exercise, gratitude journaling, and engaging in meaningful relationships can boost brain health.
◊ **Lean on Faith:** Spend time in prayer and Scripture, allowing God's presence to guide and uplift you.

Reflective Questions:

» What small step can you take today to support your mental health?
» How can faith provide strength during your healing journey?
» Who in your life can walk alongside you as you work toward recovery?

This week, take one tangible step—whether it's seeking professional advice, creating a healthy habit, or deepening your connection with God. Reflect on how these actions bring clarity and light to your path, reminding you that with the right tools and faith, healing is within reach.

Day 118: Embracing Hope

"But those who hope in the Lord will renew their strength. They will soar on wings like eagles; they will run and not grow weary, they will walk and not be faint." – Isaiah 40:31 (NIV)

Imagine hope as a guiding star in the night sky, illuminating your path through the darkest hours. Hope is more than just a feeling; it's a powerful force that can transform your outlook and fuel your journey. Isaiah 40:31 promises that those who hope in the Lord will experience renewed strength and resilience as eagles soar above the clouds.

From a neurological perspective, hope triggers the release of dopamine, the "feel-good" neurotransmitter, which enhances our mood and motivation. Our brain's reward system is activated when we focus on positive outcomes, increasing optimism and perseverance. This neurological boost supports our ability to tackle challenges and keep moving forward, even when obstacles seem overwhelming. Faith in God provides a solid foundation for hope in times of uncertainty. The Bible is rich with examples of individuals who faced daunting challenges but emerged victorious because of their unwavering hope in God's promises. For instance, despite being betrayed and imprisoned, Joseph held onto hope and eventually rose to a position of significant influence, showing us that perseverance and faith can lead to extraordinary outcomes.

When faced with adversity, envision hope as a beacon guiding you through the storm. Take small, hopeful steps and lean into your faith to transform challenges into opportunities for growth.

Practical Tips:

◊ **Focus on Positivity:** Regularly remind yourself of the positive aspects of your life and future.

◊ **Set Small Goals:** Instead of being overwhelmed by big challenges, break them into smaller, manageable actions to stay motivated and build confidence with each step.

◊ **Lean on Faith:** Draw strength from spiritual practices and scripture to reinforce your sense of hope.

Reflective Questions:

» What areas of your life could benefit from a renewed sense of hope?
» How can you actively nurture hope in your daily routine?
» What role does faith play in sustaining your hope?

This week, identify a challenge that requires more hope. Focus on positivity, set small goals, and lean on faith. Reflect on how these actions shift your perspective and enhance your resilience.

Day 119: Igniting Your Ambition

"The brain is the organ of ambition and desire." – Candace Pert

Ignite Your Inner Fire!
Picture your ambition as a powerful engine propelling you toward your dreams. According to Dr. Candace Pert, our brains are naturally wired for ambition, pushing us to reach for more. With passion and determination fueling this internal engine, you have what it takes to transform your dreams into reality. Embrace this drive and let it guide you toward achieving your goals.

When you set a goal, your brain's prefrontal cortex, the command centre for planning and decision-making, springs into action. Dopamine, the brain's reward chemical, surges, making you feel motivated and eager. This chemical boost enhances focus and strengthens your resolve to push through challenges and setbacks. In 1 Corinthians 9:24 (NIV), we read, *"Do you not know that in a race all the runners run, but only one receives the prize? So run that you may obtain it."*
This scripture encourages us to channel our ambition with purpose and faith. Just as athletes train tirelessly for a race, we are called to pursue our goals with determination and divine guidance.

Can you think of someone who faced many setbacks but kept their vision clear and unwavering? By maintaining focus and resilience, they eventually turned their dreams into achievements.

Practical Tips:

◊ **Set Clear Goals:** Define what you want to achieve and map out the steps needed.

◊ **Embrace the Journey:** View challenges as opportunities to grow and learn.

◊ **Seek Inspiration:** Surround yourself with uplifting mentors and positive influences.

◊ **Celebrate Progress:** Recognise and reward small victories along the way.

Reflective Questions:

» What are your current ambitions, and how can you break them into actionable steps?
» How can you align your goals with your faith to ensure they are purposeful?
» What challenges are you facing, and how can you use them to strengthen your resolve?

This week, set a big goal, outline steps, seek guidance, track progress, and reflect on how faith fuels your journey.

Day 120: The Infinite Power Within

"Now to him who is able to do immeasurably more than all we ask or imagine, according to his power that is at work within us." – Ephesians 3:20 (NIV)

The power within us, through the Holy Spirit, is limitless. Viewing ourselves solely from a physical perspective confines us to what we can see and measure. However, when we embrace our identity as spiritual beings, we tap into God's infinite power—far beyond anything we can comprehend.

Jesus exemplified this boundless power throughout His ministry. He healed the sick, calmed storms, and even raised the dead. These miracles were not just acts of physical healing but manifestations of God's spiritual power at work in the physical world. In John 14:12 (NIV), Jesus says, *"Whoever believes in me will do the works I have been doing, and they will do even greater things than these, because I am going to the Father."* This promise extends to us when we think and believe as spiritual beings, fully connected to God's power.

Consider David and Goliath. A young shepherd, David faced a giant warrior with nothing but a sling and stones. From a physical perspective, David stood no chance. But he didn't rely on physical strength; he trusted in God's power within him. This spiritual confidence allowed David to defeat Goliath, overcoming what seemed impossible. Like David, when we rely on God's power within us, we can conquer insurmountable challenges.

Practical Tips:

◊ **Affirm Your Identity:** Regularly remind yourself that you are a spiritual being with access to God's infinite power.
◊ Pray with Expectation: Approach prayer with the belief that God's power within you can achieve more than you can imagine.
◊ **Embrace Spiritual Abundance:** Trust in God's limitless provision and power as you face daily challenges.

Reflective Questions:

» How does recognising your spiritual identity change your approach to challenges?
» In what areas of your life can you rely more on God's power within you?
» How can you daily remind yourself of the infinite power available to you through the Holy Spirit?

By embracing your identity as a spiritual being and aligning your thoughts with God's word, you can tap into the infinite power within you and live a life of abundance and purpose beyond the physical world's limits.

PART FIVE

SELF DISCOVERY

Part 5 Introduction

In Part 5: Self-Discovery, we focus on uncovering your true identity in God and understanding how this shapes every part of your life. This journey begins with embracing who you are in Christ (Day 121) and realising your divine purpose. Throughout this section, you'll explore your spiritual nature (Day 124), discover the kingdom within (Day 123), and understand your role as God's ambassador (Day 129).

Neuroscience and psychology reveal that practices like journaling (Day 139) and self-reflection (Day 138) activate brain areas that enhance emotional resilience and decision-making. For those ready to go deeper, the Self-Discovery Toolkit at The Mindsight Academy offers additional questions and exercises to help uncover purpose and gain clarity, particularly in areas like values, strengths, and vision.

As you progress, you'll be encouraged to prioritise your passions (Day 130), set healthy boundaries (Day 142), and live with divine purpose (Day 134). This section will help you understand your identity as salt and light (Day 150) so you can confidently live a fulfilling life that truly reflects God's calling.

Day 121: Embracing Your God-Given Identity

"For we are God's handiwork, created in Christ Jesus to do good works, which God prepared in advance for us to do." —Ephesians 2:10 (NIV)

Embracing your God-given identity is about recognising who you are in Christ Jesus and seeing yourself through His love and purpose. In a world that often defines us by achievements, appearance, or social status, understanding your identity in God offers peace, confidence, and freedom from external pressures.

Neuroscience shows that when we align with positive truths—like those found in God's Word—our brain's prefrontal cortex (the part linked to self-awareness and emotional control) becomes more active. This shift decreases stress, improves emotional balance, and reinforces a deep sense of purpose. As 1 Peter 2:9 (NIV) says, *"But you are a chosen people, a royal priesthood, a holy nation, God's special possession."* This truth reminds us that our worth is rooted in God's love, not shifting worldly standards.

Imagine your identity as a diamond buried beneath layers of dirt, symbolising society's expectations and pressures. While the dirt might hide the diamond's shine, it can't diminish its inherent value. Similarly, your identity in Christ is constant, valuable, and waiting to be fully embraced.

Many people struggle with feelings of inadequacy or the urge to fit into moulds set by others. But realising you are God's creation brings freedom to live authentically. This freedom allows you to stand firm in who you are, empowered by the knowledge that you are loved, valued, and designed with purpose by God. Internalise this truth by meditating on scripture, like 2 Corinthians 5:17 (NIV): *"Therefore, if anyone is in Christ, the new creation has come: The old has gone, the new is here!"* Let these words reshape your self-image and guide your daily actions.

Practical Exercise:

◊ Choose three Bible verses about your identity in Christ.
◊ Memorise and meditate on them, especially when doubts arise.
◊ This practice will reinforce your confidence in who God says you are.

Reflective Questions:

» How does knowing you are God's masterpiece change your self-view?
» Where do you struggle to accept your identity in Christ?
» How can you live out your God-given identity in everyday life?

This exercise is a daily reminder of your worth, rooted in God's love, to help you live confidently and authentically.

Day 122: Who Am I? Whose Am I?

"It's not who you are that holds you back; it's what you think you are that holds you back."
– Myles Munroe

Understanding who you are begins with knowing whose you are.
Your identity isn't defined by your achievements or how others see you but by the truth that you are a child of God, made in His image. Recognising that your worth is rooted in God's love provides a firm foundation of confidence and purpose. Embracing your identity in Christ transforms your thinking.

Neuroscience shows that when you believe in your God-given identity, the prefrontal cortex—the brain's centre for decision-making and self-control—is activated, enhancing emotional stability and self-worth. Scripture reflects this truth in Genesis 1:27 (NIV): *"So God created mankind in his own image."* Knowing that you are made in God's image means that you carry His love, creativity, and purpose. Imagine yourself as a seed with unlimited potential. Just as a seed grows into a fertile tree when planted in fertile soil, you can flourish when rooted in God's truth. Knowing your identity in God assures you that every challenge is an opportunity for growth, with God working all things for your good. This awareness fuels your confidence and determination.

Start each day by affirming, *"I am who God says I am."* Reflect on Romans 8:28 (NIV), which reminds us, *"And we know that in all things God works for the good of those who love him."* This perspective empowers you to approach life with the assurance that you can achieve great things through God's guidance. This confidence empowers you to pursue dreams and overcome obstacles in both personal and professional contexts as you understand that your worth and success are rooted in God's plan for you.

Practical Exercise:

◊ Write three affirmations based on God's promises, like *"I am destined for greatness through Christ."*

◊ Repeat these each morning to reinforce your limitless potential.

Reflective Questions:

» How does knowing you are made in God's image inspire confidence in you?
» What limiting beliefs have held you back from living your potential?
» How can you embrace your God-given identity more fully from today?

This practice will help you embrace who you are, empowering you to live a life reflecting God's greatness and purpose.

Day 123: Discovering the Kingdom Within

"Neither shall they say, Lo here! or, lo there! for, behold, the kingdom of God is within you."
– Luke 17:21 (KJV)

Jesus' words remind us that the kingdom of God isn't a place to search for outside ourselves; it exists within each of us. This truth is transformative. Understanding that God's kingdom lives within us means we carry divine potential, wisdom, and strength wherever we go. It's realising that God has already placed everything we need to live a purposeful and abundant life inside us.

Embracing this truth rewires our brain by activating areas associated with peace, creativity, and resilience. This rewiring enhances effective decision-making and reduces stress by calming the emotional brain and the amygdala. Knowing God's presence within shifts our mindset from scarcity to abundance, empowering us to face challenges with confidence and grace.

Think of God's kingdom as vast, like the vastness of the universe, limitless and filled with divine light. Earthly boundaries do not confine this infinite power; it is ever-present, guiding and illuminating every aspect of your life. By acknowledging His divine presence, you live with assurance, knowing God's love and power guide you in every situation. This shift transforms your perspective, making you more resilient and hopeful.

Start each day by affirming, *"God's kingdom is alive and powerful within me."* Reflect on Luke 17:21 and let this truth shape your actions. This mindset helps turn obstacles into opportunities for God's glory to be revealed.

This awareness will bring inner peace and joy to your life. Professionally, it inspires you to act with integrity and purpose, trusting God's wisdom to guide you.

Practical Exercise:

◊ Spend five minutes each morning in quiet meditation, focusing on God's kingdom within.

◊ Imagine it as an infinite source of strength, love, and wisdom, empowering you throughout the day.

Reflective Questions:

» How does knowing the kingdom of God is within you change your outlook on life?

» How can you tap into the power of God's kingdom each day?

» How can this understanding influence your relationships with others?

Embracing this truth will help you stay connected to the divine power within, enabling you to live confidently and purposefully.

Day 124: Embracing our Spiritual Nature

"We are not human beings having a spiritual experience; we are spiritual beings having a human experience." – Pierre Teilhard de Chardin

Understanding that we are spiritual beings shifts how we see ourselves and our potential. At our core, beyond our physical form, we are spirits created in God's image. Even at the smallest level, atoms comprise electrons and protons vibrating with energy, reflecting the dynamic spirit God placed within us. This vibration and energy are reminders of our spiritual nature and the divine power we carry.

Science, particularly quantum physics and neuroplasticity, provides compelling evidence that our brains are not fixed; they can transform and evolve. This aligns with our spiritual essence, allowing us to reshape our thoughts and emotions. Our imagination, fueled by our spiritual connection to God, is a powerful tool that transcends physical limitations. Jesus said, *'You are in the world, but not of the world,'* reminding us that, while we live in a physical realm, our spirits connect us to God's infinite possibilities.

Imagine the universe within you, filled with endless potential. This divine spark enables us to imagine, create, and innovate. By tapping into this spiritual nature, you can achieve emotional mastery, using your thoughts and beliefs to shape your reality. Just as our brains can form new pathways, our spirits can guide us to new heights of understanding, creativity, and love.

Begin each day with the affirmation, **"I am a spiritual being with limitless potential."**

Embrace your ability to imagine and create, knowing your spirit aligns with God's power. This mindset will help you see challenges as opportunities for God's wisdom to shine through you. It will help you conquer fear and doubt in your personal life. Professionally, it empowers you to lead with vision and trust God's guidance.

Practical Exercise:

◊ Spend five minutes each morning imagining a goal or dream, seeing it clearly in your mind's eye.

◊ Imagine God's power flowing through you, helping you bring that vision to life.

Reflective Questions:

» How does recognising your spiritual nature influence your self-perception?

» How can you use your imagination to change your life positively?

DAY 125: THE CALL TO DISCIPLESHIP

"Before I was born, the Lord called me; from my mother's womb he has spoken my name." – Isaiah 49:1 (NIV)

Discipleship is answering the call God placed in your heart even before birth. In Isaiah 49, God reminds His servant of a purpose planted deep within, a purpose that aligns with His divine plan. Like Isaiah, each of us is called by name, chosen to walk a path that reflects God's love, wisdom, and guidance.

Think of a sculptor who sees a beautiful statue within a rough block of marble. With each careful chisel, the sculptor reveals the masterpiece inside. Similarly, God sees our potential and purpose. Through discipleship, we allow God to shape us, chisel away what doesn't belong, and reveal the masterpiece He intends us to be. This process requires dedication, faith, and a willingness to be moulded by God's hands.

Being a disciple is more than just following; it means living in a way that reflects Yeshua in every action, word, and choice. It's about being a light in the darkness, offering hope and extending grace. Just as Isaiah was called to be a light to the nations, you are also called to shine brightly, reflecting God's love in a world that desperately needs it.

Consider the role of a lighthouse. It doesn't shine for its own glory but stands firm, guiding ships through treacherous waters. As disciples, we are like lighthouses, standing firm in our faith and helping others navigate the storms of life with the light of God's love and truth.

Practical Exercise:

◊ Make it a habit to pray and ask God for guidance on how to show His love and grace to those around you daily.
◊ Write down a small action you can take to live out your discipleship, whether it's a kind word, a helping hand, or a moment of prayer for someone in need.

Reflective Questions:

» How do you feel God is shaping you as His disciple?
» How can you be a light to those around you today?
» How does knowing you were called by God before birth influence your daily choices?

Embrace the call of discipleship, knowing that God continually shapes you into a masterpiece that reflects His glory and love to the world.

Day 126: Who Are You Really?

"What is past is prologue." – William Shakespeare

Many people feel trapped in their current lives, believing they can't change or improve their circumstances. They view themselves as victims, not realising they hold the power to rewrite their stories. This gap between where you are and where you want to be creates frustration and unhappiness. Often, people chase fulfilment in material things or the approval of others, only to find themselves empty. True transformation begins with understanding your identity, which is rooted in God's Word.

Who are you really?

You are not defined by circumstances but by your alignment with God's truth. Life can move quickly, and before you know it, years pass without clarity. Many talk about change but fail to take action, stuck in negative thought patterns that block progress.

Your ability to think, choose, and feel shapes your life. To soar higher, you must focus on what you can do today. Taking small, consistent steps will help you overcome what once seemed impossible. True success is not measured by wealth or status, but by an inner peace and joy that comes from accepting yourself and living according to God's design.

Research shows that your thoughts directly impact your identity and perception of life. Changing negative thought patterns can reshape your mindset, allowing you to embrace your true self. One powerful technique is to journal your thoughts daily, becoming aware of limiting beliefs and replacing them with empowering truths rooted in God's Word.

Practical Exercise:

◊ Spend five minutes each day asking yourself, *"Who am I really?"* and *"What do I truly want?"*
◊ Write down your thoughts and feelings.
◊ This practice will help you gain clarity and build confidence toward living a fulfilled life.

Reflective Questions:

» What values guide your life?
» How can you become more open to discovering your true self?
» What small action can you take today to align with your deepest desires?

Day 127: Embracing Your Royal Identity

"Now if we are children, then we are heirs—heirs of God and co-heirs with Christ." – Romans 8:17 (NIV)

Have you ever considered what it truly means to be royalty?
As believers, we are more than ordinary people; we are children of the King, making us royalty. The Bible tells us that we are heirs of God and joint heirs with Christ. This is not just a metaphor; it is a profound truth that should shape how you view yourself and live your life.

Picture yourself born into a royal family. From a young age, you would learn to carry yourself with dignity and purpose, knowing you are destined for greatness. Your actions and decisions reflect the understanding that you represent something much bigger than yourself. As joint heirs with Christ, we are called to live with that same sense of purpose and responsibility.

Too many people live far below their royal status, accepting mediocrity because they don't understand their true identity. They settle for less, believing they are unworthy of the greatness God has placed within them. But being a joint heir with Christ means that God's kingdom blessings, authority, and responsibilities are yours.

You have the power to overcome obstacles and walk in the fullness of God's promises.

Visualise yourself wearing a crown, not a physical one, but a spiritual crown signifying your royal status in God's family. This crown reminds you that your identity is not defined by your past or other people's opinions but by God's declaration that you are His child.

Start each day by affirming, *"I am a child of the King, a joint heir with Christ."* Let this truth guide your actions, knowing you are empowered to live a life of purpose and victory.

Reflective Questions:

» How does recognising your royal identity in Christ influence your self-worth?
» Where are you living below your royal status?
» How can you walk more fully in the authority and blessings of being a joint heir with Christ?

It's time to embrace your royal identity, empowering you to live as the child of the King you truly are.

Day 128: God's Breath in Us

"The Spirit of God has made me, and the breath of the Almighty gives me life." – Job 33:4 (NIV)

The breath of God within us makes us more than just physical beings; it makes us spiritual beings with limitless potential. When God breathed life into humanity, He imparted His Spirit, making us unique among all creation. This divine breath within us isn't bound by physical limits or confined to time and space. We're made to live with a spiritual awareness that rises above earthly limitations.

Imagine a balloon filled with helium. As long as it's tethered, it can only rise so far. But if you cut the string, the balloon soars higher, unrestrained. Similarly, recognising God's breath within you allows your spirit to soar beyond earthly limitations. You have the power to imagine, create, and connect with God on a level that surpasses our physical reality.

This idea of being limitless and spaceless becomes real when you understand the power of God's Spirit within you. His breath allows you to think beyond your circumstances, dream big, and achieve the impossible. Your past, failures, or limitations do not define you. The Spirit of God that dwells within you defines you, enabling you to reach heights you never thought possible.

Start each day by affirming, *"God's breath gives me life, and His Spirit makes me limitless."* This mindset empowers you to face challenges, knowing God's power is at work within you, making you capable of great things.

Practical Exercise:

◊ Spend a few minutes each day in quiet reflection, focusing on your breathing.
◊ As you inhale, imagine God's breath filling you with His Spirit, empowering you to live beyond your perceived limits.
◊ Visualise overcoming obstacles and achieving your goals; knowing God's Spirit makes you limitless.

Reflective Questions:

» How does knowing God's breath is within you change your view of your potential?
» What self-imposed limits do you need to let go of?
» How can you live more fully as a limitless spiritual being today?

This practice will help you embrace your identity as a spiritual being, allowing you to live with purpose, freedom, and confidence in God's power within you.

Day 129: Living as God's Ambassador

"We are therefore Christ's ambassadors, as though God were making his appeal through us." – 2 Corinthians 5:20 (NIV)

As believers, we are called to be ambassadors of Christ, representing God's kingdom here on earth. An ambassador isn't just someone with a title; it's someone who carries out a mission with purpose and integrity. Imagine a king has sent you to a foreign land. Your words, actions, and character represent you and the king who sent you. That's what it means to be an ambassador for Christ. We are here to reflect God's love, grace, and truth to a world that needs to see His light.

Think of an ambassador's role. They understand their job description and their purpose. They know they represent something greater than themselves. As God's ambassadors, we must lead ourselves with integrity, making choices that align with God's principles. This means speaking the truth with kindness, offering forgiveness, and showing compassion. It's about living in a way that others can see God's character through us.

Consider a lighthouse standing tall in the storm, guiding ships safely to shore. As God's ambassadors, we are like that lighthouse, shining God's light in dark times and offering direction and hope. It's not about being perfect but authentic and intentional in our lives. Our actions and words can bring God's love to life for those around us, whether at work, at home, or in our communities.
Start each day by affirming, *"I am Christ's ambassador, representing God's kingdom with integrity and purpose."*
Let this guide your decisions; knowing how you live can influence others and make a lasting impact.

Practical Exercise:

◊ Think of a situation where you can act as an ambassador for God's love today.
◊ It could be offering a listening ear, standing up for someone in need, or simply showing kindness.
◊ Take a step to represent God's kingdom through your actions.

Reflective Questions:

» How does knowing you are an ambassador for Christ change your daily interactions?
» How can you reflect God's love and truth better?
» How can you lead yourself with more integrity and purpose?

This practice will help you live with intention and purpose, making a difference as a representative of God's love.

DAY 130: PRIORITISE YOUR PASSIONS

"Identity is lived every moment. An effective leader acts upon ideals and purpose, regardless of how he or she feels in each given circumstance." – Manuel de la Cruz

To live a fulfilling life, you must prioritise your passions and be intentional in everything you do. Begin each day by asking, *"What is the purpose of today?"* Knowing your purpose drives your actions. For me, it's about living fully according to God's will and being a blessing to others.

Many people let their emotions drive their actions, often choosing comfort and avoiding challenges. Decisions are often influenced by factors such as fear, anxiety, or even the weather. This habit can hinder personal growth and lower the quality of life.

Imagine life as a sailboat. If you let the wind (your emotions) decide your course, you risk drifting aimlessly. But with a clear purpose as your compass, you can navigate through any storm. Learn to steer the boat of your life, and don't let emotions control you. Don't let circumstances or negative opinions limit you.

The inability to manage emotions keeps you in your comfort zone, stalling growth. Understanding your identity and purpose will help you soar higher and live without limits.

Embrace mistakes as part of the journey. Mistakes are stepping stones to growth and teach resilience. Don't let fear build borders around your potential. You alone define your identity and determine what you can achieve. Gaining clarity about who you are empowers you to break free from limitations.

Practical Exercise:

◊ Each morning, write one passion to pursue and one area where you'll allow yourself to make mistakes.
◊ Take a small step toward your passion, embracing mistakes as opportunities to grow.

Reflective Questions:

» What is your purpose for today?
» How can you prioritise your passions over your emotions?
» What mistake have you recently made that taught you the most?

This practice will help you live intentionally, prioritise your purpose, and navigate life with confidence and resilience.

Day 131: Embracing God's Purpose

"You did not choose me, but I chose you and appointed you so that you might go and bear fruit."– John 15:16 (NIV)

Embracing God's purpose means realising you were created with a unique mission. God chose you with a specific plan, even before you were born. Living out this purpose isn't about chasing after something distant or unknown; it's about uncovering what God has already placed within you. When you align with His purpose, life becomes more fulfilling and joyful because you're living according to His design.

Think of purpose as the wind that fills your sails, pushing you forward and giving you direction. Just as a boat needs wind to move, understanding your God-given purpose propels you toward a life full of meaning. Ephesians 2:10 (NIV) reminds us, *"For we are God's handiwork, created in Christ Jesus to do good works, which God prepared in advance for us to do."* This verse reassures us that God has set meaningful work before us, bringing a deep sense of satisfaction and joy when we engage with it wholeheartedly.

When you live with God's purpose, you experience peace, knowing you are doing what you were created to do. Purpose gives clarity, helping you make choices that honour God and impact others positively. Each day feels more significant as you follow the path He set for you.

Practical Exercise:

◊ Spend time in prayer and journaling, asking God to reveal His purpose for your life.
◊ Reflect on the passions, talents, and desires God has instilled in you.
◊ Identify small actions that align with your purpose and put them into practice.

Reflective Questions:

» What has God placed on my heart to pursue in this season?
» How can embracing my purpose add more joy and meaning to my life?
» What steps can I take today to live more closely in line with God's plan?

To explore your purpose further, check out the Self-Discovery Toolkit at The Mindsight Academy. It offers questions and exercises to deepen your insights into passion, values, and vision.

Day 132: Creating a Vision for Your Life

"The best way to predict your future is to create it." – Peter Drucker

Creating a vision for your life means setting long-term goals and imagining the future you want. A clear vision provides direction and motivation, providing a roadmap for personal growth and fulfilment. It helps you align your daily actions with your dreams, making your life more purposeful.

Visualising your future engages the brain's visual and prefrontal cortexes, responsible for planning and decision-making. This process activates the brain's reward system, releasing dopamine to enhance motivation and focus. Emotions are crucial in this process; they drive you to pursue your vision, especially when obstacles arise. Connecting emotionally with your vision deepens your sense of purpose, making you more committed to your goals.

Proverbs 29:18 (KJV) states, *"Where there is no vision, the people perish."* This highlights the importance of having a vision to lead a fulfilling life. Without a clear vision, you may feel directionless and struggle with decision-making. Vision provides clarity, helping you navigate challenges and focus on what truly matters. Think of vision as a GPS for your life. Without it, you might wander aimlessly. With a clear vision, you have a destination, making it easier to stay on course. Terri Savelle Foy, a motivational speaker, often says, *"Your life moves toward your most dominant thoughts."* A clear vision guides your thoughts and actions toward your desired future.

Practical Tips:

◊ Create a vision board with images, quotes, and affirmations representing your long-term goals.
◊ Place it where you can see it daily to keep your vision at the forefront of your mind.

Practical Exercise:

>Reflect on your vision. Write your long-term goals and break them into smaller, achievable steps.
>Regularly update your vision board as your goals evolve.
>Creating a vision for your life empowers you to lead a more motivated, fulfilling, and purpose-driven life.

Reflective Questions:

» What is your vision for your life?
» How can you create a clear and inspiring vision for your future?
» How does having a vision enhance your motivation and fulfilment?

Day 133: Vision: See It, Believe It, Achieve It

"Write the vision; make it plain on tablets, so he may run who reads it." – Habakkuk 2:2 (ESV)

Creating a personal vision is about seeing beyond your current circumstances and believing in the future God has planned for you. It's about defining your goals, writing them down, and taking steps to achieve them. In Joshua 6:2 (NIV), God told Joshua, *"See, I have delivered Jericho into your hands, along with its king and its fighting men."* God encouraged Joshua to see victory even before it happened. By envisioning success, Joshua could believe in God's promises and take action to achieve them.

When you face mountains—challenges, pressures, or obstacles—God calls you to see beyond them, just like He did with Joshua. Envisioning your victory is the first step to achieving it. Habakkuk 2:3 (ESV) says, *"For still the vision awaits its appointed time; it hastens to the end—it will not lie. If it seems slow, wait for it; it will surely come; it will not delay."* Your vision provides hope and direction, keeping you motivated through the trials of life.

Steps to See, Believe, and Achieve Your Vision:

> **Pray and Envision:** Ask God to reveal His vision for your life. Picture it clearly in your mind.
> **Write It Down:** Just like God told Habakkuk, make your vision clear and tangible by writing it down.
> **Visualise Daily:** Spend time each day seeing your goals. This activates the brain's reward system, increasing motivation.
> **Take Action:** Break your vision into specific, achievable steps. Each small victory builds confidence.
> **Stay Focused:** Keep your vision in sight, even when challenges arise. Trust in God's timing and promises.

Practical Exercise:

◊ Write your vision statement. Keep it visible and reflect on it daily, seeing yourself achieving the goals God has set before you.

Reflective Questions:

» What vision has God placed in your heart?
» How can you turn your vision into actionable steps?
» How does believing in your vision help you overcome obstacles?

By seeing your vision, believing in it, and taking steps to achieve it, you align with God's plan and lead a life of purpose and fulfilment.

Day 134: Living with Divine Purpose

"Many are the plans in a man's heart, but it is the Lord's purpose that prevails." – Proverbs 19:21 (NIV)

Living with divine purpose means aligning your daily life with God's unique mission. It's about continually following God's guidance and letting His purpose shape your actions. This alignment brings fulfilment, peace, and joy. Neuroscience shows that having a sense of purpose activates the brain's reward centres, releasing dopamine, which boosts happiness and motivation. Emotionally, purpose offers stability, reduces stress, and gives a compelling reason to move forward.

Think of a painter guided by a vision for a masterpiece. Each brushstroke is intentional, contributing to the overall picture. Similarly, living with divine purpose means letting God guide your decisions and actions. When you understand your purpose, every choice becomes a step toward the life God has planned for you. Knowing your divine purpose helps you make decisions aligned with God's will in business, relationships, or personal growth. Isaiah 46:10 (NIV) states, *"My purpose will stand, and I will do all that I please."* This reminds us that God's purpose is unchanging and reliable.

True fulfilment comes from aligning our lives with His divine plan. Emotionally intelligent people recognise the power of purpose to navigate challenges and make thoughtful decisions. Aligning with God's purpose connects us to something greater, offering clarity and direction.

Practical Tips:

◊ **Start with Prayer:** Begin each day by asking God to guide you in His purpose.
◊ **Define Your Purpose:** Write down what you believe is your purpose and revisit it often.
◊ **Act with Intention:** List small, purposeful actions and integrate them into your daily life.

Reflective Questions:

» How can I live out my divine purpose today?
» What actions align with God's purpose for me?
» What challenges are keeping me from embracing my divine purpose?

Living with a divine purpose means that each action is a step toward God's beautiful plan for you, which brings true fulfilment and peace.

Day 135: Developing Mental Toughness

"The greatest glory in living lies not in never falling, but in rising every time we fall." – Nelson Mandela

Mental toughness is the ability to stay calm and perform well, even when things get tough. It's what sets apart people who thrive under pressure from those who struggle. As pressure builds, many feel fear, anxiety, and lose control over their emotions. But those with mental toughness remain confident, focused, and motivated. They see challenges as opportunities and don't get overwhelmed.

The most important factors in developing mental toughness are confidence, focus, and emotional control. Confidence comes from believing in yourself and trusting that you can handle whatever happens. Focus means keeping your mind clear and staying on track, even when there are distractions. Emotional control is about managing fear and anxiety and responding thoughtfully rather than reacting impulsively.

Mental toughness strengthens decision-making and emotional control, keeping you calm under stress. Combined with emotional intelligence, it helps you handle pressure and perform at your best. Staying grounded in your faith and purpose can help you remain composed in challenging times. Isaiah 41:10 (NKJV) reminds us, *"Fear not, for I am with you; be not dismayed, for I am your God."* This promise gives peace, reassuring you that you're never alone.

Practical Tips:
◊ **Practice Mindfulness:** Use deep breathing daily to stay centred and maintain emotional control.
◊ **Visualise Success:** Spend a few minutes picturing yourself confidently handling challenges.
◊ **Positive Self-Talk:** Use affirmations like, "I am strong," to boost confidence under pressure.

Reflective Questions:
» How do I usually respond to pressure?
» What strategies can I use to strengthen my mental toughness?
» How can my faith help me stay calm under stress?

By developing mental toughness, you can face life's challenges with resilience, remaining strong and composed under pressure.

DAY 136: EMBRACING YOUR STRENGTHS AND WEAKNESSES

"Strength and growth come only through continuous effort and struggle." – Napoleon Hill

Understanding your strengths and weaknesses is crucial for personal and professional growth. This awareness isn't about focusing on flaws; it's about recognising what you're good at and where you can improve. At The Mindsight Academy, I use *PRISM Brain Mapping Diagnostic* with my clients—a tool that reveals strengths and areas for growth. PRISM helps people see themselves more clearly, leading to increased confidence and better decision-making.

Knowing your strengths boosts your confidence, making you more effective in different areas of life. For example, if you're naturally good at communication, use that skill to lead team meetings or deliver presentations. Recognising and using strengths also releases dopamine in the brain, reinforcing positive actions and making you feel more motivated.

Weaknesses are equally important to recognise, not as limitations, but as areas for growth. If public speaking is a challenge, for instance, regular practice or training can help you improve. Working on these areas enhances your brain's plasticity, or ability to adapt and learn. This aligns with 2 Corinthians 12:9 (NIV), where God says, *"My grace is sufficient for you, for my power is made perfect in weakness."* Acknowledging our weaknesses allows God's strength to work within us.

Practical Tips:

- ◊ **Reflect Regularly:** Each week, take time to assess one strength and one weakness, noting ways to use or improve them.
- ◊ **Leverage PRISM:** Use tools like PRISM Brain Mapping, available at The Mindsight Academy, to gain deeper insights into your abilities.
- ◊ **Seek Feedback:** Ask trusted friends or mentors for feedback to gain a fuller perspective on your strengths and areas for growth.

Reflective Questions:

- » What are my top three strengths, and how can I use them daily?
- » Which weakness can I work on with specific actions?
- » How does understanding my strengths and weaknesses empower me?

Embracing both strengths and weaknesses helps you grow, turn challenges into opportunities, and let your abilities shine, all while drawing strength from God.

Day 137: Exploring Personal Values

"When your values are clear to you, making decisions becomes easier." – Roy E. Disney

Personal values are the guiding principles that shape your decisions and actions. They define who you are and what you stand for, acting as a compass that directs your life. Living in alignment with your values brings a sense of identity, fulfilment, and peace. It's important to recognise that values can either empower or limit you. Embracing positive, strong values helps you live with clarity and purpose.

Imagine your values as the foundation of a house. If the foundation is strong, the house stands firm, even in a storm. A strong foundation provides stability, guiding you to make decisions that align with your beliefs, leading to a life of integrity and purpose. However, if your values are weak or unclear, it's like building a house on shaky ground. Such a foundation will crumble under pressure, causing confusion and inconsistency in your actions. When values are negative or misaligned with your true self, you may make choices that lead to regret or dissatisfaction.

Our values are shaped by our experiences, culture, upbringing, and beliefs. The brain's decision-making processes, particularly in the prefrontal cortex, help us act according to these values. By focusing on values like honesty, kindness, and perseverance, you can navigate life's challenges more effectively and make decisions that reflect what truly matters to you.
Think of a sailor using a compass to navigate the sea. Without a reliable compass, the sailor drifts aimlessly. Your values act like that compass, keeping you on course, even in life's rough waters. By ensuring your values are strong and positive, you can make decisions that align with what is important to you.

Practical Tips:

◊ **Identify Your Core Values:** Write your top three to five values and reflect on how they guide your choices.

◊ **Live by Your Values:** Make daily decisions that reflect these core values.

◊ **Reflect Regularly:** Revisit your values to ensure your actions align with what matters most.

Reflective Questions:

» What are my core values?
» How do these values influence my daily life?
» How can I better align my actions with my values?

Understanding and living by your values brings clarity and strength, helping you face life's challenges with integrity and purpose.

Day 138: The Power of Self-Reflection

"Knowing yourself is the beginning of all wisdom." – Aristotle

Self-reflection is like looking into a mirror that reveals your inner thoughts, feelings, and motivations. It's a crucial tool for personal growth and emotional intelligence, helping you understand why you think, feel, and act as you do. By regularly reflecting on your experiences, you can make better decisions, improve emotional regulation, and grow in wisdom.

Self-reflection activates the prefrontal cortex, the part of the brain involved in planning and decision-making. This process helps you pause and respond thoughtfully, instead of reacting impulsively. In our fast-paced world, taking time to reflect can be transformative. It aligns your actions with your values and goals, leading to a more fulfilling life. Think of a gardener tending a garden. Without regular care, weeds grow, and plants can become overgrown. Self-reflection is like weeding your mind, helping you remove negative thoughts and behaviours and nurturing positive growth. Reflecting on your day allows you to recognise what went well and identify areas for improvement, much like a gardener assessing what needs attention.

Scripture emphasises the importance of self-reflection. Psalms 139: 23-24 (NIV) says, *"Search me, God, and know my heart; test me and know my anxious thoughts. See if there is any offensive way in me, and lead me in the way everlasting."* This invites God's insight, encouraging both spiritual and personal growth. Although many struggle with self-reflection due to busy schedules, its benefits are significant: better emotional control, improved decision-making, and a deeper self-understanding. Even a few minutes of quiet reflection daily can bring clarity and insight.

Practical Tips:

◊ **Daily Reflection:** Spend five minutes reviewing what went well and what to improve.

◊ **Journal Your Thoughts:** Write down insights or feelings that arise to track progress and recognise patterns.

◊ **Prayer and Meditation:** Invite God into your self-reflection for deeper insight.

Reflective Questions:

» How often do I practice self-reflection?
» What insights have I gained from my reflections?
» How can I make self-reflection a daily habit?

Daily self-reflection boosts emotional intelligence, aligns you with your values, and fosters personal growth.

Day 139: Journaling for Self-Discovery

"Journal writing, when it becomes a ritual for transformation, is not only life-changing but life-expanding." – Jen Williamson

Think of journaling as your personal sanctuary, a quiet place to sort through your thoughts, like clearing out a cluttered attic. It's more than just recording events; journaling deepens self-awareness and helps you understand your thoughts, emotions, and behaviours. This practice acts like a mirror, reflecting your inner world and revealing truths often hidden in daily life's rush.

Scientific research shows journaling can reduce stress, improve mood, and enhance overall well-being. Writing activates the brain's language and memory centres, helping you effectively organise your thoughts and process emotions. This practice boosts emotional intelligence, enabling you to manage your feelings better. Proverbs 3:1-3 (NIV) reinforces the importance of recording wisdom: *"My son, do not forget my teaching, but keep my commands in your heart, for they will prolong your life many years and bring you peace and prosperity."* This scripture highlights the transformative power of writing down your reflections.

Imagine a day filled with endless tasks and stress. Journaling for just a few minutes can feel like hitting the pause button, bringing clarity and calm. Whether you write about gratitude, challenges, or dreams, journaling offers a way to navigate life's ups and downs with perspective. It's a tool for understanding what drives you, recognising patterns in your behaviour, and celebrating your growth. Many people struggle with journaling due to busy schedules or not knowing what to write. The key is consistency. Even brief, honest entries can lead to significant self-discovery and personal growth. Journaling helps you become more self-aware, emotionally balanced, and aligned with your true self.

Practical Tips:

◊ **Start Small:** Commit to five minutes of journaling daily. Focus on honesty, not perfection.

◊ **Use Prompts:** Use questions like, *"What am I grateful for today?"* or *"What challenged me today?"*

◊ **Stay Consistent:** Choose a regular time, such as morning or bedtime, to make journaling a habit.

Reflective Questions:

» What insights have I gained through journaling?
» What challenges do I face in keeping a journaling practice?
» How can I make journaling a consistent part of my routine?

Day 140: Embracing Criticism for Growth

"Criticism, like rain, should be gentle enough to nourish a man's growth without destroying his roots." – Frank A. Clark

Feedback and criticism can feel uncomfortable, but they are essential for personal and professional growth. When you see feedback as a tool for improvement, not a personal attack, you can transform your reactions into intentional responses. Instead of feeling defensive or hurt, you use criticism to become better versions of yourself. Feedback is like a mirror, showing us where we excel and where we need some work. This awareness is vital for continuous growth.

Think of feedback as a coach guiding an athlete. A coach points out areas to improve, not to discourage the athlete but to help them maximise their potential. Similarly, feedback is meant to help us grow stronger and perform better. Receiving criticism can trigger a defensive reaction, but viewing it as an opportunity will enable you to respond thoughtfully and learn from the experience. Proverbs 15:31 (NIV) says, *"Whoever heeds life-giving correction will be at home among the wise,"* reminding us to welcome feedback as a pathway to wisdom.

Picture a gardener pruning a plant. Pruning may seem harsh, but removing unnecessary elements allows the plant to thrive. Constructive criticism works the same way—it trims away unproductive habits and attitudes, creating space for growth. Whether at work, in relationships, or in our personal lives, embracing feedback helps us improve and succeed. Many people struggle with criticism because they take it personally. It's important to separate your self-worth from the feedback you receive. Instead of viewing it as a judgment, see criticism as valuable information. This mindset will enable you to use feedback to enhance your skills, become wiser and achieve your desired goals.

Practical Tips:

◊ **Listen Carefully:** Focus on listening without interrupting or becoming defensive.

◊ **Ask for Examples:** Seek clarity to understand feedback fully, such as, "Can you give me an example?"

◊ **Reflect:** Reflect on the feedback, identify areas for growth, and develop an action plan.

Reflective Questions:

» How do I typically respond to feedback?
» What can I learn from recent criticism?
» How can I use feedback to improve myself?

Day 141: The Lord Is Your Shepherd

"True self-discovery begins when you see yourself through God's eyes—loved, valued, and guided by His everlasting love." – Maureen Chiana

Seeing God as our shepherd isn't just comforting; it determines how we live. Hebrews 13:20-21 calls God the *"great Shepherd,"* equipping us for every good work. 1 Peter 2:25 (NIV) states, *"For you were like sheep going astray, but now you have returned to the Shepherd and Overseer of your souls."* These verses show that true self-discovery starts by recognising that we are God's beloved children.

Imagine a shepherd guiding his flock, each sheep trusting him to lead them to safety and nourishment. This is how God cares for us—lovingly and faithfully. When we stray, He searches for us, not to condemn but to bring us back. This truth should encourage you to shift from striving for worldly approval to embracing your true identity and potential through God's unwavering love.

God doesn't just guide you; He empowers you with His Holy Spirit. This divine presence is like having a constant companion, providing strength and wisdom. Accepting this truth activates the brain's prefrontal cortex, enhancing your ability to stay calm, make wise decisions, and handle stress effectively. It reduces anxiety, building emotional resilience and inner peace.

Understanding God as our shepherd frees us from the need to conform to societal pressures. It grounds us in God's purpose, showing that our value is not in achievements or other people's opinions but in His love for us. Trusting God as your shepherd helps you see yourself as He does—strong, capable, and deeply cherished.

Practical Tips:

◊ **Daily Affirmation:** Start each morning with, *"I am guided, empowered, and loved by God."*

◊ **Scripture Reflection:** Meditate on Hebrews 13:20-21 and 1 Peter 2:25 to remind yourself of God's care.

◊ **Seek Guidance:** In challenging moments, pray and ask the Holy Spirit to guide and support you.

Reflective Questions:

» How does seeing God as my shepherd change my view of myself?
» Where can I trust more in God's guidance and love?
» How can I remind myself daily of my identity in God?

By embracing God as your shepherd, you embark on a true journey of self-discovery, filled with purpose, peace, and the unwavering knowledge that you are deeply loved and guided by the One who knows you best.

Day 142: Setting Personal Boundaries

"Daring to set boundaries is about having the courage to love ourselves, even when we risk disappointing others." – Brené Brown

Setting personal boundaries is like building a protective fence around your garden. Just as a fence keeps out intruders, boundaries protect your well-being from stress and negativity, allowing you to flourish. Boundaries help you define what is acceptable and what isn't, ensuring your emotional, mental, physical, and spiritual needs are respected. Research shows that setting boundaries activates the brain's prefrontal cortex, enhancing self-regulation and decision-making.

Think of your brain as a traffic controller, directing thoughts and actions to balance life. Setting boundaries enables this "traffic controller" to make decisions that align with your values, reduce stress, and promote well-being. Proverbs 4:23 (NIV) says, *"Above all else, guard your heart, for everything you do flows from it."* This scripture highlights the importance of protecting your inner peace, which boundaries help maintain.

Imagine a colleague who frequently asks you to cover their shifts, but you're already feeling overwhelmed. Without boundaries, you might agree to avoid conflict, leading to burnout. Setting a boundary and saying *'no'* protects your time and energy, allowing you to stay balanced and focused. Many people find it challenging to set boundaries due to fear of conflict or disappointing others. However, boundaries are not about being selfish; they are about caring for yourself. Setting boundaries allows you to be your best self, both for you and for those around you. Healthy boundaries foster respect and lead to stronger, more fulfilling relationships.

Practical Tips:
- ◊ **Identify Your Limits:** Recognise areas where you feel overwhelmed and set boundaries to protect your well-being.
- ◊ **Communicate Clearly:** Practice saying, *"I need some time for myself,"* or *"I can't take on more work right now,"* to express your limits kindly.
- ◊ **Learn to Say No:** Understand that saying 'no' does not mean rejecting others but prioritising your well-being.

Reflective Questions:
- » What areas of your life need stronger boundaries?
- » How can you communicate your boundaries more effectively?
- » How will setting personal boundaries improve your well-being?

Personal boundaries are an act of self-love. It creates space for peace, growth, and genuine connections.

Day 143: Soar Higher

"Surround yourself with those who lift you higher." – Oprah Winfrey

The people you surround yourself with determine your mindset and future. Spending time with those who complain, lack ambition, or settle for less is like swimming with ducks. Ducks are content to paddle in circles, never venturing beyond the familiar pond. But eagles spread their wings and soar high, seeking new heights and broader horizons.

Stop swimming with ducks and start flying with eagles to reach your full potential.

Imagine your mindset as a garden. If you plant seeds of encouragement, positivity, and ambition, it will flourish. But if you allow weeds of negativity and doubt to take over, they will choke your growth. Surrounding yourself with people who lift you up and inspire you helps your mindset grow strong, like a garden in full bloom. Eagles push each other to rise above challenges and see the world from a higher perspective. By spending time with people who embody these traits, you set yourself up to thrive.

Think of a young eagle learning to fly. If it stays among ducks, it might never learn what its wings are capable of. But when it joins other eagles, it discovers its potential, learns new skills, and gains the courage to soar. Proverbs 13:20 (NIV) says, *"Walk with the wise and become wise, for a companion of fools suffers harm."* This wisdom shows that the company we keep directly affects our mindset and direction.

Practical Tips:

◊ **Evaluate Your Circle:** Reflect on who you spend time with. Are they helping you grow or keeping you stuck?

◊ **Find Your Eagles:** Seek relationships with people who inspire, challenge, and share your values.

◊ **Set Boundaries:** Spend less time with negative influences and build connections that uplift and support your goals.

Reflective Questions:

» Who in my life encourages me to soar higher?
» How can I build more relationships that inspire growth?
» What steps can I take to distance myself from negative influences?

Flying with eagles means building a mindset of ambition and resilience. Surround yourself with people who lift you higher, and you'll gain the strength to soar to new heights.

Day 144: Vision Starts with Imagination

"Imagination is the beginning of creation. You imagine what you desire, you will what you imagine, and at last, you create what you will." – George Bernard Shaw

Imagination is the ability to see with your mind what you can't see with your eyes. It's like a spiritual womb where you conceive God's plans for your life. Proverbs 29:18 (KJV) says, *"Where there is no vision, the people perish."* Vision—birthed from imagination—provides hope and direction, guiding your actions and keeping you aligned with God's will.

Imagination shapes reality by forming mental images of what's possible. Research shows that when you vividly imagine reaching your goals, your brain responds as if you're actually achieving them. This mental practice strengthens the pathways in your brain, making it easier to turn those dreams into reality by motivating you to take the right actions. Filling your imagination with negativity limits what God can do in your life. Luke 6:45 (NKJV) reminds us, *"For out of the abundance of the heart his mouth speaks."* Your imagination reflects what fills your heart and mind.

Imagine a student aspiring to be a doctor. Although they may not yet see the end goal, they create motivation and purpose by envisioning themselves in a white coat, saving lives. This mental image builds emotional resilience, helping them push through challenges like tough exams. In your own life, using imagination to envision success, even when the path is unclear, enables you to persevere.

Practical Tips:

◊ **Visualise Daily:** Imagine your goals as if they're already achieved. See yourself thriving and fulfilling God's purpose.

◊ **Renew Your Mind:** Focus on scriptures like Romans 12:2 to align your thoughts with God's truth.

◊ **Create a Vision Board:** Use images and verses that reflect your dreams, keeping them visible to inspire your imagination.

Reflective Questions:

» How can I use my imagination to see beyond my limitations?
» What negative thoughts must I replace with God's promises?
» How can I align my imagination with God's vision for my life?

Your imagination is not just for daydreaming; it's a powerful tool that shapes your destiny. Fill it with God's truth, and you'll be empowered to reach the heights He has planned for you.

Day 145: Visualisation vs. Imagination: Understanding the Difference

"Imagination is everything. It is the preview of life's coming attractions." – Albert Einstein

Imagination and visualisation are different, but both are powerful tools. Imagination is about thinking up new ideas and possibilities that don't exist yet. It's like letting your mind dream and explore freely. Visualisation, on the other hand, is more focused. It's about taking a specific goal or dream from your imagination and picturing it clearly in your mind, almost like playing a movie of it happening.

Think of imagination as a child with a box of crayons, able to draw anything they can dream of. It's free and creative, with no limits. Visualisation is like taking one of those drawings and planning how to make it real. It's about focusing on one idea and seeing the steps to make it happen.

Research shows that when you visualise achieving something—like taking a test or delivering an excellent presentation—your brain activates in a way similar to actually doing it. This practice helps build confidence and prepares you for success. While imagination enables you to think creatively and explore new ideas, visualisation focuses your energy on making those ideas a reality. Proverbs 29:18 (KJV) says, *"Where there is no vision, the people perish."* This means having a clear picture of what you want in life is essential.

Imagination lets you dream big, while visualisation helps you concentrate on reaching those dreams.

Practical Tips:

◊ **Use Your Imagination:** Spend time daydreaming about what excites and inspires you.
◊ **Practice Visualisation:** Picture achieving a specific goal, like a career milestone or personal success.
◊ **Combine:** Dream big and use visualisation to make those dreams achievable.

Reflective Questions:

» How can I use my imagination to think of new possibilities for my life?
» What specific goals can I visualise to bring my dreams closer to reality?
» How can I use both imagination and visualisation to fulfil my purpose?

Imagination opens your mind, while visualisation helps turn those possibilities into reality.

Day 146: The Power of New Beginnings

"The secret of change is to focus all of your energy, not on fighting the old, but on building the new." – Socrates

New beginnings are like turning to a fresh page in a book, promising new adventures and opportunities. Whether starting a new job, moving to a different city, or making personal changes, these moments offer a chance to grow and reinvent ourselves.

Although change can be intimidating, it is also the doorway to new possibilities.

Imagine new beginnings as planting seeds in a garden. Each seed has the potential to grow into something beautiful, but it requires courage to plant, patience to nurture, and faith to see it bloom. Embracing change means letting go of the familiar and trusting in the growth process. Our brains are naturally wired to adapt to new situations, the process called neuroplasticity. This adaptability helps us learn and become more resilient, making it easier to face change and thrive.

Fear of the unknown is normal, but it shouldn't hold you back. Isaiah 43:19 (NIV) says, *"See, I am doing a new thing! Now it springs up; do you not perceive it? I am making a way in the wilderness and streams in the wasteland."* This scripture reassures us that God is constantly creating new opportunities and guiding us, even when we can't see the way forward.

Practical Tips:

◊ **Focus on Growth:** Embrace new beginnings by seeing them as chances to learn and develop, not as threats to your comfort.

◊ **Start Small:** Break your new beginning into small, manageable steps. Celebrate each success to build confidence.

◊ **Find Support:** Surround yourself with people who encourage and support your journey into new beginnings.

Reflective Questions:

» What new beginning am I facing, and how can I embrace it positively?
» How can I use this change as a chance to grow?
» Who can support me as I navigate this new chapter in my life?

Embracing new beginnings allows you to explore new paths and live a more fulfilling life. Focus on what you can build, not what you leave behind, and trust that each new start is an opportunity for growth and success.

DAY 147: THE ROLE OF NEUROCOACHING

"Watch your thoughts; they will become your actions. Watch your actions; they will become your destiny." – Frank Outlaw

Neurocoaching is a powerful approach that combines neuroscience with coaching techniques to help individuals achieve their full potential. It focuses on understanding how the brain works, shifting thought patterns, and developing habits that lead to personal and professional growth. By tapping into the science of how the brain processes information, neurocoaching offers a practical way to rewire your brain for success and fulfilment.

Think of your brain as a garden. Negative thoughts are like weeds that can choke out healthy growth. A neurocoach helps you remove these weeds and plant seeds of positive, empowering thoughts. This process uses the brain's natural ability to adapt, known as neuroplasticity, to allow you to replace limiting beliefs with new, constructive ones. Over time, this leads to more positive thinking, better emotional resilience, and a stronger mindset.

One significant benefit of neurocoaching is overcoming mental barriers that hold you back. Many people struggle with limiting beliefs like "I'm not good enough" or *"I can't change."* Neurocoaching helps you reframe these thoughts, opening up new possibilities. Developing a positive mindset enhances your ability to manage stress, make better decisions, and improve relationships. Proverbs 23:7 (NKJV) reminds us, *"For as he thinks in his heart, so is he."* This scripture shows that our thoughts shape our reality, making it essential to cultivate positive thinking.

Practical Tips:
- ◊ **Find a Neurocoach:** Find an experienced neurocoach who understands your goals and challenges and can help you achieve sustained results.
- ◊ **Practice Daily:** Use techniques such as visualisation and positive self-talk to reinforce new, positive thought patterns.
- ◊ **Stay Open to Change:** Be willing to challenge and shift your current beliefs to unlock new opportunities.

Reflective Questions:
- » What limiting beliefs are holding me back?
- » How can neurocoaching help me change these beliefs?
- » What steps will you take to find a neurocoach?

By engaging with neurocoaching, you harness the power of your mind to overcome obstacles, break free from negativity, and live a life that reflects your true potential.

Day 148: The Power of Creating New Memories

"Sometimes you will never know the value of a moment until it becomes a memory." – Dr. Seuss

Creating new memories is like painting a beautiful picture, with each joyful experience adding colour and life to the canvas. Positive memories serve as emotional anchors, reminding us of love, joy, and the good times in life. They offer comfort during challenges, shape our identity, and help build resilience.

Our brains are naturally wired to remember emotionally charged experiences. When you engage in activities that bring you joy, your brain releases dopamine, a neurotransmitter that strengthens memory formation. The hippocampus, which is responsible for memory storage, plays a key role in this process. Positive experiences are often stored as explicit memories—conscious recollections we can easily access. On the other hand, negative experiences can sometimes create implicit memories, which may unconsciously influence our emotional responses, like anxiety or fear. Creating positive memories helps balance these effects, promoting emotional resilience.

Think of your mind as a garden. Positive emotions are like sunlight and rain, helping the flowers of joyful memories bloom. However, negative emotions are like weeds that can grow uncontrollably if left unchecked. By intentionally creating positive experiences, you cultivate a thriving garden in your mind, filled with uplifting memories that nourish your spirit. Psalm 77:11 (NIV) says, *"I will remember the deeds of the Lord; yes, I will remember your miracles of long ago."* This verse encourages us to focus on and cherish positive memories. Even simple activities like a walk in nature, a conversation with a friend, or a family dinner can create moments that enrich your life.

Practical Tips:

◊ **Be Intentional:** Plan joyful activities like hobbies or time with loved ones.
◊ **Capture the Moment:** Journal or photograph these moments to revisit later.
◊ **Stay Present:** Practice mindfulness to fully engage in each moment, making it more memorable.

Reflective Questions:

» What recent experience brought me joy, and how can I create more of these moments?
» How can I be more intentional about creating new, positive memories?
» What upcoming activities can I plan to ensure lasting, joyful memories?

Focusing on positive experiences brings joy and builds hope.

Day 149: Balancing Self-Improvement with Self-Acceptance

"You are allowed to be both a masterpiece and a work in progress simultaneously."
– Sophia Bush

Balancing self-improvement with self-acceptance is essential for a fulfilling life. While aiming to grow and develop is important, embracing who you are is equally crucial. Focusing solely on self-improvement can lead to perfectionism and dissatisfaction, while ignoring growth may result in stagnation. Finding a balance allows you to pursue personal growth while maintaining a sense of inner peace and self-worth.

Because our brains naturally aim for progress and avoid unpleasant feelings, we can sometimes be overly critical of ourselves. The prefrontal cortex, responsible for planning and decision-making, often pushes us to do better and be better. However, this can activate the brain's stress response if not balanced with self-acceptance. Emotional intelligence teaches us to recognise our feelings and practice self-compassion, which helps calm the mind and fosters resilience. Philippians 4:11 (NIV) offers a valuable reminder: *"I have learned to be content whatever the circumstances."* This scripture encourages us to find contentment in the present, even as we work towards our goals.

Imagine a sculptor working on a statue. Each day, they carefully chip away, shaping the form. However, they also appreciate the beauty of the work in progress. They understand that each stage has its value and that the final masterpiece takes time. Similarly, in our journey of self-improvement, we must acknowledge and appreciate who we are at each moment, understanding that growth is a process, not a race.

Practical Tips:
- ◊ **Set Realistic Goals:** Aim for progress, not perfection. Celebrate minor achievements and improvements.
- ◊ **Practice Self-Compassion:** Treat yourself with the same kindness you would offer a friend when you make mistakes.
- ◊ **Embrace the Present:** Regularly remind yourself of your worth and unique qualities. Use affirmations to reinforce self-acceptance.

Reflective Questions:
- » How can I balance my desire for self-improvement with self-acceptance?
- » What are some ways I can be more compassionate towards myself?

Balancing growth with self-acceptance fosters progress and inner peace. Be kind to yourself and enjoy the journey.

Day 150: Embracing Your Identity as Salt and Light

"You are the salt of the earth... You are the light of the world." – Matthew 5:13-14 (NIV)

Understanding who you are is key to living a meaningful and impactful life. In Matthew 5:13-14 (NIV), Jesus says, *"You are the salt of the earth"* and *"You are the light of the world."* These powerful metaphors highlight our value and potential to influence the world around us positively.

Salt enhances flavour and preserves what is good. When Jesus calls us salt, He's saying we have the power to bring out the best in others and maintain goodness in our environment. This aligns with how our brains respond to positive reinforcement. Acts of kindness release dopamine, a feel-good chemical that boosts happiness and fulfilment. Realising that our actions matter improves our emotional well-being and strengthens our sense of self-worth.

Being the light of the world means we can brighten dark situations, provide guidance, and bring hope. Light brings illumination, clarity, and inspiration. When we let our light shine, we inspire and encourage those around us. This concept is linked to neuroplasticity, the brain's capacity to adapt and create new connections. Consistently focusing on being a positive influence helps create neural pathways that reinforce kindness and compassion. This not only transforms our lives but also positively impacts others.

Think of yourself as a lighthouse in a storm, guiding ships safely to shore. By embracing your role as salt and light, you acknowledge your capacity to make a significant and positive difference in the world.

Practical Tips:

◊ **Recognise Your Worth:** Reflect on how your unique qualities add value to others' lives.

◊ **Be a Positive Force:** Look for ways to encourage and uplift those around you, even in small ways.

◊ **Shine Brightly:** Use your talents and kindness to offer hope and guidance to others.

Reflective Questions:

» How can I bring out the best in my daily interactions?
» What unique qualities do I have that make a positive impact?
» How does seeing myself as salt and light change my perspective?

By embracing your role as salt and light, you recognise your true worth and the positive impact you can make. This understanding brings fulfilment, direction, and a strong sense of purpose.

PART SIX

EMOTIONAL INTELLIGENCE UNLOCKED

PART 6 INTRODUCTION

In this section, we'll explore how emotional intelligence (EQ) plays a vital role in personal growth, relationships, and leadership. Emotional intelligence isn't just about understanding emotions; it's about mastering self-awareness, managing emotional responses, and building meaningful connections with others. EQ impacts every part of our lives, it shapes how we handle stress, communicate with others, make decisions, take action (or choose not to), lead effectively, and build trust in our relationships..

During these days, you'll learn practical ways to enhance your emotional intelligence, from cultivating empathy and self-regulation to strengthening social skills and resilience. We'll explore key aspects like building trust, listening with intent, embracing self-leadership, and understanding the emotions surrounding money and decision-making. You'll also see how applying emotional intelligence can deepen your faith and improve your leadership, both in personal and professional settings.

Each topic is designed to help you maximise your potential, equipping you with the tools to navigate challenges, improve relationships, and live with purpose. Whether you're learning to be more patient, building emotional resilience, or embracing self-love, this journey will deepen your understanding of how EQ influences every aspect of life.

Day 151: Understanding Emotional Intelligence

"Emotional intelligence is the ability to make emotions work for you, instead of against you." – Lisa Feldman Barrett

Emotional Intelligence (EI), also known as EQ, is the ability to recognise, understand, and manage one's own emotions while being sensitive to the emotions of others. Imagine EQ as a toolkit for handling life's challenges, helping one navigate interactions with awareness and self-control. The key components of EQ—self-awareness, self-regulation, motivation, empathy, and social skills—work together to improve personal relationships and professional success.

Think of EQ as a steering wheel that guides your responses, especially in moments of tension. Proverbs 4:23 reminds us, *"Above all else, guard your heart, for everything you do flows from it,"* showing the importance of being aware of and managing our emotional reactions. Our brains have pathways dedicated to processing emotions and social interactions, and with regular reflection and practice, we can strengthen these pathways. When we become mindful of our emotions, we gain the power to shape our reality, respond thoughtfully to challenges, and connect meaningfully with others.

Consider a moment at work or home when a conversation grew tense. Rather than reacting impulsively, take a moment to pause, breathe, and choose a response that diffuses tension. While many people respond based purely on emotion, developing EQ allows for better mental health, reduced stress, and improved leadership. Take Josh, a manager who often became defensive during feedback sessions. Developing his EQ taught him to listen actively, empathise, and respond calmly. This shift transformed his relationships, built team trust, and increased productivity— proving how EQ can be a powerful asset in personal growth and leadership.

Practical Tips:

◊ **Notice Patterns:** Track your emotional responses to identify common triggers.
◊ **Mindfulness:** Spend a few minutes daily focusing on your breath to stay grounded.
◊ **Reflect and Grow:** After emotional reactions, take time to reflect on what you might do differently next time.

Reflective Questions:

» How often do you take time to reflect on your emotional reactions?
» What steps could help you boost your emotional intelligence?
» How might enhancing your EQ improve your relationships and career?

DAY 152: CULTIVATING SELF-AWARENESS

"Only with self-awareness can we begin self-improvement." – Frank Moran

Self-awareness, a crucial aspect of emotional intelligence, is the foundation for recognising our emotions, thoughts, and values and understanding their impact on our behaviour. Self-awareness helps us navigate our strengths, weaknesses, and emotional triggers like a compass. It involves examining our beliefs about ourselves and determining whether they are factual, constructive, and empowering. Doing so fosters personal growth, achieves inner peace, and actively shapes our reality—our character, circumstances, and overall success.

From a scientific perspective, self-awareness activates brain areas involved in introspection, helping us reflect deeply and make thoughtful decisions. Spiritually, scripture encourages self-examination. Psalm 139:23-24 (NIV) asks, *"Search me, God, and know my heart; test me and know my anxious thoughts."* Facing our true selves and emotions can be challenging, but it's better than denial or overreacting. Self-awareness allows us to pause, reflect, and respond intentionally instead of reacting impulsively.

Chioma, a manager, realised she often became defensive whenever given feedback. By becoming more self-aware, she understood this reaction stemmed from a fear of criticism. This awareness allowed her to approach feedback more openly, improving her relationships and leadership.

Practical Tips:

◊ **Daily Reflection:** Dedicate a few minutes each day to introspection, examining your thoughts and emotions. Ask yourself: *"Are these perceptions helping me grow?"*

◊ **Mindfulness:** Practice mindfulness to observe your thoughts and feelings without judgment.

◊ **Journaling:** Write down your feelings regularly to identify patterns and gain insights.

Reflective Questions:

» What are the thoughts you have about yourself? Are they positive or limiting?
» Do you listen to yourself? Do you respect and value your own feelings?
» Do you help yourself feel loved and accepted? Are you reaching your highest potential and making a difference?

Exercise: Spend 10 minutes reflecting on a recent emotional experience. Write down what you felt, your thoughts, and how you reacted. Consider whether these thoughts were helpful and how greater self-awareness could have changed your response.

DAY 153: MASTERING SELF-REGULATION

"It's not what happens to you, but how you react to it that matters." – Epictetus

Self-regulation is the process of managing our emotions, thoughts, and behaviours in different situations. It involves maintaining control, not letting emotions dictate actions, and choosing responses that align with our values and goals. Self-regulation is like having an internal thermostat—it prevents overreaction to stress and helps us stay balanced, even in challenging circumstances.

Self-regulation involves the prefrontal cortex, which is responsible for decision-making and impulse control. Practising self-regulation strengthens these brain pathways, leading to better emotional control and improved mental well-being. Self-regulation reflects the biblical principle of self-control. Proverbs 25:28 compares a person without self-control to "a city whose walls are broken down," illustrating how a lack of self-regulation can leave you emotionally vulnerable and unstable. Mastering self-regulation can help you handle difficult emotions, reduce stress, and make thoughtful decisions. Imagine being in a heated argument; instead of reacting angrily, self-regulation allows you to pause, breathe, and respond calmly. This does not only prevent escalation but also fosters healthier communication and relationships.

Ayo, a customer service representative, often encountered angry clients. Initially, she reacted defensively, which only made situations worse. By practising self-regulation, she learned to stay calm, listen actively, and address concerns with empathy, leading to more positive interactions.

Practical Tips:
- ◊ **Pause and Reflect:** When emotions run high, take a moment to pause before reacting. This simple act can prevent impulsive behaviour.
- ◊ **Healthy Coping Mechanisms:** Engage in activities like deep breathing, exercise, or meditation to manage stress effectively.
- ◊ **Set Personal Boundaries:** Know your limits and communicate them clearly to avoid feeling overwhelmed or losing control.

Reflective Questions:
- » How do you typically react when faced with stress or criticism?
- » What strategies can help you stay calm and in control in difficult situations?

Exercise: Recall a recent situation where you felt triggered. Note what happened, how you reacted, and how you could have used self-regulation to respond better.

DAY 154: DEVELOPING EMPATHY

"Empathy is seeing with the eyes of another, listening with the ears of another, and feeling with the heart of another." – Alfred Adler

Empathy is the ability to understand and share the feelings of others. It's about stepping into someone else's shoes and seeing the world from their perspective. Unlike sympathy, which is feeling for someone, empathy is feeling with them. This emotional connection strengthens relationships, improves communication, and fosters teamwork.

One fascinating part of empathy is the role of mirror neurons in our brains. Mirror neurons are special cells that activate when we observe others' emotions or actions, allowing us to "mirror" their feelings and experiences. They help us understand and feel what others are going through, even without words. Think of it as a natural tool that allows us to connect on a deeper level, picking up on subtle emotional cues. The Bible echoes this in Romans 12:15: *"Rejoice with those who rejoice; mourn with those who mourn,"* reminding us to connect and share in each other's experiences.

Empathy is essential for building trust and showing others they are valued. Imagine a situation where a colleague shares a personal struggle. Practising empathy means listening without judgment, acknowledging their feelings, and offering support. This builds a foundation of trust and shows you genuinely care. John, a manager, noticed his colleague seemed unusually quiet. Instead of overlooking it, he approached her with empathy, gently asked if she was okay, and listened to her concerns. This small act made her feel valued, lifting her morale and strengthening their working relationship.

Practical Tips:

◊ **Active Listening:** Focus fully, avoid interrupting, and show interest through eye contact and nodding.

◊ **Ask Open Questions:** Use phrases like "Can you tell me more?" to encourage sharing.

◊ **Practice Compassion:** Acknowledge their feelings, even if you disagree, and respond with kindness.

Reflective Questions:

» How often do you try to understand others' feelings?
» What steps can you take to show more empathy in your interactions?
» How might empathy improve your relationships and work environment?

Exercise: Reflect on a recent conversation. How did you respond? Note ways to show more empathy next time.

Day 155: Enhancing Social Skills

"The most important single ingredient in the formula of success is knowing how to get along with people." – Theodore Roosevelt

Social skills are a vital part of emotional intelligence. They enable us to communicate effectively, build strong relationships, and easily navigate social situations. Social skills are the bridge that connects us with others, fostering collaboration, understanding, and trust. Whether in personal or professional settings, these skills are essential for achieving shared goals and building lasting connections.

Good social skills combine empathy, self-awareness, and self-regulation. They activate the brain's social circuits, including the prefrontal cortex, helping us read social cues and respond appropriately. The Bible highlights the value of harmonious relationships. Proverbs 15:1 (NIV) says, *"A gentle answer turns away wrath, but a harsh word stirs up anger,"* highlighting the importance of kind and effective communication. Imagine a team meeting where conflict arises. Someone with strong social skills can help resolve conflicts, listen to different opinions, and steer conversations in a way that leads to a positive solution. By practising these skills, we create environments of respect and cooperation, leading to better results for everyone involved.

Alex, a team leader, noticed rising tensions during a project discussion. Using her social skills, she encouraged everyone to share their perspectives, acknowledged their concerns, and steered the conversation toward a solution. Her approach helped build trust and improved team collaboration.

Practical Tips:

- ◊ **Active Listening:** Maintain eye contact, avoid interruptions, and respond with thoughtful questions or comments.
- ◊ **Clear Communication:** Speak clearly, use specific examples, and ask for feedback to ensure understanding.
- ◊ **Build Rapport:** Highlight shared interests, smile, and use approachable body language to strengthen connections.

Reflective Questions:

- » How effectively do you handle social interactions and conflicts?
- » What steps can you take to improve your communication and relationship skills?

Exercise: Reflect on a social interaction that went poorly. Note what happened and how to improve next time.

DAY 156: CULTIVATING MOTIVATION

"Success is not the key to happiness. Happiness is the key to success. If you love what you are doing, you will be successful." – Albert Schweitzer

Motivation is the spark that lights our way and keeps us moving, even when the road gets tough. Think of it as the fuel that powers your car, pushing you toward your dreams with energy and excitement. Cultivating motivation means connecting with what brings you joy and purpose, turning challenges into stepping stones rather than obstacles.

Our brains love rewards! When you do things that make you happy or align with your values, your brain releases dopamine, the chemical that makes us feel good. This keeps you energised and focused. In the Bible, Colossians 3:23 (NIV) encourages, *"Whatever you do, work at it with all your heart,"* reminding us to approach our tasks with enthusiasm and dedication.

Imagine working on a project you're truly passionate about. Instead of feeling it's a burden, each task feels like a step toward something meaningful. Like a sunflower turning to the sun, we thrive when driven by love and purpose.

Ian, a teacher who felt burned out, found his spark again by focusing on the joy of inspiring his students. He set fun teaching goals and celebrated each student's progress, which renewed his enthusiasm and made his classes more engaging. This helped his students aim higher and achieve more.

Practical Tips:

◊ **Set Exciting Goals:** Break big goals into smaller, fun steps. Each small win keeps your motivation alive and provides a clear direction for your journey.
◊ **Connect with Your Passion:** Identify what you love about what you do—understanding your 'why' transforms tasks into joyful activities and helps you stay connected to your work.
◊ **Celebrate Your Progress:** Reward yourself for even the smallest achievements. Every step forward is a victory!

Reflective Questions:

» What activities make you feel most alive?
» How can you bring more passion into your daily life?
» What small achievements can you celebrate today to boost your motivation?

Exercise: Write down one thing you can do today that brings you joy and aligns with your goals. Celebrate each step forward, no matter how small.

DAY 157: PRACTICING EMOTIONAL EMPATHY

"Empathy is about finding echoes of another person in yourself." – Mohsin Hamid

Empathy is like a bridge that connects us to others, allowing us to feel their joys and struggles. It's more than just understanding someone's feelings—it's about truly sharing their experience. When we practice emotional empathy, we tune into the emotions of those around us, offering comfort and understanding. This ability to resonate with other people's feelings makes us human and strengthens our relationships.

Empathy activates the **mirror neurons** in our brains, allowing us to feel what others feel. It's like catching a yawn; when we see someone else yawn, we often yawn, too. Empathy works in a similar way—we mirror emotions, creating a shared connection. The Bible urges us in Romans 12:15 (NIV) to *"rejoice with those who rejoice; mourn with those who mourn."* This verse beautifully illustrates the essence of empathy: being present with others in their emotional highs and lows. Think about comforting a friend who's going through a tough time. Instead of offering advice or trying to fix their problem, empathy allows you to be there, listening and providing comfort by being present and understanding their experience. This act of compassion can be more healing than any words of wisdom.

Uche noticed her colleague looking upset after a meeting. Instead of ignoring it, she approached him and said, *"I noticed you seem down. Do you want to talk?"* This simple act of empathy made her colleague feel valued and supported, deepening their connection.

Practical Tips:

◊ **Listen with Your Heart:** When someone is talking, focus entirely on them. Listen to their words and also pay attention to their emotions.

◊ **Be Present:** Put away distractions and be fully present with the person. Your presence can be a powerful source of comfort.

◊ **Acknowledge Emotions:** Validate the other person's feelings. Sometimes, saying, *"I understand, and I'm here for you,"* is enough.

Reflective Questions:

» How often do you practice genuinely listening to others?
» How can you show empathy to someone today?
» What impact does empathy have on your relationships?

Exercise: Think of someone in your life who might need emotional support. Reach out to them today, offer a listening ear, and let them know you care. Practice being fully present and empathetic.

Day 158: Building Trust Through Consistency

"Trust is built with consistency." – Lincoln Chafee

Trust is the foundation of any strong relationship at home, work, or within your community. It's like the glue that holds everything together, making interactions smoother and more meaningful. Building trust isn't about grand gestures; it's being reliable, keeping promises, and showing up consistently. When people know they can count on you, it creates a solid bond that withstands the test of time.

Trust activates the brain's oxytocin system, often called the "bonding hormone." This chemical release fosters feelings of safety and connection, encouraging open communication and collaboration. Biblically, Proverbs 11:13 (NIV) states, *"A gossip betrays a confidence, but a trustworthy person keeps a secret."* This scripture highlights the importance of being trustworthy and consistent in our actions and words.

Consider how trust plays out in your everyday life. Imagine a manager who consistently supports their team, listens to their concerns, and follows through on commitments. Over time, the team feels safe and valued, leading to higher morale, better team engagement, retention and productivity. On the other hand, inconsistency breeds doubt and insecurity, eroding trust and weakening relationships. Lara, a team leader, regularly checked in with her team, offering support and guidance. By consistently being there for her team members and following through on her promises, she earned their trust and loyalty, creating a strong, collaborative environment.

Practical Tips:

◊ **Keep Your Promises:** Always follow through on commitments, no matter how small. Your reliability will build trust over time.

◊ **Be Honest and Transparent:** Communicate openly and truthfully. Honesty, even when difficult, strengthens trust.

◊ **Show up Consistently:** Be present and available for others. Consistency in actions and words reinforces trust and dependability.

Reflective Questions:

» How reliable and consistent are you in your relationships?
» What actions can you take to build trust with those around you?
» How does being trustworthy impact your personal and professional life?

Exercise: Reflect on a key relationship. List three ways to build trust and take one step today to show reliability.

Day 159: The Power of Patience

"Patience is the calm acceptance that things can happen in a different order than the one you have in mind." – David G. Allen

Patience isn't just about waiting; it's about managing your emotions while you wait. Whether facing an unexpected delay, a challenging project, or waiting for a personal breakthrough, patience helps you stay calm, focused, and grounded. It's a crucial part of emotional intelligence (EQ), enabling you to handle stress, frustration, and uncertainty without reacting impulsively.

Developing patience strengthens the brain's prefrontal cortex, which controls emotional regulation and decision-making. This means patience allows you to pause, think, and respond thoughtfully rather than acting out of frustration. Think of patience as building mental resilience—it teaches you to face life's delays and disruptions with grace, which helps you grow emotionally stronger and more adaptable over time.

From a spiritual perspective, patience is also about trust. It's the faith that things will unfold at the right time, trusting that God is working everything out for you, even if you can't see it yet. Patience encourages us to release control and rely on God's timing, understanding that His plan is always perfect. Galatians 5:22 refers to patience as a "fruit of the Spirit," highlighting its importance in a peaceful and purposeful life. Practising patience shows that you trust God's timing and believe that everything is unfolding for your ultimate good.

Practical Tips:

◊ **Pause Before Reacting:** Feel impatience? Pause, breathe, and think first.
◊ **Stay Calm:** Use patience to manage emotions in chaos.
◊ **Focus on Growth:** See delays as lessons in emotional management.

Reflective Questions:

» How do you usually handle situations when things don't go as planned?
» In what areas could patience help improve your emotional intelligence?
» How might practising patience change your reactions to stressful situations?

Exercise: When you feel impatient, pause, name the feeling, and think of a better way to respond. Patience brings balance and strength.

Day 160: The Power of Truly Listening

"Most people do not listen with the intent to understand; they listen with the intent to reply." – Stephen R. Covey

Listening is more than just hearing words—it's about connecting. Imagine listening as a bridge that connects hearts, making others feel valued and understood. Developing better listening skills means giving your full attention, truly understanding the message, and responding with care. It's like saying, "I see you, I hear you, and you matter."

Science shows that active listening engages brain areas related to empathy and understanding. Our mirror neurons light up, helping us feel what others feel. It's not just about using your ears but your heart, too. In the Bible, James 1:19 (NIV) encourages us, *"be quick to listen, slow to speak, and slow to become angry,"* reminding us that listening leads to understanding and peace.

Imagine sitting with a friend who's pouring their heart out. Instead of jumping in with advice, you simply listen. You nod, maintain eye contact, and this silence says, *"I'm here for you."* This simple act of listening provides more comfort than any words could. It strengthens your bond and shows your friend that they are not alone.

Practical Tips:

◊ **Be Fully Present:** Put away your phone and distractions. Focus entirely on the person speaking. Your full attention is a gift.
◊ **Hold Back:** Resist the urge to interrupt or offer solutions. Let the speaker finish their thoughts before you respond.
◊ **Show Understanding:** Reflect on the speaker's words to show you've been listening. Phrases like, "It sounds like you're feeling…" can open up deeper conversations.

Reflective Questions:

» How often do you listen without interrupting or planning your response?
» What steps can you take to improve your listening skills today?
» How can being a better listener transform your relationships?

Exercise: Next time you're in a conversation, practice listening fully. Focus on the speaker, don't interrupt, and reflect on what they say. See how this changes the interaction and deepens your connection.

Day 161: Building Emotional Resilience

"Strength doesn't come from what you can do. It comes from overcoming the things you once thought you couldn't." – Rikki Rogers

Emotional resilience is the ability to bounce back from life's challenges and adapt to stress. Think of it as a rubber band—flexible enough to stretch under pressure but strong enough to snap back into shape. Building resilience means developing coping strategies, maintaining a positive outlook, and seeking support when needed. It's not about avoiding hardships but thriving despite them.

Resilience activates the brain's reward and stress-regulation systems. When we overcome obstacles, our brains release chemicals that reduce stress and boost our sense of achievement. This process strengthens our emotional resilience over time. The Bible also speaks about this in James 1:2-3 (NIV), *"Consider it pure joy, my brothers and sisters, whenever you face trials of many kinds, because you know that the testing of your faith produces perseverance."* This scripture teaches us that challenges help build our strength and character. Think of resilience like a tree in a storm. It bends but doesn't break, and its roots grow even deeper after the storm. In the same way, when we face tough times—like losing a job or going through a personal setback—emotional resilience helps us adapt, find new paths, and stay positive.

When my client Joanne lost her job, I coached her to rewire her brain and reframe her thoughts, focusing on new opportunities instead of the loss. This shift in mindset helped her stay positive and quickly find a job aligned with her passions, proving that resilience turns setbacks into new beginnings.

Practical Tips:

◊ **Develop Coping Strategies:** Find activities that help you manage stress, such as exercise, meditation, or talking to a friend.

◊ **Keep a Positive Outlook:** Focus on what you can control and view challenges as opportunities for growth.

◊ **Seek Support:** When needed, reach out to friends, family, or professionals. Sharing your burdens can make them feel lighter.

Reflective Questions:

» How resilient are you when faced with challenges?
» What strategies can you use to build emotional resilience?
» How can increasing your resilience improve your mental health and overall life satisfaction?

DAY 162: EMBRACING SELF-LEADERSHIP

"Don't become too preoccupied with what is happening around you. Pay more attention to what is going on within you." – Mary-Frances Winters

Many people don't see themselves as leaders, but everyone has the power to lead—starting with themselves. Self-leadership is like being the captain of your own ship, guiding your life in the direction you want to go. It's about taking charge of your actions, decisions, and mindset, steering confidently even when the waters are rough.

Self-leadership begins with knowing yourself—your strengths, weaknesses, values, and dreams. It's making choices that align with who you are and where you want to be. This requires emotional intelligence, which means managing your emotions, staying motivated, and facing challenges head-on. Proverbs 3:6 (NIV) reminds us, *"In all your ways acknowledge Him, and He will make your paths straight,"* highlighting the importance of aligning our choices with our values and purpose.

Imagine you are a gardener. Self-leadership is like tending to your own garden. You choose which seeds to plant (goals), you water them daily (effort), and you pull out the weeds (negative thoughts) that could hinder growth. Just as a gardener is responsible for their garden's health, you are responsible for nurturing your own growth and well-being.

Jake didn't see himself as a leader, but when his team lacked direction, he knew he wanted to make a difference. By taking charge of his project and guiding his team, he impressed senior leaders, who rewarded him with leadership training and promotion.

Practical Tips:

◊ **Set Clear Goals:** Define your vision of success to guide your journey.
◊ **Take Charge:** Be proactive—start taking steps, no matter how small, toward your goals.
◊ **Stay Committed:** Build self-discipline by staying consistent, even when challenges arise.

Reflective Questions:

» How are you leading yourself daily?
» What actions can you take to practice better self-leadership?
» How can self-leadership positively impact your personal and professional life?

Exercise: Identify one area for improved self-leadership. Commit to one action today that will guide your life towards your goals.

Day 163: The Impact of Emotional Intelligence on Leadership

"Leadership is not about being in charge. It's about taking care of those in your charge." – Simon Sinek

Great leaders don't just manage tasks; they connect with people. Emotional intelligence (EQ) is the heart of effective leadership because it helps leaders understand, empathise, and respond to the emotions of others. Think of EQ as the heart of leadership—it builds trust, fosters strong relationships, and creates a positive work environment. With EQ, leaders can inspire and motivate their teams, making everyone feel valued and heard.

Leaders with high EQ are aware of their emotions and understand how they affect their actions. They can sense what their team members are feeling and respond thoughtfully. This awareness creates a supportive atmosphere, leading to higher morale and better productivity. As Matthew 20:26 (NIV) says, *"Whoever wants to become great among you must be your servant."* This scripture shows that outstanding leadership involves humility, empathy, and serving others—core aspects of emotional intelligence.

In my work as a neuroleadership trainer and neurocoach, I worked with a manager named Luanne, who noticed her team was burning out. Instead of pushing them harder, I guided her to use emotional intelligence. Luanne began holding meetings to listen to her team's concerns, showing empathy and adjusting their workloads. This simple act of understanding reduced stress and boosted morale, highlighting how important emotional intelligence is for high performance leadership.

Practical Tips:

◊ **Active Listening:** Truly understand what your team says and feels—listening shows you care.
◊ **Manage Emotions:** Stay calm under stress to set a positive example.
◊ **Show Empathy:** Recognise feelings and offer support to build trust and loyalty.

Reflective Questions:

» How do you use emotional intelligence in your leadership?
» What can you do to understand and support your team better?
» How can improving your EQ make you a more effective leader?

Exercise: Reflect on a recent leadership challenge. Write how you handled it and how emotional intelligence could have improved the outcome. Identify one way to apply EQ in your leadership today.

Day 164: Understanding Emotional Triggers

"When we are no longer able to change a situation, we are challenged to change ourselves."
– Viktor Frankl

Emotional triggers are moments when a word, action, or situation provokes a strong emotional response, like anger, fear, or sadness. Understanding these triggers is crucial for emotional growth and well-being. Recognising what sets you off enables you to gain the power to manage your responses and handle life's challenges with more grace and composure.

Triggers often originate from past experiences or unresolved issues. For example, criticism might trigger feelings of inadequacy if you've faced harsh judgment before. The amygdala, the brain's emotional centre, quickly reacts to these triggers, often bypassing the rational prefrontal cortex, leading to impulsive reactions. Recognising your triggers enhances your emotional intelligence by improving self-awareness, which helps you manage your responses more effectively. Proverbs 16:32 (NIV) states, *"Better a patient person than a warrior, one with self-control than one who takes a city."* This verse highlights the strength of managing emotions rather than letting them control you.

Think of your emotions as a storm. When a trigger arises, it's like storm clouds forming. Instead of being swept away, you can find shelter and wait it out, allowing the storm to pass. Identifying your triggers helps you prepare for these storms, whether through deep breathing, taking a moment to pause, or focusing on the present.

Practical Tips:

◊ **Identify Triggers:** Keep a journal to note situations that provoke strong emotional responses. Reflect on why these triggers affect you.
◊ **Practice Mindfulness:** Use meditation or deep breathing exercises to stay calm when faced with triggers.
◊ **Develop Coping Strategies:** Have a plan, such as stepping away, counting to ten, or reframing the situation positively.

Reflective Questions:

» What are my common emotional triggers, and why do they affect me?
» How can I prepare myself to respond calmly when triggered?
» What strategies can I use to regulate my emotions in challenging situations?

Understanding and managing emotional triggers leads to greater emotional stability, healthier relationships, and a more peaceful life. By practising awareness and self-control, you empower yourself to handle life's ups and downs with strength and grace.

Day 165: The Hidden Cost of Emotional Suppression

"What you resist, persists." – Carl Jung

Many people believe that suppressing emotions is a sign of strength. They think that by pushing feelings down, they can maintain control and appear strong. However, emotional suppression can actually be harmful, like trying to hold a beach ball underwater—it eventually pops up with more force. Suppressing emotions not only affects mental health but also damages relationships and overall well-being.

When you suppress emotions, your brain goes into overdrive, trying to maintain a facade of calm. This increases stress and can lead to anxiety, depression, and physical health issues such as high blood pressure. Rather than experiencing a decrease in emotions, you become even more overwhelmed. The Bible reminds us in Psalm 34:18 (NIV), *"The Lord is close to the brokenhearted and saves those who are crushed in spirit."* This verse encourages us to acknowledge our emotions, rather than suppress them, to find comfort and healing.

Imagine trying to hold back tears during a sad movie. You tense up, clench your jaw, and hold your breath. This effort takes energy and can leave you feeling drained. Similarly, suppressing real-life emotions takes a toll on your body and mind. It's important to understand that emotions are natural signals, guiding us to what matters and needs attention.

Practical Tips:

◊ **Acknowledge Your Feelings:** Instead of pushing emotions away, recognise them. Naming your feelings can help you process them.

◊ **Express Emotions Healthily:** Find constructive ways to express your feelings, whether through talking to a friend, writing in a journal, or creative outlets like art.

◊ **Practice Self-Compassion:** Be kind to yourself. Accept that it's okay to feel and express emotions. This is a sign of strength, not weakness.

Reflective Questions:

» How do you typically handle your emotions when you feel stressed or upset?
» What are some healthy ways you can express your emotions?
» How might acknowledging and expressing your emotions improve your mental well-being?

Exercise: Reflect on a recent time when you suppressed your emotions. Write down what you were feeling and how you handled it. Consider one healthy way you could have expressed those emotions instead. Practice this new approach the next time you feel overwhelmed.

DAY 166: THE TRAP OF TOXIC POSITIVITY

"It's okay to not be okay. Feelings are meant to be felt, not ignored." – Unknown

In a world that often says, *"just stay positive,"* it's easy to get caught up in toxic positivity—the belief that we should ignore negative feelings and focus only on the positive. While having a positive outlook is helpful, constantly forcing yourself to *"stay happy"* is like putting a bandage on a deep wound. Unacknowledged emotions don't go away; they build up, creating even more stress.

Toxic positivity will make you feel as though emotions like sadness, anger, or fear are wrong, encouraging you to suppress them. But avoiding these feelings can lead to shame and isolation, making you feel that you're somehow "failing" by not being cheerful. Remember, even Jesus expressed sadness and wept (John 11:35), showing us that deep emotions are part of being human. Imagine emotions as weather patterns: not every day is sunny, and that's okay. Sometimes, we face storms, and growth often happens in those rainy seasons. True healing comes from experiencing all emotions, not just the positive ones. One way to move beyond toxic positivity is to label your emotions. For example, instead of forcing yourself to *"look on the bright side,"* try naming what you feel: *"I feel disappointed"* or *"I feel hurt."* Labelling emotions helps you process them, making them easier to manage. If a friend shares that they're feeling low, instead of saying, *"just stay positive,"* try responding with, *"I'm here for you, and it's okay to feel this way."* This response validates their feelings rather than brushing them aside.

Practical Tips:

◊ **Acknowledge Emotions:** Feelings like sadness or anger are natural; don't judge them.

◊ **Name Them:** Label emotions (e.g., "I feel anxious") to understand them better.

◊ **Offer Support:** Listen and empathise when others share their feelings instead of trying to "fix" them.

Reflective Questions:

» How do you typically respond to your own and others' negative emotions?
» What are some ways you can practice accepting your feelings without judgment?
» How might acknowledging all your emotions improve your overall mental well-being?

Day 167: Embracing Self-Love

"To love oneself is the beginning of a lifelong romance." – Oscar Wilde

Self-love isn't selfish or self-centred; it's about valuing and caring for yourself, just as you would for a friend. It's recognising your worth, setting healthy boundaries, and being kind to yourself, even when you make mistakes. Imagine self-love as the foundation of a house. Without a strong foundation, everything built on top will eventually crumble. Self-love is that solid base that provides the strength and resilience needed to face life's challenges.

Many people struggle with self-love, often being their harshest critics. They may prioritise others' needs over their own or feel guilty for taking time for themselves. But remember, you can't pour from an empty cup. Practising self-love replenishes your energy, making you better equipped to care for others and handle daily stressors. As Psalm 139:14 (NIV) says, *"I praise you because I am fearfully and wonderfully made."* Recognising this truth helps us see our inherent worth and embrace self-love.

Imagine you're on a flight: you're told to put on your oxygen mask before helping others. Life works the same way—caring for yourself first makes you stronger for those around you.

Have you had a rough day? Instead of criticising yourself, practice self-love. Remind yourself that tough days happen. Take a warm bath, read, or call a friend. Kindness to yourself renews your energy and helps you bounce back.

Practical Tips:

◊ **Practice Positive Self-Talk:** Replace self-criticism with kindness. Speak to yourself the way you would speak to a friend.
◊ **Set Boundaries:** Learn to 'say no' when necessary. Setting limits is essential for protecting your well-being and energy.
◊ **Take Time for Self-Care:** Prioritise activities that recharge you, whether it's reading, exercising, or simply relaxing.

Reflective Questions:

» How do you practice self-love in your daily life?
» What are some negative thoughts you can replace with positive self-talk?
» How can embracing self-love improve your relationships and overall well-being?

Exercise: Write down three things you appreciate about yourself. Then, read them aloud every morning. Repeat daily to reinforce the habit of self-love.

DAY 168: CULTIVATING COMPASSION

"Compassion is not a relationship between the healer and the wounded. It's a relationship between equals." – Pema Chödrön

Compassion means understanding and sharing the feelings of others. It's offering help when someone is struggling, listening without judgment, and being present in their pain. Genuine compassion doesn't drain joy; it multiplies it by deepening our connections, fostering understanding, and bringing a sense of purpose.

Think of compassion as a warm light. Extending it to others brightens their world and reflects back on you, bringing light to your own life. Compassion connects us, making us feel seen and understood. It reminds us that we're not alone, building a sense of community and belonging.

Compassion is central to many Bible teachings. In Colossians 3:12 (NIV), we are told, *"clothe yourselves with compassion, kindness, humility, gentleness, and patience."* This verse highlights the importance of compassion as a key virtue in our interactions with others. Consider a time when a friend was struggling. By listening and offering support, you helped them and felt joy and fulfilment in being there. Compassion is not about fixing other people's problems; it's about showing empathy and kindness.

Imagine a colleague is visibly upset. Instead of ignoring them, you ask, *"Is everything okay? I'm here if you want to talk."* This simple act of compassion can lift their spirits and remind them they're not alone.

Practical Tips:

- ◊ **Listen Actively:** Pay attention to others without interrupting. Sometimes, being heard is all someone needs.
- ◊ **Practice Kindness:** Small gestures, like a smile or kind words, can significantly uplift someone's day.
- ◊ **Show Empathy:** Try to put yourself in other people's shoes. Understand their feelings, even if you don't agree.

Reflective Questions:

- » How do you show compassion to those around you?
- » What small acts of kindness can you add to your daily routine?
- » How does practising compassion impact your joy and fulfilment?

Exercise: Identify someone who might need compassion. Reach out with a kind word or gesture. Observe how this act of compassion affects both you and them.

Day 169: The Dangers of Comparison

"Comparison is the thief of joy." – Theodore Roosevelt

Comparing yourself to others can make you feel inadequate. Whether it's scrolling through social media, hearing about a friend's promotion, or seeing a neighbour's new car, comparison can swiftly steal your joy. Like a shadow that dims your light, comparing yourself to others not only diminishes your joy but also erodes your self-worth, diverting your focus from your blessings to what you lack.

Comparison breeds feelings of inadequacy, jealousy, and resentment. It distracts you from your own path and leads to a cycle of never feeling good enough. Remember, everyone has their own unique journey. What you see on the surface often hides the struggles others face. As Galatians 6:4 (NIV) advises, *"Each one should test their own actions. Then they can take pride in themselves alone, without comparing themselves to someone else."* This scripture encourages us to focus on our own progress and achievements.
Think of life as a race, but instead of competing against others, you're running your own marathon. The goal isn't to beat the person next to you but to reach your personal best. By focusing on your own growth, you can celebrate your progress and find fulfilment in your unique journey.

Have you ever felt a twinge of envy when you saw a friend's success shared online? Instead of letting jealousy take over, take a moment to reflect on your achievements and what makes you unique. Celebrate their success, but stay focused on your own goals and path.

Practical Tips:

◊ **Practice Gratitude:** Focus on what you have, not what others have. Gratitude helps shift your mindset from lack to abundance.

◊ **Limit Social Media:** Spend less time on platforms that encourage comparison and invest in activities that make you happy and fulfilled.

◊ **Celebrate Your Wins:** Acknowledge your achievements, no matter how small. This reinforces your sense of self-worth.

Reflective Questions:

» How often do you compare yourself to others?
» What are some unique qualities or achievements you can be proud of?
» How can focusing on your own journey improve your happiness?

Exercise: Write down three things you're proud of about yourself. Reflect on these daily to reinforce your sense of self-worth and reduce the urge to compare yourself to others.

Day 170: Prioritising Mental Health and Mental Fitness

"You can't pour from an empty cup. Take care of yourself first." – Unknown

Mental health is as vital as physical health, but it often takes a backseat. In today's fast-paced world, prioritising your mental well-being and mental fitness is not a luxury—it's essential. Just as you maintain your physical fitness to stay healthy, mental fitness requires consistent care and attention. Think of it like exercising your brain. By practising mental fitness, such as mindfulness, stress management, and emotional regulation, you build resilience and the capacity to face life's challenges head-on.

Neglecting mental health can lead to burnout, overwhelm, and even physical health problems. It is critical to pay attention to how your mind feels and take proactive steps to recharge. Proverbs 17:22 (ESV) says, *"A joyful heart is good medicine, but a crushed spirit dries up the bones,"* showing how closely linked our mental and physical health are.

Think of your mind as a well-maintained home. If you neglect it, clutter—like stress and negative thoughts—begins to pile up, making it difficult to function. But by regularly taking time to declutter, organise your thoughts, and focus on positivity, you create a space where your mind can thrive. Prioritising your mental well-being isn't just about managing stress; it's about strengthening your mind to handle life's challenges with clarity and resilience.

Imagine you're feeling overwhelmed by a long to-do list. Instead of pushing through, you step outside for fresh air or call a friend to share your thoughts. That short break allows you to return feeling refreshed and mentally stronger, ready to handle your tasks with renewed energy.

Practical Tips:

◊ **Practice Mental Fitness:** Spend a few minutes each day focusing on deep breathing and clearing your thoughts. This strengthens your mind and reduces stress.

◊ **Take Breaks:** Avoid burnout by taking short, regular breaks. These moments help reset your mind and keep you mentally fit.

◊ **Build Support Networks:** Connect with friends, family, or colleagues who can offer emotional support and perspective.

Reflective Questions:

» How do you currently prioritise your mental fitness?
» What activities help you recharge and maintain mental clarity?

Exercise: Choose one activity to strengthen your mental fitness, such as meditation, exercise, or connecting with loved ones. Practice it daily for a week, and reflect on how it improves your mental well-being.

Day 171: Cultivating the Fruit of the Spirit through Emotional Intelligence

"But the fruit of the Spirit is love, joy, peace, forbearance, kindness, goodness, faithfulness, gentleness, and self-control. Against such things there is no law." – Galatians 5:22-23

Galatians 5 describes the fruit of the Spirit—qualities that bring us closer to God and shape our character. Emotional Intelligence (EQ) is vital for nurturing these qualities, helping us manage our emotions and interact more meaningfully with others. Love and joy, for instance, are deeply tied to self-awareness. Recognising emotional triggers allows us to pause and choose responses rooted in love instead of frustration. Imagine feeling annoyed; by shifting focus to gratitude, you cultivate joy and a heart full of love.

Emotional regulation is essential for peace and patience, especially in stressful situations. When stress hits, we sometimes experience an **amygdala hijack**—a response where the amygdala, our brain's emotional centre, takes over, bypassing the prefrontal cortex (our rational thinking area) and causing us to react impulsively. EQ helps us counter this, engaging the prefrontal cortex so we can respond calmly instead of reacting emotionally. Instead of allowing frustration to dominate, we can trust God's timing, letting His peace guide us.

Empathy, another core aspect of EQ, empowers us to show kindness, goodness, and gentleness. By understanding others' emotions, we respond with compassion, deepening our connections and fostering trust. Lastly, self-control is crucial for both EQ and spiritual growth. Self-control allows us to resist impulsive actions and choose behaviours that align with God's will. Through prayer and intentionality, we can grow in self-discipline, nurturing a life that reflects God's purpose.

Practical Tips:

◊ **Pause and Pray:** When facing a challenge, pause, pray, and respond thoughtfully.

◊ **Start with Gratitude:** Begin each day by listing what you're thankful for to maintain a joyful heart.

◊ **Ground Yourself:** Use deep breathing or prayer to stay calm in stressful moments.

◊ **Practice Active Listening:** Acknowledge others' feelings and respond with kindness.

Reflective Questions:

» How can EQ help you nurture the fruit of the Spirit?
» How can you manage your emotions in difficult situations?

Day 172: Building a Network of Positive Influences

"As iron sharpens iron, so one person sharpens another." – Proverbs 27:17 (NIV)

The people we spend time with shape our thoughts, emotions, and overall well-being. Building a network of positive influences means surrounding yourself intentionally with those who uplift, inspire, and challenge you to grow. Think of it like tending a garden—plants thrive in a nurturing environment, and so do we when surrounded by supportive, caring people. Positive relationships do more than brighten your mood; they foster personal growth, confidence, and fulfilment.

Studies show that positive social interactions activate areas in the brain linked to reward and well-being. Being around encouraging people boosts your mood, reduces stress, and supports mental health. This idea echoes Hebrews 10:24-25, which encourages us to uplift one another. By surrounding ourselves with positive people, we create a nurturing environment where we can thrive mentally and emotionally.

Take the story of my client, Pam. She felt stuck in her career but found new momentum after joining our Mindsight Women's Network, an encouraging community of women dedicated to growth and support. With guidance from neurocoaching and support within the community, she gained the confidence to explore new career paths. With this support, she wasn't just working toward her goals—she was thriving in ways she hadn't imagined. This is the power of positive influences: when surrounded by those who challenge and uplift us, we experience growth in unexpected, impactful ways.

It's important to remember that emotions are contagious. When you're around positive, joyful people, their energy positively impacts your outlook, helping you maintain a more optimistic, empowered perspective.

Practical Tips:

- ◊ **Seek Positive Relationships:** Connect with those who inspire and encourage you, whether friends, family, mentors, or colleagues.
- ◊ **Engage in Uplifting Activities:** Join groups or activities filled with positive energy, like workshops or volunteering.
- ◊ **Be a Positive Influence:** Remember, your energy affects others. Spread positivity to those around you.

Reflective Questions:

- » Name three positive influences in your life.
- » How can you strengthen these relationships?
- » How can building a network of positive influences enhance your personal growth?

Day 173: Cultivating EQ for Effective Church Leadership

"But the wisdom from above is first pure, then peaceable, gentle, open to reason, full of mercy and good fruits, impartial and sincere." – James 3:17 (ESV)

Emotional intelligence (EQ) is essential for effective church leadership. It involves understanding and managing our own emotions while being sensitive to the emotions of others. By cultivating EQ, church leaders can mirror Christ's love, patience, and kindness, fostering a supportive and compassionate environment within their communities.

Research shows high EQ enhances empathy, communication, and conflict-resolution skills. These are vital for building strong relationships and leading with wisdom. In a Christian context, EQ aligns with the biblical command to love our neighbours as ourselves (Matthew 22:39) and to carry each other's burdens (Galatians 6:2). By developing EQ, leaders can serve their congregations better, showing compassion and understanding in every interaction. Think of EQ as the oil that keeps the gears of a church community running smoothly. As oil reduces friction and allows parts to work harmoniously, EQ helps leaders navigate relationships and manage conflicts without unnecessary tension. By being aware of their own emotions and those of others, church leaders can respond with grace, promoting peace and unity within their communities.

Imagine leading a church group where members are feeling stressed and tense. Instead of reacting defensively, you take a moment to listen, empathise, and address concerns with understanding. This approach helps resolve the conflict and rebuild trust, showing the power of EQ in action.

Practical Tips:

◊ **Practice Self-Awareness:** Check in with your emotions to respond thoughtfully, not impulsively.

◊ **Cultivate Empathy:** Understand others' perspectives to lead with compassion.

◊ **Develop Self-Control:** Stay patient and wise in challenges, setting a positive example.

Reflective Questions:

» How can developing your EQ enhance your church leadership?

» What steps can you take to practice self-awareness and empathy daily?

Exercise: Think of a recent emotional situation. How could emotional intelligence have improved the outcome? Choose one action to boost your EQ in similar situations.

Day 174: Embrace the Unexpected

"People are more comfortable with the familiar discomfort than they are with an unfamiliar new possibility." – Lisa Nichols

Life is full of surprises, and not everything goes as planned. Embracing the unexpected is important for personal growth and resilience. Often, we stick with what we know, even if it's uncomfortable, because the unknown seems more frightening. However, stepping into the unfamiliar can lead to new opportunities, growth, and learning that we would otherwise miss by staying in our comfort zones. Embracing the unexpected means being open to change and seeing new possibilities as opportunities for growth. It's about shifting your mindset from resistance to acceptance, viewing unexpected events not as distractions but as chances to explore new paths. This openness allows you to grow beyond your current limits and experience life in richer ways.

Think of life as a journey with many paths. Sometimes, we stick to a familiar road filled with discomfort simply because it's familiar. When an unexpected detour appears, it might lead to smoother paths or unexpected joy. Being open to these new paths allows you to find happiness and opportunities where you least expect them. Imagine losing a stable job unexpectedly. Instead of focusing on the loss, view it as an opportunity to explore new career paths or develop new skills. This openness to change can lead to greater personal fulfilment.

Practical Tips:

◊ **Stay Open-Minded:** See new possibilities as chances to grow. Flexibility helps you embrace the unexpected.

◊ **Trust the Process:** Believe that change can lead to positive outcomes. Let go of control and trust the journey.

◊ **Take Calculated Risks:** Step out of your comfort zone and embrace new opportunities, even if they're intimidating.

Reflective Questions:

» How do you typically react to unexpected changes?
» What can help you feel more comfortable with the unfamiliar?
» How can embracing the unexpected promote personal and spiritual growth?

Exercise: Think about a recent unexpected event. How did you respond? Write one way to embrace new possibilities positively next time.

Day 175: Quit Complaining

"Do everything without grumbling or arguing." – Philippians 2:14 (NIV)

Complaining may seem harmless, but it can negatively impact your mindset, relationships, and overall well-being. When you complain, you focus on the negative, fueling frustration, discontent, and stress. These emotions shape your actions, making you irritable, less productive, and distant from others. Over time, complaining creates a cycle of negativity that drains energy and clouds our perspective.

Emotions are powerful and contagious. When you complain, you spread negativity to those around you, leading to a toxic environment where dissatisfaction and resentment thrive. In contrast, choosing gratitude shifts your emotions and mindset towards positivity, improving your outlook and uplifting those around you. Think of complaining as carrying a heavy backpack filled with rocks. Each complaint adds another rock, making the load heavier and difficult to carry. By quitting complaining, you remove those rocks, lighten our burden, and make room for more positive, uplifting thoughts. This helps us and creates a more positive atmosphere for everyone around us.

Imagine a co-worker who constantly complains about work. Instead of joining in, you focus on what's going well and discuss ways to improve the situation. Your positive approach sets a constructive example, encouraging others to focus on solutions.

Practical Tips:

◊ **Practice Gratitude:** Focus on what's good in your life instead of what's wrong. Gratitude helps shift your mindset from negativity to positivity.

◊ **Be Solution-Focused:** When faced with challenges, look for solutions rather than complaining. This proactive approach promotes personal growth.

◊ **Reframe Your Thoughts:** Turn complaints into constructive statements. For example, instead of saying, *"I hate this traffic,"* say, *"This time gives me a chance to listen to an interesting podcast."*

Reflective Questions:

» How often do you catch yourself complaining?
» What steps can you take to focus on solutions?
» How can quitting complaining improve your well-being and your environment?

Exercise: Avoid complaining for the next week. Practice gratitude and look for positive aspects in every situation. Observe how this impacts your mood, actions, and interactions with others.

Day 176: Overcoming the Disease to Please

"Am I now trying to win the approval of human beings, or of God?" – Galatians 1:10 (NIV)

The **"disease to please"** is the habit of constantly seeking approval from others, often at the expense of your own well-being. Driven by a fear of rejection or conflict, this behaviour can lead to stress, anxiety, and burnout. Striving to please everyone can prevent you from living authentically and aligning your actions with God's purpose for your life.

Neurotransmitters and hormones play a role in this behaviour. Pleasing others triggers dopamine, creating a temporary emotional high. Over-activation of estrogen, particularly in women, can heighten the need to seek approval to maintain harmony and connection. However, relying on these chemical responses can lead to emotional exhaustion and a cycle of dependency where your self-worth is tied to others' approval rather than your own values and beliefs.

Emotions like fear and guilt often fuel the disease to please. You're afraid of disappointing others and feel guilty if you don't meet their expectations. True peace, however, comes from seeking to please God rather than people. Setting boundaries and learning to say *'no'* is essential for protecting your emotional health and achieving balance.

Do you always say *'yes'* to avoid disappointing others, feeling constantly exhausted? Instead, practice saying 'no' kindly, with respect and honesty. This simple shift will help you protect your well-being, focus on what truly matters, and feel more balanced and at peace.

Practical Tips:

◊ **Practice Self-Awareness:** Regularly check your motivations. Are you acting out of genuine desire or fear of disapproval?

◊ **Set Boundaries:** Start saying *'no'* when necessary. Protecting your well-being is not selfish; it's vital for your mental health.

◊ **Seek God's Approval:** Focus on aligning your actions with God's will rather than seeking approval from others. This brings true peace and fulfilment.

Reflective Questions:

» How often do you find yourself trying to please others at the expense of your own well-being?

» What steps can you take to set healthier boundaries?

» How can focusing on God's approval rather than human approval bring peace and reduce stress?

Day 177: Biblical Examples of Emotional Intelligence

"A soft answer turns away wrath, but a harsh word stirs up anger." – Proverbs 15:1 (ESV)

Emotional intelligence (EQ) is the ability to understand, manage, and respond to emotions effectively. The Bible offers powerful examples of EQ, demonstrating how this trait leads to wisdom, compassion, and effective leadership. By learning from these biblical figures, we can apply EQ in our own lives.

Joseph is a prime example. Despite being sold into slavery by his brothers, Joseph chose forgiveness over revenge, saying, *"You meant evil against me, but God meant it for good"* (Genesis 50:20 ESV). His ability to manage his emotions and see a higher purpose not only restored his family relationships but also saved many lives during a famine.

King Solomon also displayed emotional intelligence. When two women claimed to be the mother of a baby, Solomon suggested cutting the baby in half, knowing the true mother would reveal herself by her willingness to give up her claim to save the child (1 Kings 3:16-28). His understanding of human nature and emotions brought a peaceful resolution.

Jesus Christ embodies the highest level of emotional intelligence. He showed empathy, patience, and compassion, even in betrayal and suffering. Jesus' calmness under pressure and His forgiveness of those who wronged Him are ultimate examples of EQ. When a friend betrays your trust, instead of reacting with anger, you take a moment to understand their perspective and choose to forgive. This act of empathy will heal your relationship and bring you inner peace.

Practical Tips:

◊ **Practice Forgiveness:** Like Joseph, choose forgiveness over resentment. It brings peace and healing.
◊ Seek Wisdom: Like Solomon, use discernment to resolve conflicts effectively.
◊ **Show Compassion:** Follow Jesus' example by showing empathy and kindness, even in challenging situations.

Reflective Questions:

» How do Joseph, Solomon, and Jesus inspire your emotional intelligence?
» When can you choose forgiveness or understanding instead of anger?
» How can showing empathy improve your relationships?

Exercise: Reflect on a recent emotional challenge. Using these biblical examples as a guide, write one way you could respond with more emotional intelligence.

DAY 178: EMOTIONS AROUND MONEY

"If you always do what you always did, you will always get what you always got." –
Unknown

Money is a powerful tool, and your emotions around it can significantly impact
your life. While money itself is neutral, how you think and feel about it can lead to
either empowerment or stress. Viewing money as a tool for good helps develop a
healthy relationship with it, allowing it to come to you and work for you, serving
your goals and needs.

In his book *"We Don't Need Permission,"* Eric Collins emphasises that money should
be seen as a means to create opportunities, not as an end goal. By shifting your
mindset from seeing money as something to hoard to viewing it as a resource
to invest in your dreams, communities, and futures, you open yourself to new
possibilities. This disruptive thinking will enable you to use money as a catalyst for
positive change.

Think of money as a hammer. In the hands of a skilled builder, it can construct
homes and create beauty. In the wrong hands, it can cause damage. It's not the tool
itself that holds power but how you use it. Money can create opportunities, foster
growth, and make a lasting impact when managed wisely and with intention.

If you feel constantly stressed about money, try viewing it as a tool for positive
change: create a budget, set clear goals, practice gratitude, and seek financial advice
to shift from worry to confidence and control.

Practical Tips:

◊ **See Money as a Resource:** Use money to achieve goals and make a difference
rather than view it as a source of stress.
◊ **Invest in Growth:** Allocate money towards personal development, education,
or community projects.
◊ **Practice Generosity:** Sharing resources can bring joy and positively influence
your relationship with money.

Reflective Questions:

» How do your emotions around money affect your decisions?
» What steps can you take to view money more positively?
» How can using money as a tool for growth and generosity improve your life?

Exercise: Reflect on your current financial mindset. Write down one way you can
use money to invest in your personal growth or help others.

Day 179: You Don't Need Permission

"Don't wait for permission to take charge of your own life. You hold the power to create your path." – Unknown

Many people wait for approval from others before taking action, believing you need someone else's permission to pursue your dreams. However, true empowerment comes from realising that you don't need permission to live the life you desire. Waiting for validation will trap you in fear and doubt, preventing you from achieving your desired reality.

God has given each of us unique gifts and a purpose. Believing that you don't need human permission to fulfil your God-given mission helps you live boldly in faith. The Bible encourages us to be courageous, trusting that God equips us for the paths He sets before us. Focusing on God's purpose will help you overcome fear, ignore others' judgments, and build the confidence to act with faith.

Emotional intelligence (EQ) plays a crucial role in this process. Developing EQ allows you to become more aware of your emotions and understand the motivations behind your need for approval. This self-awareness helps rewire your brain from fear-based thinking to confidence. Managing your emotions effectively enables you to take proactive steps toward your goals without waiting for external validation. Think of life as a blank canvas, and you are the artist. Waiting for permission is like holding a paintbrush but being too afraid to paint. Realising you don't need approval lets you boldly create your life into a masterpiece. Taking action without waiting for permission empowers you and builds confidence.

If you want to start a new project but hesitate, take the first step alone. Pray, trust your instincts and build confidence, relying less on others' opinions.

Practical Tips:

◊ **Trust Your Instincts:** Believe in your abilities and decisions.
◊ **Take Small Steps:** Start with one action toward your goal to build confidence.
◊ **Reframe Failure:** View mistakes as learning opportunities.

Reflective Questions:

» What goals have you put on hold, waiting for approval?
» How can you begin to trust your instincts and take action today?
» How would taking control of your choices improve your emotional well-being?

Exercise: Write down one thing you've wanted to do but felt you needed permission for. Take one step toward it today, trusting in your ability.

DAY 180: THE MIND-BODY CONNECTION

"The mind is its own place and in itself, can make a Heaven of Hell, a Hell of Heaven." – John Milton

As we conclude our journey through emotional intelligence, it's crucial to understand how thoughts, feelings, and body sensations work together to shape reality. The brain's neuroplasticity—the ability to form and reorganise connections—allows you to change how you think, feel, and respond. Mastering this connection is essential for living a fulfilling and productive life.

Thoughts trigger emotional responses in the brain, engaging the amygdala (which handles fear and stress) and the hippocampus (which stores memories). These emotions show up physically, affecting heart rate, muscle tension, and overall body state. Negative thoughts can lead to anxiety, causing a racing heart and tense muscles, while positive thoughts can promote calmness and relaxation.

Being aware of your body's signals—such as tight shoulders or a racing heart— helps you trace these feelings back to the thoughts causing them. This awareness is the first step in recognising and managing your emotions. Recognising that your thoughts create feelings that affect your body gives you control. By consciously choosing positive thoughts, you can use neuroplasticity to rewire your brain for better emotional health and resilience.

The Bible reminds us of the importance of aligning our thoughts with faith, hope, and love. Mindful thinking can transform your brain's wiring, fostering emotional well-being and spiritual growth. When you feel your shoulders tense and your heart race before a challenging task, pause and notice these feelings. Identify the anxious thoughts behind them, then shift to thoughts of calm and confidence, reminding yourself of past successes. This change helps calm your body and mind.

Practical Tips:
- ◊ **Body Awareness:** Notice signs of stress, such as a racing heart or tense muscles, to identify negative thought patterns.
- ◊ **Link Thoughts to Emotions:** Acknowledge the thoughts behind your physical sensations to manage your emotional reactions.
- ◊ **Reframe Negative Thoughts:** Replace them with positive affirmations or scripture to gradually rewire your brain.

Reflective Questions:
- » How do your physical sensations reflect your emotional state?
- » What negative thoughts can you start to reframe positively?
- » How can connecting thoughts, feelings, and body improve your well-being?

PART SEVEN

LETTING GO OF THE PAST

PART 7 INTRODUCTION

Letting go of the past is an important step toward living a happier, more fulfilling life. In this section, you'll learn how to release the emotional baggage that holds you back—whether it's regrets, past mistakes, or unmet expectations. Each day will help you understand the impact of your past and guide you through practical steps to heal and move forward.

You'll explore how past experiences shape your thoughts and feelings today and how you can break free from old patterns. By using techniques from neuroscience, emotional intelligence, and scripture, you'll discover how to let go of guilt, regret, and self-doubt. This section will help you forgive yourself, reframe painful memories, and find new meaning in past struggles.

Through reflection, simple exercises, and daily insights, you'll learn how to build resilience, create new positive memories, and embrace change. Letting go of the past isn't about forgetting; it's about freeing yourself to grow and live a life that aligns with who you are today and the future you want to create. Each step you take will help you heal from within and embrace a fresh start.

DAY 181: UNDERSTANDING THE IMPACT OF THE PAST

"The past is a place of reference, not a place of residence; the past is a place of learning, not a place of living."—Roy T. Bennett

Our past, with its joys and pains, shapes who we are today. Each memory influences our thoughts, emotions, and behaviours. Understanding how the past affects us is essential to navigating the present with clarity and intention.

Our brain acts like an archivist, storing past experiences as subconscious memories encoded in neural pathways. When these memories are triggered, the amygdala, the brain's emotional centre, gets activated, causing us to relive those emotions. The hippocampus aids in recalling these memories, which influences our actions, reactions and decisions in the present.

Consider someone who survived a car accident. Each time they drive, the memory may trigger anxiety, even in safe situations. This shows how past events can shape our present emotional responses. I experienced this myself after skidding off an icy road and landing in a ditch. Every time it snowed and I had to drive, my heart would start palpitating rapidly, and I'd become extremely nervous. It wasn't until I worked on rewiring my brain that I could face these situations calmly.

Many people find it difficult to let go of past traumas, often stuck in recurring thoughts and emotional pain. These unresolved issues can lead to negative behaviours, such as avoidance or anger, making it difficult to move forward. Recognising the impact of the past enables you to process and address these experiences. This awareness will help you break free from negative patterns, enhancing emotional resilience and mental well-being.

Practical Tips:

◊ Spend 15 minutes writing about a past experience that affects you.

◊ Reflect on your feelings and consider how you can start to let go, trusting in Jeremiah 29:11 that a hopeful future is possible.

Reflective Questions:

» What past experiences continue to affect you today?
» How do these experiences shape your thoughts and behaviours?
» What steps can you take to begin letting go?

Day 182: Healing Through Acknowledging Triggers

"The first step toward change is awareness. The second step is acceptance."—Nathaniel Brande

Recognising what sets off your emotions is a big step in moving on from the past. Triggers often reflect unresolved wounds. By understanding what provokes strong reactions, you can begin to heal and respond more mindfully rather than being controlled by past experiences.

Triggers activate the brain's amygdala, starting a "fight, flight or freeze" response. This quick reaction often bypasses rational thought (conscious awareness), drawing from past experiences stored in the hippocampus. For instance, someone who faced rejection might feel anxiety or anger when ignored, reflecting unhealed past hurts. A person who experienced frequent criticism as a child; as an adult, even constructive feedback can trigger feelings of inadequacy. This reaction is more tied to past wounds than to what's happening in the present. A colleague's abrupt tone might trigger feelings of worthlessness due to past belittlement.

Recognising the link between past criticism and current feelings reminds you that your worth isn't defined by other people's opinions, allowing for a more grounded response. This awareness of emotional triggers builds emotional intelligence and self-control. Proverbs 25:28 (NIV) teaches, *"Like a city whose walls are broken through is a person who lacks self-control."* Developing self-awareness and resilience helps fortify our emotional boundaries, protecting inner peace.

Practical Tips:

◊ **Recognise Your Triggers:** Pay attention and recognise situations that evoke strong emotions in you.
◊ **Develop Self-Awareness:** Use deep breathing to activate your parasympathetic nervous system, calming the amygdala and allowing your prefrontal cortex to manage emotional reactions more effectively.
◊ **Positive Affirmations:** Replace negative thoughts with affirmations reinforcing your worth and control.

Reflective Questions:

» What situations trigger strong emotions in me?
» How can mindfulness help me pause and respond calmly?
» What affirmations remind me of my strength?

Practical Exercise: Identify one common trigger and journal about it. Explore your feelings and why the trigger affects you. Write down a calming strategy and a positive affirmation to use when the trigger arises. This will empower you to let go of the past.

Day 183: Releasing the Grip of the Past

"Letting go gives us freedom, and freedom is the only condition for happiness." – Thich Nhat Hanh

Letting go of the past is like releasing a rope tied around your heart. Holding onto old hurts, mistakes, or regrets keeps us bound, preventing us from moving forward. By letting go, you free yourself to experience peace and joy. Imagine your mind as a backpack. Every time you cling to anger, resentment, or regret, you add a rock to that backpack. Eventually, it becomes heavy, slowing you down. Letting go is like taking out those rocks, making your journey lighter and more enjoyable.

Neuroscience shows that holding onto past hurts keeps the amygdala—the brain's emotional centre—on high alert, triggering stress responses and releasing cortisol, which can lead to anxiety and physical health issues. Letting go helps activate the prefrontal cortex, the part of the brain that manages rational thought and emotional regulation, allowing us to feel calm and in control.

Emma felt betrayed by a friend, and for years, she replayed the event, feeling the pain repeatedly. She felt a weight lift when she chose to let go, finding joy in new relationships and experiences. Letting go of the past allowed her to embrace the present fully.

Letting go improves mental and physical health, helps us live in the present, and opens the door to new opportunities. Philippians 3:13-14 reminds us to forget what lies behind and press forward to what lies ahead.

Practical Tips:

- ◊ **Visualise Letting Go:** Imagine removing a rock from your backpack each time you release a painful memory.
- ◊ **Practice Gratitude:** Focus on the positives in your life to shift your mindset.
- ◊ **Use Affirmations:** Remind yourself, "I am free to move forward."

Reflective Questions:

- » What past events are you still holding onto?
- » How can letting go improve your present life?
- » What step can you take today to start letting go?

Exercise: Write down any grudges or regrets. Tear up the paper, symbolising your decision to let them go. Feel the relief that comes with release.

Day 184: Forgive Yourself

"Forgive yourself for not knowing what you didn't know before you learned it." – Maya Angelou

Forgiving yourself is like releasing a heavy burden that holds you back. It's essential for emotional healing, freeing you from guilt, shame, and self-blame and allowing you to move forward with peace and positivity. Self-forgiveness reduces negative emotions and fosters self-compassion. It rewires the brain to create a healthier self-image and boosts emotional resilience. By practising self-forgiveness, you calm the amygdala, which is responsible for fear and anxiety, and strengthen the prefrontal cortex, which handles rational thought and self-reflection.

Imagine making a mistake at work that causes a minor setback. You might feel guilty and replay the error over and over in your mind. Practising self-forgiveness allows you to acknowledge the mistake, learn from it, and focus on moving forward instead of being stuck in regret. Forgiving yourself is often harder than forgiving others. Self-blame can become a habit, keeping you trapped in the past and making it difficult to grow. Without self-forgiveness, mistakes can weigh you down, leading to feelings of unworthiness and holding back your progress.

Self-forgiveness is a powerful way to boost self-esteem, build emotional resilience, and improve your mental health. It helps you accept your mistakes, learn from them, and let them go. By freeing yourself from self-blame, you create space for growth, new opportunities, and a happier, more fulfilling life.

Practical Tips:

◊ **Practice Self-Compassion:** Speak to yourself kindly, as you would to a friend. Acknowledge mistakes without harsh judgment, focusing on growth.

◊ **Reframe:** Notice when self-criticism arises. Take a deep breath and replace negative thoughts with affirmations of self-worth.

◊ **Reflect on Growth:** Write down what you've learned from your mistakes and how they've helped you grow.

Reflective Questions:

» What past mistakes do you need to forgive yourself for?
» What steps can you take today to practice self-compassion?

Exercise: Spend 10 minutes writing a letter to yourself, acknowledging a mistake, offering forgiveness, and noting what you've learned. Revisit it when guilt resurfaces to remind yourself of the power of self-forgiveness.

Day 185: Releasing Regret

"Regret is insight that comes a day too late." – Anonymous

Regret can feel like an anchor dragging you through life, holding you back from moving forward. Whether it's about missed opportunities, choices you can't change, or dreams that slipped away, clinging to regret prevents you from enjoying the present and embracing the future.

Regret isn't just a passing thought. It lingers in your mind, influencing how you see yourself and your possibilities. Constantly replaying past mistakes keeps the brain's emotional centre, the amygdala, in a heightened state of alert. This can cause feelings of guilt, sadness, and self-doubt, all of which weigh on your sense of self and your future goals. When you dwell on regret, you might start to believe it's too late to change or that you've missed your chance at success.

Think about a time you regretted not following a passion. Maybe you stayed in a job that didn't fulfil you because it seemed safer. The regret of missed chances can lead you to believe there's no time left to pursue new goals. However, research on neuroplasticity shows that you can rewire your brain, forming new neural pathways by focusing on the present and future. This process can shift your mindset from one of regret to one of opportunity. Imagine trying to drive a car while constantly looking in the rearview mirror. You wouldn't get very far, would you? Regret works the same way. It slows your progress and keeps you stuck. But by letting go of regret, you free up mental space for growth, creativity, and forward movement.

Letting go of regret doesn't mean forgetting the past; it means learning from it. By releasing regret, you can take on new challenges and succeed in areas that still excite you.

Practical Tips:

◊ Be Kind To Yourself: Recognise your mistakes but avoid harsh self-judgment.
◊ Focus Forward: Set goals based on what you can do today.
◊ Reframe Regrets: See them as lessons, not failures.

Reflective Questions:

» What regrets are holding you back?
» How can releasing regret help you grow?
» What positive step can you take today?

Exercise: Write down a regret and reflect on what you've learned from it. Then, write a new goal that aligns with your current values.

DAY 186: REFRAMING PAST EXPERIENCES

"You can't change the past, but you can change how you view it." – Anonymous

We all have moments from our past that weigh us down—times we regret or feel ashamed of. But how you look at these experiences can shape your future. Reframing them can turn those moments into valuable lessons instead of letting them hold you back. The **FACED Framework—Focus, Accept, Challenge, Embrace, Decide**—can help you see things differently.

Focus: Start by thinking about the experience that bothers you. Don't push it away; allow yourself to feel it. Facing it is the first step to healing.
Accept: Accept what happened without blaming yourself. Everyone makes mistakes, and facing challenges is part of life. Accepting doesn't mean you agree with what happened; it just means you recognise it's part of your story.
Challenge: Challenge your negative thoughts about the experience. Are these thoughts fair? Are they true? Sometimes, we hold on to beliefs that aren't helping us and keep us stuck.
Embrace: Look for the lessons in what happened. What did you learn about yourself, others, and life? Turning a bad experience into a learning moment helps you grow.
Decide: Choose to move forward with a new outlook. See your past as steps that have brought you to where you are today, not as mistakes holding you back. Use what you've learned to make better choices from now on.

If you regret not pursuing a different career, use *FACED*. Focus on those feelings, accept what happened, challenge the belief that it's too late, embrace what you've learned, and decide to explore new opportunities now.
Reframing your past helps lighten your emotional burden, strengthens you, and turns pain into power.

Practical Tips:

◊ **Write It Down:** Use a journal to review each *FACED* step.
◊ **Practice Regularly:** Use this technique whenever painful memories come up.
◊ **Talk to Someone:** Share your experience with a trusted friend or neurocoach.

Reflective Questions:

» What past experience do you need to reframe?
» How can the FACED technique help you see it differently?
» What positive lessons can you take from it?

Exercise: Pick an experience that still affects you. Reframe it using the *FACED* technique and write down each step to see how your feelings change.

Day 187: Finding Meaning in Adversity

"The struggle you're in today is developing the strength you need for tomorrow." – Robert Tew

Life's challenges can feel like walking through a dark tunnel with no end in sight. But even in the darkest times, there's always a glimmer of light—finding meaning in your struggles can be that light. Adversity has a way of shaping us, building strength and character we didn't know we had. Your brain is incredibly adaptable. When you face tough times, it's like your brain is lifting emotional weights, getting stronger with each challenge. The amygdala, your brain's emotional centre, triggers stress, but your prefrontal cortex steps in to find solutions and make sense of the situation. This is how we turn pain into purpose. Viktor Frankl, who survived the horrors of the Holocaust, taught that finding meaning even in suffering can bring hope and resilience. He believed that no matter how difficult life gets, we can choose how we respond.

Imagine you've lost your job. The fear and uncertainty are real. But what if this loss is an opportunity in disguise? Maybe it's the push you need to pursue a passion you've always put on hold, or perhaps it's a chance to find a job that truly aligns with your values. Seeing the situation this way turns a setback into a new beginning. Romans 5:3-4 (ESV) reminds us, *"We rejoice in our sufferings, knowing that suffering produces endurance, and endurance produces character, and character produces hope."* This verse shows us that hard times are not just obstacles but stepping stones to building a stronger, more hopeful self. Consider someone who faced a health scare and used that experience to become an advocate for healthy living, inspiring others along the way. Their adversity became their mission.

Practical Tips:

◊ **Look for the Lesson:** What can this challenge teach you? Maybe it's patience, resilience, or empathy.

◊ **Set New Intentions:** Use this time to set goals that align more closely with your values.

◊ **Focus on Gratitude:** Even in tough times, there's always something to be thankful for.

Reflective Questions:

» What challenges are you facing now?
» How can you find meaning in the situation?
» What steps can you take today to turn this adversity into a positive force?

Exercise: Write down a recent challenge and what it taught you. Then, list one action to turn it into a meaningful step forward.

Day 188: Letting Go of Unmet Expectations

"Expectations are resentments waiting to happen." – Anne Lamott

We all have dreams about how our lives should turn out. Maybe you imagined a different career, a perfect relationship, or hitting certain milestones by now. When things don't go as planned, it's easy to feel disappointed and stuck in the past. Letting go of these unmet expectations is crucial for finding peace, fully embracing the present and achieving your desired future.

Expectations often come from our hopes and what we see around us. You feel frustrated or sad when reality doesn't match up, replaying *"what if"* scenarios. This keeps you anchored to the past. Letting go of these expectations helps you realise that while you can't control everything, you can control how you respond. This shift frees you from the weight of the past and allows you to see the possibilities right before you. Think about a time when a relationship didn't work out as you hoped. Maybe you've been holding onto how things should have been, replaying conversations and moments, feeling regret. Holding onto those unmet expectations keeps you stuck. But when you decide to let go, you create space for new relationships and experiences that bring you joy.

Proverbs 19:21 (NIV) says, *"Many are the plans in a person's heart, but it is the Lord's purpose that prevails."* This verse reminds us that our plans don't always go how we want, but trusting that God is in control will help you let go of unmet expectations and have hope in the future outcome.

Practical Tips:

◊ **Shift Your Focus:** Look for the opportunities and blessings in your current situation, even if they're different from what you expected.

◊ **Practice Acceptance:** Recognise your feelings about unmet expectations, then consciously choose to release them.

◊ **Stay Present:** Focus on what you can enjoy today instead of dwelling on what you thought should happen.

Reflective Questions:

» What expectations from the past are you holding onto?
» How could letting go of these expectations open up new possibilities for you?
» What can you appreciate about your life right now?

Exercise: Write down one expectation from your past that didn't turn out as planned. Reflect on how holding onto it has affected you. Write down one positive outcome or opportunity from letting go of an unmet expectation. Commit to focusing on what you can enjoy and appreciate today.

DAY 189: UNDERSTANDING REGRET

"Regret doesn't remind us that we did badly—it reminds us that we know we can do better." – Kathryn Schulz

Everyone experiences regret at some point. Whether it's a missed opportunity, an unspoken word, or a choice you wish you'd made differently, regret can feel like a weight on your shoulders, holding you back from moving forward. However, understanding and processing regret can turn it into a powerful tool for personal growth.

Regret happens when you believe you made a wrong choice or missed out on something important. It often triggers feelings of anxiety and stress because the brain's emotional centre, the amygdala, is activated. Dwelling on regret can make you feel stuck, replaying mistakes repeatedly. But here's the good news: neuroscience shows that when we reflect on regret constructively, it activates the parts of the brain involved in learning and decision-making. This allows us to grow from the experience and make better choices in the future.

Can you recall a time when you wished you'd contacted a friend sooner? That feeling may have been painful, but it can also teach you to be more present and open in your relationships. Understanding that regret is natural can shift your focus from what went wrong to how you can improve. Proverbs 28:13 (NIV) reminds us, *"Whoever conceals their sins does not prosper, but the one who confesses and renounces them finds mercy."* When we acknowledge our regrets and learn from them, we allow ourselves to grow and heal, making room for better decisions in the future.

Practical Tips:

◊ **Acknowledge Your Regret:** Accept that regret is a normal and natural part of life.
◊ **Reflect, Don't Dwell:** Use regret as a tool to learn from, not a reason to punish yourself.
◊ **Focus on Growth:** Let your regrets inspire positive changes in your behaviour and choices.

Reflective Questions:

» What regrets are you holding onto?
» How can understanding these regrets help you grow?
» What lessons can you learn from your past decisions?

Exercise: Write down one regret you've been holding onto. Reflect on what it taught you about yourself and identify one positive change you can make because of that experience.

DAY 190: STRATEGIES TO OVERCOME REGRET

"Don't regret the past, just learn from it." – Ben Ipock

Regret can feel like a burden, weighing you down and keeping you stuck in the past. But regret doesn't have to control your life. By using effective strategies, you can overcome regret, learn from your experiences, and move forward with a lighter heart. Holding onto regret is like carrying a backpack full of heavy stones. It drains your energy and keeps you from focusing on the present and future. Letting go of regret helps reduce stress and activates areas of the brain involved in planning and positive thinking. By developing healthy coping strategies, you can transform regret from a source of pain into a catalyst for growth.

Imagine wanting to follow a passion but never starting. You might regret waiting so long, and that regret could stop you from trying now because you're afraid it's too late. Letting go of regret helps you move forward, try new things, and live a more fulfilling life. Isaiah 43:18-19 (NIV) reminds us, *"Forget the former things; do not dwell on the past. See, I am doing a new thing!"* This verse encourages us to let go of past regrets and embrace the new possibilities that lie ahead.

Lucy regretted not pursuing her passion for art when she was younger. She spent years in jobs that didn't fulfil her, always thinking it was too late to change. But by focusing on strategies to overcome regret, Lucy began taking art classes in the evenings and now paints joyfully. She used her regret as motivation to explore her creativity, now realising it's never too late to follow her passions.

Practical Tips:

◊ **Practice Self-Compassion:** Treat yourself with the kindness you would offer a friend who feels regretful.

◊ **Reframe Your Thoughts:** Instead of focusing on what you did wrong, think about what you can do differently now.

◊ **Set New Goals:** Use regret as a motivator to set goals that align with your current values and desires.

Reflective Questions:

» How does holding onto regret affect your happiness?
» What steps can you take to let go of regret?
» How can you use past regrets to inspire positive changes today?

Exercise: Write down a regret you've been carrying. Identify one lesson you've learned from it. Then, set a goal or action step you can take today that reflects this lesson and helps you move forward.

DAY 191: BUILDING A POSITIVE FUTURE

"Forgetting what is behind and straining toward what is ahead, I press on toward the goal to win the prize for which God has called me heavenward in Christ Jesus." – Philippians 3:13-14 (NIV)

Imagine trying to drive while only looking in the rearview mirror. You wouldn't get far without crashing. Building a positive future means letting go of what's behind and focusing on what's ahead. It's about setting goals, making a plan, and taking action to create a life that excites and fulfils you. When you set goals, your brain releases dopamine, the "feel-good" chemical that boosts motivation and keeps you focused. This shift helps you move from past regrets to the exciting possibilities of the future. Instead of being stuck in "what ifs," you become energised by what you can achieve.

Think of someone who regrets not following their passion for writing. Instead of letting that regret define them, they start a blog or write in their free time. This action reignites their joy, turning regret into motivation and a sense of purpose for the future. It's normal to feel discouraged if past mistakes make you doubt your ability to achieve your goals. Breaking big goals into smaller, manageable steps can help you celebrate progress and build momentum. Each small victory makes the past feel less significant. Setting and achieving goals boosts confidence, provides purpose, and improves overall happiness. Focusing on the future frees you from the past, opening doors to new growth and opportunities.

When I started my Neuroleadership business, my subconscious brain reminded me of past failures, whispering fears of another failure. I battled those doubts but focused on my passion and vision. Thank God I did because now I'm doing what I love and impacting people globally. This is a reminder that the past doesn't define the future; moving forward does.

Practical Exercise:

◊ Choose one goal that excites you.
◊ Break it into three smaller, actionable steps. Start with one today.
◊ Notice how focusing on your future helps you let go of the past.

Reflective Questions:

» What goals do you have for your future?
» How can you break these goals into smaller steps?
» What can you do today to start moving toward your dreams?

Day 192: The Role of Brain-Based Coaching

"The first step toward getting somewhere is to decide that you are not going to stay where you are." – J.P. Morgan

Everyone needs a coach. Whether you're trying to overcome challenges, break free from negative patterns, or achieve new goals, having a guide can make all the difference. Neurocoaching—also called brain-based coaching—takes this further by using the science of how your brain works to help you create lasting change and unlock your potential.

Your brain holds onto past experiences, particularly negative ones, as a way of protecting you. These experiences form neural pathways that shape how you think, react, and make decisions. Neurocoaching helps you understand these patterns and, more importantly, change them. Through the power of neuroplasticity—the brain's ability to rewire itself—you can let go of limiting beliefs, adopt empowering thoughts, and create a future focused on growth and success.

Imagine feeling stuck because of a past failure, like missing an important opportunity or making a decision that didn't go as planned. Neurocoaching can help you recognise how these experiences influence your current mindset. It allows you to reframe your thoughts, see possibilities instead of barriers, and take action with clarity and confidence. As Isaiah 43:18 (NIV) says, *"Forget the former things; do not dwell on the past."* Neurocoaching helps you do just that—shifting your focus from regrets to the possibilities ahead.

Practical Steps to Get Started:

◊ **Find a Neurocoach:** Look for a coach who specializes in brain-based coaching to guide you through rewiring your thought patterns.

◊ **Reflect:** Consider areas of your life where you feel stuck. How might neurocoaching help you move forward?

◊ **Take Action:** Commit to working with a neurocoach to set clear goals and develop new ways of thinking that support your growth.

Reflective Questions:

» What challenges or thought patterns are holding you back?
» How could a neurocoach help you address these?
» What first step can you take today to explore neurocoaching?

Investing in a neurocoach is an investment in your future. Neurocoaching empowers you to rewire your thoughts, break free from limitations, and maximise your full potential.

Day 193: The Role of Therapy and Counselling

"Plans fail for lack of counsel, but with many advisers, they succeed." – Proverbs 15:22 (NIV)

Therapy and counselling provide a safe space to explore and address past traumas, emotional pain, and harmful behavioural patterns. With professional guidance, you can develop healthier coping mechanisms, understand your emotions better, and learn how to move forward with a lighter heart.

Various therapies, such as cognitive-behavioural therapy (CBT), psychodynamic therapy, and Eye Movement Desensitization and Reprocessing (EMDR), are highly effective in treating mental health issues. These therapies work by helping to rewire the brain, creating new, healthier thought patterns and behaviours. For example, CBT focuses on changing negative thinking, while EMDR helps process and heal from traumatic memories, allowing for emotional release and recovery.

If you're dealing with anxiety and depression, regular counselling sessions can help you uncover the root causes of your emotions, like past traumas or ongoing stress. A therapist can guide you in understanding and developing effective strategies to manage these feelings. Over time, you feel more in control of your emotions and start experiencing improved mental well-being. Seeking therapy can be daunting. Many people feel a stigma or fear of being vulnerable about their struggles. Admitting the need for help may feel like admitting weakness, but it's a sign of strength and a step toward healing. Therapy can significantly improve mental health, emotional regulation, and overall well-being. It provides tools to manage stress, anxiety, and other mental health issues effectively. Therapy also helps you gain insights into yourself, build healthier relationships, and find a renewed sense of purpose and joy.

Practical Tips:

◊ If you're struggling with past traumas or emotional pain, consider seeking therapy.
◊ Find a licensed therapist specialising in the areas you need help with. Therapy is an investment in your mental and emotional health.

Reflective Questions:

» How can therapy help you address past traumas and emotional pain?
» What fears or hesitations do you have about seeking therapy?
» How could professional guidance improve your mental and emotional well-being?

Disclaimer: This content is for informational purposes only and is not a substitute for professional medical or psychological advice, diagnosis, or treatment.

Day 194: Rewire the Past with Scripture

"Healing doesn't mean the damage never existed. It means the damage no longer controls our lives." – Unknown

Spiritual practices like prayer, meditation, and reading scripture offer powerful tools for healing past wounds. These practices connect you with God, providing comfort, peace, and a sense of purpose. Engaging in these practices helps you release past hurts and find the strength to move forward.

Studies show that spiritual practices significantly reduce stress and improve emotional regulation. Research in the Journal of Religion and Health highlights that these practices lower cortisol levels, the body's main stress hormone. Brain imaging studies reveal that prayer and meditation activate the prefrontal cortex, which manages emotions and self-control, helping you handle stress better. They also reduce activity in the amygdala, the brain's fear centre, making you less reactive to anxiety. Moreover, spiritual practices boost serotonin and dopamine, neurotransmitters that enhance mood and promote well-being. This combination creates a calmer, more centred state, making it easier to handle emotional pain and life's challenges.

Setting time aside daily for prayer or meditation enables you to reflect and provides solace and strength when you feel overwhelmed. Reading scripture offers guidance and comfort, helping to heal emotional wounds and bring clarity. Regular spiritual practices lead to emotional healing, increased resilience, and inner peace. They offer a foundation and connection to God, supporting you through life.

Practical Tips:

◊ Dedicate a specific time each day to spiritual practices.
◊ Whether you start your day with prayer, end it with scripture, or take a moment for meditation, consistency is key to spiritual growth and healing.

Reflective Questions:

» How can spiritual practices help you heal from past emotional wounds?
» Which spiritual practices resonate most with you, and why?
» How can making time for these practices improve your overall well-being?

Exercise: Spend a few minutes each day reflecting on a scripture. Write down your thoughts and how God's word applies to your life.

Day 195: Creating New Memories

"Forget the former things; do not dwell on the past. See, I am doing a new thing!" – Isaiah 43:18-19 (NIV)

Life is like a book with many chapters, and you have the power to write the next one. Creating new memories is vital to letting go of past hurts and embracing a brighter future. By focusing on the present and seeking new experiences, you can fill your life with joy, replacing old, painful memories with positive ones.

Your brain is like a garden; the memories you focus on are the seeds you water. Creating new, positive experiences plants fresh seeds that can grow and push out the weeds of past pain. Neuroscience shows that our brains can form new pathways when we engage in joyful activities. These new connections make it easier to focus on the good and less on past pain.

Think of a time when you felt stuck. Maybe you tried something new, like joining a cooking class or volunteering. Those new experiences brought joy and a sense of accomplishment. Over time, these moments became new memories that lifted your spirit and shifted your focus from the past to the possibilities of the future. Sticking to routines is easy, especially when the past feels heavy. But taking small steps, like trying a new hobby or exploring a different place, can start to change your outlook and how you feel and think about life.

Creating new empowering memories fills your life with positive energy, reduces stress, and boosts happiness. It opens your heart to new possibilities and helps you see life with fresh eyes.

Practical Tips:

◊ Make a list of simple, new activities to try, like visiting a local park, learning a new hobby, or meeting new people.
◊ Start with one and notice how it changes your mood.

Reflective Questions:

» What new experiences can you try to replace old, negative memories?
» How can trying new things help you feel more alive?
» What steps can you take today to start building positive memories?

Exercise: Plan a "new experience day" each month. Do something new, like exploring a new place or learning a new skill. Write down how it made you feel.

DAY 196: BUILDING RESILIENCE FOR THE FUTURE

"Do not judge me by my success, judge me by how many times I fell down and got back up again." – Nelson Mandela

By building resilience, you create the capacity to bounce back from setbacks, disappointments, and painful memories. Resilience helps you survive challenges and thrive despite them, enabling you to let go of the past and embrace a hopeful future.

Resilience is the ability to adapt and recover from adversity. It's a vital skill that helps you manage stress, overcome obstacles, and continue moving forward, no matter what life throws at you. Studies show that resilient people are better at regulating their emotions, maintaining a positive outlook, and finding solutions to problems. Building resilience strengthens the neural pathways in your brain associated with problem-solving and emotional regulation, making you better equipped to handle future challenges.

Think of a time when life didn't go as planned—like losing a job or facing a personal setback. People who build resilience use these moments to learn and grow. They see challenges not as roadblocks but as opportunities for personal development. This mindset helps them navigate life's ups and downs with grace and optimism.

Building resilience doesn't happen overnight. It requires practice and patience. Staying positive when things go wrong can be challenging, but resilience allows you to see beyond the immediate pain and look toward a brighter future. Developing resilience helps you let go of past hurts, reduce anxiety, and build confidence. It also provides a foundation for handling future difficulties and keeps you focused on growth and healing.

Practical Tips:

◊ Practice resilience by setting small, achievable goals.
◊ Celebrate each success, no matter how minor, to build confidence.
◊ Surround yourself with supportive people who encourage you.

Reflective Questions:

» How can building resilience help you let go of the past?
» What steps can you take today to strengthen your resilience?
» How have past challenges helped you grow and become stronger?

Exercise: Reflect on a past challenge you overcame. Write down what you learned from that experience and how it strengthened you. Use this reflection to remind yourself of your resilience.

DAY 197: MOVING FORWARD WITH CONFIDENCE

"Believe you can, and you're halfway there." – Theodore Roosevelt

Confidence is the foundation that helps you take the next step, no matter how uncertain the path may seem. Moving forward confidently means trusting in your abilities and the lessons you've learned from the past. It's about having faith that, even if you face challenges, you are equipped through Yeshua to handle them and continue growing.

Confidence is not about being fearless; it's about taking action despite the fear. Neuroscience shows that confidence can actually change the way your brain operates. When you confidently approach situations, your brain releases chemicals like dopamine, which enhance motivation and help you stay focused. This positive mindset activates the prefrontal cortex, the part of the brain responsible for planning and decision-making, helping you navigate challenges more effectively.

Imagine walking into a room full of strangers for a networking event. If you enter confidently, believing in your ability to connect and communicate, you're more likely to engage with others and leave a positive impression. Even if you feel nervous, acting confidently can change the outcome and your perception of the experience. It's normal to feel unsure, especially after experiencing failure or setbacks. Doubt can creep in from your subconscious mind, making you question your abilities. But moving forward with confidence doesn't mean having all the answers; it means trusting that you can figure things out along the way. Confidence helps you make decisions more easily and quickly, pursue opportunities you might otherwise avoid, and handle criticism or failure gracefully. It gives you the courage to try new things, knowing that each step forward is a step toward growth.

Practical Tips:

◊ Start each day with a positive affirmation about your abilities.
◊ Remind yourself of past successes and how you overcame challenges.
◊ This practice can boost your self-esteem and prepare you for the day ahead.

Reflective Questions:

» What areas of your life would benefit from more confidence?
» How can past challenges you've overcome boost your confidence now?
What small steps can you take today to act with more confidence?

Exercise: List three things you're confident about. Reflect on how these strengths have helped you and how they can support you moving forward.

Day 198: Rebuilding Self-Esteem

"No one can make you feel inferior without your consent." – Eleanor Roosevelt

Letting go of the past is essential to nurturing your self-worth and seeing yourself as God sees you: a beloved child, a joint heir with Jesus Christ, part of a royal priesthood, and God's special possession.

Self-esteem is the inner voice that tells you how valuable you are. When that voice is shaped by past mistakes or harsh criticism, it can lead to self-doubt and insecurity. Rebuilding self-esteem means replacing those negative messages with positive truths. Studies show that individuals with healthy self-esteem experience lower levels of anxiety, make better choices, and are more resilient in the face of adversity. This shift transforms how you feel about yourself and how you approach the world around you.

Psalm 139:14 (NIV) says, "I praise you because I am fearfully and wonderfully made." 1 Peter 2:9 (NIV) says, *"But you are a chosen people, a royal priesthood, a holy nation, God's special possession..."* These scriptures remind us of our inherent worth, encouraging us to let go of past failures and embrace our true identity.

Letting go of past negativity and rebuilding self-esteem leads to better mental health, stronger relationships, and the courage to pursue your dreams without fear.

Practical Tips:

◊ Keep a journal of positive affirmations and achievements.
◊ Write down three things you appreciate about yourself daily to shift your focus from past negativity to present strengths.

Reflective Questions:

» What past experiences are affecting your self-esteem?
» How can focusing on your God-given identity help rebuild your confidence?
» What small habits can you start to boost your self-worth?

Exercise: Stand in front of a mirror and affirm confidently, "I am fearfully and wonderfully made." Practice this daily to nurture self-esteem and build confidence.

Day 199: Letting Go with Self-Compassion

"You are imperfect, you are wired for struggle, but you are worthy of love and belonging." – Brené Brown

Self-compassion means treating yourself with the same kindness and understanding you'd offer a close friend, especially when dealing with past mistakes or regrets. It's about accepting your humanity and recognising that you are worthy of forgiveness and grace. Practising self-compassion helps you let go of the past and adopt a more positive outlook on life.

Research by Dr. Kristin Neff shows that self-compassion reduces anxiety, depression, and self-criticism. It provides an emotional safety net, allowing you to acknowledge pain without being consumed by it. Think of self-compassion as a gentle hug for your soul, helping you soothe yourself rather than resort to harsh judgment. This practice releases oxytocin, the "love hormone," promoting feelings of comfort and connection, which support emotional healing.

Psalm 34:18 (NIV) says, *"The Lord is close to the brokenhearted and saves those who are crushed in spirit."* This scripture reminds us of God's love in our brokenness. Practising self-compassion allows you to mirror this divine love towards yourself. Picture spilling coffee on yourself during a meeting. Instead of criticising yourself for being clumsy, practice self-compassion by saying, "It's okay. Everyone makes mistakes." This approach helps you handle daily mishaps with grace, reducing the emotional burden of self-criticism. Many believe being hard on themselves leads to improvement. However, studies show that self-compassion actually enhances motivation and personal growth more effectively than harsh self-criticism.

Self-compassion helps you let go of past mistakes, reduces shame, and promotes well-being. It builds resilience, enabling you to handle challenges calmly and confidently.

Practical Tips:

◊ When you notice negative self-talk, pause and ask, *"How would I comfort a friend?"*
◊ Offer yourself those same kind words.

Reflective Questions:

» How do you usually respond to your own mistakes?
» What can you do to practice more self-compassion?

Exercise: Write a compassionate letter to yourself about a recent mistake. Focus on understanding and forgiveness. Re-read it when you need a reminder to be kind to yourself.

Day 200: Embracing Change To Let Go

"There is a time for everything, and a season for every activity under the heavens." –
Ecclesiastes 3:1 (NIV)

Embracing change is essential for letting go of the past. It means being open to new
experiences and adapting to new circumstances. Accepting change allows you to
heal, grow, and thrive in ways you never imagined, freeing you from the grip of
past regrets or failures.

The brain's ability to adapt helps form new connections when you face new
experiences. Embracing change activates this process, breaking old patterns and
fostering healthier ways of thinking. Think of neuroplasticity as your brain's way
of clearing out old, unhelpful thoughts to make space for positive ones. Letting
go of the past and accepting change enhances creativity, emotional resilience, and
personal growth.

Ecclesiastes 3:1 (NIV) reminds us, *"There is a time for everything, and a season for every
activity under the heavens."* This scripture encourages us to trust in God's timing
and release the past, understanding that each new season brings opportunities
for growth and renewal. Leaving an old job that no longer fulfils you can be
challenging. However, starting a new role offers fresh opportunities, new skills, and
a sense of purpose. By embracing this change, you let go of past dissatisfaction and
move forward with excitement.

Letting go of the past can be challenging because it feels safe and familiar. Fear of
the unknown can make change uncomfortable. However, focusing on the growth
potential can help you rewire your brain to overcome this fear and adapt more
quickly. Letting go of the past by embracing change fosters personal growth,
builds resilience, and opens up new opportunities. It enables you to navigate life's
transitions with confidence and hope.

Practical Tips:

◊ When facing change, remind yourself it's a chance to grow.
◊ Focus on what you can learn and how you can improve.
◊ A positive mindset can make transitions smoother.

Reflective Questions:

» How can embracing change help you let go of past hurts or regrets?
» What areas of your life need a fresh perspective?
» How can you stay positive when facing change?

Exercise: Identify an area in your life where you need to let go of the past and
embrace change. Write down simple steps to adapt, highlighting the benefits of this
change.

Day 201: Healing from Within

"Your genetics load the gun. Your lifestyle pulls the trigger." – Dr. Mehmet Oz

The link between our past, our genes, and our health is powerful. While genetics plays a role in our predispositions, the study of epigenetics shows that our lifestyle choices, thoughts, and emotions significantly influence how our genes are expressed. Letting go of past emotional pain can positively impact health, reducing the risk of disease and promoting well-being. **Epigenetics** reveals that while our DNA is fixed, our environment and emotional state can alter gene expression. Stress, trauma, and negative emotions can activate genes linked to inflammation, heart disease, anxiety, and depression. Conversely, positive lifestyle choices—such as forgiveness, reducing stress, and maintaining a positive mindset—can positively influence gene expression, promoting healing and well-being. Think of your genes as light switches that your thoughts and actions can turn on or off.

Proverbs 17:22 (NIV) says, *"A cheerful heart is good medicine, but a crushed spirit dries up the bones."* This scripture highlights the healing power of a positive outlook and the harm caused by holding onto emotional pain. Embracing forgiveness and joy can lead to healing both emotionally and physically.

Imagine someone constantly replaying past mistakes, resulting in chronic stress. This stress can manifest physically as headaches, high blood pressure, or digestive issues. By choosing to let go, practice forgiveness, and focus on positive thoughts, they can reduce stress and improve mental and physical health. Letting go of the past can feel difficult, especially when it's ingrained in your identity. However, understanding that your mindset affects your physical health makes releasing past burdens essential for overall well-being. Releasing past hurts and embracing positivity can improve health, reduce inflammation, and lower the risk of chronic diseases. It promotes overall well-being and empowers you to take control of your health.

Practical Tip:

◊ Practice meditation, deep breathing, or regular exercise to focus on the present, encouraging healthier gene expression.

Reflective Questions:

» How might your past emotions affect your physical health?
» What steps can you take to let go of past hurts?

Exercise: Write down past grievances you're holding onto. Reflect on how they might affect your health. Commit to a daily practice of letting go through prayer, meditation, or talking with a trusted friend.

Day 202: New Wine in New Wineskins

"And no one pours new wine into old wineskins. Otherwise, the new wine will burst the skins…" – Luke 5:37 (NIV)

Letting go of the past is like replacing old wineskins with new ones to hold fresh wine. If you cling to old habits, thoughts, or past hurts, you can't fully embrace life's new opportunities and growth. To live a fulfilled and transformed life, you need to create space for positive change by releasing outdated patterns and emotional baggage.

Old wineskins symbolise a rigid, fixed mindset way of thinking and feeling. Trying to hold on to past hurts or negative beliefs is like storing fresh wine in brittle, old skins—it leads to a breakdown. Letting go of the past allows you to create new 'wineskins'—a growth mindset and healthier emotional spaces. Doing this opens you to personal and professional growth, healing, and new possibilities to enable you to achieve your desired goals.

Holding onto past hurt makes it hard to fully connect in a new relationship. Emotional baggage from the past can damage fresh opportunities, just like trying to pour new wine into old wineskins—it doesn't work. To experience love fully, you need to let go of the pain and make room for something new. Letting go of past pain allows you to trust and love again. Letting go can be scary because it feels like losing a part of yourself. But holding onto the past prevents new growth. It's not about forgetting but learning from past experiences to move forward stronger. By letting go of the past, you embrace new experiences with an open heart. This fosters personal growth, emotional healing, and healthier relationships. Becoming a 'new wineskin' prepares you to receive life's blessings fully.

Practical Tips:

◊ Identify something you need to release from your past—old hurt, regret, or limiting belief.

◊ Focus on how letting go can make room for new growth.

Reflective Questions:

» What old habits or thoughts are holding you back from embracing new opportunities?

» How can letting go of the past help you grow?

» What steps can you take today to be a 'new wineskin' ready for new blessings?

Exercise: Write down one past hurt or belief you're holding onto. Reflect on how releasing it will create space for new experiences. Commit to one small action today.

Day 203: Navigating Emotions from the Past

"You don't have to control your thoughts; you just have to stop letting them control you." – Dan Millman

Navigating emotions from the past is essential for letting go. Past experiences can linger, causing emotions like guilt, anger, or sadness to resurface. Managing these emotions will give you peace and allow you to progress rather than be stuck in what has already happened.

Our brains are wired to remember emotional events, especially intense or painful ones. These memories shape how we react to new situations. Through neuroplasticity, you can change your response to old emotions by forming new thought patterns. When triggers bring up past feelings, it's your brain signalling unresolved pain. Navigating these emotions shifts you from automatic reactions to thoughtful responses.

A comment from a colleague might trigger feelings of inadequacy rooted in a past job. Instead of reacting defensively, acknowledge the emotion as a remnant of your past. Use emotional intelligence (EQ) strategies like deep breathing and reframing your thoughts. Remind yourself, *"This is about my past, not my present. I choose to respond differently."*

Emotions that have become habitual can easily trap you. Accepting these feelings without judgment and using tools like mindfulness and journaling can help process them, reducing their hold on you. Navigating past emotions brings emotional freedom, reduces stress, and encourages personal growth. It empowers you to make choices based on your present, improving your relationships and overall well-being.

Practical Tips:

◊ Practice mindfulness.
◊ When past emotions surface, pause, breathe, and acknowledge the feeling.
◊ This approach rewires your brain for calm and resilience.

Reflective Questions:

» What past emotions tend to resurface for you?
» How can acknowledging these emotions help you manage them better?
» What strategies can help you navigate these emotions?

Exercise: When past emotions arise, write down what you're feeling. Reflect on how you can respond in a way that supports your growth.

Day 204: Breaking Free from the Magnetic Pull of the Past

"If you want to fly, you have to give up what weighs you down." – Roy T. Bennett

The past can act like a magnet, pulling you back into old memories, regrets, and pain. This pull can be powerful, making it difficult to move forward. However, recognising and resisting this pull is crucial for personal growth and living a fulfilling life. By breaking free, you can embrace the present and look forward to the future with hope.

The brain tends to dwell on past events, especially those with strong emotional impact. Memories linked to strong emotions can create a cycle of negative thinking, constantly pulling people back into old patterns. Neuroscience shows that the brain can change through neuroplasticity, allowing people to form new, healthier pathways. By consciously choosing to focus on the present, you can weaken the magnetic pull of the past and create new habits that promote growth.

Starting a new project might bring up doubts from past failures, making the fear of repeating mistakes feel like a magnet pulling you back. Acknowledge these feelings, but shift your focus to the present task. Use affirmations like, *"I am capable and prepared,"* to counteract the pull of the past.

Many people feel trapped by their past, believing it defines them. Breaking free requires recognising the past's influence but choosing not to let it control your future. Resisting the pull of the past frees you to engage fully with the present and create a future based on your current choices, not past regrets. This shift increases confidence, reduces anxiety, and fosters empowerment.

Practical Tips:

◊ When past thoughts arise, practice grounding techniques, such as deep breathing or focusing on your senses, to bring your attention back to the present.

Reflective Questions:

» What aspects of your past tend to pull you back?
» How can you shift your focus to the present and future?
» What steps can you take today to break free from the magnetic pull of the past?

Exercise: Identify a recurring thought from your past that pulls you back. Please write it down, then write a counter-statement that reflects your present reality and future aspirations. Repeat this counter-statement whenever you feel the past pulling at you.

DAY 205: LETTING GO OF PAST EXPECTATIONS

"Sometimes we create our own heartbreaks through expectation." – Unknown

Past expectations can weigh heavily on your present life, whether set by you or others. These expectations can make you feel inadequate, guilty, or even like a failure if you haven't met them. Letting go of these past expectations is essential for finding peace and success. Holding onto unmet expectations can cause lingering feelings of disappointment and frustration. Neuroscience shows a close connection between our brain's reward system and meeting expectations. When these expectations aren't met, our brain reacts with feelings of dissatisfaction, which can lead to a cycle of negative thinking and self-criticism. By letting go of these unrealistic or outdated expectations, you free your mind from this cycle, allowing for greater self-acceptance and a clearer perspective on your true goals and desires.

Consider the expectations you had for your career path. Perhaps you thought you'd be in a different position by now, and not meeting that expectation has left you feeling frustrated or unfulfilled. By acknowledging that those expectations were based on past desires or circumstances that have changed, you can let go and focus on your progress and the opportunities available now and in future. Many people struggle with letting go of past expectations because they feel it means accepting failure. However, letting go is not about giving up but about adapting to what's realistic and fulfilling now. It's about reassessing what truly matters and aligning your actions with your present values and goals. Releasing the weight of past expectations reduces stress and increases self-compassion. It empowers you to set realistic, meaningful goals that align with your current situation, leading to greater satisfaction and well-being.

Practical Tips:

◊ Practice gratitude for what you have achieved rather than focusing on what you haven't.

◊ Regularly review your goals and expectations to ensure they align with your current reality and values.

Reflective Questions:

» What past expectations are you still holding onto?

» What new goals can you set that align better with your current values and situation?

Exercise: Write down a past expectation that has been weighing you down. Reflect on how it has impacted your current mindset. Now, rewrite this expectation into a goal that aligns with your present life and aspirations.

Day 206: Rewriting Your Story

"You can't go back and change the beginning, but you can start where you are and change the ending." – C.S. Lewis

Your past is like a book you've already written. While you can't erase the chapters, you can change how you interpret them and write the next ones. Rewriting the narrative of your past means viewing your experiences with fresh eyes, finding the lessons, and choosing perspectives that empower rather than hold you back.

Your story about your past shapes how you see yourself and your future. If you focus on mistakes or painful experiences, you will feel stuck or defined by them. But thanks to neuroplasticity, your brain can form new thoughts and beliefs. Think of your mind as a garden: if you keep nurturing weeds of regret, they'll flourish. Instead, plant seeds of resilience and wisdom, and watch your strength grow.

By reframing your past—seeing setbacks as learning opportunities—you transform your story from failure to growth and resilience.

If you have faced a business or career failure and see yourself as a failure, it's time to rewrite your story and view the experience as a stepping stone toward greater success. This shift will empower you to see new possibilities rather than being defined by past setbacks.

Rewriting your story helps release feelings of shame and inadequacy. It promotes self-compassion, boosts confidence, and opens the door to new opportunities.

Practical Tips:

◊ Practice positive self-talk.
◊ When reflecting on the past, focus on what you've learned and how those experiences have made you stronger.

Reflective Questions:

» What story do you currently tell yourself about your past?
» How can you reframe your past experiences positively?
» What new narrative can you create to empower your future?

Exercise: Write a letter to your past self, acknowledging your struggles, expressing forgiveness, and highlighting the strengths you've gained. Keep this letter as a reminder of your growth.

DAY 207: FROM DISCRIMINATION TO DETERMINATION

"Out of suffering have emerged the strongest souls; the most massive characters are seared with scars." – Kahlil Gibran

Discrimination can feel like a heavy chain holding you back, limiting your potential. But by transforming discrimination into determination, you can break free from its grip. This shift isn't just about overcoming obstacles; it's about reclaiming your power and creating a brighter future. Experiencing discrimination can leave lasting emotional scars, impacting your self-worth and mental health. Repeated negative experiences can create neural pathways that reinforce feelings of fear and inadequacy. Our brains naturally remember painful events more vividly than positive ones, making it easy to get trapped in a cycle of self-doubt. However, the brain's neuroplasticity means you can change these patterns. Choosing determination over despair allows you to forge new pathways that build resilience and self-confidence.

Emotional intelligence helps you recognise and manage the emotions triggered by discrimination, enabling you to respond thoughtfully rather than react impulsively. Romans 8:28 reassures us, *"And we know that in all things God works for the good of those who love him, who have been called according to his purpose."* This verse reminds us that God can use even painful experiences to strengthen and prepare us for a greater purpose.

When I was overlooked for promotions due to my gender, it felt like hitting a brick wall. Rather than letting bitterness take root, I focused on personal growth. I enrolled in courses, developed new skills, and committed to my goals. Eventually, I left that environment and secured a senior role in a company that valued my contributions. By turning frustration into fuel, I advanced my career and became a role model for others facing similar challenges.

Practical Tips:

◊ When facing discrimination, focus on what you can control—your actions and reactions.

◊ Use these experiences to motivate yourself to grow and set goals aligned with your values.

Reflective Questions:

» How have experiences of discrimination influenced your self-view?
» What strengths have you developed from overcoming challenges?
» How can you use your experiences to help others facing discrimination?

Exercise: Think about a time you faced discrimination. Write down how it affected you and what you learned.

DAY 208: BUILDING DISCOMFORT TOLERANCE

"Life begins at the end of your comfort zone." – Neale Donald Walsch

Stepping out of your comfort zone can feel like walking a tightrope without a safety net, but developing discomfort tolerance is vital to growth and moving beyond the past. Embracing discomfort opens doors to new experiences, skills, and opportunities that can transform your future.

We're naturally inclined to avoid pain and seek comfort, which can trap us in familiar habits that may no longer be beneficial. The science of neuroplasticity shows that repeatedly facing discomfort rewires the brain, creating new neural pathways that make handling challenging situations easier over time. It's like training a muscle—the more you practice, the stronger you become. Emotional intelligence helps you recognise and manage your response to discomfort so you can thoughtfully respond rather than impulsively react.

In 1 Peter 1:6-7, we are reminded: *"In all this you greatly rejoice, though now for a little while you may have had to suffer grief in all kinds of trials. These have come so that the proven genuineness of your faith—of greater worth than gold...—may result in praise, glory, and honor when Jesus Christ is revealed."* This scripture teaches that discomfort isn't just something to endure—it's an opportunity to strengthen our faith and build resilience.

I remember my first five-minute talk during teacher training. My knees were shaking so badly I could hardly stand still. This fear stemmed from a high school memory where a teacher made fun of my answer in class, making me dread public speaking. This experience shows the deep impact words can have on us. Over time, I had to reframe that memory and remind myself that I am a great communicator. With each instance of discomfort that I confronted, I observed a remarkable growth in my confidence as fear gradually evolved into a source of strength. Avoiding discomfort feels safe, but it prevents your brain from forming new pathways for growth. By building discomfort tolerance, you strengthen your resilience, boost your confidence, and learn to navigate change with more ease.

Practical Tip:

◊ Challenge yourself to do one small thing each day that makes you uncomfortable, like speaking up or trying something new.

Reflective Questions:

» What areas of your life do you avoid due to discomfort?
» How can embracing discomfort help you grow?
» What small steps can you take today to build your discomfort tolerance

Day 209: Break Free from Automatic Patterns

"Awareness is the greatest agent for change." – Eckhart Tolle

Sometimes, it might feel like your actions are on autopilot, repeating the same mistakes. These automatic patterns, shaped by past experiences, can control your responses without you even realising it. Understanding and addressing these patterns will help you reclaim control over your life, leading to true healing and progress.

Our brains are designed to respond automatically to quick actions, especially in dangerous situations. However, not all automatic responses are helpful. Past traumas or negative experiences can be stored in our subconscious brain, leading to behaviours that no longer serve us. Neuroscience shows these patterns become hardwired into our neural pathways, causing us to react without conscious thought. Becoming aware of these patterns is the first step to change. Through neuroplasticity, the brain's ability to rewire itself, we can replace harmful responses with healthier ones. Emotional intelligence helps us recognise these reactions and manage them intentionally.

Justina kept choosing emotionally unavailable partners and reacted with panic during breakups. In therapy, she discovered this behaviour was rooted in a childhood memory of feeling abandoned and alone. She learned to make healthier relationship choices by processing and reframing this memory.
You might have habits you want to change, like avoiding public speaking or feeling anxious without knowing why. These are often automatic responses linked to past experiences stored in your subconscious brain. Recognising and changing automatic patterns will help reduce anxiety, improve relationships, and help you make choices that align with your true values. This will lead to greater self-awareness, emotional freedom, and a more fulfilling, purpose-driven life.

Practical Tips:

◊ Notice your automatic reactions in stressful situations.
◊ Identify where these responses might come from and consciously choose a different response.

Reflective Questions:

» What automatic behaviours do you wish to change?
» How might these behaviours be linked to past experiences?
» What steps can you take to rewire your brain for healthier responses?

Exercise: Reflect on a recurring behaviour that holds you back. Write down when it happens and how you usually react. Imagine a healthier response and practice it the next time the situation arises.

Day 210: Embracing a New Beginning

"Every moment is a fresh beginning." – T.S. Eliot

Letting go of the past is like clearing out a cluttered closet. By making space, you create room for what truly matters. Embracing a new beginning means moving forward and leaving behind old mistakes, regrets, and painful memories. It's your chance to rewrite your story and build a future that excites you. Your brain naturally gravitates toward familiar patterns, even unhealthy ones, because familiarity feels safe. This makes it hard to move beyond past hurts. But here's the good news: neuroplasticity shows that you can create new, healthier neural pathways.

Emotional intelligence helps you manage your emotions so you can face life with resilience and hope instead of fear and regret. Focusing on the present and future allows you to break free from limiting patterns and develop positive, empowering habits. Remember that God is constantly working to bring you new beginnings and fresh opportunities. Trust that letting go of what's behind is the first step toward embracing what's ahead.

Picture a butterfly emerging from its cocoon. It doesn't cling to its old form but spreads its wings to embrace new life. You have that same power. Moving beyond past wounds enables you to step into a future full of hope and potential. It's natural to feel anxious about letting go of the familiar, even if it's painful. But embracing a new beginning is about trusting that better things are ahead. Each small step toward a fresh start builds your confidence and opens new doors. Embracing a new beginning helps you grow into the best version of yourself, unburdened by past limitations. With a fresh start, you can approach life with renewed energy and optimism.

Practical Tips:

◊ Visualise your new beginning.
◊ Imagine your life free from the weight of the past.
◊ Write down your goals and dreams and take small, consistent steps toward them daily.

Reflective Questions:

» What parts of your past are you ready to let go of?
» How can embracing a new beginning change your outlook on life?
» What steps will you take today to start this new chapter?

Exercise: Create a "New Beginnings" vision board with images, words, and quotes that inspire you. Place it where you'll see it daily to remind yourself of the new life you're creating.

PART EIGHT

TURN YOUR DREAMS INTO REALITY

PART 8 INTRODUCTION

Setting goals is a powerful way to create a future different from today. It fuels motivation, brings clarity, and gives you direction.

Part 8 guides you through goal setting, supported by the **Soar Higher eToolkit from The Mindsight Academy.** This approach is based on four pillars: Self-Discovery, Reframe Your Mind, Reset Yourself, and Reform Your Life. It will help you align your goals with your core values and strengths, whether you're focused on personal growth or professional success.

Neuroscience shows that setting goals rewires the brain, releasing dopamine, the "feel-good" chemical that strengthens motivation. However, the journey can be challenging, and emotional intelligence helps us embrace the ups and downs. As Proverbs 16:9 (NIV) says, *"In their hearts, humans plan their course, but the Lord establishes their steps,"* reminding us to trust the process even when our path takes unexpected turns.

You'll also briefly explore the SMARTEST goal-setting framework.

This journey will equip you to dream big, start small, and sustain momentum. Let's begin!

Day 211: Self-Discovery – The Foundation of Goal Setting

"Your vision will become clear only when you can look into your own heart." – Carl Jung

Before diving into setting goals, it's crucial to truly understand yourself—your values, passions, beliefs, and strengths. We explored Self-Discovery in depth in Part 5, and now we'll build on that foundation.

Neuroscience tells us that the goals most aligned with our deepest desires—the ones that come from the "heart"—are rooted in the subconscious brain, particularly the emotional centres like the limbic system. When your goals resonate with your subconscious self, the brain releases dopamine, which fuels motivation and enables you to progress.

But if your goals don't align with these deeper, subconscious drivers, you may feel disconnected or even drained by them. This is because the subconscious mind holds your core beliefs and values, which drive much of your behaviour. When your goals reflect these subconscious desires, you activate the brain's reward system, making it easier to stay motivated. Goals driven by external pressures— what society or others expect of you—tend not to trigger the same emotional engagement, leaving you feeling unfulfilled.

Emotional intelligence helps you tune into these subconscious motivations. Psalm 139:23 (NIV) says, *"Search me, God, and know my heart. "* This verse encourages you to look within and align your goals with what truly matters. Setting goals that align with your inner values is like planting seeds in fertile soil—they grow with energy and purpose.

Practical Tips:

◊ Reflect on what truly excites you.
◊ Revisit your notes from Part 5 to reconnect with your core passions and values.

Reflective Question:

» Are the goals you've set in the past rooted in external expectations, or do they come from your authentic desires?

Exercise: Write down three things you deeply care about and three strengths you possess. Use this to create one goal that reflects who you truly are and excites you on a deeper level.

Day 212: Turning Self-Discovery into Action

"Change the way you look at things, and the things you look at change." – Wayne Dyer

After exploring your values, strengths, and passions through self-discovery, the next step is to take that knowledge and turn it into action. How you think about your abilities and potential can either help you move forward or hold you back. The good news is that your brain can change! Neuroplasticity means your brain is flexible and can rewire old, limiting thoughts into new ones that help you grow and reach your goals.

Sometimes, during self-discovery, you might uncover beliefs that need to be challenged. For instance, maybe you've always loved creativity but told yourself, *"I'm not the creative type"* or *"I'm too old to start something new."* These thoughts are barriers that keep you from setting and achieving meaningful goals. This is where emotional intelligence comes in. It helps you recognise these limiting beliefs when they pop up, and gives you the tools to challenge them.

Philippians 4:13 (NKJV) reminds us, *"I can do all things through Christ who strengthens me."* This powerful verse shows that, through faith, you can change your mindset and embrace a more positive and empowered outlook. Reframing your thinking is like cleaning a foggy window—suddenly, you can see clearly, and what seemed impossible becomes possible.

Practical Tips:

◊ When you notice a limiting belief, ask yourself, "Is this really true, or is it just a story I've been telling myself?"
◊ Replace it with a positive, empowering thought.

Reflective Question:

» What limiting beliefs are holding you back from setting exciting goals?

Exercise:

> Write down one limiting belief you've identified.
> Reframe it into a positive belief. For example, "I'm not good enough" can become "I have what it takes to succeed."
> Reflect on how this new thought changes the way you approach your goals.

Day 213: Reset Yourself

"People are not lazy. They simply have impotent goals—that is, goals that do not inspire them." – Tony Robbins

As you continue on your journey of self-discovery and reframing your mindset, it's time to Reset Yourself by setting goals using the **SMARTEST Framework**. You might already be familiar with SMART goals (Specific, Measurable, Achievable, Realistic, and Time-bound), but the SMARTEST framework takes goal setting to a deeper level by adding three key elements: **Emotional, Significant and Transformative**.

Today, let's focus on the "E" for Emotional.

Why is this important? Because when your goals connect with your emotions, they become more than just tasks on a to-do list; they become a driving force. Neuroscience shows that emotionally charged goals activate the brain's reward system, releasing dopamine and keeping you motivated even when challenges arise. If a goal doesn't stir you emotionally, it's likely to lose its power over time.

Think of a goal like "getting a promotion." Now, what's the emotional reason behind it? Perhaps it's the desire to provide a better life for your family or to feel more fulfilled in your work. When the emotional aspect is clear, the goal takes on new meaning. Emotional intelligence also reminds us that we must recognise and harness our feelings to stay motivated and focused.

Proverbs 16:3 (NIV) encourages, *"Commit to the Lord whatever you do, and He will establish your plans."* When we align our goals with our emotions and deeper purpose, we position ourselves for success.

Practical Tips:

◊ When setting goals, ask yourself, *"What's the emotional reason behind this?"*
◊ Write it down to remind yourself why it matters.

Reflective Questions:

» Are your current goals emotionally charged?
» Do they inspire you on a deeper level?

Exercise: Pick one of your current goals and ask yourself, "How will achieving this goal make me feel?" Write down the emotional impact and use it as motivation moving forward.

Day 214: Reform Your Life – Bringing It All Together

"The only way to do great work is to love what you do." – Steve Jobs

You've already explored Self-Discovery, Reframing Your Mind, and Resetting Yourself to set meaningful goals. Now it's time to take everything you've learned and put it into action. Reforming your life means turning your goals into daily habits.
Remember, setting goals isn't something you do just once—it's a process that keeps growing and evolving as you do.

Real change happens when you set goals and work on them daily. Science shows that building new habits and reaching long-term goals takes time and effort. Your brain has the power to rewire itself, but it needs you to keep repeating those new actions until they stick. Every time you follow through, you strengthen those habits and make success easier to reach.

Emotional intelligence helps you stay connected to the reason behind your goals. When you know why you want something, it's easier to stay motivated, even when things get tough. The Bible also reminds us in Galatians 6:9 (NIV), *"Let us not become weary in doing good, for at the proper time we will reap a harvest if we do not give up."* So, keep going—you'll see the results if you stay committed.
As you move forward, ask yourself: *"Are my goals helping me build the life I really want?" "Do I need to adjust them as I grow and change?"*

Practical Tips:
   ◊ Keep checking in with yourself.
   ◊ Make sure your goals still match your passions and values.
   ◊ If they need tweaking, that's okay—goals should grow with you.

Reflective Question: How can I stay focused on my goals when things get hard?

Exercise: Review your goals. What's one small step you can take today to move closer to your most important goal? Start with something simple to build momentum.

For additional support and tools to help you along your goal-setting journey, visit The Mindsight Academy [*www.themindsightacademy.com*] and explore the Soar Higher eToolkit.
This toolkit is designed to help you further refine your personal and professional goals by applying the SMARTEST framework.

Day 215: The Power of Specificity in Goals

"The more specific you are, the clearer your path becomes." – Unknown

When it comes to setting goals, clarity is crucial. A vague goal is like embarking on a journey without a destination—you might be moving, but you won't make meaningful progress. That's why being specific is the first critical step in the SMARTEST framework. Specificity gives your brain clear instructions on where to go and what to focus on, creating a direct path to success.

Neuroscience shows us that the brain thrives on clarity, particularly when it understands the *'why'* behind a goal. When you set a specific goal, the prefrontal cortex—the part of your brain responsible for decision-making and planning gets activated. Vague goals leave your brain scrambling, often resulting in procrastination or confusion.

For example, if your goal is "to get healthier," it's too broad to drive meaningful change. Instead, make it specific and personal: *"I will eat three servings of vegetables daily and exercise for 30 minutes five times a week because I want to feel energetic and strong so I can feel confident in my own body."* That 'why' matters.

When your goal taps into a personal reason—such as wanting more energy, strength, or confidence—it creates an emotional connection. This emotional tie is what keeps you motivated when obstacles arise. Your brain does not only need clarity, it also needs to know that the goal matters to you. Without this emotional connection, goals can easily slip through the cracks. The more specific and emotionally connected your goal, the better your brain and heart work together to push you toward success.

Proverbs 21:5 (ESV) reminds us, *"The plans of the diligent lead surely to abundance, but everyone who is hasty comes only to poverty."* Being specific helps you avoid rushing and cutting corners, setting you on a path to lasting success.

Practical Tips:

◊ When setting your next goal, ask yourself: Is this specific enough?

◊ Could someone else understand exactly what I want to achieve just by reading it?

Reflective Question: How can I make my current goals more specific, and what details can I add to create a clearer plan?

Exercise: Rewrite one of your broader goals with more specific details. Identify exactly what you want to achieve, by when, and how you'll measure success.

Day 216: Measurable Goals – Track Your Progress

"What gets measured gets managed." – Peter Drucker

Once you've set specific goals, the next step is to make them measurable. If you don't track your progress, it's hard to know if you're moving forward or stuck in the same place. Measurable goals give you clear benchmarks to see how far you've come, which helps keep you motivated and focused.

When you measure progress, your brain gets a boost of dopamine, a chemical that makes you feel good and keeps you motivated. Neuroscience shows that seeing even small wins gives us the energy to keep going. By breaking your goals into measurable steps, you make it easier for your brain to notice progress and stay on track.

For example, instead of saying, "I want to save more money," make it measurable: "I will save £500 in the next three months." Now you have a clear target, and each pound you save feels like progress. Measuring your progress makes every step feel like a small win, boosting your confidence and commitment.

In Luke 14:28 (ESV), we are reminded, *"For which of you, desiring to build a tower, does not first sit down and count the cost, whether he has enough to complete it?"* This scripture shows us the importance of planning and measuring progress in achieving success. Tracking progress allows you to adjust your efforts if needed, keeping you on course.

Whether you're working on personal goals like fitness or professional ones like completing a project at work or in your business, measuring your progress helps you stay accountable and keeps you from losing track.

Practical Tips:

◊ Set clear benchmarks for your goals—use numbers, deadlines, or frequency.
◊ Check-in regularly to see how you're doing.

Reflective Question: How can I make my current goals measurable, and what can I track to see progress?

Exercise: Take one goal and make it measurable. Write down how you'll track it and create a system for regularly checking your progress.

Day 217: Actionable – Turning Goals into Tangible Steps

"Vision without action is merely a dream." – Joel A. Barker

A clear vision is essential, but turning it into action makes it real. The next step in the SMARTEST framework is making your goals actionable—breaking them down into specific tasks that you can execute daily. An actionable goal gives you a clear roadmap for achieving it. Without this, even the most exciting goals can remain distant dreams.

Neuroscience shows that breaking a goal into smaller, actionable steps makes it easier for your brain to handle. When the brain sees a large, overwhelming task, it activates the stress responses. However, by breaking that task down into smaller actions, your brain shifts into problem-solving mode, boosting motivation and reducing anxiety. This creates a powerful sense of progress.

For example, if your goal is to "write a book," that can feel daunting and overwhelming. Making it actionable looks like this: *"I will write 500 words a day for the next 90 days."* This turns the large goal into a series of smaller, manageable tasks that feel achievable. Doing this gives you an explicit action to take every day, which builds momentum.

Scripture supports this concept in James 2:26 (NIV): *"As the body without the spirit is dead, so faith without deeds is dead."* It's not enough to have a goal or intention; you must take action to bring it to life.

Actionable goals also create accountability. They help you measure your progress and ensure you're consistently working toward your vision.

Practical Tips:

◊ Break each goal into smaller, daily or weekly tasks.
◊ This creates a clear action plan to follow.

Reflective Question: Are my goals actionable? How can I break them into smaller, manageable tasks?

Exercise: Take one of your large goals and break it into three actionable steps. Write down what you can do today to start moving forward.

Day 218: Create an Action Plan

"A goal without a plan is just a wish." – Antoine de Saint-Exupéry

Creating a compelling vision for your life is only half the work. Even the most heartfelt goals can feel overwhelming without a clear Action Plan. An action plan helps you break down your grand aspirations into manageable actions, turning your goals into tangible outcomes. It also connects you emotionally, giving you tangible steps to fuel your sense of progress.

We now know that the brain craves clarity. When your brain is presented with a detailed plan, it reduces the uncertainty that often leads to stress. Your prefrontal cortex, the part of your brain responsible for planning and decision-making, becomes more active. This reduces the feeling of being overwhelmed and provides emotional relief. Each time you complete a step in your action plan, your brain releases dopamine, the 'feel-good' chemical. This reinforces your motivation and gives you a sense of accomplishment.

Emotional intelligence plays a vital role in goal-setting because, as humans, we are driven by how we feel. Setting an action plan helps you break through emotional barriers like fear, doubt, or feeling stuck. By creating an action plan—such as *"I will research the market this week and start creating a website next week"*— you empower yourself to take small, manageable steps toward your larger vision. This eases anxiety and builds emotional resilience, making you feel more empowered and in control of your journey.

Scripture emphasises the importance of planning in Proverbs 16:9 (ESV): *"The heart of man plans his way, but the Lord establishes his steps."* By planning prayerfully and wisely, you set yourself up for success while remaining open to divine guidance, which can make you feel supported and hopeful in your journey.

Practical Tips:

◊ Break down your goals into small, actionable steps with deadlines.
◊ This creates emotional momentum and provides clarity.

Reflective Questions:

» Do I have a step-by-step action plan for my goals?
» How can I break it down further to ease stress?

Exercise: Take one goal and create three actionable steps with clear deadlines. Reflect on how achieving each step will make you feel.

Day 219: Realistic Goals – Ground Your Dreams in Reality

"Dream big, but start small." – Robin Sharma

Dreaming big is important for growth, but ensuring your goals are realistic is also vital. A realistic goal doesn't mean you're playing it safe—it's about balancing your big dreams with what's possible based on your time, energy, and resources. The goal should stretch you but not be so overwhelming that it feels impossible.

Neuroscience shows that when we set goals that feel too far out of reach, our brains can become overwhelmed. This leads to stress, which lowers our motivation. Conversely, when a goal is realistic but still stretches you, your brain stays engaged and focused. When you start achieving small wins, your brain releases dopamine, making you feel good and motivating you to continue, even when things get challenging.
For example, if your dream is to write a book, setting the goal to finish it in one month might set you up for failure, especially if you don't have the time. A better approach would be: *"I will write for 30 minutes every day."* This way, you're still making progress, but in a way that fits your life and keeps you moving forward.

Emotional intelligence helps you manage the feelings that come with pushing beyond your comfort zone. Setting realistic goals builds emotional resilience, allowing you to stay focused even when things get tough. Proverbs 21:5 (ESV) reminds us, *"The plans of the diligent lead surely to abundance, but everyone who is hasty comes only to poverty."* Being diligent means you take steady, realistic steps toward your dreams without rushing.

Practical Tip: Set goals that stretch you and ask, "Is this realistic given my time, energy, and resources?" Adjust if needed.

Reflective Question: Are my goals stretching me while still being realistic, or do they need tweaking?

Exercise: Break one big dream into smaller, realistic goals. Write down the first step you'll take today to move closer to that dream.

DAY 220: TIME-BOUND – SET DEADLINES

"A goal without a deadline is just a dream." – Napoleon Hill

Setting deadlines transforms vague aspirations into actionable goals. Deadlines create a sense of urgency, which drives action and keeps your brain focused. When your goals are time-bound and clearly tied to why they matter to you, you're far more likely to stay on track. The combination of a meaningful purpose and a deadline creates urgency, pushing you to prioritise and take consistent, focused steps toward your objective. The emotional connection to why you want to achieve the goal fuels your drive, while the deadline keeps you accountable and moving forward.

Neuroscience reveals that deadlines activate the brain's prefrontal cortex, which is responsible for decision-making, planning, and self-control. Setting time limits gives your brain a clear timeline, preventing procrastination. Having deadlines is important because it helps the subconscious brain see these new actions as part of an organised plan, not as a threat. Without deadlines, your goals can seem chaotic, triggering the brain's resistance to change. Deadlines provide structure, making the process feel safer and more manageable.

For example, if you set a goal to "learn a new language" but don't include a deadline, it's easy to postpone it. However, by reframing it as *"I will complete 30 language lessons by the end of the month because I want to communicate confidently during my trip,"* you create both a timeline and an emotional connection that keeps you motivated and consistent.

Emotionally, time-bound goals help relieve the stress of feeling stuck. Deadlines build momentum by providing a finish line that, when crossed, releases a sense of accomplishment. This boosts your motivation for future tasks, making goal-setting more rewarding and sustainable.

Ecclesiastes 3:1 (NKJV) says, *"To everything there is a season, a time for every purpose under heaven." Deadlines ensure that every goal has its season.*

Practical Tip: Break larger goals into smaller, time-bound tasks with clear deadlines.

Reflective Question: Are my current goals time-bound, and how can deadlines increase my focus?

Exercise: Take one goal and set a specific deadline for completion. Break the goal into smaller steps, and assign a timeline to each task.

DAY 221: THE SIGNIFICANT FACTOR

"If it doesn't challenge you, it doesn't change you." – Fred DeVito

One of the most important aspects of the **SMARTEST** framework is ensuring your goals are **significant.** A significant goal goes beyond simply being achievable—it must hold deep personal meaning, pushing you to grow and transform. It should challenge you, excite you, and have a lasting impact on your life. Significant goals drive you toward change because when something truly matters to you, you're more motivated to achieve it.

When you pursue goals that resonate more deeply emotionally, your brain engages more actively. Significant goals tap into your limbic system, the part of the brain responsible for emotion and motivation. When your goals align with what you care about most, your brain rewards progress by releasing dopamine, keeping you energised and focused.

A significant goal stirs passion and commitment. For instance, if your goal is to *"save money,"* but it doesn't connect to something that truly matters, it may lose its power. However, if you reframe that goal as *"save money to take my family on a life-changing vacation"* or *"to have financial security,"* it becomes significant, giving you a reason to keep going, even when it's tough.

Scripture reminds us of the importance of pursuing what matters. Matthew 6:21 (NIV) states, *"For where your treasure is, there your heart will be also."* When your goals reflect your values and purpose, they become significant, leading to long-lasting impact.

Practical Tips:
  ◊ Reflect on whether your goals are significant.
  ◊ Do they inspire deep meaning, or are they surface-level?
  ◊ Align your goals with what truly matters.

Reflective Questions:
  » Are my goals deeply significant to me?
  » How can I make them more aligned with my values?

Exercise: Identify one significant goal and explain why it matters to you emotionally. How will achieving it change your life?

DAY 222: THE TRANSFORMATIONAL FACTOR

"Transformation is a process, and as life happens there are tons of ups and downs. It's a journey of discovery." – Rick Warren

The last element of the **SMARTEST** framework is ensuring that your goals are transformational. A transformational goal changes not only your circumstances but also you. It pushes you beyond surface-level achievements, leading to profound personal growth, new perspectives, and lasting change in your life.

Transformational goals engage the brain's emotional and cognitive parts. This blend of emotion and logical planning stimulates neuroplasticity, allowing the brain to rewire through new experiences and challenges. Pursuing transformational goals creates lasting changes in how one thinks, acts, and perceives the world. These goals challenge old patterns and force one to develop new habits, strengthening the brain's ability to adapt and grow.

Emotionally, transformational goals often bring discomfort because they require you to face your fears, overcome doubt, and push past your current limitations. However, emotional intelligence helps you stay grounded in these moments of uncertainty, reminding you that growth comes through challenge. For example, if your goal is to improve your leadership skills, the transformation goes beyond simply learning new techniques—it involves changing how you interact with others, make decisions, and inspire those around you.

Scripture encourages transformation as part of our spiritual and personal journey. Romans 12:2 (NIV) states, *"Do not conform to the pattern of this world, but be transformed by the renewing of your mind."* Transformational goals help you renew your mind, leading to deeper, more fulfilling change.

Practical Tips:
   ◊ Set goals that challenge your skills, mindset, and behaviour.
   ◊ Focus on how achieving them will transform you.

Reflective Question: Are my current goals just about achievement, or will they transform who I am becoming?

Exercise: Write down one transformational goal. Identify how achieving it will change your circumstances, perspective, mindset, and behaviour.

Day 223: Aligning Goals with Core Values

"Success without fulfilment is the ultimate failure." – Tony Robbins

Setting goals is powerful, but if those goals don't align with your core values, they may lead to success without fulfilment. Core values are the principles and beliefs that matter most to you. When your goals are in harmony with these values, you create a sense of purpose and long-term satisfaction that goes beyond just reaching milestones.

When your goals align with your core values, you activate the brain's reward system more effectively. This happens because achieving a value-aligned goal brings deeper emotional satisfaction, releasing more dopamine—the chemical responsible for feelings of happiness and accomplishment. On the other hand, when goals contradict or don't align with your values, the brain experiences cognitive dissonance, leading to stress, internal conflict, and even burnout.

Emotional intelligence plays a significant role in this process. Recognising and understanding your emotions and values allows you to set meaningful and motivating goals. For example, if one of your core values is family, but your career goals pull you away from spending time with loved ones, you may feel unfulfilled despite professional success. Real fulfilment comes when your goals are ambitious and reflect what you care about most.

Psalm 37:23 (NIV) states, *"The Lord makes firm the steps of the one who delights in him."* Aligning your goals with your values helps you stay grounded in purpose and ensures your path leads to lasting success that brings personal fulfillment and meaningful impact.

Practical Tips:

◊ Take time to reflect on your core values.
◊ Write them down and assess whether your current goals align with them.
◊ If not, adjust your goals to reflect what truly matters to you.

Reflective Question: Are my current goals aligned with my core values, or am I chasing success that doesn't deeply fulfil me?

Exercise: List your top three core values and one goal for each that reflects those values. Evaluate how these goals contribute to your sense of fulfilment and purpose.

DAY 224: WHY NEW YEAR'S RESOLUTIONS FAIL

"A double-minded man is unstable in all his ways." – James 1:8 (KJV)

Millions of people set New Year's resolutions every January, hoping for a fresh start. However, statistics show that most resolutions fail by mid-February. Why? It's not because people don't want change—it's because they often set goals that are disconnected from their *core values, identity and purpose.*

Resolutions fail when they are based on external desires or societal expectations rather than on who God says you are. You can choose to change a habit, but true transformation will not happen until you see yourself differently. When your perceived identity conflicts with your goals, it creates a gap between your actions and your core beliefs, leading to failure. Self-discovery is essential because it grounds your goals in your divine identity. When you know who you are in Christ, your decisions align with that truth.

The brain's **reticular activating system (RAS)** filters information based on your beliefs about yourself. If you set a goal but your core belief contradicts it (e.g., trying to lose weight while subconsciously believing you're not worthy of health), your brain will sabotage your efforts. That's why discovering your true identity is critical. When you align your goals with the identity that God has given you, your brain begins to support those decisions.

The difference between deciding and merely choosing is vital. A choice is often fleeting—it's based on preference and external factors. But a decision comes from within, rooted in conviction and a clear sense of identity. James 1:8 reminds us that being double-minded leads to instability. When you decide based on who God says you are, you gain clarity and direction, reducing the likelihood of giving up when challenges arise.

Practical Tips:

◊ Before setting new goals, spend time reflecting on your true identity in Christ.
◊ Decide from that place, not based on external pressures.

Reflective Questions:

» Do my current goals reflect my true identity, or are they based on external expectations?
» How can I make decisions that align with who God says I am?

Exercise: Reflect on a past resolution that failed. Write down what identity you believed about yourself when you set it. Then, ask yourself how you can realign your goals with the identity God has given you.

Day 225: How Vision Boards Fuel Success

"See things in the mind's eye before you can see them with your eyes." – Zig Ziglar

A vision board is more than a fun project—it's a powerful tool for rewiring your brain and making your dreams a reality. By making your goals visible and engaging with them daily, you keep your focus sharp and your motivation strong. This regular engagement can instil a sense of discipline and focus in pursuing your goals.

From a neuroscience perspective, regularly looking at your vision board activates your brain's reticular activating system (RAS). The RAS helps filter the information around you, ensuring you notice things related to your goals. This process works with neuroplasticity, which allows your brain to form new pathways through repeated focus and action. The more you engage with your vision board, the more your brain adapts to help you achieve those goals.

Vision boards connect your goals to your heart emotionally. When you see images of what you want—a successful career, a healthy lifestyle, or strong relationships—your brain releases dopamine, the 'feel-good' chemical. It also releases adrenaline, which gets you energised and ready to act. This emotional boost keeps your goals feeling real and within reach, fostering a deeper commitment and connection to your aspirations.
Scripture also highlights the power of vision. Proverbs 29:18 (KJV) says, *"Where there is no vision, the people perish."* Keeping your vision in front of you is essential for staying on track and aligned with God's purpose for your life.

Practical Tips:

◊ Create or update your vision board with images and words that reflect your biggest goals.
◊ Place it where you'll see it daily to keep your brain and heart focused on your dreams.

Reflective Question: What images represent the life you want to create, and how do they inspire you to take action?

Exercise: Add three meaningful images or words to your vision board. Review them for a few minutes every day and visualise your success.

Day 226: Breaking Big Goals Into Small Steps

"The journey of a thousand miles begins with one step." – Lao Tzu

Big dreams and ambitious goals can feel exciting, but they can also be overwhelming. It's easy to get discouraged when the path to your goal seems too long or complicated. The key to making progress is breaking large, overwhelming goals into smaller, actionable steps. This approach helps prevent procrastination, diminishes fear, and helps you stay focused on what's achievable right now.

When faced with an enormous task, your brain's amygdala, the centre for fear and anxiety, can become activated, causing you to freeze or avoid action. However, when you break that large goal into smaller, manageable steps, your brain feels less threatened. Each completed step activates the brain's reward system, releasing dopamine, the "feel-good" chemical which keeps you motivated and reinforces positive habits.

For instance, if you want to write a book, thinking about the entire project can feel overwhelming and lead to procrastination. Instead, break it down into smaller tasks—just like I've done with this guide, committing to write 15 days of content each day. Focusing on one section at a time makes the goal feel achievable, and with each completed part, I build momentum. Over time, these small steps add up, and before long, the guide is complete and ready for you to read.

Breaking down goals into smaller steps helps prevent burnout and frustration. Focusing on small wins builds confidence, and this emotional resilience helps carry you through the more challenging parts of your journey. As Proverbs 21:5 (ESV) says, *"The plans of the diligent lead surely to abundance, but everyone who is hasty comes only to poverty."* Diligence in taking steady, consistent steps ensures you're always moving closer to success, even when the progress seems slow.

Practical Tips:

◊ Break your large goal into smaller, time-bound tasks.
◊ Focus on one step at a time, and celebrate each small win.

Reflective Question: How can I break my big goals into smaller, manageable tasks that will reduce my fear of failure?

Exercise: Break one large goal into five smaller, actionable steps. Write down the first step you'll take today.

DAY 227: CREATING DAILY HABITS TO SUPPORT YOUR GOALS

"First we make our habits, then our habits make us." – John Dryden

Long-term success is not about grand actions; it's built on the foundation of consistent, daily habits. Establishing small, intentional habits aligned with your goals ensures you're taking steps toward your dreams every day. Though simple, these habits accumulate over time, leading to significant progress.

Neuroscience explains that the basal ganglia, the brain region that manages routine behaviour, governs daily habits. Once a habit forms, it becomes automatic and requires less mental energy. This frees up the brain to focus on other important tasks. Each time you complete a habitual action, your brain rewards you with a hit of dopamine, reinforcing the habit and keeping you motivated.

The **If-Then technique** is a powerful way to build daily habits. It works by creating a mental shortcut, linking a specific action to a particular situation. For example, *"If I feel overwhelmed with work, then I'll take a 10-minute walk at lunchtime."* This method simplifies forming new habits by giving you a clear situation and action. Over time, these responses become automatic, making new behaviours easier to adopt and maintain as part of your routine.

Daily habits, though small, are powerful. If your goal is to improve your health, a daily habit like taking a 20-minute walk can lead to significant changes over time. When repeated consistently, this habit becomes part of your routine, effortlessly moving you closer to your goal. These daily habits provide a sense of control and accomplishment. They break down larger goals into manageable actions, reducing anxiety. Proverbs 13:4 (NIV) reminds us, *"A sluggard's appetite is never filled, but the desires of the diligent are fully satisfied."* Diligence in building daily habits ensures steady progress.

Practical Tips:

◊ Use the If-Then technique to create a habit.
◊ Link a simple action to a daily event to reinforce it.

Reflective Question: How can I use the If-Then technique to develop daily habits that align with my goals?

Exercise: Choose a goal and create an If-Then habit to support it. Practice it for 30 days and track how this habit brings you closer to your goal.

DAY 228: THE POWER OF REFLECTION AND ADJUSTMENT

"Life is 10% what happens to us and 90% how we react to it." – Charles Swindoll

Achieving long-term success isn't just about setting goals and pushing forward; it's also about reflection and adjustment. Life rarely goes exactly as planned, so regularly reviewing and adapting your goals helps you stay aligned with your purpose and adjust to changes that arise. This process keeps you motivated and on the right track.

The brain thrives on feedback, so when you reflect on your progress, your brain processes what's working and what isn't, allowing you to make informed decisions about how to move forward. This process activates the prefrontal cortex, which governs planning, problem-solving, and decision-making. Reflection helps you rewire your brain to focus on what's effective, ensuring you learn from your experiences and make necessary adjustments.

Reflection provides clarity. Without it, you may continue pursuing goals that no longer align with your values or circumstances, leading to frustration or burnout. Regularly reflecting allows you to reassess whether your goals are still meaningful and achievable. If not, adjusting them becomes essential to staying motivated and aligned with what truly matters. For example, if you've been working toward a goal for months but find it's no longer fulfilling, reflection allows you to explore why. Is the goal still relevant, or do you need to pivot? Adjusting your approach is not a sign of failure—it's a smart way to ensure that your efforts always align with your true purpose.

Proverbs 4:26 (NIV) reminds us to *"Give careful thought to the paths for your feet and be steadfast in all your ways."* Reflection ensures that you remain mindful and deliberate about your goals, adjusting as needed.

Practical Tips:

◊ Take some time each week or month to pause and reflect on how far you've come.

◊ Ask yourself if your current goals are still meaningful and if any adjustments are necessary.

Reflective Question: How often do I reflect on my goals, and how can I adjust to stay aligned?

Exercise: Write down your current goals and assess whether they still align with your values and circumstances. Adjust them as needed to stay on track.

Day 229: Facing Obstacles with Resilience

"Achievers are not afraid of challenges, rather they relish them and use them profitably." – Unknown

No goal-setting journey is without obstacles. Whether it's unexpected setbacks, failures, or delays, challenges will arise along the way. But how you handle these obstacles determines whether you move forward or give up. Developing resilience is key to staying committed to your goals, even when things don't go as planned.

Resilience is something you can strengthen over time. The prefrontal cortex—the part of your brain that helps with clear thinking and managing emotions—keeps you calm and focused when facing challenges. The amygdala, which handles stress and fear, can sometimes trigger panic or frustration. By building resilience, you train yourself to rely more on problem-solving skills, helping you stay steady instead of letting stress take over.

Emotionally, resilience is about viewing setbacks as growth opportunities rather than failures. Every time you overcome an obstacle, you build emotional strength and confidence in your ability to handle future challenges. This emotional fortitude allows you to maintain focus on your long-term goals, knowing that setbacks are temporary and a part of the journey.

For example, if your goal is to launch a new business and you face financial difficulties or delays, resilience means adjusting your approach. Instead of seeing it as the end of the road, it becomes an opportunity to refine your business plan or seek new partnerships. As James 1:2-4 (NIV) reminds us, *"Consider it pure joy, my brothers and sisters, whenever you face trials of many kinds because you know that the testing of your faith produces perseverance."*

Setbacks develop perseverance, which ultimately strengthens your ability to achieve long-term success.

Practical Tips:
◊ When faced with setbacks, reflect on how to use them to your advantage.
◊ Adjust your plan rather than give up.

Reflective Question: How can I cultivate resilience when faced with setbacks?

Exercise: Think of a recent setback. Write down what you've learned and how to adjust your approach to keep moving forward.

Day 230: Finding Your Why – The Power of Purpose

"He who has a why to live can bear almost any how." – Friedrich Nietzsche

Setting specific goals is crucial, but the real power comes when you connect those goals to a deeper purpose—your personal 'why'.
Purpose fuels perseverance, making you unstoppable even when the road gets tough. It's easy to stay motivated when things are going well, but it's your deeper 'why' that will pull you through the challenging times.

When our goals are tied to something personally meaningful, the limbic system—the part of the brain that controls emotion and motivation—becomes highly active. This emotional connection triggers the release of dopamine, which keeps us motivated and drives us forward, even during setbacks. Connecting your goals to your life's purpose transforms them into more than just tasks; they become a mission that fuels every step forward.

For example, imagine your goal is to build a successful business. If you only focus on profits, the journey might get overwhelming and unfulfilling. But if your 'why' is to create financial freedom for your family or to make a lasting impact on your community, you tap into a deeper purpose. That purpose will keep you moving forward when things don't go as planned.

Having a strong sense of purpose can help you become more emotionally resilient. It transforms obstacles from roadblocks into stepping stones. Setbacks don't derail you, they strengthen your resolve with a strong 'why'. Proverbs 19:21 (NIV) says, *"Many are the plans in a person's heart, but it is the Lord's purpose that prevails."* Your 'why' aligns your goals with something greater, giving your journey profound meaning.

Practical Tips:
   ◊ When setting a goal, ask yourself: "Why does this matter to me?"
   ◊ Dig deep until you find the core reason.

Reflective Question: Is my current path aligned with my deeper purpose, or am I chasing goals that lack meaning?

Exercise: Take one of your goals and write down your 'why'. How does this purpose give your goal deeper meaning, and how will it sustain you?

Day 231: Visualising Success – How Mental Imagery Fuels Achievement

"The way you view the world determines how it appears to you. Things can be made beautiful or terrible by your thinking. Your mind is the world." - Marcus Aurelius

Visualisation is not just about dreaming of a better future—it's a practical tool that can help you shape that future. When you picture yourself achieving your goals, you prime your brain to believe that success is possible, which builds confidence and motivates you to take action. By imagining yourself succeeding, you start aligning your thoughts and actions with that vision.

Visualising activates the same brain areas used when you are actually performing the task. When you mentally practice something—like giving a presentation, running a race, or leading a project—your brain responds as though you're actually doing it. This strengthens the pathways in your brain, making it easier to succeed when the time comes to take action.

Visualisation isn't just about seeing the end result. It's about imagining the entire process—the steps, the obstacles, and how you'll overcome them. For example, if you're working toward a fitness goal, visualise not only reaching the end result but also pushing through tough workouts and staying committed. This mental practice prepares your brain to handle challenges and builds your inner strength.

Visualising success also boosts your confidence and prepares you for setbacks. It helps you stay focused and determined. As Proverbs 4:25 (NIV) reminds us, *"Let your eyes look straight ahead; fix your gaze directly before you."* Keeping your mind focused on success changes how you approach your goals and challenges.

Practical Tips:

◊ Spend 5 minutes daily visualising yourself achieving a specific goal.
◊ Focus on the steps you'll take and how it will feel to overcome obstacles.

Reflective Questions:

» How often do I visualise the steps to achieving success, not just the end goal?
» What challenges can I mentally prepare for to feel more confident when they arise?

Exercise: Choose a specific goal and visualise achieving it. Imagine how you'll handle difficulties and stay committed.

Day 232: The Importance of Accountability in Goal Achievement

"Two are better than one, because they have a good return for their labor." – Ecclesiastes 4:9 (NIV)

Accountability is a powerful tool that can significantly boost your chances of achieving your goals. Having someone to check in with, whether it's a friend, neurocoach, mentor, or accountability group, provides external motivation, encouragement, and a sense of responsibility. While personal discipline is crucial, knowing that someone else is holding you accountable can make a significant difference in staying on track.

When you share your goals with someone else, your brain releases dopamine, the chemical responsible for motivation and reward. This release makes the goal feel more real, and the sense of responsibility to others drives you to follow through. Additionally, accountability partners or groups provide positive reinforcement, which reinforces your commitment to your goals.

Accountability helps you manage setbacks more effectively. Knowing you have someone to lean on during tough times can make obstacles feel less overwhelming. It's easier to push through challenges when you have the support and encouragement of someone who believes in your ability to succeed. For example, if your goal is to improve your fitness, having a workout partner can help keep you motivated, especially on days when you feel like giving up.

Scripture emphasises the value of partnership in Ecclesiastes 4:9 (NIV): *"Two are better than one because they have a good return for their labour."* Working together amplifies the impact of your efforts, making success more attainable. Accountability ensures that you're not walking the path alone—it provides strength and guidance along the way.

Practical Tips:

◊ Find an accountability partner or join a group to support your goals.
◊ Schedule regular check-ins to discuss progress and challenges.

Reflective Questions:

» Who can I ask to hold me accountable in my goal-setting journey?
» How can I be an effective accountability partner for someone else?

Exercise: Identify a goal you're working on and find someone to hold you accountable. Set up a regular meeting or check-in to track progress and offer support.

DAY 233: EMOTIONAL INTELLIGENCE AND GOAL SETTING

"The only way to change someone's mind is to connect with them from the heart." – Rasheed Ogunlaru

Setting and achieving goals is not just about strategy and discipline—it's also about managing the emotional journey that comes with it. This is where emotional intelligence (Emotional Quotient - EQ) plays a crucial role. Emotional intelligence is the ability to recognise, understand, and manage your emotions, as well as the emotions of others. By developing EQ, you can stay in tune with how you feel throughout your goal-setting process, which helps you manage the ups and downs with more resilience and focus.

Neuroscience shows that emotional intelligence activates your prefrontal cortex, the brain's centre for decision-making and emotional regulation. This part of the brain helps you process emotions logically, allowing you to respond to challenges thoughtfully rather than reactively. High emotional intelligence prevents you from being derailed by frustration, fear, or anxiety when things don't go as planned, helping you stay committed to your goals.

Emotionally intelligent people are more likely to set goals that align with their values and personal fulfilment. For example, if you're pursuing a goal that doesn't truly resonate with your deeper needs, emotional intelligence helps you recognise this disconnect early on. It allows you to course-correct before frustration or burnout sets in. EQ also enables you to navigate setbacks with grace. Instead of getting overwhelmed by failure, you can approach it with a growth mindset, seeing obstacles as learning opportunities. Proverbs 16:32 (NIV) reminds us, *"Better a patient person than a warrior, one with self-control than one who takes a city."* Emotional intelligence is about having the patience and self-control to manage the emotional challenges of goal setting and staying focused on the bigger picture.

Practical Tips:

◊ When setting goals, regularly check in with your emotions.
◊ Ask yourself how you're feeling and if your goals still align with your core values.

Reflective Questions:

◊ How do my emotions affect my ability to stay focused on my goals?
◊ How can I use emotional intelligence to manage setbacks and stay resilient?

Exercise: Take 5 minutes to reflect on your current emotional state regarding your goals. Write down any emotions that may be affecting your progress and how you can manage them better.

Day 234: Faith and Goal Setting – Trusting the Process

"Commit to the Lord whatever you do, and He will establish your plans." – Proverbs 16:3 (NIV)

Many people often see goal setting as a purely practical or strategic endeavour, but a spiritual dimension adds depth and purpose to the journey. Faith is crucial in helping us trust the process, knowing that the path to success is not always straightforward or predictable. When we set goals with faith, we surrender to the idea that the journey is as important as the destination, and we trust in God's timing to guide us toward what is best for us.

Neuroscience teaches us that uncertainty can trigger stress and anxiety. The amygdala, responsible for fear and survival instincts, often kicks into overdrive when we're unsure of the outcome. But when you trust in a higher divine purpose, your prefrontal cortex—the brain's planning and problem-solving centre—helps regulate those emotions. Faith allows you to manage uncertainty with grace, reducing anxiety and keeping you focused on your goals, even when you don't see immediate results.

Faith also reminds us to embrace the lessons that come with setbacks and delays. These moments of waiting or challenge can be times of growth and reflection. They teach us patience, perseverance, and humility. Trusting the process means recognising that the road may have unexpected turns, but every experience serves a purpose in God's plan.

Faith gives us a sense of peace and assurance that we are not alone in our journey. As Philippians 4:6-7 (NIV) reminds us, *"Do not be anxious about anything, but in every situation, by prayer and petition, with thanksgiving, present your requests to God. And the peace of God…will guard your hearts."* This peace equips you to move forward confidently, knowing that your goals are aligned with God's higher purpose.

Practical Tips:

◊ When facing uncertainty in your goals, remind yourself that the process is part of the plan.

◊ Trust that the timing will unfold as it should.

Reflective Questions:

◊ How can I deepen my faith in the process of goal setting?

◊ Am I trusting in God's timing, or am I trying to control every outcome?

Exercise: Reflect on one goal you've set. Write down how you can release control and trust the process, focusing on the journey rather than the destination.

Day 235: Pacing Yourself – The Key to Sustainable Success

"It does not matter how slowly you go, as long as you do not stop." – Confucius

Success isn't about sprinting to the finish line—it's about learning to pace yourself over the long haul. Achieving your goals requires energy and perseverance, but if you burn yourself out early on, you'll struggle to make it to the end. That's why finding the right pace is essential for sustainable progress.

The brain's prefrontal cortex, which handles decision-making and long-term planning, works best when not overloaded. Trying to do too much, too fast, can lead to burnout and poor decision-making, as the brain becomes overwhelmed. Multitasking or constantly task-switching is incredibly draining, as the brain must adjust between tasks, decreasing efficiency and focus. Instead, focusing on one task at a time while pacing yourself allows the brain to stay sharp and productive.

Emotional intelligence plays a role here, too. It's easy to become impatient and want immediate results, but pacing yourself helps manage those emotions. Being aware of how you're feeling—whether stressed, rushed, or anxious—allows you to adjust your pace and take the necessary steps to avoid burnout. For example, if you're working toward a significant career goal, taking on too much at once can lead to exhaustion. Instead, breaking tasks down into smaller, manageable steps helps you maintain a steady rhythm that keeps you moving forward without crashing.

Scripture also emphasises the importance of pacing. Ecclesiastes 3:1 (NKJV) reminds us, *"To everything there is a season, a time for every purpose under heaven."* This passage reminds us that progress doesn't have to happen all at once—each season of life has its own pace.

Practical Tips:

◊ Break your goals into smaller steps with achievable milestones.
◊ Set a realistic schedule for rest and recovery, ensuring steady progress.

Reflective Questions:

» Am I pacing myself well, or am I trying to accomplish too much too quickly?
» How can I balance ambition with the need for sustainability in my goals?

Exercise: Pick a goal and adjust your timeline for balance. Plan breaks and set a sustainable pace for long-term success.

DAY 236: CONQUER SELF-DOUBT AND RECLAIM CONFIDENCE

"Doubt kills more dreams than failure ever will." – Suzy Kassem

Self-doubt can quietly creep in and prevent you from reaching your goals. It makes you question your abilities and weakens your confidence. But remember, self-doubt is often more about how you see things than what is really true. By learning to recognise and challenge your doubts, you can take control of your path and confidently move forward.

Self-doubt activates the amygdala, the part of your brain that triggers fear and hesitation. This leads to a "fight-flight-or-freeze" response, causing you to second-guess yourself or avoid taking action altogether. However, when you engage your prefrontal cortex, the brain's centre for rational thinking, decision-making, and planning, you will have the ability to counterbalance that doubt with precise, logical thoughts. Reframing doubts into productive thinking helps your brain shift from fear-driven reactions to more focused, goal-oriented actions.

One common trap that feeds self-doubt is focusing too much on minor details. This is called the 80/20 rule—spending 80% of your time on things that only give you 20% of your progress. Instead of trying to perfect everything, focus on the most important tasks that will move you forward. This shift will help you avoid getting stuck in doubt and perfectionism. Emotional intelligence is also key to overcoming self-doubt. By becoming aware of your emotional triggers, you can stop doubt before it takes over. It's normal to feel self-doubt, but it shouldn't control you. Proverbs 3:5-6 reminds us, *"Trust in the Lord with all your heart... and He will make your paths straight."* Trust in your abilities and your purpose, knowing that you are on the right path.

Practical Tips:

◊ When doubt arises, rewire your brain by focusing on your strengths and the actions that matter most.

◊ Redirect your attention away from minor details and repetitive doubts.

◊ This shift creates positive neural pathways, boosting focus and confidence to move forward with ease.

Reflective Questions:

» What parts of my goals cause self-doubt, and how can I shift my mindset?

» How can I focus on the 20% of actions that matter most?

Exercise: Identify one area of self-doubt. Write down one action you will take today, focusing on progress rather than perfection.

Day 237: Take Action, Even If You're Scared

"Courage is not the absence of fear, but the triumph over it." – Nelson Mandela

Fear often feels like the biggest roadblock between you and your goals. The bigger your dream, the stronger the fear. But waiting for the fear to disappear will keep you stuck. Doing it scared means acknowledging the fear but taking action anyway. When you act despite fear, you start to rewire your brain, moving closer to your desired future.

From a neuroscience perspective, fear activates the amygdala, the part of your brain responsible for the fight-or-flight response. This can cause hesitation or make you avoid action. However, when you take even small steps forward, you engage your prefrontal cortex, the area that controls rational thinking and problem-solving. This shift helps rewire your brain from fear-based reactions to clear, focused action. Over time, your brain becomes better at managing fear, making future challenges less daunting.

For example, someone who is afraid of public speaking may avoid jobs that require it. However, they gradually reduce that fear by taking small steps—practising in front of a mirror or speaking to small groups. This method of rewiring your brain applies to any goal: starting a business, making a career change, or pursuing a passion. The key is to act, even if fear still lingers.

Taking action in the face of fear builds resilience and self-trust. Every step forward reinforces the truth that fear is not a barrier but a signal of growth. Proverbs 28:1 (NIV) says, *"The wicked flee though no one pursues, but the righteous are as bold as a lion."*

Boldness means taking action despite fear, trusting that each step brings you closer to your goals.

Practical Tips:

◊ Break your goals into smaller, manageable steps.
◊ Take one action daily, even if fear is present. This rewires your brain to build confidence and reduce fear over time.

Reflective Questions:

» What fears are holding me back, and how can I act despite them?
» How can I break down my big goals to make fear feel manageable?

Exercise: Identify one task you've been avoiding due to fear. Commit to doing it this week, no matter how small the action.

Day 238: Busy vs. Productive – Avoiding Productive Procrastination

"You may delay, but time will not." – Benjamin Franklin

Have you ever found yourself busy all day but feeling like you didn't actually achieve anything?

That's productive procrastination—the act of staying busy with tasks that feel productive but don't move you any closer to your goals. It's one of the biggest hidden traps in goal setting. You might be organising, planning, or tackling low-priority tasks, but in reality, you're avoiding the work that really matters.

Productive procrastination activates the brain's reward system. Doing more manageable tasks gives you a quick sense of accomplishment, releasing dopamine, the feel-good chemical. But while this temporary boost feels satisfying, it often distracts from meaningful progress. The brain naturally gravitates toward more manageable tasks to avoid the discomfort of the more challenging ones that would move you closer to your goals. For example, you might spend hours cleaning your desk, organising files, or answering emails—tasks that feel necessary but don't directly contribute to completing a major project. These small tasks make you feel busy, but they often mask the fear or discomfort of tackling bigger, more significant tasks.

Emotionally, productive procrastination can create frustration and stress. You feel like you're working hard but still falling behind. Recognising this pattern is vital to breaking it. Emotional intelligence helps you become aware of when you're avoiding important work by filling your time with distractions.

Scripture encourages focus and diligence. Proverbs 12:11 (ESV) says, *"Whoever works his land will have plenty of bread, but he who follows worthless pursuits lacks sense."* The key to real productivity is aligning your time and energy with tasks that truly matter.

Practical Tip: Identify one high-priority task each day and commit to working on it first, before any lower-priority tasks.

Reflective Questions:

> » How often do I fill my time with non-essential tasks to avoid more important ones?
> » What is the most important task I can focus on today to truly move me forward?

Exercise: List three tasks you often use as "productive" distractions. Then, pick one important task and commit to finishing it before anything else today.

Day 239: The Power of Saying 'No' – Guard Your Time and Energy

"You have to decide what your highest priorities are and have the courage—pleasantly, smilingly, non-apologetically—to say 'no' to other things." – Stephen Covey

In today's busy world, one of the most powerful tools you can use to protect your time and energy is the ability to say 'no'. Many people feel pressure to say 'yes' to every request, commitment, or opportunity that comes their way. However, constantly saying yes can drain your energy, dilute your focus, and prevent you from working on what truly matters.

Neuroscience shows that decision fatigue—the mental exhaustion from making too many decisions—lowers your ability to prioritise and think clearly. Each time you say 'yes 'to something that isn't aligned with your goals, you're depleting your mental and emotional resources. In contrast, learning to say 'no' frees up space for more important decisions and allows you to focus on tasks that align with your highest priorities.

Saying 'no' doesn't have to be hostile or rude. It's about recognising your limits and protecting your time so that you can focus on meaningful goals. For example, if you're working on launching a business but find yourself constantly agreeing to social commitments or unnecessary projects, it can lead to burnout and hinder progress. Saying 'no' allows you to create boundaries that keep you focused on the long-term vision.

Saying 'no' can be empowering. It demonstrates self-awareness and emotional intelligence, allowing you to recognise when you're spreading yourself too thin. Proverbs 4:25 (NIV) reminds us, *"Let your eyes look straight ahead; fix your gaze directly before you."* By saying 'no' to distractions, you stay focused on what truly matters.

Practical Tips:

◊ Practice saying 'no' by assessing whether each commitment aligns with your goals.
◊ If it doesn't, decline politely but firmly.

Reflective Questions:

» Where in my life do I need to start saying 'no' to protect my time and energy?
» How can saying 'no help me stay more focused on my goals?

Exercise: Identify one area where you've been saying 'yes' too much. This week, practice saying 'no' to one request that doesn't serve your bigger vision.

Day 240: The Cost of Perfectionism – When Perfect Holds You Back

"Done is better than perfect." – Sheryl Sandberg

Perfectionism might seem like a strength, but it often keeps you stuck. When you aim for things to be "just right," you can end up overthinking, delaying taking action, and missing growth opportunities. Instead of helping you succeed, perfectionism slows you down. Perfectionism triggers the amygdala—the part of your brain responsible for fear and stress. This can make even small tasks feel overwhelming, activating your body's stress response by putting you into "fight-flight-or-freeze" mode as if facing a real threat. Perfectionism also leads to obsessive thinking, where your brain loops through over-analysing details and worrying about mistakes. This fixation is partly due to imbalanced serotonin, a chemical that affects mood and emotional balance. When serotonin is low, it's hard to feel satisfied, making you focus on unimportant details.

Additionally, perfectionism reduces dopamine—the brain's "reward" chemical. Dopamine fuels motivation by giving you a sense of achievement after completing tasks. But when you're fixated on perfection, your brain misses out on the satisfaction of small wins, leading to frustration and low motivation. The prefrontal cortex, which helps with planning and decision-making, also struggles under perfectionism. Instead of focusing on what's important, it gets bogged down in minor details, draining your energy and keeping you from making progress.

Emotionally, perfectionism can lead to burnout. It makes you overly critical, often blinding you to the progress you've made. Ecclesiastes 11:4 (NIV) reminds us, *"Whoever watches the wind will not plant; whoever looks at the clouds will not reap."* Waiting for the "perfect" moment stops you from acting. Instead, take action, learn, and improve along the way.

Practical Tips:

◊ Release the need for perfection.
◊ Focus on completing tasks and learning from them instead of making everything flawless.

Reflective Questions:

» How does perfectionism hold me back?
» Where could focusing on progress over perfection improve my life?

Exercise: Choose one task you've delayed due to perfectionism. Focus on progress, not perfection, and commit to finishing it this week.

Day 241: Purpose + Profit – Building a Mission Beyond Yourself

"The secret of success is making your vocation your vacation." – Mark Twain

Success isn't just about financial gain—it's about using your profits as a tool to achieve a greater purpose. When your mission becomes bigger than yourself, you unlock the power to create meaningful change. By aligning your purpose with profit, you can make a real impact on the world around you. This blend of purpose + profit creates the fuel that keeps you excelling and thriving, even when challenges arise.

Neuroscience shows people are more motivated and resilient when their work connects to a greater *"why."* The prefrontal cortex—the part of your brain responsible for planning and long-term decision-making—is activated when you have a purpose-driven goal. This keeps you focused, engaged, and driven, especially when short-term rewards (like money) lose their motivational power. The bigger your mission, the more your brain aligns with that vision, driving you to take meaningful action.

Take a moment to check in with yourself: What motivates you to get up and work every day? Is it simply to earn money, or do you see money as a tool to accomplish something greater? Perhaps it's to support your family, give back to your community, or fund a cause that matters to you. The more you continue to ask why your goals matter, the closer you get to your true purpose.

Emotionally, you gain clarity and power when you make your mission about something bigger than yourself. It becomes less about the day-to-day grind and more about fulfilling a more profound need. As Proverbs 16:3 (NIV) reminds us, *"Commit to the Lord whatever you do, and He will establish your plans."* Purpose aligned with faith amplifies your ability to achieve lasting success.

Practical Tips:

◊ Reassess your goals by asking yourself why they matter.
◊ Keep exploring until you uncover a deeper purpose behind your work.

Reflective Question:
What is my deeper "why" behind my goals, and how does it shape my motivation?

Exercise: Write down your current goals and ask yourself why each one matters. Continue asking 'why' until you connect them to your deeper purpose.

PART NINE

ELEVATING YOUR RELATIONSHIPS

PART 9 INTRODUCTION

Relationships are at the heart of both our personal and professional lives. In Part 9: Elevating Your Relationships, we'll explore how to strengthen connections using the science of rewiring your brain. Through neuroplasticity, your brain is constantly adapting, and with the right focus, you can enhance trust, empathy, communication, and understanding in your relationships.

This section will guide you through practical steps for better communication, handling conflict, and fostering deeper connections. Using neuroscience and emotional intelligence, you'll learn how to improve the quality of your interactions, whether at home or in the workplace.

By rewiring your brain, you can move beyond surface-level relationships and build meaningful, lasting connections that enrich both your life and the lives of others.

Day 242: The Importance of Healthy Relationships

"Healthy relationships are built on trust, respect, and mutual support." - Unknown

Healthy relationships are vital to our overall well-being. They provide emotional support, foster growth, and create a sense of belonging. Neuroscience explains that when we feel secure in our relationships, our brain releases oxytocin, the "bonding hormone," strengthening our connections and promoting trust. On the other hand, strained or unhealthy relationships trigger the release of cortisol, the stress hormone, which can negatively affect our emotional and physical health.

Building healthy relationships begins with trust and respect. Scripture in 1 Corinthians 13:4-7 reminds us that love is patient and kind, offering a clear guide for how we should engage with others. Emotional intelligence also plays a critical role, enabling us to understand and manage our emotions while empathising with others. This helps create an environment where open communication and mutual respect can thrive.

Consider a workplace where the team leader consistently respects and trusts their employees. Over time, this builds a culture of loyalty and collaboration. Similarly, when individuals feel heard and respected in personal relationships, it fosters deeper bonds and mutual understanding.

Practical Tips:

◊ Practice active listening in your daily interactions.
◊ Giving others your full attention communicates respect and helps build trust over time.

Reflective Question: How can you intentionally foster trust and respect in your key relationships?

Exercise:

> Identify one relationship in your life that could benefit from greater respect or trust.
> Take one concrete action today, such as offering sincere appreciation or being fully present in a conversation, to strengthen that relationship.
> Focusing on trust, respect, and connection can help establish relationships that support personal and mutual growth.

Day 243: Shifting from 'What Can I Get?' to 'What Can I Give?

"The purpose of a relationship is not to find someone who completes you, but to find someone with whom you can share your completeness." -Unknown

Too often, people enter relationships with the mindset of what they can gain rather than considering what they can contribute. This approach can leave relationships feeling transactional and unfulfilling. The real purpose of any relationship—whether romantic, personal, or professional—is to express the best version of yourself, not to extract value from the other person. Relationships are an opportunity to decide how you want to show up in the world, to embody the qualities you value most, and to offer that fullness to someone else.

From a neuroscience perspective, focusing on what you can contribute to relationships stimulates the brain's reward system. Giving and sharing activates the brain's dopamine release, creating satisfaction and joy. Conversely, entering relationships with a "take" mentality breeds frustration and disconnection when expectations aren't met. Scripture teaches us in Acts 20:35 (ESV), *"It is more blessed to give than to receive."* This timeless wisdom aligns with the idea that relationships are most fulfilling when built on mutual giving rather than self-serving demands. Emotional intelligence further supports this concept by encouraging us to be aware of our motives and to foster empathy and generosity in our interactions, which are key to a giving mindset.

Consider a romantic relationship in which both people focus on what they can offer—support, love, encouragement—rather than expecting the other to "complete" them. This mindset fosters a deeper bond and allows both individuals to grow independently while enriching the relationship.

Practical Tips:

◊ In your relationships, shift from *"What can I get?"* to *"What can I give?"*
◊ Focus on adding value through support, kindness, or understanding.

Reflective Questions:

» Take a moment to reflect on your relationships.
» Which of them are you focused more on getting than giving?
» How can you change that approach?

Exercise: In one important relationship, give something—time, patience, or encouragement—without expecting anything in return. Notice how it changes your perspective and connection. Giving creates relationships based on respect, fulfilment, and genuine connection.

Day 244: Your First Relationship Is With Yourself

"Love yourself first and everything else falls into line." - Lucille Ball

The foundation of all healthy relationships begins with your relationship with yourself. If you don't see yourself as worthy of love, respect, and kindness, offering those things to someone else becomes incredibly difficult. When you honour yourself—your strengths, flaws, and everything in between—you create a firm foundation from which all other relationships grow. When you nurture positive self-perception, your brain's reward centres light up, reinforcing feelings of confidence and security. In contrast, poor self-esteem can trigger feelings of inadequacy and anxiety, making it difficult to form healthy relationships with others. When you see yourself as worthy, your brain responds by boosting feelings of connection and happiness.

Scripture echoes this truth in Mark 12:31 (NIV), *"Love your neighbour as yourself."* Notice that the command begins with loving yourself. Emotional intelligence is a crucial part of this journey, helping you be aware of how you treat yourself and giving you the tools to manage your internal dialogue. Self-compassion is a liberating force—it's about extending the same kindness to yourself that you would to someone you love deeply.

Consider a person who is constantly critical of themselves. Their inner dialogue might affect their relationships by making them overly dependent on external validation or prone to resentment. Now imagine the opposite—someone who is secure in their worth. They naturally offer more patience, understanding, and love to others because they don't seek external validation to feel complete.

Practical Tips:

◊ Begin each day by affirming your worth.
◊ Acknowledge your strengths, and when you fall short, offer yourself the same compassion you would extend to a loved one.

Reflective Questions:

» How does your relationship with yourself impact your other relationships?
» Are you as kind to yourself as you are to others?

Exercise: Write three qualities that you love about yourself. Reflect on how those qualities enhance your relationships. Practice speaking kindly to yourself today, especially when faced with a challenge.

Building a strong, loving relationship with yourself elevates your self-worth and enriches every other connection in your life.

Day 245: Building Trust and Respect

"Respect is how to treat everyone, not just those you want to impress." – Richard Branson

Trust and Respect are the cornerstones of any meaningful relationship. Without trust, relationships struggle to grow and feel secure. When respect is missing, communication falters, leading to misunderstandings and feelings of neglect. However, when trust and respect are present, relationships thrive, becoming sources of strength, encouragement, and mutual support.

Trust stimulates the release of oxytocin, often referred to as the "bonding hormone," which deepens emotional connections and fosters a sense of safety. When trust is broken, the brain releases cortisol, the stress hormone, which creates tension and can erode the bond between individuals. Similarly, respect provides an environment where people feel valued, appreciated, and heard, laying a foundation for deeper understanding. Emotional intelligence helps us navigate this balance by understanding how our actions and words affect others.

Romans 12:10 (NIV) tells us to *"honor one another above yourselves."* This is a powerful reminder that respect isn't about what we can get from others—it's about showing genuine care. Trust and respect in any relationship, whether at work or in our personal lives, are built through consistent actions, honesty, and open communication. These aren't just words; they are the foundation of strong, lasting connections.

Think of a colleague who always delivers on their promises—over time, this consistency builds trust. Now imagine a friendship where both parties actively listen and support each other. In such environments, the relationship flourishes. When promises are broken or someone's feelings are disregarded, the bond weakens.

Practical Tips:

◊ Foster trust by being reliable and following through on your commitments.
◊ Demonstrate respect by actively listening and valuing other people's perspectives.

Reflective Questions:

» Where in your relationships can you strengthen trust and respect?
» What small changes can you make to improve them?

Exercise: Focus on one relationship today. Take action to build trust or show respect, like keeping a promise or listening attentively. When nurtured, trust and respect build lasting, fulfilling relationships.

Day 246: Mastering the Skill of Communication

"Wise men speak because they have something to say; fools because they have to say something." – Plato

Good communication is at the heart of every strong relationship—whether at work, with friends, or with family. It's not just about talking but also about listening, paying attention to body language, and responding with care. Misunderstandings happen because we speak without really listening or assume others know exactly what we mean. But mastering communication can completely change how you connect with others.

When you communicate clearly and empathetically, your brain releases feel-good chemicals that strengthen your bond with others. Engaging in thoughtful, meaningful conversations activates the brain's reward system, making you feel more connected and trusted. The real key to this skill is emotional intelligence—being aware of your emotions and the emotions of others during conversations. It's like having a special tool that makes every conversation more meaningful.

Proverbs 18:2 (ESV) says, *"A fool takes no pleasure in understanding, but only in expressing his opinion."* This reminds us that real communication is about listening to understand, not just speaking to be heard. When you truly listen, you learn more and deepen your relationships.

Imagine a leader at work who takes the time to listen to their team before making decisions. This will not only build trust but encourage collaboration. In your personal life, communication improves when both sides feel heard and understood.

Practical Tips:
- ◊ If you want to have a more effective conversation, practice active listening by speaking less and listening more.
- ◊ Let the other person finish their thoughts fully before responding.

Reflective Question: What specific actions will you take to improve your listening and communication skills in everyday conversations?

Exercise: During your next conversation, focus on listening without interrupting or planning your response. Ask at least one question to clarify their thoughts and see how it strengthens your connection.

Mastering communication can truly elevate your relationships, helping you create more trust and understanding with the people around you.

Day 247: The Power of Active Listening

"Listening is not hearing; it is taking a vigorous human interest in what is being told to us." – Andrew Carnegie

Active listening is not just a skill, it's a transformational tool in any relationship. It's about more than just hearing words; it's about fully engaging with the person speaking, understanding their perspective, and responding with empathy. In a world filled with distractions, many conversations become exchanges where people talk over one another or formulate responses without fully absorbing what's being said. But active listening has the power to change that.

Active listening strengthens relationships by fostering trust and connection. When we listen attentively, the brain releases oxytocin, the "bonding hormone," which promotes feelings of closeness and trust. On the other hand, when we are not genuinely being listened to, it can trigger stress responses in the brain, increasing cortisol levels and creating emotional distance between individuals.

The Bible reminds us in James 1:19 (NIV) to *'be quick to listen, slow to speak.'* Active listening aligns with this wisdom and plays a crucial role in reinforcing emotional intelligence. It helps us to understand others' emotions and provides the space for meaningful communication, fostering a deeper level of empathy and understanding.

Imagine a professional setting where leaders actively listen to their team, valuing and allowing their voices to be heard. This will build a sense of value and trust and foster a culture of respect and appreciation. In contrast, a conversation in which someone interrupts or disregards the speaker leads to frustration and disconnect.

Practical Tips:
- ◊ During your next conversation, focus solely on what the speaker is saying.
- ◊ Let them finish their thoughts without interruption, and use nonverbal cues like eye contact and nodding to show engagement.

Reflective Question: Do you often find yourself preparing a response before fully hearing what the other person has to say?

Exercise: The next time you engage in a conversation, actively listen by summarising the speaker's points after they've finished talking. This helps ensure you've truly understood their message and allows the speaker to feel heard.

By embracing active listening, you'll find that your relationships deepen, communication improves, and others feel more valued in your presence.

Day 248: Strengthening Family Bonds

"Family is the compass that guides us; it is the source of strength and comfort." – Brad Henry

Your family is often your strongest source of love and support, but maintaining those deep connections takes intentional effort. Relationships, especially within families, don't grow stronger on their own. They need consistent nurturing, patience, and understanding. When life's stresses build up, it's easy for frustration to spill over into family interactions. But when you take a moment to pause, breathe, think, and respond with calmness, you shift the energy of the whole dynamic. Staying balanced in the face of stress doesn't just help you—it influences everyone around you positively. By managing your emotions, you create space for understanding and connection, strengthening the bonds that hold your family together.

The Bible's wisdom in Ephesians 4:2 (NIV) teaches us to *"Be completely humble and gentle; be patient, bearing with one another in love."* It's a reminder that family's foundation isn't just in the big moments but in the small, everyday choices to be patient, kind, empathetic and understanding. It's in how you choose to listen rather than react and how you show up even when things get difficult. Picture a moment of tension in your family—an argument, possibly a disagreement. Now, imagine pausing, breathing deeply, and choosing to respond with patience rather than frustration or anger. This small act of restraint and empathy can turn conflict into connection, reminding you and your loved ones that you're all in this together.

Practical Tips:

◊ When family stress builds up, remember the transformative power of a pause.
◊ Before reacting, take a deep breath and focus on responding calmly and carefully.
◊ This simple act empowers you to take control of the situation and steer it towards a positive outcome.

Reflective Question: How can you become more present and patient during challenging family moments?

Exercise: This week, when you encounter a tense family situation, pause before responding with patience and understanding. Notice the difference it makes. Patience and understanding strengthen family bonds, helping you face challenges and build a hopeful, optimistic future together.

DAY 249: DEVELOPING DEEP AND MEANINGFUL FRIENDSHIPS

"A friend is someone who knows all about you and still loves you." — Elbert Hubbard

Developing strong and lasting friendships is critical for emotional and mental wellness. Research shows that strong social relationships reduce stress, promote happiness, and improve physical health by lowering blood pressure and strengthening the immune system. However, lasting friendships do not come by happenstance; they involve intention, trust, and reciprocal effort.

In today's fast-paced society, friendships can quickly become shallow or transactional. Genuine friendships are distinguished by empathy, loyalty, and persistent support. Studies have shown that deep friendships engage the brain's reward centres, producing dopamine and serotonin, which are connected with enjoyment and bonding. This is why being part of a close-knit community can make us feel more fulfilled and less lonely.

Proverbs 18:24 (NIV) emphasises the value of solid friendships: *"One who has unreliable friends soon comes to ruin, but there is a friend who sticks closer than a brother."* This verse emphasises the value of friendship over quantity—genuine friends stick around through life's ups and downs. Similarly, emotional intelligence is critical in developing these partnerships. Being aware of one's own and others' emotions allows one to respond with empathy and develop a stronger connection.

Think of a time when you felt truly supported by a friend. That feeling of being understood and valued did not stem from superficial conversations but from genuine concern and care. Friendships lacking emotional depth fade over time, leaving both people unsatisfied.

Practical Tips:
◊ Invest time and attention in meaningful friendships.
◊ Regular, meaningful encounters, whether through conversation or group activities, develop friendships and foster trust.

Reflective Question: How can you cultivate connections that add the most value to your life?

Exercise: Set aside time this week to connect closely with a friend. Share a personal story and listen carefully, with the goal of establishing trust and understanding. By investing in deep and lasting friendships, you improve your relationships and overall well-being, forming bonds that will help you get through life's problems

DAY 250: NURTURING ROMANTIC RELATIONSHIPS

"Love is not something you look for. Love is something you become." – Loretta Young

In a romantic relationship, both individuals should come together whole and complete, not seeking someone else to "complete" them. Imagine two trees with solid roots growing side by side—each drawing its strength from the soil, not from leaning on the other. Similarly, when your identity and self-worth are grounded in Christ, you bring a solid foundation into the relationship, freeing you from needing your partner to validate or complete you. This independence and freedom in Christ is a beautiful aspect of a healthy relationship.

Healthy relationships thrive on mutual understanding, not on trying to change each other. It's like receiving a gift—you appreciate it as it is rather than wishing it were something else. When you focus on accepting and understanding your partner instead of trying to mould them to fit your expectations, the relationship becomes a space of growth and connection, not frustration. The Bible addresses this in Ephesians 4:2-3: *"Be completely humble and gentle; be patient, bearing with one another in love."* This encourages us to be patient and receptive, understanding that true love is about growing together rather than demanding change. Learning to respond with empathy and active listening rather than responding in fury strengthens your bond.

For example, rather than being irritated because your partner handles stress differently, take a step back and try to understand why. Perhaps they need some time to reflect before discussing an issue. Accepting them for who they are offers a safe environment in which both of you may thrive.

Practical Tip: Focus on becoming whole in Christ so that your love comes from a place of fullness, not need.

Reflective Question: Are you allowing your partner to be themselves, or are you trying to change them to fit your expectations?

Exercise: This week, when faced with a difference, practice patience. Instead of reacting, take a moment to understand your partner's perspective.

When you approach relationships with understanding and wholeness, they become a space where love thrives and grows stronger over time.

Day 251: Navigating Gender Differences in Communication

"The way we communicate with others and with ourselves ultimately determines the quality of our lives." - Tony Robbins

Caroline Leaf's He Said/She Said book discusses the surprising disparities in how men and women communicate. According to her, the variances stem from how our brains are wired. Men typically process information in a more compartmentalised manner, focusing on problem-solving and concrete conclusions, whereas women frequently process information holistically, striving to comprehend emotional nuances and develop connections.

Understanding these disparities can significantly affect how we interact with one another. Rather than viewing these different communication styles as barriers, see them as complementing assets. For example, a woman may want to talk about her emotions and experiences, whereas a man may look for a quick solution. Recognising this distinction and responding with empathy and patience will improve the connection rather than lead to dissatisfaction.

Ephesians 4:29 (NKJV) says, *"Let no corrupt word proceed out of your mouth, but what is good for necessary edification, that it may impart grace to the hearers."* This is consistent with the premise that learning and adjusting to each other's communication styles strengthens the relationship rather than weakens it.

Consider it a dance: each partner has their own rhythm, but when you discover a way to synchronise, the movement flows smoothly and beautifully. The same is true for communication—knowing and respecting each other's rhythms allows you to move together in harmony.

Practical Tip: The next time communication becomes difficult, take a step back and consider how your spouse, friend, or colleague processes information. Adjust your approach to match their style.

Reflective Question: How can you tailor your communication to respect and enhance your partner's natural style?

Exercise: During your next conversation, pay attention to your partner's communication style. Try tailoring your responses to address their specific needs.

Recognising and valuing the variations in how men and women communicate can turn potential misunderstandings into opportunities for deeper connection.

Day 252: Bridging the Gap in Emotional Processing

"The greatest gift you can give someone is your full attention." – Jim Rohn

In her book, *He Said/She Said*, Caroline Leaf sheds light on the distinct ways men and women handle emotions. Men typically take more time to process their emotions internally before expressing them, while women often process emotions verbally, using conversation to comprehend and manage their feelings. Understanding these fundamental differences can be empowering, as it can prevent potential misunderstandings and foster a deeper emotional connection.

For instance, a woman may want to talk through a stressful situation, seeking emotional connection and validation, while a man might need time to reflect on his feelings alone before discussing them. Neither approach is wrong; they're just different. Recognising these differences can reduce frustration and help build a deeper emotional connection.

Colossians 3:13 (NIV) reminds us to *"bear with each other and forgive one another if any of you has a grievance."* This scripture highlights the importance of patience and understanding in bridging emotional processing differences. Instead of expecting your partner to respond like you do, allow them the time and space they need to process emotions in their own way. This reassurance can bring a sense of calm to your relationship.

Imagine these emotional differences like two roads leading to the same destination. One is winding and scenic, and the other is more direct. Both roads will get you where you need to go, but they offer different journeys. The key is respecting the route your partner needs to take, whether it's talking things through immediately or taking time to reflect.

Practical Tips:
- ◊ The next time you share feelings with your partner, try to understand how they process emotions.
- ◊ Be patient if they need more time or approach the situation differently than you would.

Reflective Question: How can you better support your partner's emotional processing style while also honouring your own?

Exercise: In your next emotionally charged conversation, practice patience. Give your partner space to process and express their feelings. By acknowledging and embracing emotional differences, you nurture a relationship in which both parties feel valued and understood, thereby strengthening the emotional connection.

Day 253: How Mirror Neurons Shape Our Relationships

"What we see in others is a reflection of what we cultivate within ourselves." - Maureen Chiana

Our ability to connect deeply with others stems from powerful mirror neurons. These neurons are found in areas like the premotor cortex and the parietal lobe of the brain. Their job is to "mirror" what we see in others. For example, when you see someone smile, your mirror neurons make you feel like smiling, too. This helps us feel what others feel and understand them better.

Mirror neurons are important in building relationships because they allow us to experience empathy. When someone is sad, your mirror neurons fire, making it easier for you to share their feelings and offer comfort. However, this also means that negative emotions, like frustration or anger, can spread quickly. When you are conscious of how your actions and words impact others, you are better equipped to foster positive and healthy relationships, giving you the ability to assert control over your emotional influence.

Proverbs 27:17 says, *"As iron sharpens iron, so one person sharpens another."* This means we influence each other, for better or worse. When you bring patience, kindness, and understanding into your relationships, those around you will likely reflect that back to you. Emotional intelligence helps you manage your emotions to create a positive environment in your relationships.

Consider a work environment where a calm leader helps the whole team stay relaxed, even under pressure. Or consider a personal relationship in which responding to frustration with patience can turn a tense moment into an opportunity for connection.

Practical Tips:

◊ Pay attention to the emotions you bring into your interactions.
◊ Positive energy can help others feel calmer and more connected to you.

Reflective Questions:

» How do your emotions affect those around you?
Are you creating an environment of positivity or tension?

Exercise: This week, be mindful of how your mood affects others. When you notice negative emotions spreading, pause, take a deep breath, and shift your response toward calm and empathy.

By understanding how mirror neurons work, you can use them to create healthier, more empathetic relationships that build trust and connection.

Day 254: Strengthening Relationships with the 5C Model

"Trust is built in very small moments." – Brené Brown

Every personal or professional relationship needs trust, respect, and communication to thrive. That's where the **5C Model** comes in. It's a simple framework for strengthening any relationship by focusing on five key areas: **Condition, Certainty, Control, Connection, and Communication.** **Condition** is about creating the right environment for your relationships to grow. Think of it like planting a garden—if the soil isn't healthy, the plants won't thrive. When you create a positive and supportive atmosphere, it's much easier for trust and respect to blossom. **Certainty** helps people feel secure by setting clear expectations. When others know what to expect from you, it builds confidence and reduces anxiety. **Control** is giving others the freedom to make their own choices. When you allow people space to be themselves, you show respect and foster trust. **Connection** is all about building deeper, genuine relationships. True connection happens when you take the time to empathise and share meaningful moments with others. Finally, **Communication** is the key to making it all work by sharing your thoughts and listening to others clearly and honestly. Without communication, misunderstandings happen, trust breaks down, and relationships weaken.

Think about the relationships in your life. Are you creating a positive atmosphere? Are you being clear about what others can expect from you? Do you give others the space to make their own decisions? Are you really connecting with people or just going through the motions? And most importantly, how well are you communicating?

Practical Tips:

◊ **Pick One Area:** Choose one of the 5C's to focus on this week (e.g., Communication or Connection).

◊ **Set a Goal:** If you're focusing on communication, define a small goal, such as having one clear, open conversation each day.

◊ **Reflect and Adjust:** Notice any positive changes in your relationships as you apply this focus and adjust as needed.

Reflective Questions:

» Which of the 5C's needs more attention in your relationships?
» What can you change today?

Explore the EQ for Leadership course at The Mindsight Academy to learn more about using the 5 C Model in relationships. This course is designed to help leaders master emotional intelligence and build trust-filled connections.

DAY 255: THE ROLE OF EMPATHY IN STRENGTHENING RELATIONSHIPS

"Empathy is the language of connection; it speaks louder than words." – Maureen Chiana

Empathy is one of the most powerful tools for deepening relationships. It's more than just understanding someone's words; it's about feeling their emotions and truly seeing the world from their perspective. When you practise empathy, you allow others to feel heard, appreciated, and understood, fostering trust and connection.

From a scientific perspective, empathy activates mirror neurons in the brain, helping you experience the emotions of those around you. When you see someone joyous or in pain, your brain mirrors those feelings, enabling you to share in their experience. This natural connection is key to developing deeper personal and professional relationships.

Romans 12:15 (NIV) encourages us, *"Rejoice with those who rejoice; mourn with those who mourn."* This scriptural wisdom shows us that empathy isn't just about sharing in someone's struggles but also celebrating their joys. Whether you're offering support during tough times or sharing in someone's happiness, the joy of celebrating their successes through empathy strengthens your bond.
Think about a time when you felt truly understood by someone. That moment likely created a deep connection because they didn't just hear your words—they felt your emotions. This is the essence of empathy in relationships.

Practical Tips:

◊ In your conversations, practice empathy by focusing on the other person's emotions rather than just their words.

◊ Listen without judgment and offer support without needing to fix things.

Reflective Questions:

» How often do you practice empathy in your relationships? What can you do to be more emotionally available to others?

This question encourages careful reflection and gives you a deeper understanding of your own empathetic capabilities.

Exercise: This week, engage in one conversation in which your sole goal is to understand the other person's feelings. Don't rush to offer solutions—listen and empathise. Notice how this deepens the connection.

Practising empathy builds trust, fosters understanding, and creates meaningful connections that stand the test of time.

Day 256: How Community Builds Strong Relationships

"A strong community provides the foundation for growth, support, and shared purpose."– Maureen Chiana

Community is important in our personal and professional lives because it provides us with support, accountability, and a sense of belonging. Being a part of a community, whether in your family, office, network group, church or with a group of friends, deepens your relationships and gives you a sense of purpose. When individuals come together, they form a network of trust and compassion that benefits everyone.

Research has shown that being part of a supportive community triggers the brain's reward system, producing dopamine and oxytocin—chemicals that make us feel good and foster connection. This leads to lower stress levels, more emotional resilience, and a stronger sense of belonging. The resulting sense of connectedness fosters trust and enables us to feel more secure in our relationships.

Ecclesiastes 4:9-10 reminds us that *"two are better than one because they have a good return for their labour: if either of them falls down, one can help the other up."* Community is about encouraging one another, providing assistance when needed, and celebrating one another's accomplishments. It's during these shared experiences that deep, long-lasting ties are built.

Consider a time when your community, whether friends, family, or colleagues, came together to assist you. The sense of belonging to something larger than yourself fosters trust and connection, allowing you to thrive while also giving back.

Practical Tips:

◊ Actively engage with your community, whether it's through offering help, sharing advice, or simply being present.

◊ Remember, a strong community thrives on mutual support, and your active participation is key to its success.

Reflective Question: How are you contributing to the communities in your life, and how can you foster deeper connections within them?

Exercise: This week, reach out to one member of your community who may need support or encouragement. Take the time to strengthen your bond, whether it's a phone call, a kind word, or practical help.

By embracing the power of community, you strengthen your own relationships and contribute to the growth and well-being of everyone around you.

Day 257: Setting Boundaries in Relationships

"Healthy boundaries are the foundation of mutual respect and trust in relationships." – Maureen Chiana

Setting boundaries in relationships is different from personal boundaries. While personal boundaries protect your own well-being, boundaries in relationships establish the limits needed for respect, trust, and understanding between two people. They help define acceptable behaviour, ensuring both individuals feel valued and respected without overstepping each other's emotional or physical space.

Healthy boundaries in relationships allow both parties to maintain their individuality while still growing together. For example, in a friendship, clear boundaries might include respecting personal time or understanding emotional limits during tough conversations. In a romantic relationship, boundaries can involve communicating needs regarding personal space or emotional availability. Establishing boundaries in relationships activates the prefrontal cortex, which helps with decision-making and emotional regulation. This part of the brain enables you to make thoughtful decisions about boundaries, ensuring they align with your values and the nature of the relationship.

Galatians 6:2 (NIV) says, *"Carry each other's burdens, and in this way you will fulfill the law of Christ."* While this verse encourages helping others, it's important to remember that setting boundaries doesn't mean you stop supporting those you care about. Instead, it helps ensure your support is healthy, sustainable, and balanced. Consider a situation where a friend consistently relies on you for emotional support but rarely offers the same in return. Setting boundaries and communicating your needs fosters a healthier relationship where both parties can give and receive.

Practical Tips:

◊ When setting boundaries in relationships, be clear and kind.

◊ Explain your limits in a way that prioritises respect for both yourself and the other person.

Reflective Question: What boundaries could you set in your key relationships to maintain balance and mutual respect?

Exercise: This week, identify one relationship where boundaries need to be strengthened. Practice communicating those boundaries kindly and clearly, and notice how it impacts the relationship dynamic. Setting boundaries strengthens relationships by fostering respect and ensuring both parties feel valued. This leads to more fulfilling and balanced relationships.

Day 258: When People Show You Who They Are, Believe Them

"When actions speak louder than words, trust what you see, not just what you hear." –
Maureen Chiana

We often hear the phrase, "Actions speak louder than words," but how often do we
truly pay attention?
In relationships, it's easy to get caught up in what we hope or wish someone will
be. But the truth is, people show us who they are through their actions, not just
their words. When someone's behaviour repeatedly shows their true character, it's
important to trust what you see rather than holding on to false expectations.

Think of it like reading a book. If the pages keep showing you the same plot,
you can't rewrite it just because you want a different ending. People's consistent
behaviour is like the pages of that book. If someone constantly lets you down or
fails to respect your boundaries, it's time to believe their actions rather than make
excuses for them. This can be tough, especially if you care about the person, but
acknowledging reality helps you protect your emotional well-being.

Psychologically, ignoring someone's true behaviour can lead to cognitive
dissonance, a mental conflict in which the mind tries to reconcile the difference
between what it wants to believe and what's actually happening. This can create
stress and tension, draining emotional energy.

Proverbs 27:19 (NIV) says, *"As water reflects the face, so one's life reflects the heart."*
This scripture reminds us that people's actions reflect their true selves. Pay
attention to those reflections because they tell you more than any words can.

Practical Tip: If someone's behaviour consistently shows a pattern that conflicts
with their words, trust their actions. Don't ignore the signs.

Reflective Question: Are there any relationships in your life where you're ignoring
someone's actual behaviour because it doesn't match what you hope for?

Exercise: Reflect on one relationship where the person's actions have been
inconsistent with their words. Ask yourself if their behaviour is showing you
something important about who they are. Make a decision based on the truth you
see, not just the words you hear.

Trusting people's actions, rather than hoping for change, leads to healthier and
more authentic relationships.

Day 259: Self-Discovery Through Forgiveness

"Forgiveness isn't just about others—it's about freeing yourself to become who you're meant to be." – Maureen Chiana

Forgiveness is not only a powerful act of grace toward others but also a profound journey of self-discovery. When you choose to forgive those who have wronged you, you release yourself from the chains of past hurt and anger. Forgiveness allows you to explore who you are without the weight of resentment holding you back. It creates space for healing, growth, and transformation, opening up your heart to new possibilities and deeper connections.

Think of unforgiveness as a heavy stone you carry everywhere. The longer you carry it, the more it weighs you down, making it difficult to move forward. By forgiving, you're not just letting go of the stone; you're freeing yourself to walk more lightly on your journey.

Neuroscience reveals that harbouring resentment causes your brain to stay stressed, repeatedly triggering your fight-or-flight response. This can cloud your thinking, limit your emotional growth, and trap you in patterns of fear and anger. When you forgive, your brain releases tension, promoting emotional clarity and inner peace. This process allows you to rediscover your strength, resilience, and purpose.

Matthew 6:14 (NIV) reminds us, *"For if you forgive other people when they sin against you, your heavenly Father will also forgive you."* This scripture invites us to release the weight of past wrongs, not just for others, but to restore our own peace and purpose.

Practical Tip: Start by forgiving yourself. Sometimes, the hardest person to forgive is yourself, but this is vital to self-discovery. Release past mistakes and allow yourself to move forward with grace.

Reflective Questions:

» How has holding onto past hurts affected your personal growth?
» What would forgiving those who have wronged you (or yourself) unlock in your journey?

Exercise: This week, reflect on one unresolved hurt or grudge. Write down what happened and how it affected you. Then, choose to forgive—either through prayer, reflection, or journaling—and notice how it lightens your emotional burden.

Through forgiveness, you uncover new layers of strength and purpose, opening up a path to deeper self-awareness and personal growth.

Day 260: Let Go of the 'Should-Have' Mindset

"Unspoken expectations are pre-meditated disappointments." – Maureen Chiana

How often do you catch yourself thinking, *"They should have known,"* or *"I shouldn't have to explain this"*?

The should-have mindset can lead to disappointment and frustration in relationships. Expecting others to know precisely what you need without telling them is a recipe for misunderstandings and resentment. No one can read your mind, and relying on assumptions can weaken your connection and trust.

Relationships thrive on clear communication, not on silent expectations. Neuroscience shows that our brains seek clarity, and when we assume others should know what we need, it causes stress and confusion. It's like setting a trap in your own mind—waiting for someone to fall into it without even realising the rules. Letting go of these assumptions frees both you and the people in your life from unnecessary conflict.

Imagine trying to bake a cake without a recipe, expecting it to turn out perfectly. You wouldn't expect that in the kitchen, so why expect it in relationships? People need clear directions to understand your needs. Without them, you're both left guessing and frustrated. Proverbs 18:2 (ESV) states, *"A fool takes no pleasure in understanding, but only in expressing his opinion."* This highlights the importance of understanding and clear communication rather than assuming others will automatically know.

Practical Tips:

◊ Swap assumptions for clear communication.
◊ The next time you catch yourself thinking, "They should-have known," pause and communicate your needs directly.

Reflective Questions:

» Do you expect others to read your mind?
» How can you communicate your expectations more clearly?

Exercise: Identify one situation where you've been holding onto unspoken expectations. Have a direct conversation with the person, expressing your needs clearly and without assumptions.

Letting go of the *'should-have'* mindset allows you to embrace honest, open communication, building stronger, more trusting relationships.

Day 261: The Hidden Gift of Rejection

"Rejection isn't the end of your journey—it's often the beginning of your greatest growth."
– Maureen Chiana

We all face rejection, and it can hurt deeply. But what if rejection is actually pushing you toward something even better? In the Bible, David experienced this when his family didn't invite him to meet the prophet Samuel. David was left out, forgotten in the fields. But during this time, he developed the skills and courage that later helped him defeat Goliath and become one of Israel's greatest leaders.

When you face rejection—whether in your job, relationships, or personal goals—it's a chance to grow stronger, just like David did. Neuroscience shows that rejection activates the same areas of the brain as physical pain, which is why it can feel overwhelming. But here's the good news: facing challenges like rejection can strengthen our brains, increasing our ability to bounce back. By rewiring your brain through emotional intelligence, you can see rejection as a moment to learn and adjust your path rather than something that defines your worth.

Romans 8:28 (NIV) reminds us, *"And we know that in all things God works for the good of those who love him, who have been called according to his purpose."* Even when rejection feels painful, it could be guiding you toward something better than you imagined.

Think about a time when rejection made you grow—maybe it led you to learn new skills or find a different path. Like David, it's often in these moments that we gain the strength, wisdom, and courage we need for future success.

Practical Tips:

◊ Next time you face rejection, pause and ask, "What can I learn from this?"
◊ Use it as a stepping stone to grow instead of letting it define you.

Reflective Questions:

» How has rejection helped you grow in ways you didn't expect?
» What strengths have you developed because of it?

Exercise: Think of a recent rejection you faced. Write down what you learned from it and how the experience might prepare you for future opportunities.

By viewing rejection as a valuable gift, you can transform it into a powerful tool that fosters personal and professional growth and propels you towards new levels of success in all areas of your life.

Day 262: Protecting Yourself from Toxic People

"You cannot control others, but you can always control how you respond to them."
– Maureen Chiana

By establishing and maintaining healthy boundaries, you are not only safeguarding yourself from the negative impact of toxic individuals but also equipping yourself to preserve and enhance your emotional well-being. Whether in personal relationships or professional environments, this practice allows you to navigate challenging interactions without sacrificing your peace or personal growth.

When you're around toxic people, your brain releases cortisol, the "stress hormone," making you feel anxious and drained. Prolonged exposure to negativity can harm your mental, emotional, and physical health. Setting boundaries helps you control how much time and energy you invest in these relationships, protecting your mind from absorbing their negativity.

Proverbs 4:23 (NIV) reminds us, *"Above all else, guard your heart, for everything you do flows from it."* Guarding your heart means being intentional about the energy you let in and the people you allow close. Emotional intelligence helps you recognise when someone's negativity is affecting you and enables you to set boundaries that maintain your peace. Although you have no control over other people's actions, you have complete control over your own responses. You take charge of your well-being by staying aware of your feelings and managing your actions.
Think of your heart like a garden. Not everyone may walk through its gates. Boundaries are the fence that keeps your garden safe from harm, allowing it to grow and flourish in a healthy environment.

Practical Tip: Learn to set clear boundaries with toxic people. This could mean limiting time with them, saying 'no' more often, or emotionally detaching from their negativity.

Reflective Questions: Are there any relationships in your life that drain your energy? Recognising these relationships is the first step towards setting healthier boundaries to protect your well-being.

Exercise: This week, identify one toxic relationship and practice setting a boundary. Whether it's limiting contact or managing how their energy affects you, notice how this shift affects your peace.

Remember, protecting your emotional well-being is not just important, it's essential. By setting boundaries, you create space for positive, healthy connections and allow yourself to thrive.

DAY 263: MANAGING YOUR EXPECTATIONS OF PEOPLE

"Releasing unrealistic expectations opens the door to true understanding and authentic connection." – Maureen Chiana

Expectations can be tricky in relationships. While it's natural to hope that others will act in certain ways, holding onto unrealistic expectations often leads to disappointment and frustration. When we expect people to behave in ways that align with our desires rather than their own abilities or nature, we set ourselves up for conflict and misunderstandings.

Managing expectations doesn't mean lowering your standards but recognising that everyone is different. People have their own perspectives, limitations, and ways of doing things. Research shows that when our expectations aren't met, the brain's reward system is disrupted, releasing cortisol—the "stress hormone." This leads to irritation, disappointment, and even friction in relationships. However, by changing your expectations to reflect the reality of the situation and the person's abilities, you can be more understanding and at peace.

Psalm 118:8 (NIV) reminds us, *"It is better to take refuge in the Lord than to trust in humans."* This verse highlights the importance of releasing control and trusting God's plan, rather than relying on others to meet all your expectations. By shifting your focus from unrealistic demands to grace and understanding, you create space for healthier and more fulfilling relationships. Imagine expecting someone to meet all of your emotional needs without ever expressing them. That's like expecting a plant to thrive without giving it water or sunlight. People need clarity and communication to meet expectations—without them, we're setting them up for failure and ourselves for disappointment.

Practical Tips:

◊ Let go of rigid expectations and embrace open communication.

◊ Share your needs clearly, empowering yourself and understanding that people will respond from their own abilities and limitations.

Reflective Questions:

» Where in your relationships have you held unrealistic expectations?

» How can you adjust those expectations for healthier interactions and foster growth?

Exercise: This week, reflect on one relationship where your expectations have led to frustration. Practice communicating your needs clearly and releasing any unrealistic demands you may hold onto.

DAY 264: TRUSTING GOD IN YOUR RELATIONSHIPS

"Trust in the Lord with all your heart and lean not on your own understanding;"
—Proverbs 3:5 (NIV)

Trust is one of the most important aspects of any relationship, but it isn't just about the people in your life—it's also about trusting God with your relationships. When you surrender your worries, fears, and expectations to Him, you allow God to guide your connections, giving you the wisdom and strength to handle challenges with grace.

When we let go of control and trust, the brain responds by lowering stress levels, allowing us to feel more at peace. Emotional intelligence helps us let go of our need to control everything and, instead, rely on God's guidance. Trusting in His plan enables you to approach relationships with more patience, openness, and faith. This patience is essential for understanding and accepting the intricacies of relationships.

Proverbs 16:9 (NIV) reminds us that *"In their hearts humans plan their course, but the Lord establishes their steps."* While having hopes and desires for your relationships is natural, trusting God means releasing the need to micromanage every detail and allowing His plan to unfold in its own time. This brings a sense of relief, knowing that we don't have to carry the burden of controlling every aspect of our relationships.

Practical Tips:

◊ When you feel anxious about a relationship, pause and pray.
◊ Trust that God has a plan for both you and the other person, and lean on His wisdom.

Reflective Questions:

» Are there areas in your relationships where you've struggled to let go of control?
» How can trusting God bring more peace into these situations?

Exercise: This week, reflect on one relationship where you've felt the need to control outcomes. Practice mindfulness and gratitude, and pray for the strength to trust God with the direction of that relationship.

By trusting God with your relationships and applying brain-rewiring practices like mindfulness and gratitude, you release the pressure to control everything, allowing your relationships to grow with love, peace, and purpose.

Day 265: Stop Pleasing People and Start Pleasing God

"You can't live your life for other people. You've got to do what's right for you, even if it hurts some people you love." – Nicholas Sparksans

People-pleasing can be exhausting, leaving you feeling drained and disconnected from your true purpose. While it might feel easier to meet other people's expectations, constantly seeking approval from people instead of God leads to frustration and a lack of fulfilment. Your purpose isn't in pleasing others but in living according to God's will.

From a neuroscience perspective, people-pleasing activates your brain's reward system, giving you a temporary sense of satisfaction. But this validation fades, leaving you trapped in a cycle of constantly seeking approval. Shifting your focus to pleasing God rewires your brain for lasting peace and fulfilment. Emotional intelligence helps you recognise when you're acting out of a desire for validation, allowing you to realign your thoughts and actions with God's purpose.

Matthew 6:33 (NIV) reminds us to *"But seek first His kingdom and His righteousness."* Pleasing people often leads to compromising your values, but when you prioritise pleasing God, you find true joy and peace.

Imagine carrying a load of expectations, each adding more weight. The more you try to meet everyone's needs, the heavier the load becomes. By choosing to please God, you release that burden and embrace a life aligned with His purpose.

Practical Tips:

◊ When you catch yourself trying to please others, pause and ask, *"Is this in line with God's will, or am I seeking human approval?"*

Reflective Questions:

» Where are you prioritising people's approval over God's?
» How can you focus more on pleasing God?

Exercise: This week, identify one area where you've been people-pleasing. Make a conscious choice to align your actions with God's will, even if it means saying 'no' to others.

By letting go of people-pleasing and focusing on God, you'll find freedom and deeper fulfilment in your purpose.

DAY 266: THE NEUROSCIENCE OF NEGOTIATION IN RELATIONSHIPS

"In business as in life, you don't get what you deserve, you get what you negotiate." – Chester L. Karrass

Negotiation offers a pathway to compromise and understanding. It's not about winning or losing but about finding a middle ground where all parties feel valued and respected. When approached with empathy and clarity, negotiation becomes a powerful tool for strengthening connections and fostering trust.

Successful negotiation involves the activation of the prefrontal cortex, the brain region responsible for logical reasoning, decision-making, and empathy. This area helps you think critically and balance your needs with those of others. However, in moments of conflict, the limbic system—the emotional centre of the brain—can take over, triggering the fight-or-flight response. This makes you defensive and less likely to listen. Emotional intelligence is crucial in regulating this response, allowing you to remain calm, listen, and work toward a solution that satisfies both sides.

Proverbs 15:1 (NIV) reminds us, *"A gentle answer turns away wrath, but a harsh word stirs up anger."* This scripture emphasises the power of a calm, thoughtful approach in negotiations. You can defuse tension and create positive outcomes by effectively managing your emotions and focusing on understanding. Imagine negotiating with a partner over how to manage time or responsibilities. If both of you approach the conversation with empathy, seeking to understand the other's point of view, you create an atmosphere of cooperation rather than conflict. This shared empathy can bridge the gap between your perspectives, leading to a more harmonious outcome.

Practical Tips:

◊ Before entering a negotiation, take a deep breath to calm your emotions.
◊ Practice thinking logically and empathetically to find a solution that benefits everyone.

Reflective Question:

» How can you harness the power of emotional regulation during negotiations to foster better communication and understanding?

Exercise: Practice staying calm and listening actively before responding in your next negotiation. Notice how controlling your emotions improves the conversation. You can negotiate with grace by mastering the balance between empathy and logic, ensuring both sides feel valued and heard.

DAY 267: THE SCIENCE OF PERSUASION IN RELATIONSHIPS

"Persuasion is about helping others see new perspectives, not about control." – Maureen Chiana

Persuasion is a valuable skill in any relationship. It's not about manipulating people but about guiding them to understand your point of view while creating trust. When used effectively, persuasion can improve communication and strengthen relationships.

Persuasion involves the prefrontal cortex (the part responsible for logical thinking and empathy) and the limbic system (the part dealing with emotions). An essential factor in persuasion is dopamine, a chemical that makes you feel good when you're rewarded. When dopamine is released, it makes people more open to new ideas and creates a sense of satisfaction. This means that when you use persuasion well, you can create a positive emotional response in others, making them more likely to agree with you.

Think of it this way: when you connect with someone emotionally and then offer logical reasons for your idea, you engage their brain in a way that makes them feel good and more open to your perspective. As neuroscientist Antonio Damasio once said, *"We are feeling machines that think."*

Emotions play a huge role in how we make decisions. For example, if you're trying to convince a colleague to try an alternative approach at work, start by acknowledging their concerns and showing empathy. This connects with their emotions. Then, give them clear, logical reasons why the new method is beneficial. This approach activates dopamine, making them more receptive to your idea.

Practical Tips:

◊ Start by connecting with someone's emotions—listen to their concerns.
◊ Then, use clear reasoning to back up your point.

Reflective Question: How can you balance emotions and logic when persuading someone?

Exercise: In your next conversation, focus on first understanding the other person's feelings and then offer logical reasons to support your idea. Notice how they respond.

Understanding how persuasion works in the brain allows you to communicate better and build stronger relationships.

DAY 268: ELEVATING CONVERSATIONS TO INSPIRE GROWTH

"Great minds discuss ideas. Average minds discuss events. Small minds discuss people." –
Eleanor Roosevelt

This quote by Eleanor Roosevelt challenges us to think about the quality of
our conversations. The way we communicate deeply affects our relationships.
Engaging in conversations that focus on meaningful ideas, regardless of the setting,
helps cultivate stronger personal and professional connections. These discussions
help elevate relationships and encourage personal and collective growth. It's easy
to get caught up in talking about everyday events or gossip. While these topics
can fill time, they don't lead to deeper understanding or growth. Surface-level talk
often leaves you feeling disconnected. Instead, when you engage in discussions
that explore new ideas or perspectives, you're more likely to feel energised
and connected. These types of conversations strengthen your relationships and
stimulate your brain's creative and problem-solving centres.

Your brain is designed to adapt through neuroplasticity, which means you can train
it to focus on more meaningful discussions. When you prioritise conversations
about ideas or solutions, you activate areas in the brain responsible for creativity
and deep thinking. Over time, this rewires your brain, making you more inclined to
seek out and enjoy thoughtful discussions.

Elevating Conversations:

> **Be Intentional:** Choose discussions that challenge your thoughts and encourage
> growth.
> **Pause and Reflect:** Before speaking, ask yourself, *"Will this conversation bring
> value?"*
> **Reinforce Positive Habits:** Regularly remind yourself to seek deeper, more
> meaningful conversations.

Manage your emotions and focus on others to keep conversations meaningful.
Empathy and listening build strong relationships.

Practical Tip: In your next conversation, steer the discussion toward an idea or
challenge that stimulates thought and growth.

Reflective Question: How can focusing on ideas improve the quality of your
conversations?

Exercise: In your next conversation, try discussing a new idea or challenge. See
how it impacts your connection with the other person.

Day 269: Overcoming Envy and Jealousy

"A heart at peace gives life to the body, but envy rots the bones." – Proverbs 14:30 (NIV)

It's natural to feel moments of envy or jealousy when you see others succeeding in areas where you're struggling. However, it's crucial to understand that holding onto these feelings will rob you of your peace and significantly damage your relationships. Envy and jealousy make you focus on what you lack rather than appreciating what you have. They create a sense of dissatisfaction that can ripple into other areas of your life.

When you're caught up in envy or jealousy, your brain's amygdala—the emotional centre—gets activated, triggering the release of cortisol, the stress hormone. This leaves you feeling tense, anxious, unfulfilled, and disconnected from yourself and those around you. You might start comparing your achievements to those of others, seeking a fleeting sense of control or validation. But this feeling doesn't last—envy and jealousy drain your energy over time, pulling you away from your own journey and distracting you from your unique path.

Proverbs 14:30 says, *"Envy rots the bones,"* reminding us that jealousy drains our peace. But a heart at peace—rooted in gratitude and self-awareness—brings life and fulfilment. When you focus on your own growth and release comparisons, you create space for joy and progress. Think back to a time you felt envious of someone else's success. Instead of letting those feelings settle, take a moment now to reflect on your own journey. What milestones have you reached? What strengths make you unique? This simple shift in focus can bring calm and remind you that your path is yours alone to walk.

Practical Tips:

◊ The next time envy or jealousy arises, pause and take stock of your own achievements.
◊ Gratitude is a powerful way to shift your mindset and reduce stress.

Reflective Questions:
In what areas of your life do envy and jealousy show up most often?
How can focusing on your own growth bring you peace?

Exercise: When you feel envious or jealous this week, write down three things you're proud of. Notice how reflecting on your own progress shifts your perspective. Letting go of envy and jealousy allows you to celebrate not only your journey but also the successes of others. Doing so creates more space for peace and deeper connections in your relationships.

DAY 270: OVERCOMING THE HABIT OF BEING JUDGMENTAL

"Why do you look at the speck of sawdust in your brother's eye and pay no attention to the plank in your own eye?" – Matthew 7:3 (NIV)

We've all been guilty of making snap judgments about others based on first impressions or incomplete information. These quick judgments, however, are often misleading and can prevent you from truly understanding the people around you. They also prevent you from extending empathy and building authentic relationships.

These snap judgments are made in the amygdala, the part of the brain responsible for emotional reactions, including fear and anger. When triggered, the amygdala can cause you to react impulsively without considering the whole story. While this part of the brain helps us make fast decisions, it's also prone to bias and overreaction. However, the prefrontal cortex—the part of the brain responsible for rational thought and empathy—can help you pause, reflect, and override these initial emotional responses.

Jesus reminds us in John 8:7 (NIV), *"Let any one of you who is without sin be the first to throw a stone."* This scripture teaches that none of us are perfect, and judging others based on limited information overlooks the struggles they may be facing. By engaging your prefrontal cortex, you can shift from judgment to understanding, fostering more meaningful connections. Think about a time when you judged someone too quickly, only to realise later that you misunderstood the situation. Next time, pause and engage your prefrontal cortex by asking, *"What's the full story here?"* This allows you to respond with empathy instead of criticism.

Practical Tips:
- ◊ When you feel judgment coming on, pause for a moment.
- ◊ Take a deep breath and engage your prefrontal cortex by asking yourself, *"Do I know the whole story?"*
- ◊ Replace judgment with curiosity.

Reflective Questions:
- » Where in your life are you quick to judge others?
- » How can you engage empathy and understanding instead of criticism?

Exercise: This week, when you catch yourself judging someone, pause and reflect on your own flaws. Consider the challenges the other person might be facing to help shift your focus from criticism to curiosity.

By learning to control the urge to judge and engaging your prefrontal cortex, you create space for empathy, compassion, and stronger, more authentic relationships.

DAY 271: THE ROLE OF SPINDLE CELLS IN SNAP JUDGMENTS

"For wisdom will enter your heart, and knowledge will be pleasant to your soul." –
Proverbs 2:10 (NIV)

We all make snap judgments—those quick decisions in the heat of the moment.
Whether it's reacting to a situation at work or handling an emotional conversation,
it feels like we're acting on instinct. But these fast decisions are powered by special
brain cells called **spindle cells**, which play a big role in helping us make choices
quickly by linking our emotions and thoughts.

The Role of Spindle Cells
Spindle cells, found in a part of the brain called the cingulate cortex, work like
your brain's *"speed processors."* They allow you to quickly sort through complex
information and emotions, especially when things are stressful or emotional. Their
unique shape helps them transmit information faster than other brain cells, giving
you the ability to make split-second decisions. But here's the key: they can only
make good decisions based on what you've already learned and experienced.

Your brain is always growing and adapting through neuroplasticity. This means
that the more you learn and experience, the better equipped your spindle cells
become to make smart, quick decisions. If you've spent time developing your
mind—whether through learning new skills or gaining life experience—your brain
has a stronger foundation for making wise snap judgments. In emotionally intense
situations, like disagreements at work or high-pressure choices, spindle cells help
balance your emotions with logic. This gives you the power to stay calm and think
clearly, even when emotions are running high.

Practical Tips:
One effective way to enhance your snap judgments is to prioritise lifelong learning
and continuous improvement. The more knowledge and experience you gain, the
better your brain will be at making smart, quick decisions in stressful situations.

Reflective Question:
How can you continue to build your knowledge and experience so your quick
decisions are more informed and effective?

Exercise: This week, try learning something new—whether it's reading a book,
taking a course, or practising a skill. Pay attention to how this knowledge helps you
make quicker, better decisions in challenging situations.
Understanding your spindle cells shows that snap judgments aren't just gut
feelings; they're shaped by your learning and experience over time.

DAY 272: THE DANGERS OF MIND READING

" But who can discern their own errors? Forgive my hidden faults." – Psalm 19:12 (NIV)

Mind reading—when we assume we know what others are thinking or feeling—can be a dangerous habit in relationships. Without realising it, you might be projecting your own fears, insecurities, or assumptions onto others, leading to misunderstandings and unnecessary conflict. None of us can accurately know what another person is thinking unless they tell us directly.

Our brain tries to predict other people's behaviours and emotions through 'mentalising', where we use our own experiences to guess what someone else might be thinking. While this can help us empathise with others, it can also lead to errors when we rely on assumptions rather than facts. This habit triggers the brain's amygdala, causing emotional responses like fear or anxiety, often based on nothing more than misinterpretation.

When you engage in mind reading, you rob yourself of the opportunity to communicate effectively. Instead of asking someone how they feel, what they need, or what they mean, you act based on assumptions, which often leads to tension or resentment. Scripture warns against relying on our own understanding. Proverbs 3:5 reminds us to trust the Lord with all our hearts and not rely on our understanding. This highlights the importance of seeking clarity rather than making assumptions.

Thinking a colleague is upset with you because they seemed distant, only to learn later they were actually dealing with personal issues. By mind reading, you misjudged the situation and likely added unnecessary stress to your own life.

Practical Tips: When you catch yourself trying to *"read someone's mind,"* pause and ask them directly how they're feeling or what they're thinking. Clear communication prevents misunderstandings.

Reflective Questions:
  » Where in your life have you made assumptions about others' thoughts or feelings?
  » How can you shift to clearer communication?

Exercise: This week, when you feel the urge to mind-read, stop and ask for clarification instead—practice asking open-ended questions to foster more understanding and direct communication.

By avoiding the trap of mind reading and embracing clear communication, you foster trust and prevent misunderstandings in your relationships.

Day 273: Resolving Conflicts

"A gentle answer turns away wrath, but a harsh word stirs up anger." – Proverbs 15:1 (NIV)

Conflict is inevitable in any relationship, whether personal or professional. However, handling conflict can either strengthen or weaken our connections with others. While some see conflict as negative, it can actually foster deeper connections if managed effectively. The key is learning how to resolve conflicts effectively, with empathy and clear communication.

Neuroscience tells us that during conflict, the amygdala—the brain's emotional centre—can hijack our responses, triggering the fight-flight-or-freeze reaction. This can cause us to react impulsively, say hurtful things, or shut down emotionally. However, the prefrontal cortex, responsible for rational thinking and empathy, helps regulate this emotional response and encourages thoughtful problem-solving. Engaging the prefrontal cortex allows us to stay calm and approach conflicts with a clearer mind, leading to more effective resolutions.

Ephesians 4:26 (NIV) reminds us, *'In your anger, do not sin:'* This scripture calls us to manage our emotions in a way that honours others, even when we feel wronged. Instead of letting anger control you, approach conflict with the goal of understanding and resolution. Imagine a disagreement with a colleague over a project deadline. If you let emotions take over, the conversation can quickly escalate into blame and frustration. But if you pause, take a deep breath, and calmly express your concerns while listening to theirs, you create space for compromise and understanding.

Practical Tips: During conflicts, pause and take a deep breath to calm your emotions. Engage your prefrontal cortex by focusing on finding a solution instead of reacting out of anger or frustration.

Reflective Questions:
- » How do you typically respond during conflicts?
- » How can you manage your emotions better to resolve conflicts with empathy and understanding?

Exercise: This week, practice resolving a conflict by calmly expressing your thoughts and actively listening to the other person's perspective. Notice how this approach affects the outcome.

Resolving conflicts with empathy and clear communication builds stronger, healthier relationships based on mutual respect and understanding.

Day 274: Building a Network of Positive Influences

"Walk with the wise and become wise, for a companion of fools suffers harm." – Proverbs 13:20 (NIV)

Picture life as a garden. The people around you are like sunlight and water, helping you grow, or like weeds, holding you back. Just as a plant needs a healthy environment, you need positive influences to thrive emotionally, spiritually, and professionally. When you're surrounded by people who uplift and encourage you, your "garden" blossoms. But toxic relationships act like weeds, sapping your energy and choking your growth.

Our relationships impact our brains. Positive interactions release oxytocin, the "bonding hormone," which builds trust, reduces stress, and makes us feel connected and supported. In contrast, negative influences trigger cortisol, the stress hormone, leading to anxiety and fatigue. Over time, this can damage our well-being and distract us from our goals.

Think back to a time when someone constantly criticised you or pulled you into negative thinking—you likely felt drained and defeated. Now, remember when someone believed in you and encouraged you to chase your dreams. That conversation probably left you feeling energised and hopeful. This is why building a network of positive influences is essential for growth.

Proverbs 13:20 reminds us, *"Walk with the wise and become wise."* Positive influences act like mentors, sharing wisdom and helping you through challenges. But just as a gardener removes weeds, you must also set boundaries with negative influences.

Practical Tips:

◊ Review your relationships.
◊ Who inspires and supports your growth?
◊ Nurture meaningful connections and set boundaries with energy-drainers.

Reflective Question:

» Who are the "sunlight and water" in your life?
» How can you invest more in these relationships?

Exercise: This week, reach out to someone who has positively influenced you and discuss your goals for deepening that relationship.

Building a network of positive influences is like cultivating a garden. The more you connect with those who uplift you, the more you'll flourish in every area of your life.

Day 275: Balancing Independence and Togetherness

"Though one may be overpowered, two can defend themselves. A cord of three strands is not quickly broken." – Ecclesiastes 4:12 (NIV)

Balancing independence and togetherness can be challenging in relationships. You want to maintain your individuality and personal space, but you also need emotional closeness and support from your partner or loved ones. Achieving this balance allows both you and your relationships to flourish.

Healthy relationships stimulate the release of oxytocin, the "bonding hormone," which fosters trust and intimacy. However, personal autonomy is equally important for mental and emotional well-being. According to research, individuals who possess a sense of independence experience an increase in self-worth and a decrease in stress levels, ultimately positively impacting their relationships. Scripture supports this balance: Galatians 6:5 (NIV) reminds us, *"For each one should carry their own load."* This highlights the importance of managing your own responsibilities while still being connected to others.

In a healthy relationship, both individuals are like trees planted side by side. They grow independently but have roots that intertwine, providing support without suffocating one another. Similarly, pursuing personal hobbies and interests while also spending meaningful time together is important. This balance creates mutual respect and space for personal growth and emotional intimacy. Imagine a couple in which one partner feels suffocated because they don't have enough personal space to pursue their interests while the other feels neglected. This imbalance can lead to frustration and misunderstandings. However, when both partners prioritise their independence and their togetherness, the relationship becomes more harmonious and fulfilling.

Practical Tips: Schedule personal time for yourself and quality time with your partner. This will help you meet your needs for autonomy and connection.

Reflective Questions:

  » How well do you balance your independence and togetherness in relationships?
  » Are there areas where you could improve?

Exercise: This week, plan a personal activity that you enjoy, and also set aside intentional time to spend with your partner or loved ones. Notice how this balance makes you feel.

By balancing independence and togetherness, you foster both personal growth and deeper connection, building resilient and rewarding relationships.

PART TEN

NEUROLEADERSHIP: UNLOCKING CAREER AND BUSINESS SUCCESS

PART 10 INTRODUCTION

Success in your career or business isn't just about hard work—it's about working smart. In this section, you'll explore how neuroleadership—combining brain science and leadership—can help you achieve high-level sustained success.

Your brain is your greatest tool. By understanding how it works, you can rewire it to boost focus, make better decisions, and build resilience. Neuroplasticity—your brain's ability to adapt—allows you to grow and evolve at any stage of your career.

However, success also depends on emotional intelligence (EQ), which is understanding yourself and others. Leading with EQ helps you build strong relationships, navigate workplace challenges, and inspire those around you. It's essential to creating lasting success in a fast-paced world.

In the coming days, we'll explore practical strategies to develop the habits, skills, and mindset needed for career growth. From building a personal brand to mastering work-life balance, each topic will be guided by neuroscience, EQ, and scripture.

As Proverbs 16:3 (NIV) says, *"Commit to the Lord whatever you do, and He will establish your plans."* Let this journey of growth be a reflection of your faith and dedication to success.

Are you ready to maximise your potential in leadership? Let's begin.

Day 276: Unlock Your Future with New Skills

"If you're not willing to learn, no one can help you. If you're determined to learn, no one can stop you." – Zig Ziglar

Think of your brain as a city with roads. Every time you learn something new, you're building a new road to a fresh destination. The more skills you develop, the more paths you create that lead to success. This is how neuroplasticity works—your brain rewires itself as you challenge it, strengthening connections and preparing you to take on even bigger tasks down the road.

Just like David in the Bible, who learned how to use a slingshot while watching over his sheep (1 Samuel 16), the skills you gain today might seem small but are setting the stage for bigger opportunities tomorrow. Whether you're learning new software, improving your leadership, or mastering communication, each new skill rewires your brain, making you more effective and adaptable.

Take Mariam, for example. She was a software developer who struggled with keeping up with new coding languages. She committed to spending 15 minutes each day learning a new language. Over time, her small daily practice rewired her brain, improved her skills, and opened doors to leading innovative projects at her company. That consistent effort transformed her career.

Practical Tips:

◊ Start small. Dedicate 15 minutes each day to learning a skill that will help your career or business.

◊ Whether it's improving your time management or mastering a new tool, this daily habit will rewire your brain and make what seems difficult today feel natural tomorrow.

Reflective Questions:

» What skill have you been hesitant to learn?
» How could mastering it shape your future?

Exercise: Pick one skill you want to develop today. Spend 15 minutes practising it and track your progress over time. Reflect weekly on how your brain is adapting as you stay committed.

Learning new skills isn't just about growth—it's about unlocking your future potential. Each new road you build in your brain is a path to greater success in your career, business, and life. Keep building, and see where those roads lead you.

Day 277: Adaptability: Thriving in a Changing World

"It is not the strongest that survive, but those most adaptable to change." – Charles Darwin

In today's world, everything moves fast. Technology changes, industries shift, and unexpected challenges pop up. The key to success is adaptability—being open to change and learning to adjust. Your ability to adapt isn't just a skill; it's a mindset that helps you thrive when others get stuck.

When you try something new, your brain forms new connections, making you more flexible and able to handle challenges better. This helps your brain grow stronger. Think of it like training your brain as you would a muscle. The more you work on adapting to changes, the easier it becomes. It's a bit like learning to ride a bike. At first, it feels awkward, but you gain balance and confidence with each attempt.

In the Bible, Paul talks about this kind of adaptability: *"I have learned to be content whatever the circumstances"* (Philippians 4:11 (NIV). His ability to adjust wasn't natural—it came from practice and the right mindset.

Adaptability might mean learning new tools, changing how you work with others, or even rethinking your goals in your job or business. Instead of fighting change, see it as an opportunity. The more adaptable you become, the easier it is to face the unknown.

When everything shifted to digital, Mark, a small business owner, had to move his business online. At first, it was overwhelming, but his business thrived after he embraced the change and learned new skills.

Practical Tips: Start small. Tackle one change you've been avoiding. It could be a new task at work or a different way of solving a problem. The more you practice adapting, the stronger your brain becomes at handling the unexpected.

Reflective Questions:

  » How do you usually respond to change?
  » Is there something in your work or life that you've been resisting?

Exercise: Identify one area where change is happening. Take one small step today to embrace that change, and reflect on how it might benefit you in the long run.

The more you practice adapting, the easier it becomes to face whatever life throws at you—and thrive!

DAY 278: DON'T LET YOUR DREAMS BE BURIED

"The future belongs to those who believe in the beauty of their dreams." – Eleanor Roosevelt

Have you ever had a dream that excited you, but over time, life got in the way? Maybe responsibilities, fear, or doubt buried it. But here's the truth: your dream is still there, waiting for you. It might be hidden, but it's still present. When life gets in the way, responsibilities, fear, or doubt bury dreams like seeds in the soil. Nevertheless, it is worth remembering that dreams, when given the proper attention, have the potential to blossom into something extraordinary.

When you think about your dreams, your brain releases dopamine, which makes you feel good and motivates you to take action. But when you push your dreams aside, it can leave you feeling stuck and unfulfilled. God has plans for you, and those dreams He placed in your heart aren't by accident. As Jeremiah 29:11 (NIV) says, *"For I know the plans I have for you…plans to give you hope and a future."* Your dreams are part of His bigger plan for your life.

Think of David. When Samuel came to anoint the next king, David's own family didn't even consider him. But while tending sheep, David's dream didn't die—his time in the fields prepared him for the moment he would face Goliath. Like David, your dream may feel distant or forgotten, but everything you're going through now is preparing you for something greater.

David dreamed of starting his own business, but fear held him back. One day, he decided to attend a business seminar. That simple action reignited his passion and set him on the path to launching his dream.

Practical Tips: Take one small step toward your dream today. It could be researching, writing your ideas, or even telling someone about it. The important thing is to take action, no matter how small.

Reflective Questions:
  » Is there a dream you've set aside?
  » What small step can you take today to bring it back to life?

Exercise: Write down one dream you've been holding back. This week, commit to taking one action to move closer to it. Reflect on how it feels to revive that dream.

Your dreams are still alive. Don't let them stay buried—take that first step, and watch what happens!

Day 279: The Path to Mastery

"No matter what happens to you, the important thing is what happens in you"– John Maxwell

Mastery doesn't happen overnight. It results from consistent effort, learning, and dedication. Whether it's mastering a skill, a craft, or a discipline, true mastery comes from small, intentional steps taken daily. Neuroscience shows that the brain strengthens neural pathways through repetition. The more you practice, the stronger and more efficient your brain becomes at that skill.

Mastery is like climbing a mountain. The peak can seem far away, but with each step, you get closer. It takes more than talent; persistence is also important. The Bible also speaks about this in Proverbs 22:29 (NIV), which says, *"Do you see someone skilled in their work? They will serve before kings."* The reward of mastery is personal satisfaction and the ability to impact others meaningfully.

To achieve mastery in your career or business, you must constantly refine your abilities. There are several ways to achieve this, such as practising leadership skills, acquiring knowledge in a new craft, or dedicating yourself to becoming an expert in your field. It's about showing up every day and putting in the work, even when it feels tedious. Each repetition builds you into someone who can achieve great things.

Think about a skill you've been wanting to master. Instead of feeling overwhelmed, try dedicating just 30 minutes each day to practice. Over time, those small, consistent efforts will add up, and soon, you'll see new opportunities and progress that you hadn't imagined possible.

Practical Tips:
◊ Focus on one area of your life where you want to achieve mastery.
◊ Dedicate a set amount of time each day—15 minutes to an hour—to practice.
◊ The key is consistency. Over time, the minor efforts will lead to significant improvement.

Reflective Questions:
» What area of your life or work do you want to master?
» How can you commit to practising consistently, even in small steps?

Exercise: Choose one skill or area you want to master. Set aside time each day to practice it. At the end of the week, reflect on your progress.

Mastery is a journey, not a destination. Every step you take, no matter how small, brings you closer to becoming the best version of yourself.

Day 280: Stop Waiting for Opportunities—Create Them

"Success doesn't come to you; you go to it." – Marva Collins

It's easy to think that opportunities will eventually come your way if you wait long enough. But the truth is, waiting can leave you stuck. Real success happens when you take control and create your own opportunities. Whether in your career, business, or personal life, you have the power to shape your future by taking bold action.

Neuroscience tells us that our brains are wired for problem-solving and action. When you actively pursue opportunities, you engage your brain's reward system, which motivates you to keep going. But when you sit back and wait, you miss out on chances to grow and make progress. The Bible encourages us in James 2:17 (NIV): *"Faith by itself, if it is not accompanied by action, is dead."* Believing is important, but it's action that brings results.

Think of it like planting a garden. If you wait for seeds to fall into your hands, you'll never start. But you'll see growth when you choose to plant, nurture, and water those seeds. In the same way, by taking action—whether it's networking, learning new skills, or launching a project—you create opportunities for yourself that wouldn't exist otherwise.

Instead of waiting for a promotion, seek out new responsibilities at work, offer ideas to improve processes or network with decision-makers. By taking initiative, you create your own path to advancement.

Practical Tips:

◊ Identify one area of your life where you've been waiting for something to happen.
◊ Take one bold step today—reach out to someone, start a new project, or take a class.
◊ The key is to act now.

Reflective Questions:

» What opportunity have you been waiting for?
» How can you take action today to create it instead of waiting?

Exercise: Choose one action you can take today to create an opportunity in your life. Whether big or small, commit to making it happen and track the results over time.

Don't wait for things to happen—make them happen! You hold the power to create the opportunities that will shape your future.

Day 281: Courage to Step Into Your Moment

"...you have come to your royal position for such a time as this" – Esther 4:14 (NIV)

In life and leadership, there are defining moments when you're called to step up, take action, and make a difference. These moments are often uncomfortable and can be scary, but they are also filled with potential. Esther's story reminds us that we must rise to the occasion when the time comes, even when fear tries to hold us back.

Esther was placed in a position of significant influence, but it wasn't for her comfort or personal gain. When the survival of her people was at stake, she had to find the courage to step into her purpose. We know that fear activates the amygdala, which is part of the brain responsible for the "fight, flight or freeze" response. But when you face fear with courage, the prefrontal cortex (the decision-making centre) overrides the amygdala, allowing you to make bold, intentional choices that align with your goal and purpose.

These defining moments often come when you least expect them in business and personal life. Maybe you're facing a challenge at work, or perhaps you've been given a leadership role that feels overwhelming. The key is to remember that you've been placed there for a reason. Just as Esther found the strength to face the king and save her people, you can overcome your challenges with God's guidance. Imagine negotiating a key client deal or streamlining your business operations. The pressure feels immense, but you rise to the occasion instead of shying away. With every decision you make, you will notice your confidence growing and eventually understand that this was the exact moment you were meant to shine.

Practical Tips: When you're faced with a tough decision or challenge, take a moment to pause and reflect. Ask yourself, *"What would happen if I courageously stepped into this moment?"* Embrace the discomfort, and trust that you are being prepared for something greater.

Reflective Questions:

> » Are you facing a moment that feels bigger than you?
> » How can you draw on Esther's courage to step into that moment with faith and confidence?

Exercise: Identify one area where you need to step up. Write down the fears or doubts holding you back, and then commit to taking one bold step toward your purpose this week.

You are not in this moment by accident. Just like Esther, you were created for such a time as this. Embrace it!

DAY 282: LEADING WITH INTEGRITY

"Whoever walks in integrity walks securely, but whoever takes crooked paths will be found out." – Proverbs 10:9 (NIV)

Integrity is the cornerstone of true leadership. It's about doing the right thing even when no one is watching, staying true to your values, and being honest in all areas of life. Without integrity, trust crumbles, and relationships lack depth, whether in business or personal life. Trust and authenticity activate the brain's reward centre, releasing oxytocin, which strengthens bonds and fosters collaboration. On the other hand, dishonesty triggers the brain's stress response, leading to feelings of insecurity and instability.

Think of your integrity as the foundation of a building. No matter how impressive the structure appears, the entire building is at risk of collapse if the foundation is weak. Integrity gives you stability, allowing you to lead confidently and earn the trust of others. The Bible reinforces this in Proverbs 11:3 (NIV): *"The integrity of the upright guides them, but the unfaithful are destroyed by their duplicity."* Having integrity earns respect and also positions you for long-term success.

In your career, integrity shows up in the small decisions—being transparent, admitting mistakes, and treating others fairly.
Leaders with integrity inspire loyalty and confidence, while those who compromise their values lose trust quickly. Imagine you're offered a major contract that could bring in a lot of money, but you realise the terms are unfair to one side. Choosing integrity means walking away, knowing it's the right thing to do. You trust that by staying honest, better opportunities will come along.

Practical Tips:

◊ Reflect on your daily actions.
◊ Are they aligned with your core values?
◊ When faced with a tough decision, pause and ask, *"Am I acting with integrity?"*
◊ Let your values guide you.

Reflective Questions:

» Where in your life have you compromised integrity?
» How can you commit to living more authentically?

Exercise: Identify one area where you've been tempted to compromise your values. Today, commit to making choices that align with integrity.

Living with integrity may be challenging, but it builds a lasting foundation.

DAY 283: LEADERSHIP IS ABOUT THEM, NOT YOU

"The greatest leader is not necessarily the one who does the greatest things. They are the one who gets the people to do the greatest things." – Ronald Reagan

Neuroleadership, the science of how our brains influence our leadership style, teaches us that leadership is not about one fixed approach. It's about understanding the people you lead and adapting your style to best serve them. Many leaders fall into the trap of using a style that works for them but may not work for their team.

When you apply emotional intelligence (EQ) in leadership, you tap into neuroleadership principles by recognising both your own emotions and those of your team members. Neuroscience shows that when leaders use empathy and adjust their approach, they engage the brain's trust and collaboration circuits, releasing oxytocin. This chemical strengthens relationships, improves engagement, and fosters a more collaborative environment. However, when leaders stick rigidly to their preferred style, team members may feel undervalued, triggering stress responses that lead to disengagement.

It is like coaching a sports team—each player has different strengths and needs. A good coach adjusts to bring out the best in each player. In business, neuroleadership means understanding the unique strengths of your team members and adapting your style to help them thrive. For example, one business leader realised that a team member performed best when given more creative freedom. By applying neuroleadership principles and adjusting her style, she empowered that employee to deliver exceptional results.

Practical Tips:

◊ Apply neuroleadership by learning about your team's individual needs.
◊ Ask yourself, *"Am I leading in a way that taps into their potential, or just what's comfortable for me?"*
◊ Adjust your leadership to meet their needs and help them grow.

Reflective Questions:

» Are you stuck in a leadership style that suits you but not your team?
» How can you apply neuroleadership to adapt your approach and serve them better?

Exercise: Identify one team member whose needs you may have missed. Adjust your leadership style to support their unique strengths, and notice the impact.

Leading with Neuroleadership and EQ means adapting to people's needs and helping them succeed while bringing you deeper fulfilment as a leader.

DAY 284: AMBITION WITH EMOTIONAL INTELLIGENCE

"Ambition is enthusiasm with a purpose." – Frank Tyger

Ambition is a God-given drive, a call to rise, lead, and make a difference. Scripture tells us that we are *"the head and not the tail"* (Deuteronomy 28:13 (NIV)), meant to step boldly into our purpose. However, ambition reaches its highest potential when paired with emotional intelligence (EQ). When ambition is balanced with EQ, it becomes more than just a personal pursuit—it becomes a force that lifts others.

Ambition stirs us to pursue big dreams, activating our brain's reward system, which releases dopamine as we reach our goals. This excitement drives us forward, but unchecked ambition can be purely self-focused. EQ keeps us grounded, helping us pursue our dreams with patience, wisdom, and grace, even through challenges.

When ambition and EQ work together, the prefrontal cortex—the part of the brain that handles decision-making, planning, and focus—functions with a purpose beyond ourselves. Instead of pushing forward blindly, ambition becomes intentional and is fuelled by self-awareness and empathy.

Proverbs 16:32 (NIV) captures this balance: *"Better a patient person than a warrior, one with self-control than one who takes a city."* With EQ, ambition isn't just about achieving; it's about growing, serving, and making an impact.

Reflect on a time when you faced a setback with your goals. Rather than charging through, did you ever pause to consider an alternative approach, wait patiently, or seek God's guidance? When EQ shapes ambition, we can turn roadblocks into valuable lessons and achieve success with integrity. This kind of ambition allows us to achieve in ways that lift others along the way.

Practical Tips:

◊ Regularly take a moment to review your goals.
◊ Ask, "Is my ambition aligned with God's purpose? Am I also benefiting those around me?"

Reflective Question:
How can you pursue your dreams in ways that bless both you and others?

Ambition, when guided by EQ, leads to success that honours God and serves others. Let your drive be anchored in compassion and purpose, and you will create an impact that uplifts everyone it touches.

DAY 285: ASK FOR WHAT YOU WANT

"…you do not have because you do not ask." – James 4:2 (NKJV)

Many people hesitate to ask for what they want, fearing rejection, conflict, or the possibility of appearing demanding. But what if the very act of asking is the key that unlocks the doors to your desires? Asking for what you want is not only about communicating your needs; it's about embracing your self-worth and recognising that you matter and your voice matters.

Neuroscience shows that asking engages deeper parts of the brain, particularly the anterior cingulate cortex (ACC). This region helps regulate the discomfort of asking, especially when faced with the fear of rejection. By learning to push through that discomfort, you develop emotional resilience, allowing you to ask with clarity and purpose. Also, the ventromedial prefrontal cortex (vmPFC), responsible for self-worth and decision-making, gets activated when you assert yourself. This process reinforces your belief in your own values and sharpens your ability to make confident decisions.

Emotionally intelligent leaders understand that asking is not a sign of weakness but a strategic move toward growth. The Bible reminds us to ask with boldness: *"Ask, and it will be given to you; seek, and you will find;…"* (Matthew 7:7 (NKJV)). When you ask, you are demonstrating faith not only in others but also in yourself.

Practical Tip: Start by asking for more minor things to build confidence. Notice how your brain reacts to the discomfort and how, over time, it becomes easier. This practice strengthens your emotional resilience.

Example: Imagine being overlooked for a promotion. Instead of waiting, you request a meeting with your supervisor to discuss your achievements and express your interest. This act of asking shows your confidence and opens doors that might have stayed closed.

Reflective Question: What are you afraid to ask for? How could asking with clarity, boldness and confidence change your situation?

Exercise: Write down one thing you want but haven't asked for. Take a step this week to ask for it, and reflect on how asking affects your emotions and mindset.

Asking for what you want isn't just about getting something—it's about knowing your worth and believing your voice matters.

Day 286: Drop the "But" – Words That Hold You Back

"The only limits you have are the limits you believe." – Wayne Dyer

Have you ever noticed how often you say, "I would, but…"?

That little word *"but"* has a lot of power. It's often the excuse we use to avoid action, to explain why we can't move forward, or why something is too difficult. Your "but's" can create invisible barriers that keep you from reaching your potential.

When you say "but," your brain listens. Using limiting language like "but" can trigger the amygdala, the brain's emotional response centre that handles fear and avoidance. This is what stops you from taking action by reinforcing negative thinking patterns. This is what causes you to procrastinate. When you reframe your thoughts and replace *"but"* with *"and,"* your brain's prefrontal cortex—the area responsible for decision-making and problem-solving—becomes more engaged, helping you see possibilities rather than obstacles.

Think about it this way: when you say, *"I want to launch my idea, but I'm not ready,"* you're closing off a path to success. Replace that with *"I want to launch my idea, and I'll start preparing now."* Suddenly, you shift from being stuck to taking action.

The Bible teaches the importance of our words in Proverbs 18:21 (NIV), *"The tongue has the power of life and death."* How you speak about your goals can either limit or empower you. Instead of saying, *"I'd like to pursue that opportunity, but I don't have enough experience,"* say, *"I'd like to pursue that opportunity, and I'll start building the skills I need."*

Practical Tips:

◊ Pay attention to how often you use "but" when thinking or discussing your goals.
◊ Practice switching it to "and" to open yourself up to new possibilities.

Reflective Questions:

» How often do you find yourself saying "but"?
» How could shifting your language change the way you pursue your goals?

Exercise: For the next week, catch yourself every time you use *"but"* when discussing your goals. Replace it with *"and"* to reframe your thinking and open new doors for action. Changing how you speak can change how you act. Watch your "but's" and start turning obstacles into opportunities.

Day 287: Neuro-Success: Rewiring for Achievement

"The trouble with most people is that you think with your hopes or fears or wishes rather than with your minds." – Will Durant

Your brain is a powerful tool that can be trained to create success. Neurosuccess taps into this potential by intentionally rewiring how you think and act. Thanks to neuroplasticity, your brain adapts and forms new connections whenever you push through a challenge, learn something new, or practice positive thinking. This means you can reshape your mindset toward achievement.

When you pursue a goal, your brain releases dopamine, the chemical that boosts motivation. Dopamine is like fuel for your brain, rewarding you for small wins and pushing you to keep going. Each small step forward strengthens the brain's pathways, making you more resilient and determined. However, success isn't just about reaching goals—it's also about how you handle the inevitable setbacks. Obstacles often trigger fear and self-doubt, which can derail progress. But by using emotional intelligence, you can train your brain to see setbacks as opportunities to grow, not failures, thereby fostering a positive and growth-oriented mindset.

Imagine you're climbing a mountain. Every step up is progress, but there are rocks along the way. Neurosuccess is about learning to navigate those rocks, knowing they're part of the journey rather than a reason to stop. Proverbs 24:16 (NIV) says, *"Though the righteous fall seven times, they rise again…"* Success lies not in never falling but in continuing to rise. If the thought of taking on a leadership role intimidates you, start by volunteering for small tasks that allow you to guide others. Each positive experience builds your confidence and reinforces that you can lead effectively.

Practical Tips:

◊ Catch yourself when negative thoughts hold you back.
◊ Reframe those thoughts into positive, action-focused statements, and focus on small wins that push you forward.

Reflective Questions:

» What thoughts or fears are limiting your progress?
» How can you shift your focus toward positive actions that lead to success?

Exercise: This week, reframe one limiting thought into an opportunity for growth. Track how it changes your mindset and motivates action.

By rewiring your brain with the right mindset and emotional resilience, you'll achieve success and handle life's challenges with strength and determination.

Day 288: Persuasion for Leadership and Success

"The ability to influence people without irritating them is the most profitable skill you can learn." – Napoleon Hill

Persuasion is more than just getting people to agree with you—it's about guiding others toward a shared goal while maintaining respect and trust. Effective persuasion shapes decisions with integrity, using influence to benefit everyone involved. Great leaders understand that persuasion isn't about forcing a point of view but creating a vision others want to be part of. When you persuade effectively, you activate the mirror neurons in the brain, which makes people more empathetic and receptive to your message. This is the foundation of rapport. By stimulating the brain's reward system with positive reinforcement, you build lasting trust and increase openness to new ideas. This is especially important in business, where emotional intelligence combined with logical arguments can turn hesitation into commitment.

Leaders who excel at persuasion know how to balance ethos *(credibility)*, pathos *(emotional connection)*, and logos *(logical reasoning)*. For example, in a business setting, a leader trying to implement a new policy might begin by acknowledging the team's hard work and commitment (building emotional connection), then share data that supports the policy's benefits (providing logical reasoning) and finally, express confidence in the team's ability to succeed with this new approach (building credibility). A department head persuading the team to adopt a new workflow could initially highlight how the current process limits growth and then show how the new approach will increase efficiency and reduce burnout. This method addresses their concerns and also appeals to their desire for improvement.

Practical Tips:
- ◊ Focus on understanding what motivates your audience.
- ◊ Instead of trying to change their minds, find common ground and present your case in a way that aligns with their values and needs.

Reflective Questions:
- » How do you use persuasion in your leadership?
- » Are you focusing on what motivates others or pushing your agenda?

Exercise: Identify a current leadership challenge. Use persuasion by focusing on the needs and values of your team. Notice how they respond differently.

Persuasion isn't about convincing others—it's about showing them why your vision matters and how their involvement leads to shared success.

Day 289: Creating Sustainable Value

"Strive not to be a success, but rather to be of value." – Albert Einstein

In today's fast-paced world, it's easy to chase quick wins. But real, lasting success comes from creating sustainable value—something that grows, benefits others, and holds its worth over time. In leadership, career, or business, building sustainable value means making a lasting impact, not just for yourself but for everyone it touches.

Our brains naturally seek quick rewards because of the dopamine released when we achieve something. However, creating lasting value requires using the prefrontal cortex. This area helps us plan for the long term, make thoughtful decisions, and practice patience instead of chasing instant gratification. When you focus on creating lasting value, you engage this part of your brain, making decisions that go beyond the present moment and setting the foundation for future success.

Creating sustainable value also requires emotional intelligence, especially the ability to connect with others and understand their long-term needs. As a leader, it's not just about hitting targets today—it's about building systems, relationships, and solutions that continue to benefit your team, clients, or business over time.

The Bible reminds us of this in Proverbs 13:11 (ESV): *"Wealth gained hastily will dwindle, but whoever gathers little by little will increase it."* Sustainable value comes from steady, thoughtful growth. Instead of focusing solely on short-term gains, invest in personal or employee development, understanding that a more skilled workforce will bring long-term value to the company for years.

Practical Tips:

◊ Ask yourself how your decisions today will benefit you and others tomorrow.

◊ Focus on creating lasting value by building meaningful relationships, long-term strategies, and investing in your growth.

Reflective Questions:

» Are you focusing on quick wins or building value that will last?

» How can you shift your mindset toward creating something that endures?

Exercise: Choose one area in your life or work to create lasting value. Take one step this week to build something that benefits others long-term. True success is about creating value that grows and serves the future.

Day 290: Getting Unstuck and Building with God

"Opportunities don't happen, you create them." – Chris Grosser

When you align your plans with God's guidance, you tap into a strength that helps you break free from stagnation. Trusting in God's direction allows you to move from a place of fear or doubt into faith and clarity, which is essential to getting unstuck and building a purposeful life.

Committing our plans to God activates the prefrontal cortex, the brain region responsible for decision-making and long-term planning. This shift helps us approach challenges with clarity and make thoughtful decisions rather than acting out of fear or uncertainty. Faith, when combined with action, opens up space for hope and new possibilities to replace doubt.

Building with God means inviting Him into every part of your journey—seeking His guidance as you set goals and take action. It's not about relying solely on your strength but leaning on His wisdom. Doing so lets you find balance and confidence, knowing you're not walking the path alone.

For example, consider a business owner struggling with a stagnant project. Instead of rushing forward, they pause and seek God's direction. Realigning their plans with God's purpose gives them the clarity needed to move forward in the right direction, ultimately finding renewed success.

Practical Tips:

◊ When you feel stuck, pause and pray for guidance.
◊ Take a small, intentional step forward, trusting that God is leading your path.

Reflective Questions:

» In what areas of your life do you feel stuck?
» How can you invite God into those situations to help guide your next steps?

Exercise: This week, commit one challenge or area of your life to God. Take one small step in faith, trusting that He will provide the clarity and guidance you need to move forward.

Building with God gives you the strength to get unstuck and move forward confidently, knowing your actions align with His greater purpose.

Day 291: Effortless Success

" For my yoke is easy and my burden is light." – Matthew 11:30 (ESV)

Success doesn't have to be exhausting. True success comes when you work from a place of rest—where your thoughts and mindset are aligned with your purpose. Instead of constantly striving, you flow effortlessly toward your goals. This shift in mindset rewires your brain to embrace ease over struggle, making success more sustainable and fulfilling.

Think of your mind like a well-tuned car. When the engine is aligned and taken care of, the journey is smooth. But when it is misaligned, every mile feels exhausting. Your brain functions in a similar way. When you align with your purpose, your prefrontal cortex—responsible for planning and decision-making—operates more efficiently. You activate the dopamine system, rewarding progress and making work more fun.

Jesus invites us to embrace this in Matthew 11:30 (ESV): *"My yoke is easy, and my burden is light."* When your thoughts and actions are in harmony with God's plan, you stop struggling against life's challenges and instead work from a place of peace. It's important to work from a place of rest, not rest after exhausting work. This mindset shift changes everything. A stressed entrepreneur shifts their mindset, focusing less on minor setbacks and more on building strong client relationships. By aligning their work with what they love, success begins to flow naturally.

Practical Tips:

◊ Pay attention to tasks that feel like a grind.
◊ Reframe your thinking to see them as opportunities for growth.
◊ Focus on tasks that align with your strengths and passions, trusting that this alignment brings natural success.

Reflective Questions:

» Where are you pushing too hard?
» How can you reframe your mindset to work from rest and alignment?

Exercise: Pick one overwhelming task this week and reframe it by focusing on how it aligns with your strengths and purpose. Notice the difference.

Effortless success comes from working in harmony with your purpose, allowing your brain to rewire for joy rather than exhaustion.

Day 292: Lead Like Christ (Yeshua)

"Instead, whoever wants to become great among you must be your servant" – Matthew 20:26 (NIV)

To lead like Yeshua is to embrace a style of leadership rooted in humility, compassion, and service. While the world often teaches that leadership is about power and control, Yeshua showed us that true leadership is about serving others. His example of servant leadership is a powerful model for both personal and professional life. It's not about being above others but about lifting others up, guiding them with love, and creating a lasting impact.

When you lead like Christ, you engage in empathic leadership—a style grounded in understanding, patience, and sacrifice. Neuroscience shows that when leaders exhibit empathy and humility, they activate mirror neurons in the brain, fostering trust and connection. This bond strengthens relationships and motivates people to follow their example. The emotional intelligence that Yeshua displayed—knowing when to correct, comfort, and guide—is essential for any leader who wishes to inspire lasting change.

In John 13:14-15 (NIV), Jesus washes the feet of His disciples and says, *"Now that I, your Lord and Teacher, have washed your feet, you also should wash one another's feet."* This act is a profound lesson in leadership, reminding us that no task is beneath us when we serve with love. Leading like Christ means recognising the needs of those around us and meeting those needs without seeking recognition. Imagine a manager who sees a struggling team member. Instead of criticising, they offer support, helping them improve. This leadership style builds trust and inspires loyalty, just as Christ inspired His followers.

Practical Tips: Look for opportunities to serve those you lead. This could be helping a team member with a task, offering encouragement, or simply being present and listening. Your actions will speak louder than your words.

Reflective Questions:
  » Are you leading in a way that serves others?
  » How can you model Christ-like leadership in both your personal relationships and interactions with those you lead?

Leading like Christ isn't about authority; it's about love, service, and lifting others up. This kind of leadership transforms those you lead and you as a leader.

Day 293: Achieving Work-Life Balance

"Balance is not better time management, but better boundary management." – Betsy Jacobson

Achieving work-life balance doesn't mean everything is evenly divided; life isn't designed to work that way. Instead, it's about setting priorities that align with God's purpose for your current season and creating boundaries to honour those priorities. The reality is that life ebbs and flows, and balance is about adjusting to the shifts with intentionality rather than striving for perfection.

Pursuing an unrealistic version of balance can lead to stress and burnout, triggering the brain's amygdala and making it harder to focus or make wise decisions. However, when you set clear boundaries and allow yourself time to rest, your prefrontal cortex—the brain's centre for planning and decision-making—functions at its best, helping you navigate responsibilities more effectively.

Even Yeshua understood the need for rest and reflection. In Luke 5:16, He withdrew to pray, despite the overwhelming demands of His ministry. This act of stepping back not only restored His strength but also refocused His purpose. His example teaches us that making space for rest is not just wise—it's essential to living a purpose-filled life.

I've experienced this firsthand. In the past, I stretched myself too thin, trying to juggle everything at once. By creating intentional boundaries, like dedicating specific evenings to family and unplugging from work, I found renewed energy and clarity, both personally and professionally.

Practical Tips:

◊ **Set priorities:** Determine what matters most right now, and let that guide your focus.
◊ **Honour Boundaries:** Protect time for rest, family, and spiritual reflection.
◊ **Adjust as Needed:** Be flexible and willing to realign when life shifts.

Reflective Questions:

» Are your actions aligned with God's purpose for this season?
» What steps can you take to protect time for rest and connection?

Exercise: Choose one area where you feel stretched thin. Set a boundary this week to protect your time and energy, and notice how it impacts your overall well-being.

Work-life balance isn't about achieving the impossible—it's about aligning your life with God's purpose and creating space for what truly matters.

Day 294: Owning Your Time

"It's not enough to be busy. The question is: what are we busy about?" – Henry David Thoreau

Managing time effectively is like steering a ship—without direction, you'll drift, feeling busy but unproductive. Time management isn't about doing more but focusing on what matters. When you control your time, you clear mental clutter and make room for actual productivity.

I use time blocking, and it has transformed how I manage my day. I create a clear structure and prevent distractions by scheduling specific time slots for tasks. It helps me focus on one task at a time, making the day less overwhelming.

The Pomodoro Technique is another excellent tool. Working in 25-minute focused bursts followed by short breaks is like sprinting for short distances, keeping energy high and preventing burnout.

Effective time management rewires your brain to handle tasks more efficiently. When you focus on one task, you strengthen neural pathways related to concentration. Over time, your brain adapts and becomes better at staying engaged. This process improves your brain's ability to stay focused and productive.

Jesus understood the importance of being intentional with time. He regularly withdrew to pray and recharge, showing us that balance and rest are key to maintaining focus and productivity. A project manager who felt overwhelmed began using time blocking for specific tasks. This structure allowed her to complete tasks more quickly while feeling less stressed.

Practical Tips:

◊ Try time-blocking a couple of tasks each day.
◊ Combine it with the Pomodoro Technique for short bursts of focused work.

Reflective Questions:

» Do you intentionally manage your time or let distractions take over?
» How could time blocking help you focus better?

Exercise: Choose one task that overwhelms you. Block out time for it, use the Pomodoro Technique, and notice the improvement in focus and productivity.

Mastering time management creates focus and discipline, helping you achieve more with clarity and purpose.

Day 295: Be Visionary: Seeing Beyond the Now

"The only thing worse than being blind is having sight but no vision." – Helen Keller

Being visionary means leading with a clear sense of purpose and direction, moving beyond the present to create a meaningful future. Visionaries don't just react to today's events; they set goals, plan for growth, and inspire others to join them in building something enduring. This foresight is invaluable in careers, businesses, and personal life, as it establishes a path for progress and fulfilment.

Vision isn't just about grand ideas—it's about putting them into action. A visionary leader combines creativity with strategy, actively working toward their goals. Neuroscience shows that when we visualise future outcomes, the brain's prefrontal cortex—responsible for planning and problem-solving—comes to life. This mental exercise boosts motivation and sharpens our decision-making skills. The brain's reward system releases dopamine, fueling excitement and determination as we see ourselves moving closer to our vision.

Proverbs 29:18 (KJV) says, *"Where there is no vision, the people perish."* This verse highlights the importance of vision as a guiding force. Jesus exemplified this by revealing the Kingdom of God as a present reality and calling us to live actively in alignment with that vision, regardless of current challenges. A powerful vision keeps us moving with purpose, grounded in faith, and focused on our calling.

Consider a business owner who had previously focused only on short-term gains. After clarifying her long-term vision, she shifted to strategic planning, which led to sustainable growth. By defining her purpose, she could lead her team with confidence and intention.

Practical Tips:

◊ Start by writing down your vision.
◊ Break it into actionable steps to keep you focused and motivated.

Reflective Questions:

» Do you have a clear vision for your future?
» Are your current actions aligned with your long-term goals?

Exercise: This week, take 15 minutes to outline your three-year vision. Identify one small action you can take today to start moving toward it.

Being a visionary isn't just about dreaming; it's about taking meaningful steps now to bring your future into focus.

Day 296: Destroy Doubt

"The only limit to our realisation of tomorrow is our doubts of today." – Franklin D. Roosevelt

Doubt is a silent dream killer. It often creeps in just when you're about to take a big step forward, causing hesitation and fear. Left unchecked, doubt can rob you of opportunities, growth, and success. But the truth is, doubt is not a reflection of your ability—it's simply a mindset that can be changed. Doubt triggers the brain's amygdala, the part responsible for fear and anxiety, which can block your ability to think clearly and take action. However, when you intentionally challenge doubt with confidence and faith, you engage the prefrontal cortex, which helps with logical thinking and decision-making. This shift rewires your brain to face challenges head-on rather than shrink back in fear.

In James 1:6 (NIV), we are told, *"But when you ask, you must believe and not doubt, because the one who doubts is like a wave of the sea, blown and tossed by the wind."* This scripture highlights how doubt can leave you feeling unstable and powerless, but belief brings focus and strength. To destroy doubt, start by acknowledging it. Once you recognise it, you can replace it with faith and action. Taking small, courageous steps gradually weakens doubt's hold over your mind.

An entrepreneur who struggled with self-doubt in networking avoided attending industry events, fearing she wouldn't measure up. Determined to grow, she started by connecting with just one new person at each event. Each successful conversation boosted her confidence and built valuable connections. Over time, networking became natural, opening doors to partnerships and clients that elevated her business.

Practical Tips:

◊ When doubt creeps in, identify it and counter it with a positive truth about yourself.
◊ Take one small step toward your goal, even if you feel unsure.

Reflective Questions:

» In what areas of your life does doubt hold you back?
» How can you replace doubt with faith and take small, actionable steps?

Exercise: This week, identify one area where doubt has kept you from moving forward. Take a small, brave step toward that goal and reflect on the outcome.

Doubt may seem powerful, but with the right mindset and action, you can destroy it and unlock your potential.

Day 297: Financial Success: Mindset and Consistency

"Don't judge each day by the harvest you reap but by the seeds that you plant." – Robert Louis Stevenson

Have you ever wondered how to take control of your financial future? It starts with your mindset and small, consistent actions. You don't achieve financial success overnight, but each day offers a chance to sow the seeds of growth.

Take Buky's story. She once felt overwhelmed by her financial goals and didn't know where to start. Rather than giving up, she began by saving just £50 a month. She didn't worry about how small it seemed; she focused on building the habit. Month after month, that consistency grew her savings. Over time, she increased her savings and invested wisely, watching her financial situation steadily improve. Buky's success wasn't about sudden breakthroughs but steady, deliberate progress.

Consistency is key. Each time Buky saved, her brain released dopamine, rewarding her for taking positive action. Through neuroplasticity, her brain rewired itself, making saving a natural habit. The same process can work for you: By taking small, consistent financial actions, you train your brain to focus on long-term rewards instead of short-term gratification.

Think of your financial habits like planting a garden. Every deposit or investment is a seed that, with time and care, will grow into something bigger. Galatians 6:7 (NIV) reminds us, *"A man reaps what he sows."* What you plant today will determine the harvest you reap tomorrow. Imagine saving just £10 a week. At the end of the year, that adds up to £520, showing how small actions lead to significant results over time.

Practical Tips:

◊ Start small. Choose an amount you can consistently save each month.
◊ At the start, the most important thing is the habit, not the quantity.

Reflective Questions:

» What financial seeds are you planting today?
» How can you make saving a consistent habit?

Exercise: This week, set a small savings goal. Stick to it and watch how consistent effort leads to growth.
Your financial success depends on the seeds you plant today. Care for them consistently, and they will flourish.

Day 298: Consistent Habits for Success

"Habits are the compound interest of self-improvement."—James Clear

Career and business success aren't about making instant giant leaps; they're about taking small, consistent steps every day. In his book Atomic Habits, James Clear describes habits as the "compound interest" of self-improvement. Just as small, regular investments add up to significant returns over time, so do daily habits. The key to long-term success is focusing on improving by just 1% daily rather than waiting for an instant breakthrough.

Think of your career as climbing a staircase. You may not be able to see the top, but each small step—whether it's learning new skills, networking, or refining your work processes—brings you closer to your goals. Over time, these small, daily actions build momentum, leading to success you couldn't have imagined when you started. Every time you repeat a habit, your brain strengthens the neural pathways associated with that behaviour. This helps you develop automatic habits that require less mental effort over time. This means that the small, consistent actions you take today will improve your skills and make it easier for you to maintain productive habits in the future.

Proverbs 10:4 (NIV) reminds us, *"Lazy hands make for poverty, but diligent hands bring wealth."* Success results from diligent, consistent effort—showing up and doing the work, even when progress seems slow.

A business owner who spends 20 minutes a day learning digital marketing will see significant results. This reminds me of when I started editing my podcast: small daily efforts built my confidence and skills over time. Consistency truly leads to progress.

Practical Tip: Start small. James Clear advises identifying one habit that supports your career or business goals and committing to it daily. Focus on getting just 1% better each day.

Reflective Questions:

- » What small, consistent actions are you taking daily to support your career or business?
- » How can you commit to improving by 1% each day?

Exercise: Choose one habit that aligns with your career or business goals. Practice it every day for the next 30 days and monitor your progress.

Success is about taking that first step and trusting that every small action brings you closer to your ultimate goal.

DAY 299: ENHANCING CAREER SUCCESS THROUGH LEARNING

"Learning never exhausts the mind." – Leonardo da Vinci

Have you thought about how your brain develops when you learn something new? Whether you're learning a new skill at work or enhancing your communication skills, your brain has a remarkable ability to adapt and strengthen through learning. The brain rewires itself in response to new information and experiences. It's similar to strengthening muscles through regular exercise; the more you work at it, the stronger it gets.

Learning isn't just about cramming information into your brain; it's about building habits that support your growth over time. When you learn something new, your brain uses short-term memory (or working memory) to handle immediate tasks, and with repeated practice, that information is stored in long-term memory. This process, known as memory consolidation, often happens during sleep, so rest plays a vital role in your ability to learn and succeed.

Creating daily learning habits doesn't just help with hard skills like mastering a new software program—it also strengthens emotional intelligence (EQ). Developing EQ helps you manage workplace relationships, handle stress, and lead with empathy. Whether you're building technical skills or improving how you connect with other people, these small daily habits make a huge difference in your career or business over time.

As you practice these habits, your brain forms stronger connections, making it easier for you to adapt and grow. Neuroplasticity is the secret to lifelong learning and staying competitive in today's fast-paced world. Spending just 15 - 30 minutes a day learning something new in your field will boost your confidence and prepare you for bigger opportunities. You'll feel more equipped in meetings, and over time, those small daily efforts can lead to promotions or business success. Small steps lead to significant results.

Practical Tips:

◊ Set time aside each day to learn something new.
◊ It could be as simple as reading an article, practising a skill, or listening to a podcast.

Reflective Questions:

» What are you doing daily to grow your career or improve your business?
» How can you develop a learning habit that helps you move forward?

By consistently learning and practising, you're setting yourself up for long-term success in your career.

Day 300: Don't Be a Drifter on the Sea of Life

"If you don't know where you are going, any road will get you there." – Lewis Carroll

Do you ever feel overwhelmed, like you're being pulled in different directions? Are you struggling to find focus, feeling like life is happening to you rather than for you? It can be frustrating, leaving you anxious and uncertain, as though you're drifting through life without a clear purpose. This feeling of drifting can be emotionally draining, especially in your career, business or personal life. Without clear goals, it's easy to feel lost and stuck in a cycle of reacting to circumstances rather than shaping your future. Clear goals activate the prefrontal cortex, the brain's executive centre for planning and problem-solving. When this part of your brain is active, you feel more in control, less overwhelmed, and better equipped to manage life's challenges.

Think of yourself as the captain of a ship. If you don't set a destination, you're at the mercy of the wind and waves, constantly changing direction without purpose. But when you know where you're going, you can navigate through setbacks and storms, adjusting course as needed, without losing sight of your destination. Setting goals provides emotional stability and a sense of purpose, enabling you to confront challenges with confidence instead of fear.

Proverbs 4:25 (NIV) says, *"Let your eyes look straight ahead; fix your gaze directly before you."* This is a powerful reminder to stay focused, no matter what distractions or challenges life throws your way. Feeling stuck in your career and moving from job to job without a clear plan can be exhausting. But when you have a clear vision, everything changes—you set goals, pursue growth, and confidently tackle challenges. The key difference is having a strong sense of direction.

Practical Tips:

◊ Take time to reflect on your goals.
◊ Write them down, break them into smaller steps, and regularly check your progress.

Reflective Questions:

» Are there areas of your life where you feel emotionally drained or lost?
» How can setting clear goals help you regain control and move forward?

Exercise: Choose one goal you've been avoiding or drifting away from. Write it down, break it into actionable steps, and take one small step toward it today.

Take control, set your course, and steer toward your desired life. You don't have to drift aimlessly.

DAY 301: THE PRICE OF HOLLOW SUCCESS

"What does it profit a man to gain the whole world, yet forfeit his soul?" – Mark 8:36 (NIV)

Have you ever pursued success so intensely that, in the end, it felt empty? In a world that glorifies wealth and status, it's easy to get caught up in achieving external recognition. But at what cost? The emotional toll of hollow success is real. You may feel a high from reaching your goals, but without purpose, balance, and God at the centre, that satisfaction fades quickly. You might ask, "Is this all there is?" Success without deeper meaning can lead to burnout, strained relationships, and a loss of peace.

Focusing on external success activates the brain's reward system by releasing dopamine, but this satisfaction is short-lived. When your success is focused only on external rewards like money or titles, it doesn't last. True success comes from aligning your goals with your values and, most importantly, with God's will.

Mark 8:36 (NIV) reminds us, *"What does it profit a man to gain the whole world, yet forfeit his soul?"* The success that pulls you away from God, your peace, or your purpose isn't a real success. Real fulfilment comes from staying close to God, letting the Holy Spirit guide your choices, and ensuring your success honours God and brings genuine goodness into your life.

Obi built a thriving business, but along the way, he sacrificed time with his family and lost touch with his relationship with God. Despite his financial success, he felt unfulfilled. When he realigned his priorities, reconnecting with God and investing time with his loved ones, his success gained true meaning—blessing his family, renewing his closeness with God, and bringing him lasting peace and purpose.

Practical Tips:

◊ Reflect on whether your goals align with God's purpose.
◊ Let the Holy Spirit guide your decisions, focusing on glorifying God through your achievements.

Reflective Questions:

» Are you sacrificing your relationship with God for worldly success?
» How can your success bring glory to God?

Exercise: Reflect on a recent achievement. Did it glorify God and align with His purpose? Make one adjustment to ensure future success serves both God and your good. True success enriches your soul and glorifies God. Stay close to Him, and your success will have lasting meaning.

Day 302: Transforming "What Ifs" into a Productivity Plan

"The secret of getting ahead is getting started." – Mark Twain

It's easy to get stuck in the "what ifs" that flood our minds when facing new challenges.
What if I fail? What if I'm not ready? What if everything falls apart?

These questions can feel like roadblocks, making it hard to take action. But what if you turned these fears into a **to-do list** instead of letting them hold you back? Shifting your "what ifs" into actionable steps can be the productivity superpower that keeps you moving forward. When you break your fears into small, manageable actions, your brain feels more in control, reducing anxiety and boosting confidence.

Here's how you can turn your *"what ifs"* **into a powerful productivity plan:**

> **What if it all fails?** – Create a backup plan. Knowing you have a Plan B eases worry and keeps you focused on moving forward.
> **What if I'm not ready?** – Start small. Choose one simple task you can do today to gain a sense of progress, even if you don't feel fully prepared.
> **What if it's too overwhelming?** – Break it down. Divide big projects into smaller, doable steps to make them feel less intimidating.
> **What if I don't have time?** Prioritise. List your top three tasks and use time management techniques, such as time blocking or the Pomodoro method, to get things done.
> **What if I fail?** – See failure as a lesson, not an end. Each setback is an opportunity to learn and grow.

When I closed my salon business, I was afraid of starting another business. The "what ifs" weighed me down, but instead of letting them stop me, I rewired my thinking and began small with consultancy work. From there, I gained momentum and built my online academy, which has become more successful than I'd ever imagined.

Practical Tips: Turn each "what if" into a step on your to-do list. This shift transforms fear into fuel, empowering you to act.

Reflective Questions:

» What *"what ifs"* are keeping you stuck?
» How can you turn them into actionable steps to move forward?

Exercise: Write three *"what ifs"* about a goal and turn each into an action step for today. Turning fears into actions boosts productivity and helps you move forward with purpose.

Day 303: Stop Wasting Time

"Time is what we want most, but what we use worst." – William Penn

How often do you catch yourself saying, *"I just don't have enough time,"* yet you find yourself scrolling through social media or procrastinating on important tasks? We all have the same 24 hours, but how you choose to use them can either propel you forward or hold you back. Wasting time often comes from a lack of clarity or fear of starting something new. The brain's reward system seeks immediate gratification, making distractions like social media or non-essential tasks tempting. However, when you focus on meaningful, productive activities, your brain releases dopamine, which reinforces positive behaviour, creating momentum and motivation to keep going.

The key is to stop wasting time on activities that do not serve your goals. Imagine your time as a limited resource, like water in a bucket with a small hole. Every moment spent on distractions leaks your potential, leaving less time to achieve what truly matters. But by plugging the hole and focusing on what counts, you maximise your productivity and feel more fulfilled. Proverbs 12:11(NIV) reminds us, *"Those who work their land will have abundant food, but those who chase fantasies have no sense."* It's a call to focus on what's important, not fleeting distractions that waste our precious time.

I used to feel like I never had enough time to work on different aspects of my business. After committing to time blocking and scheduling focused work periods, I saw a massive improvement in my productivity. Instead of feeling overwhelmed, I now accomplish more with less stress.

Practical Tips:

◊ Use **time-blocking techniques** to allocate specific periods for tasks, ensuring you stay focused.
◊ **Limit distractions** by setting clear boundaries with your phone, social media, or other time-wasting habits.

Reflective Questions:

» How are you currently wasting time?
» What small adjustments can you make to spend your time more wisely?

Exercise: Identify three common time-wasters in your day. Replace each one with a productive task or break them into manageable steps to create momentum.

Your time is precious—don't let it slip away. Focus on what truly matters, using it wisely to reach your goals and live a fulfilling life.

DAY 304: BUILD YOUR PERSONAL BRAND

"A good name is more desirable than great riches; to be esteemed is better than silver or gold." – Proverbs 22:1 (NIV)

Your personal brand is how you present yourself to the world, both in your career and personal life. It's more than a logo or catchy tagline—it's the reputation you build through your actions, values, and how you connect with others. Building a solid personal brand gives you credibility and influence, allowing you to stand out in your field.

Neuroscience shows that pattern recognition is key to building a memorable personal brand. When people consistently experience positive interactions with you, your brand becomes imprinted in their brains, activating their prefrontal cortex—the area responsible for decision-making and trust. This consistency forms strong neural connections, making you the go-to person in your area of expertise.

In the professional world, your emotional intelligence (EQ) plays a critical role in building your brand. Being aware of how you communicate, handle stress, and connect with others is essential for building a reputation based on trust, empathy, and reliability. People remember how you make them feel, and those emotional connections are a vital part of your personal brand.

Proverbs 22:1 (NIV) reminds us that *"a good name is more desirable than great riches."* Your personal brand should reflect your core values and integrity, ensuring that your actions align with your beliefs. When you ground your brand in truth and faith, you honour God and create a lasting impact.

I've built my personal brand around integrity, faith, and leadership. I've consistently reflected on these values, creating trust and credibility in my community and business. People know what to expect from me, and that consistency has opened doors I never imagined.

Practical Tips:

◊ Define the core values you want your personal brand to represent.
◊ Ensure your actions align with these values in every personal or professional interaction.

Reflective Questions:

» What does your current personal brand say about you?
» How can you ensure your brand reflects your values and faith?

Building a strong personal brand requires intentionality, consistency, and alignment with your values.

Day 305: Navigating a VUCA World

"Life is 10% what happens to you and 90% how you react to it." – Charles R. Swindoll

We live in a **VUCA** world—an environment defined by **Volatility, Uncertainty, Complexity, and Ambiguity.** Navigating this ever-changing landscape can feel overwhelming, especially when external circumstances are beyond your control. However, with the right mindset, you can thrive despite the chaos.

In a VUCA world, your brain's amygdala often reacts to uncertainty by triggering a fear response, which can cloud your judgment and make you feel paralysed. Engaging the prefrontal cortex—responsible for planning, decision-making, and problem-solving—helps you shift from fear-driven reactions to thoughtful responses. By practising mindfulness, meditation, emotional regulation, and strategic thinking, you can train your brain to stay calm and focused, even in the face of volatility and uncertainty.

Emotional intelligence (EQ) becomes a critical skill in navigating complexity. Being aware of your emotions, managing stress, and understanding the emotions of others allows you to lead with clarity and empathy. In a world where change is constant, leaders with high EQ adapt more quickly and guide their teams with confidence and resilience. Psalm 27:1 reminds us not to be afraid, even in the most uncertain times. Trusting in God as our stronghold provides the inner stability and strength to navigate uncertainty with peace. When you put your trust in Him, you become equipped to face the challenges of a VUCA world without being overwhelmed by them. During the COVID-19 pandemic, many businesses faced unprecedented challenges. Leaders who stayed calm, focused, and flexible were able to pivot their strategies and come out stronger. Those with rigid plans struggled to adapt, while those with a clear vision and the ability to adjust thrived.

Practical Tips:

◊ Embrace uncertainty by focusing on what you can control.
◊ Develop a flexible mindset and plan for different scenarios, allowing you to adapt quickly when things change.

Reflective Questions:

» How are you managing the uncertainty in your life right now?
» How can you strengthen your emotional resilience and trust in God as your anchor?

Exercise: Identify one area in your life where volatility or uncertainty is affecting you. Write down a flexible plan for navigating it, focusing on what you can control, and trust God with the rest.

Day 306: Soar High Like an Eagle

"Your wings already exist, all you have to do is fly." – Anonymous

Eagles are known for soaring above storms, using the wind to lift them higher instead of letting it weigh them down. When challenges come your way, think of them as wind meant to help you rise. Instead of letting obstacles hold you back, use them as opportunities to grow and reach new heights.

When you face difficulties with a growth mindset, your brain engages in neuroplasticity—the ability to rewire itself. The prefrontal cortex, responsible for decision-making and focus, strengthens as you navigate adversity. Challenges become like resistance training for your brain, making you more adaptable and resilient. Like an eagle riding wind currents, you can rise above life's storms by shifting your mindset and using challenges to propel you forward.

Eagles don't panic during storms; they glide with purpose. Similarly, managing your emotions, staying calm, and responding thoughtfully helps you soar through difficult times. When you handle challenges with grace, others look to you for leadership and guidance.

Isaiah 40:31 (NIV) reminds us, *"Those who hope in the Lord will renew their strength. They will soar on wings like eagles."* Trusting in God is like catching the wind beneath your wings. When you rely on His strength, He helps you rise above the obstacles that could hold you back. When I encountered setbacks in building my business, I saw them as growth opportunities. By trusting in God and learning from each challenge, I was able to soar beyond what I initially imagined.

Practical Tips:

◊ When faced with a challenge, ask, *"How can this help me grow?"*
◊ See difficulties as stepping stones to rise higher.

Reflective Questions:

» What challenges in your life could help you soar higher?
» How can you shift your mindset to see it as an opportunity?

Exercise: Identify one challenge you're facing. Write down how you can use it to grow and take one small action today to rise above it.

You are meant to soar like an eagle. Let God guide you and use the winds of life to lift you higher.

PART ELEVEN

LIVING A FULFILLED AND PURPOSEFUL LIFE

PART 11 INTRODUCTION

Living a fulfilled life is more than simply achieving goals or material success; it's about aligning your mind, body, and spirit with God's divine purpose. In 'Living a Fulfilled and Purposeful Life' section, we will explore how you can harness the power of neuroscience, emotional intelligence (EQ), and scripture to live intentionally, thrive, and make a positive impact. This section will guide you through daily practices and reflections that help you cultivate key qualities like perseverance, love, knowledge, and self-control, as outlined in 2 Peter 1:5-9.

Through the lens of neuroscience, you'll learn how to rewire your brain to build positive habits and create new neural pathways that support growth and resilience. Using EQ, you'll discover how to manage your emotions with greater wisdom and mastery. With scripture as your foundation, you'll find spiritual grounding that empowers you to navigate life's challenges with faith, trust, and confidence.

Each day's content will blend practical tools with spiritual wisdom, equipping you to experience a life of purpose, joy, and fulfilment. As you move forward, you'll be encouraged to embrace growth in every season, trusting that God has prepared you to thrive, not just survive.

DAY 307: WHAT IT MEANS TO LIVE A FULFILLED LIFE

"Fulfillment is not a matter of getting what we want, but of being satisfied with who we are." — Unknown

Living a fulfilled life is about more than achieving goals or accumulating wealth—it's about inner contentment and living in alignment with your values and purpose. Fulfilment comes from satisfying deeper emotional needs like connection, purpose, and growth. When these needs are met, the brain releases oxytocin and dopamine, creating a sense of joy, contentment, and well-being. True fulfilment goes beyond temporary satisfaction; it involves living a life that feels meaningful.

People often confuse success with fulfilment, striving for external validation through achievements or material possessions. However, fulfilment is more about the 'why' behind our actions than the 'what'. Scripture tells us in Matthew 6:33 (NIV), *"But seek first his kingdom and his righteousness, and all these things will be given to you as well."* This reminds us that everything else falls into place when we align with our higher purpose.

To apply this, start by reflecting on what brings you deep joy. Is it helping others? Growing personally? Making a difference in your work or community? The key is to identify your core values and live in a way that honours them.

Take Ama, for example. She climbed the corporate ladder, landing her dream job. Yet, something was missing. After reflecting, she realised that mentoring young professionals gave her far more joy than any promotion. By dedicating more time to mentoring, Ama found fulfilment—living in line with what truly mattered to her.

Practical Exercise:
Take 5 minutes today to write three things that make you feel fulfilled. Then, make a plan to incorporate more of those into your week.

Reflective Questions:

- » What aspects of your life give you lasting satisfaction, and how can you focus more on those areas?
- » What's one area in your life that brings temporary happiness but lacks deeper fulfilment?

Day 308: Be Fruitful – Live a Life of Lasting Impact

"You will know them by their fruits." — Matthew 7:16 (NIV)

Being fruitful isn't about accumulating success or wealth—it's about using your gifts and talents to impact others positively. When we contribute meaningfully, the brain's prefrontal cortex (responsible for decision-making and empathy) and the ventral striatum, a key part of the brain's reward system, are activated. This does not only release dopamine, the "feel-good" chemical but also activates areas of the brain responsible for feelings of purpose and fulfilment.

Scripture encourages us to bear good fruit, reflecting God's love through our actions. Galatians 5:22-23 reminds us of the *"fruit of the Spirit,"* which includes love, joy, peace, patience, kindness, goodness, faithfulness, gentleness, and self-control. Bearing fruit means living in a way that mirrors these qualities.

Take Maria, a team leader at a marketing firm. Instead of focusing only on results, she made it her mission to mentor her team members and help them grow. Maria took time to understand their strengths and weaknesses, providing personalised guidance to help them improve where they struggled. She celebrated their achievements and encouraged them to take ownership of their roles. As a result, her team didn't just meet expectations—they exceeded them. Maria's leadership helped her team deliver better outcomes, not because she demanded them but because she empowered them. Through her support, she built not only a successful team but also fostered personal and professional growth among her team members. By leading with kindness, patience, and faithfulness, Maria's leadership reflected values that created lasting impact.

Engaging in meaningful contributions strengthens self-awareness, empathy, and social skills, enhancing emotional intelligence and fostering deeper, more impactful connections in both personal and professional relationships.

Practical Exercise:

◊ Identify one area in your life where you can be more fruitful.

◊ Set a goal to take one small, meaningful action this week—whether it's offering encouragement, sharing your skills, or helping someone in need.

Reflective Questions:

» How are you using your gifts to bear fruit in the lives of others?

» What's one small change you can make today to impact those around you positively?

By living fruitfully, you enrich the lives of others while cultivating a deeper sense of purpose and joy within yourself.

Day 309: Be Valuable – Create a Lasting Impact

"Try not to become a person of success, but rather a person of value." — Albert Einstein

Being valuable is about more than contributing—it's about creating a lasting impact. When you focus on being valuable, it strengthens neural connections in the brain's reward system, releasing dopamine and reinforcing feelings of purpose and fulfilment. The more value you bring, the more your brain recognises it as meaningful, motivating you to keep making a difference.

Being valuable isn't about seeking rewards; it's about making a positive difference. Scripture reminds us in Matthew 5:16 (NIV), *"Let your light shine before others, that they may see your good deeds and glorify your Father in heaven."* When we focus on creating value, we uplift others and reflect God's goodness through our actions.

Consider Peter, an entrepreneur who runs a digital marketing agency. Rather than focusing only on profit, he prioritised delivering value by understanding each client's needs and providing tailored solutions. His genuine care for his client's success led to strong relationships and business growth through referrals. Peter proved that being valuable goes beyond offering a service—it's about making a lasting impact.

When you focus on being valuable, it benefits everyone around you. Your efforts positively impact others, and you experience a deeper sense of fulfilment and purpose in what you do.

Reflective Questions:

» How are you adding value in your personal or professional life?
» What's one way you can increase the value you bring today?

Exercise:
This week, identify one area where you can add more value. Focus on providing support, sharing your expertise, or improving an aspect of your work or personal life that can benefit others.

Day 310: Stand Strong – Be Like a Tree by Living Waters

"He is like a tree planted by streams of water, which yields its fruit in season and whose leaf does not wither—whatever they do prospers." — Psalm 1:3 (NIV)

Imagine a tree by a flowing stream, its roots stretching deep, drawing nourishment from the constant water. That tree remains strong, no matter the storms or dry seasons, because it's anchored in the right source. In the same way, when we root ourselves in God—His promises, instructions, and truth—we flourish, no matter the challenges.

Just as a tree adapts to its environment, neuroplasticity allows us to rewire our brains. When we immerse ourselves in God's Word, place our faith in Yeshua's sacrifice, and regularly pray and seek God's guidance, we strengthen the neural pathways that help us handle life's challenges with resilience and emotional mastery. By rooting ourselves in faith, God's promises, and His truth, we become less easily shaken, training our brains to respond to life with hope, strength, and confidence. This is the power of being deeply rooted in God.

Scripture reinforces this idea in Psalm 1:3, describing a person whose life is anchored in God's truth—yielding fruit, prospering, and remaining strong through all seasons. When we root ourselves in God, His promises, and His instructions, we become like that tree—flourishing no matter what comes our way.

Consider Ify, who was facing significant stress at work. Instead of giving in to anxiety, she rooted herself in God's Word, meditating daily on scriptures that reminded her of His peace and provision. Over time, her stress decreased as she rewired her brain to trust God. She became more emotionally grounded and able to navigate difficult situations without feeling overwhelmed.

Practical Exercise:

◊ This week, reflect on one of God's promises that nourishes you.
◊ Meditate on it daily and take one action to root yourself more deeply in His Word.

Reflective Questions:

» What are the streams of living water in your life?
» How are you staying rooted in God's promises and instructions?

DAY 311: GET BACK UP WHEN YOU FALL

"The righteous may fall seven times, but they rise again." — Proverbs 24:16 (NIV)

Falling isn't a sign of failure; it's an opportunity to rise again, stronger than before. Setbacks are inevitable in your personal life, career, or relationships. What matters most is how you respond when you fall. Our brain has an amazing ability to bounce back, thanks to neuroplasticity. Each time you get back up after a setback, you're actually rewiring your brain, strengthening the pathways that help you become more resilient and determined.

From an emotional intelligence perspective, learning to manage setbacks without letting them define you is crucial. It's not about avoiding failure but developing the emotional mastery to rise each time you stumble. Scripture reminds us in Proverbs 24:16 that even the righteous may fall multiple times but always rise again. This is the essence of resilience—falling but choosing to get back up.

Consider Robert, who unexpectedly lost his job. Instead of staying down, he took time to reflect, learn new skills, and rebuild. Through faith, perseverance, and hard work, he discovered a new opportunity that better aligned with his passions. Each time he got back up, he grew stronger, more resilient, and more in tune with God's plan for his life.

The key to bouncing back is to view falling not as the end but as a learning experience. You are not defeated by the fall; instead, you are strengthened by the rise.

Practical Exercise:

◊ Reflect on a recent setback.
◊ Write down one lesson you learned from it and one action you can take to rise again.
◊ Focus on moving forward, trusting that each fall is a stepping stone toward your growth.

Reflective Questions:

» How do you respond when you fall?
» What can you learn from your past setbacks to help you get stronger?

Day 312: The Power of Surrender

"Surrender to God, and you will have peace; then prosperity will come to you." — Job 22:21 (NIV)

Surrendering is often misunderstood as a weakness, but it's one of the most powerful actions you can take. When you surrender, you release the need to control everything and open yourself up to a more profound, deeper and fulfilling life. When we let go of stress and the struggle for control, the emotional brain relaxes, allowing the prefrontal cortex—the part of the brain responsible for decision-making and peace—to get activated. This leads to greater clarity, peace, and emotional balance.

Surrendering is about trusting God's sovereignty and plan, even when things don't make sense. It's about placing your trust in His divine plan, knowing He has your best interests at heart. Surrendering doesn't mean giving up, but rather letting go of the anxiety and pressure of trying to control every outcome. When we surrender to God, we allow His strength to take over, enabling us to see the new opportunities and insights we might never have considered.

Scripture speaks to this in Job 22:21, which encourages us to surrender to God to find peace and prosperity. It's not about passivity; it's about active trust in His wisdom and timing.

Consider Uzoma, who had been overwhelmed with career decisions for months. Frustrated and unsure, she finally surrendered her worries to God, trusting He would guide her through His plan. After spending time in prayer, studying scripture, and listening to God, she began to notice new opportunities and felt a peace she hadn't experienced in years. Surrendering didn't mean giving up her career goals—it meant trusting God's timing and aligning her life with His purpose.

Practical Exercise:

◊ This week, identify one area you feel overwhelmed.
◊ Surrender it to God in prayer and trust His guidance.
◊ Notice how letting go brings peace and opens up new possibilities.

Reflective Questions:

» What areas of your life are you holding onto too tightly?
» How can surrendering to God open you up to deeper peace and clarity?

Day 313: Overflowing Blessings

"You prepare a table before me in the presence of my enemies. You anoint my head with oil; my cup overflows." — Psalm 23:5 (NIV)

Imagine sitting at a beautifully prepared table, filled with everything you could ever need or dream of, right in front of those who once doubted or opposed you. This is the image of Psalm 23:5—a promise that God provides abundantly, even in the face of challenges. The overflowing cup symbolises more than just enough; it speaks to an abundant life filled with peace, blessings, success and God's favour.

Our mindset shifts when we focus on what we have rather than what we lack. Practising gratitude activates the brain's reward centres, releasing dopamine—the "feel-good" chemical. This helps us feel content and more able to see the good around us, even when life is challenging. It's like focusing on the overflowing cup instead of worrying about what's missing.

Eliza was going through a tough time financially. Instead of focusing on the stress of bills, she decided to thank God for what she had—a supportive family, a job, and good health. As she meditated on Psalm 23:5 and focused on God's gift to her of overflowing blessings, she began to see small blessings and new opportunities she hadn't noticed before. Though it seemed empty initially, her cup began to overflow with her abundance of blessings, gratitude, peace, and joy.

Applying God's principles gives us access to His blessings. It's like living in our wealthy Father's house—rather than constantly asking for permission or living like a pauper surrounded by abundance, we can confidently use the blessings He has already provided.

Practical Exercise:

◊ Each day this week, write down one blessing that you notice, no matter how small.

◊ Reflect on how God fills your cup, even in tough times.

Reflective Questions:

» Where in your life can you see God's overflowing blessings?

How can you shift your focus from lack to abundance?

DAY 314: TRUSTING GOD'S GUIDANCE

"The Lord is my shepherd; I shall not want." — Psalm 23:1 (NIV)

Psalm 23 gives us a beautiful image of God as our shepherd, guiding, protecting, and providing for us. Just like a shepherd carefully tends to his flock, leading them to green pastures and still waters, God leads us through the different seasons of life. Trusting Him as our shepherd isn't just a comforting thought—it's a powerful way to live.

Think of life as a journey through unknown landscapes. Like sheep, we don't always know the way, but the shepherd does. When you surrender control and trust God's guidance, you find peace in knowing He is leading you toward provision and protection. Trust reduces anxiety and stress, calming the brain's fear centres and allowing you to focus on what truly matters.

Psalm 23:1 reminds us that we will lack nothing with God as our shepherd. This doesn't mean you won't face difficulties, but it reassures you that God knows what you need and provides for you in His time. This assurance of His provision is a source of security, enabling you to choose to trust Him rather than letting fear or frustration rule. Trusting God's leadership brings peace, stability, and emotional balance.

You may be navigating a difficult season in your life. Instead of allowing worry to take over, choose to lean on Psalm 23, reminding you that God is your shepherd. Through prayer and trust, even in uncertainty, you will find a sense of calmness and direction.

Practical Exercise:

This week, reflect on Psalm 23. Each day, declare, *"The Lord is my shepherd, I shall not want,"* and trust that God is guiding you through every situation with care and purpose.

Reflective Questions:

» What areas of your life feel uncertain, and how can you trust God's guidance more?
» How can you embrace God's care and provision like a sheep trusts its shepherd?

Day 315: The Kingdom of God is Within You

"The Spirit of God, who raised Jesus from the dead, lives in you." — Romans 8:11 (NLT)

The Kingdom of God is not a place you seek externally—it resides within you, empowered by the Holy Spirit. This is a transformative truth: the same Spirit that raised Christ from the dead lives inside you, giving you access to God's wisdom, strength, and peace. This understanding should change how you view yourself and your ability to navigate life's challenges.

You're not powerless—you're filled with divine power.

Our thoughts actively shape the pathways in our brains. When you focus on the truth that the Holy Spirit lives within you, you start to rewire your mind, building new connections that foster confidence, self-worth, peace, and resilience. This shift empowers you to overcome fear and anxiety as your mind learns to rely on God's strength within you instead of depending solely on your own.

Scripture tells us in Romans 8:11 that the same Spirit that raised Jesus from the dead lives in you. This means you don't have to face life's struggles alone. The Kingdom of God—His wisdom, peace, and guidance—is accessible to you right now. It's not something you need to search for or earn; it's already been given to you through the Holy Spirit.

Think about those moments when you've felt stuck, overwhelmed, or unsure of what to do next. What if, instead of striving to figure things out on your own, you paused and reminded yourself that God's Kingdom is alive within you? The Holy Spirit is your counsellor, your guide, and your source of strength. By surrendering your worries and listening for His guidance, you open yourself up to peace, clarity, and purpose.

Practical Exercise:

◊ This week, take time each day to sit quietly and reflect on Romans 8:11.
◊ Acknowledge that the Spirit of God is living inside you.
◊ When challenges arise, pause and ask the Holy Spirit for guidance, trusting in the Kingdom of God within.

Reflective Questions:

» How does knowing the Holy Spirit lives within you change how you view challenges?
» In what areas of your life can you trust more deeply in the power of God's Kingdom within you?

Day 316: Grow Your Wings

"Faith is the bird that feels the light when the dawn is still dark." — Rabindranath Tagore

Growing your wings means stepping out in faith, even when the path ahead is uncertain. Just like a bird that senses the coming light even before it can see it, we must trust that God has placed the potential for greatness within us. It's in taking bold steps of faith that we learn to fly and discover the strength and purpose that God has given us.

When we challenge ourselves and take risks, our brain forms new neural pathways that help us grow and adapt. This is similar to how a bird strengthens its wings by flying. When we step beyond our comfort zones and rely on God's guidance, we experience growth and resilience. Trusting in God's plan helps us navigate the unknown, knowing He has equipped us for every step of the journey.

Isaiah 40:31 tells us that those who hope in the Lord will renew their strength and soar like eagles. This means that when we trust God's timing and provision, we are lifted by His strength, enabling us to rise above life's challenges and grow in ways we never thought possible.

Think about a time in your life when fear held you back from pursuing a dream or goal. Growing your wings means taking that leap of faith, trusting that God's presence will carry you. Every time you take a step in faith, you build inner strength. Like a bird's wings growing stronger with each flight, you develop resilience and confidence.

Each step rewires your mind to trust God more deeply, shaping you into someone who soars above fear and doubt.

Practical Exercise:

◊ This week, take one small step in an area where you've been hesitant to act.
◊ Trust that God will give you the strength and guidance to soar as you grow your wings.

Reflective Questions:

» Where in your life do you need to take a step of faith and grow your wings?
» How can trusting in God's provision help you move forward?

Day 317: You Get What You Confess

"Whatever you believe with feeling becomes your reality." — Brian Tracy

Your words are like seeds, planting the future you will eventually experience. Just as a farmer plants crops and expects a harvest, the words you speak today create the life you will live tomorrow. When you confess hope, faith, and possibility, you cultivate an environment where blessings can grow. But when you speak words of doubt or negativity, you're planting seeds of failure and fear.

The brain processes language in ways that shape thoughts and behaviour. When you consistently speak positively, your brain builds neural connections that reinforce optimism, resilience, and creativity. Over time, these connections become stronger, and your mindset shifts to one of possibility. Conversely, negative self-talk activates the brain's fear centre, feeding stress and limiting your potential to overcome challenges.

Think of your words like a thermostat. If you set the thermostat for warmth, the environment will adjust to match that temperature. Similarly, what you confess with your mouth sets the temperature of your life. If you speak life, hope, and faith, your mind, heart, and actions will align with those truths, creating a future full of promise.

Consider Mia, who had struggled with self-doubt for years. Whenever she faced a challenge, her automatic confession was, *"I can't do this."* But when she learned the power of confession, she replaced those negative words with faith-filled statements like, *"I am capable"* and *"God is with me."* Over time, Mia's confidence grew, and she began to take steps toward her goals. Her life changed significantly because her words changed.

Practical Exercise:

◊ This week, write three positive confessions based on God's promises and repeat them daily.

◊ Notice how this small shift in words changes your mindset and your outlook.

Reflective Questions:

» What words have you been speaking over your life?

» How can you begin confessing faith-filled, positive words, even in challenging situations?

Day 318: Emotions Are Good Advisors, But Terrible Masters

"You must learn to let go. Release the stress. You were never in control anyway." — Steve Maraboli

Emotions are powerful guides in our lives, but when they control our actions, they can steer us away from the path of fulfilment. To live a truly fulfilled life, it's essential to recognise that emotions should inform your decisions, not dominate them. Emotions can be helpful signals, alerting you to something important, but if you let them dictate your actions, they can lead you to make impulsive choices that don't align with your values or goals.

When emotions take over, they can cloud your judgment. Strong feelings like fear, anger, or excitement activate the brain's emotional centres, which can hijack rational thought if left unchecked. But when you allow your conscious thinking brain to guide you alongside your emotions, you make more balanced, thoughtful decisions that lead to a fulfilling life.

Imagine how this applies to your own life. Perhaps you've felt anxiety or fear when presented with new opportunities—maybe a promotion, a new business idea, or even stepping out in faith toward a personal goal. When you allow these emotions to dominate, they can hold you back from achieving the fullness of life God has planned for you.

Ben felt anxious whenever he faced new responsibilities at work, often turning down projects that could help him grow. But once he saw anxiety as a signal, not a master, he prepared thoroughly and trusted in his abilities—and God's promise to guide him. This shift helped him embrace opportunities he'd previously avoided, allowing him to grow with confidence. By acknowledging his emotions without letting them control him, Ben built confidence and unlocked his true potential. In the same way, recognising your emotions and responding with balance can help you move toward the fulfilled life you desire.

Practical Exercise:

◊ This week, when you feel strong emotions, take a moment to pause.
◊ Ask yourself what the emotion is signalling, and then choose a response that aligns with your values and long-term goals rather than reacting impulsively.

Reflective Questions:

» How often do you let emotions guide your decisions?
» What steps can you take to acknowledge your emotions without letting them control your actions?

DAY 319: TAKE TIME TO ENJOY HAPPINESS

"Plenty of people miss their share of happiness, not because they never found it, but because they didn't stop to enjoy it." — William Feather

Many people live life in a hurry, always thinking about the next task or goal. They believe happiness is waiting for them after they achieve something big. But happiness doesn't just come from reaching goals—it's found in the small, everyday moments. They often miss out on joy, not because it isn't there, but because they're too busy to notice it.

Think of life like a beautiful garden. If you rush through it, you'll miss the flowers blooming right in front of you. Likewise, if you're constantly focused on the next thing, you won't see the happiness already here. When we slow down to appreciate the present, our brain releases dopamine, the "feel-good" chemical, helping us experience a deeper sense of contentment.

In the Bible, Ecclesiastes 3:13 (NIV) reminds us, *"That each of them may eat and drink, and find satisfaction in all their toil—this is the gift of God."* God's gift isn't just in the big moments but in the simple pleasures of everyday life. Think about your own life. Are you so focused on achieving the next goal—whether it's a promotion, a personal milestone, or something else—that you forget to celebrate the little victories along the way? Maybe you've been working hard but haven't stopped to appreciate how far you've already come. What would change if you paused for a moment to enjoy the present? You may discover that your happiness grows along the journey, even before reaching your ultimate goal. By learning to savour each step, you open yourself up to more joy and fulfilment right now.

Happiness isn't just waiting for you at the finish line. It's in the quiet moments, the small wins, and the daily blessings. All you have to do is stop and enjoy it.

Practical Exercise:

◊ Each day this week, take five minutes to reflect on something that brought you joy.
◊ Write it down and thank God for it.

Reflective Questions:

» Are you rushing through life, missing the happiness right in front of you?
» How can you pause to enjoy the blessings you already have?

Day 320: Go Forth with Courage and Boldness

"Be strong and courageous. Do not be afraid; do not be discouraged, for the Lord your God will be with you wherever you go." — Joshua 1:9 (NIV)

Living a fulfilled life requires courage and boldness. It's about stepping out in faith, even when the road ahead feels uncertain. Imagine yourself as a mountain climber, staring up at the peak you want to reach. It may seem daunting, but each step you take—no matter how small—brings you closer to your goal. Courage isn't the absence of fear; it's the decision to move forward despite it, trusting that God is guiding you and has equipped you for the journey.

Self-belief is like the anchor that holds you steady, no matter how rough the winds of doubt may blow. You become unshakeable when you believe in yourself and the gifts God has placed within you. When you cultivate confidence, your brain strengthens the pathways that make resilience and perseverance easier to access. The more you act boldly, the more you build the mental strength to face challenges with courage.

Think of a tree standing tall during a storm. Its roots run deep, and while the wind may try to knock it down, it stands firm. In the same way, your belief in yourself and in God's promises allows you to stay rooted, even when life's storms come. Joshua 1:9 reminds us to *"be strong and courageous"* because God is with us every step of the way. You don't need to wait until you feel fully ready—God is already walking alongside you, providing the strength you need.

Perhaps you've been holding back on a dream, waiting for the right moment. But boldness means starting now, trusting that God's presence will carry you as you take that first step.

Practical Exercise:
This week, take one courageous step toward a goal. Even if it's small, trust that God is with you and has given you everything you need to succeed.

Reflective Questions:
- » What is one area where you need to move forward with courage and confidence?
- » How can you deepen your self-belief to become more unshakeable?

Day 321: Thrive, Don't Just Survive

"I came that they may have life and have it abundantly." — John 10:10 (ESV)

God's plan for you is not just to survive life's challenges but to thrive through them. Survival means just getting by, managing stress, and holding things together. Thriving is about flourishing, growing, and living abundantly and in flow, even when the world feels chaotic. Jesus Christ didn't come to offer a life of mere survival—He came to give you life to the fullest.

Thriving requires a shift in mindset. It's about changing your focus from merely managing problems to seeing growth opportunities. Neuroscience tells us that when we move from a survival mode, driven by fear and anxiety, to a thriving mindset, the brain's prefrontal cortex—responsible for problem-solving and higher thinking—becomes more active. This shift allows you to navigate challenges with creativity and resilience.

Imagine a plant in a drought. A surviving plant barely holds on, conserving energy to stay alive. But a thriving plant, when nourished, stretches toward the sun, its roots deepening and branches reaching out. You're not meant to just hold on— you're meant to grow, expand, and live fully. Anchored in God's truth and love, you are assured of flourishing, no matter the challenges.

Think about your life right now. Are you just surviving the daily grind, or are you embracing God's promise to live abundantly? Thriving doesn't mean you'll never face struggles, but it means those struggles won't define you. You'll grow stronger and more resilient through them because you are deeply rooted in God's love and His purpose for you.

Practical Exercise:

◊ Identify one area of your life where you've been in survival mode.
◊ This week, take one small action to shift toward thriving—whether it's investing in your growth, focusing on gratitude, or deepening your connection with God.

Reflective Questions:

» Where in your life are you merely surviving instead of thriving?
» How can you shift your mindset and start living the abundant life God has promised?

DAY 322: REPLENISH AND DOMINATE

"Then God blessed them, and God said to them, 'Be fruitful and multiply; fill the earth and subdue it; have dominion over the fish of the sea, over the birds of the air, and over every living thing that moves on the earth.'"— Genesis 1:28 (NIV)

God's original mandate to humanity is one of purpose, growth, and influence. "Replenish and dominate" is more than a call to survive—it's a divine invitation to fill your life with abundance and take charge of the world around you. To replenish is to restore, refresh, and bring forth life. To dominate is to lead with authority, using the gifts and talents God has given you to influence and shape your environment.

Replenishing yourself is crucial. You can't pour from an empty cup. When you take time to rest, recharge, and nourish your mind, body, and spirit, you equip yourself to step into the fullness of your calling. Rest and renewal enhance brain function, improving clarity, creativity, and decision-making. Just like a battery that needs recharging, we thrive when we intentionally pause to replenish.

Once replenished, God calls you to dominate—not with aggression, but with purpose and authority. Dominating means living out the influence God has given you, using your skills and strengths to make a lasting impact. It's about leading in your sphere of influence, whether it's your family, career, ministry, or community. Domination isn't about control but confidently taking charge of what God has entrusted you.

Think of it like a garden. You need to water and nurture the plants to keep them healthy. But to truly dominate the garden, you must also prune, shape, and direct its growth, making it flourish according to your vision. In your own life, replenishing allows you to lead and influence with strength and clarity.

Practical Exercise:

◊ This week, dedicate time to rest and replenish.
◊ Then, identify one area where you can step into greater leadership or influence.
◊ Make a plan to lead with purpose and confidence.

Reflective Questions:

» How are you replenishing yourself physically, emotionally, and spiritually?
» What steps can you take to dominate and excel in your God-given area of influence?

Day 323: Step Out of the Boat

"Come," he said. Then Peter got down out of the boat, walked on the water and came toward Jesus. — Matthew 14:29 (NIV)

Stepping out of the boat requires faith and courage. It means moving beyond the familiar, beyond the safe, and into the unknown, where God calls you to trust Him completely. In Matthew 14, Peter stepped out onto the water, not because he had all the answers but because he had faith in Jesus' call. Stepping out is the beginning of a journey into the extraordinary, where the impossible becomes possible.

Years ago, I read John Ortberg's book - "If You Want to Walk on Water, You've Got to Get Out of the Boat". It inspired me to take a bold step I had long dreamed of—setting up my first big business. The fear of failure was real, and so were the doubts. But the call to step out of my comfort zone was stronger. Inspired by the book and grounded in my faith, I took the leap, trusting that God had placed this vision in my heart for a reason. Like Peter stepping onto the water, I moved forward, reassured by the knowledge that what seemed impossible at first became a reality through faith, hard work, and God's unwavering guidance.

Stepping into uncertainty helps our brains develop resilience and adaptability. Every time we take a step of faith, we create new neural pathways that build confidence and courage. The more you challenge yourself, the more your brain rewires itself to grow and adapt, preparing you to face greater challenges with strength and grace. Over time, this makes you more capable and resilient, ready to overcome any obstacle that comes your way.

Think about the boat you're currently sitting in. What dream or vision has God placed in your heart? It may seem intimidating, but stepping out in faith will lead to growth and fulfilment you never thought possible.

Practical Exercise:

◊ Identify one area in your life where you've been hesitant to take a step.
◊ This week, take bold action toward that goal, trusting that God is with you as you walk on the water of faith.

Reflective Questions:

» What "boat" are you sitting in that God is calling you to step out of?
» How can you trust God more fully as you take bold steps toward your dream?

Day 324: The Four Stages of Competence

"Your potential is endless; it's your mindset that sets the boundaries." — Unknown

Mastery begins with understanding the journey through the four stages of competence: **unconscious incompetence, conscious incompetence, conscious competence, and unconscious competence**. These stages map the process of learning and skill development, showing how you can go from not knowing something to mastering it effortlessly. As you progress through these stages, your brain rewires itself to support new skills, and you become more capable of handling greater challenges, moving you closer to becoming truly limitless.

In **unconscious incompetence**, you are unaware of what you don't know. At this stage, the unconscious brain is running the show, and you might think you're doing fine when you're missing key skills or knowledge. For example, someone may think they're good at managing stress but are unaware of the deeper emotional triggers. The first step to mastery is becoming aware of these gaps, which leads to the next stage.

In **Conscious incompetence**, you become aware of what you lack. This can feel uncomfortable or humbling because you realise how much you don't know. However, this awareness is crucial for growth. The brain starts to rewire itself as you gather knowledge and skills, pushing you to improve and address the gaps you've identified.

Conscious competence is the stage where you actively work on the skill, but it still requires effort and focus. Your brain is developing stronger neural connections as you repeatedly practice the skill. For example, learning to drive takes conscious effort at first—thinking about every action. As you practice, the brain reinforces these connections, and it becomes easier with time.

When the skill becomes second nature, you reach **unconscious competence**. Your brain has rewired itself so effectively that you can perform the task without thinking about it. This is the stage where you've mastered the skill, and it no longer requires conscious effort, much like riding a bike or driving a car with ease.

By understanding and embracing these stages, you realise limits are often self-imposed. Mastering each step allows you to grow continuously, pushing the boundaries of your potential. With consistent effort and the rewiring of your brain, you truly become limitless.

Reflective Questions:

» Where in your life are you still operating from unconscious incompetence?
» How can understanding this process help you move forward and unlock new potential?

DAY 325: THE PATH TO AMPLIFIED RESULTS

"Motivation gets us in the game. Learning keeps us playing. Creativity helps us adapt, and performance amplifies the results beyond expectations." — Maureen Chiana

Success is a journey made up of several stages. Motivation is the initial spark—it's what pushes you to take that first step. But it's just the beginning. Like a runner at the starting line, motivation gets you moving, but it's learning that builds your endurance. Learning keeps you in the race, helping you grow stronger as you face challenges.

Imagine driving a car. Motivation is the fuel that gets you going, but learning is like understanding the rules of the road. Without it, you wouldn't know how to navigate the twists and turns. Creativity is your GPS, steering you through obstacles and helping you find alternative routes when the road ahead seems blocked. Being able to think creatively and adapt to life's changes is important. Finally, performance is how you drive. When you perform well—balancing your motivation, learning, and creativity—you go beyond where you thought you could, exceeding your own expectations.

In Colossians 3:23 (NIV), Scripture reminds us, *"Whatever you do, work at it with all your heart, as working for the Lord."* This means starting strong and committing to excellence throughout the journey. Motivation gets you in the game, but you truly thrive through learning and creativity.

Ngozi started her bakery full of motivation, but as she continued, her skills grew by learning more about running a business. When she faced stiff competition, her creativity kicked in, allowing her to create unique products that made her bakery stand out. Through consistent effort and improvement, she exceeded her own expectations, growing the business beyond what she had initially dreamed.

Practical Exercise:

◊ This week, focus on one project or goal.

◊ Identify where you need to improve—whether in motivation, learning, creativity, or performance—and take one action to amplify your results.

Reflective Questions:

» Where are you in your journey—fuelling up with motivation, learning the road ahead, or navigating creatively?

» How can you use what you've learned to amplify your performance and exceed expectations?

Day 326: Rewiring for Healing

"By His wounds, we are healed." — Isaiah 53:5 (NIV)

Our brains have an incredible capacity to support healing, both mentally and physically. Neuroplasticity allows the brain to rewire itself, creating new pathways that encourage resilience and physical recovery. We strengthen these positive connections by choosing thoughts of faith, hope, and peace, supporting our body's natural healing processes.

Neurogenesis—the brain's ability to create new neurons—also plays a role in resilience, especially in areas like the hippocampus, which is essential for memory and emotion management. Research shows that neurogenesis can improve our ability to handle stress, helping us adapt and grow stronger. Neuroplasticity and neurogenesis enable us to reshape our mental and physical health through intentional focus and a hopeful mindset. The impact of mindset on physical health is profound. There's a story of a man misdiagnosed with terminal cancer who believed he had only weeks to live. He passed away shortly after, despite an autopsy revealing he didn't have advanced cancer. His belief in his imminent death triggered what's known as the nocebo effect—the negative counterpart to the placebo effect. While placebos improve health through positive expectations, nocebos show the harm that can arise when negative beliefs take root.

This story illustrates how crucial it is to align our thoughts with faith and hope. When we believe in God's promise of healing, we activate the brain's potential for resilience and renewal. Isaiah 53:5 reminds us, *"By His wounds we are healed,"* affirming Jesus' sacrifice brings spiritual salvation with physical and emotional healing. Trusting in this promise builds the mental pathways needed to support a mindset of healing and strength. I experienced this personally when dealing with intense pain from prolapsed discs and sciatica. Instead of giving in to despair, I focused on God's promises and my body's ability to heal. Through prayer, physical therapy, and affirmations, I gradually rewired my brain to support recovery. Over time, healing came, showing how faith, neuroplasticity, and neurogenesis work together to build resilience and health.

Practical Exercise:

◊ Replace a negative belief about your health with a positive affirmation rooted in scripture.

◊ Repeat this affirmation daily, trusting in God's healing power and your brain's ability to support recovery.

Reflective Question:

» What limiting beliefs might be holding you back from healing?

Day 327: Be a Finisher – Finish What You Start

"Finishing is better than starting. Patience is better than pride." — Ecclesiastes 7:8 (NLT)

Starting new projects is exciting, but finishing them takes mental discipline. The brain's neurochemicals, especially dopamine and serotonin, affect our focus and persistence. When dopamine levels are high, creativity and impulsivity increase, which can lead to jumping between projects without completing them. Meanwhile, low serotonin in the brain's planning areas can make it difficult to stay on track, especially when dopamine urges you toward something new.

To become a finisher, it's important to balance these brain chemicals. You want dopamine's motivation without letting it pull you away from tasks. If dopamine is overactive, you may jump from task to task, leaving projects unfinished. Low serotonin can make you feel distracted or restless, making it tough to stick with one goal until completion.

What Should You Do?

> **Break Tasks Into Smaller Goals:** Divide a big task into smaller, manageable steps. This gives your brain multiple chances to release dopamine as you complete each step, keeping your motivation up without getting sidetracked.
> **Establish a Finishing Routine:** Make it a habit to finish what you start, even with self-imposed deadlines. Building a routine activates serotonin, helping you stay calm and focused on completing tasks.
> **Minimise Distractions:** When dopamine tempts you with new ideas, limit distractions. Try time-blocking your day, dedicating focused periods to one task at a time.
> **Visualise Success:** Imagine the sense of accomplishment that comes with finishing a task. This can boost both dopamine and serotonin, giving you the clarity and focus to follow through.

Notice how finishing each step boosts your focus and sense of achievement.

Reflective Questions:

» Are you starting more projects than you finish?
» How can you balance the excitement of starting with the discipline to finish?

DAY 328: CREATING A POSITIVE IMPACT AND LEAVING A LEGACY

"No act of kindness, no matter how small, is ever wasted." —Aesop

Living a fulfilled life is about more than personal achievements—it's about the legacy you leave behind. Your personal achievements, no matter how small, contribute to the larger legacy you create. True fulfilment comes when you create a lasting, positive impact beyond your life, influencing others and future generations. Whether through acts of kindness, leadership, or mentoring, the positive seeds you plant today shape the world of tomorrow. Your brain is wired to thrive when you make a difference, giving you a lot of joy. When you help others, the brain's reward system releases dopamine, which boosts your mood and motivation. This enhances your sense of purpose and strengthens the brain's pathways for empathy and compassion. The result? A life of deeper connection and meaning, where you aren't just surviving but thriving by making an impact.

Think of legacy as planting a tree. You may not always see the tree reach its full height, but others will benefit from its shade, fruit, and beauty long after you're gone. Every small act—whether it's mentoring a colleague, teaching someone a valuable lesson, or showing kindness—adds to this legacy. These actions create ripples that continue to grow and affect others, sometimes in ways you can't foresee.

Scripture teaches us the importance of leaving a legacy through good deeds. In Matthew 5:16 (NIV), Jesus says, *"Let your light shine before others, that they may see your good deeds and glorify your Father in heaven."* Your impact today not only influences the present but leaves a lasting mark that others will remember, shaping future generations in ways that reflect God's love and purpose. Think about the people who have impacted your life. Their kindness, mentorship and guidance shaped who you are today. By being intentional with your actions, you can be that person for others, creating a legacy that lives on through the people you touch.

Practical Exercise:

◊ This week, take one step to leave a positive legacy intentionally.

◊ Whether helping someone, mentoring a colleague, or showing kindness, think about how your actions will impact the future.

Reflective Questions:

» What kind of legacy are you creating with your actions today?

» How can you make small but meaningful contributions that will continue to impact others?

DAY 329: ALIGNING SPIRIT, SOUL, AND BODY

"May your whole spirit, soul and body be kept blameless at the coming of our Lord Jesus Christ." — 1 Thessalonians 5:23 (NIV)

Aligning your spirit, soul, and body is the key to living a truly fulfilled life. When these three parts are in harmony, you experience mental clarity, emotional balance, and physical well-being.

When the brain is in a state of balance, it releases feel-good chemicals like serotonin and dopamine, which create a sense of peace and satisfaction. The prefrontal cortex—the part of your brain that manages decision-making and emotions—helps you regulate your thoughts and feelings. This balance mirrors the alignment between your soul (mind, will, and emotions), spirit, and body. Grounding your spirit in faith calms your soul, and your body responds by lowering stress, helping you function better.

Emotionally, alignment gives you stability, especially during tough times. When your spirit is connected to God's truth, your mind and emotions (soul) find peace. Isaiah 26:3 (NIV) reminds us, *"You will keep in perfect peace those whose minds are steadfast because they trust in you."* This peace starts in your spirit, flows to your soul, and reflects in your body, making you emotionally strong.

Spiritually, alignment means staying rooted in God. Your spirit connects with God through prayer, scripture, and faith. When you nourish your spirit, it impacts your thoughts, feelings, and actions. This spiritual nourishment is the key to aligning your soul and body, leading to a balanced, joyful life.

Think of it like tuning a musical instrument. Just as a piano needs each key to be in tune, your spirit, soul, and body need regular alignment to stay in harmony. This isn't a one-time thing—it's an ongoing process that helps you face life's challenges with peace and confidence.

Practical Exercise:

◊ This week, take time to align your spirit, soul, and body.
◊ Pray, reflect on your emotions, and engage in physical activity. Notice how this alignment helps you live more fully.

Reflective Questions:

» Where do you feel out of alignment—spiritually, emotionally, or physically?
» How can you strengthen the connection between your spirit, soul, and body?

Day 330: Your Decisions Shape Your Destiny

"We are the sum total of the decisions we make every day." — Albert Camus

While you're born with traits from your parents, the choices you make shape the person you become. Your decisions build your character, determine your path, and define your destiny. Your future is greatly influenced by the consistent, small choices you make each day. Every decision you make strengthens your thought patterns and behaviours, making them easier to repeat. Positive choices build resilience, discipline, and healthy habits, while poor decisions reinforce negative patterns that can be hard to break. Fortunately, every day brings the opportunity to choose differently, giving you the power to steer your life in a new direction.

Your decisions don't just affect your emotions; they shape your entire well-being. Good choices contribute to mental clarity, physical health, and stronger relationships. Choosing actions that align with your values reduces stress and creates a sense of purpose. This emotional stability impacts your physical health—lower stress levels lead to better sleep, improved energy, and a healthier body. Spiritually, aligning your decisions with God's guidance brings fulfilment and peace, knowing that you are living in accordance with His plan. The Bible reminds us of the importance of choices: *"I have set before you life and death, blessings and curses. Now choose life, so that you and your children may live"* (Deuteronomy 30:19 NIV). Every decision you make can bring life or lead you away from your purpose.

Your life is like a road trip. Though you start with the vehicle you were given (your upbringing and circumstances), the route you take is determined by your choices. Every turn, stop, or detour can move you closer to or farther from your goals. While you may not control where you begin, you control the direction you take. Even if you were born into challenging situations, you can still change your life. By becoming more self-aware, educating yourself, making empowered choices, and building healthy relationships, you shape a future defined by your decisions, not your starting point. The journey of self-awareness is powerful, inspiring, and motivating you to take charge of your life and shape your future.

Practical Exercise:

◊ This week, reflect on one major decision.
◊ Write down the potential outcomes and choose the option that best aligns with your long-term vision and values.

Reflective Questions:

» What key decisions are you facing today?
» How can you ensure your choices align with your values and goals?

DAY 331: CHRIST IN YOU, THE HOPE OF GLORY

"Christ in you, the hope of glory." — Colossians 1:27 (NIV)

Embracing a personal relationship with God is the most profound gift one can receive. This is not a mere adherence to religious rituals, but a living reality of Christ dwelling within you. When you truly know God and experience Christ in you, you tap into the hope of glory—a hope that transcends circumstances and fills your life with peace, purpose, and joy. This relationship offers a profound transformation, enabling you to see the world through His eyes.

Imagine having a best friend who is always with you, guiding, comforting, and empowering you. That's what it's like to have Christ in you. This personal relationship brings a sense of closeness, belonging, and confidence. It's not just knowing about God but experiencing Him daily. When Christ lives in you, His presence becomes your source of hope and strength, a constant companion through all your challenges. This hope isn't fleeting; it's anchored in the eternal glory of God.

Scripture encourages this deep connection. Colossians 1:27 (NIV) tells us, *"Christ in you, the hope of glory."* It means that when you invite Christ into your life, His spirit dwells in you, giving you access to God's peace, wisdom, and love. James 4:8 further reminds us, "Draw near to God, and He will draw near to you." This intimate relationship transforms how you think, live, and relate to others.

When you understand that Christ lives in you, it changes everything. You are never alone or without guidance. His presence in your life brings clarity and direction, aligning your actions with His will. In moments of doubt, you can find assurance knowing that the hope of glory is within you, shaping your journey and giving you strength.

Practical Exercise:

◊ Meditate on Colossians 1:27 this week.
◊ Spend a few moments each day acknowledging Christ in you and invite His presence into every aspect of your life.
◊ Notice how this awareness brings peace and hope.

Reflective Questions:

» Is your relationship with God a personal one, where you experience Christ in you daily?
» How does the knowledge of Christ living in you change your perspective on life's challenges?

Day 332: Navigating Grief

"Blessed are those who mourn, for they will be comforted." — Matthew 5:4 (NIV)

Grief is an intense and often overwhelming experience. Whether it's the loss of a loved one, a relationship, or a dream, grief shakes you to your core. Elisabeth Kübler-Ross's five stages of grief — denial, anger, bargaining, depression, and acceptance — provide a framework for understanding how we process loss. These stages aren't linear; you may revisit them multiple times. Knowing this can help you navigate the stormy seas of grief and find your way toward healing.

When I lost my mum suddenly, I felt like I was sinking with no way out. I went through denial, unable to grasp that she was gone. Anger and questions filled my mind — *"Why did this happen?"* I sank into a deep sadness. But even in that dark place, by the grace of God, I held onto Him with the bit of strength I had left. During this time, I discovered the power of neuroplasticity and how I could rewire my brain. It was the beginning of my journey to where I am now. I learned that changing my thought patterns could lead to healing, even in the depths of grief. Through every tear and prayer, I felt His presence. This experience has shaped my current work—teaching others the power of neuroplasticity through neurocoaching and training, helping them navigate their own grief.

Grief is like a stormy sea. The waves crash over you, but as you allow yourself to process each stage, you start to find calmer waters. The Bible reassures us in Matthew 5:4, *"Blessed are those who mourn, for they will be comforted."* God sees your grief and walks with you, offering comfort and hope.

Practical Exercise:

◊ This week, allow yourself to feel your grief.

◊ Write down your emotions and offer them to God in prayer, asking for His comfort and strength.

Reflective Questions:

» What stage of grief are you in right now?

» How can you hold onto God's comfort during this time?

DAY 333: GOD IS FAITHFUL

"Your word is a lamp to my feet and a light to my path." — Psalm 119:105 (NIV)

It's easy to feel lost and overwhelmed in times of pressure and uncertainty. Despite the ever-changing world, God's faithfulness remains unwavering. When everything else seems uncertain, the Word of God acts as a lamp, guiding us through the darkest valleys and giving us hope. His faithfulness provides a foundation of certainty that we can rely on, no matter how turbulent life is.

The Bible is filled with reminders of God's unwavering faithfulness. In Lamentations 3:22-23 (NIV), we read, *"Because of the Lord's great love we are not consumed, for His compassions never fail. They are new every morning; great is your faithfulness."* This promise assures us that God's faithfulness is our anchor, even when life feels like a storm. His Word illuminates our path, showing us the way forward when we can't see what lies ahead.

Imagine navigating a dense forest at night with a small lamp to guide you. Without the lamp, you would be disoriented as the path is uncertain. But each step you take with that lamp reveals just enough to keep you moving forward safely. In the same way, God's Word is that reliable lamp for your life. It doesn't always reveal the entire path but gives you enough light to take the next step confidently. When you focus on His promises rather than the chaos around you, you find peace and certainty, knowing He is guiding you.

In my journey, especially during times of grief and uncertainty, God's faithfulness carried me through. His Word, filled with transformative promises, became my source of comfort and direction. Whenever I felt lost, I turned to scripture and found that even in the darkest moments, God's promises were like beams of light leading me forward.

Practical Exercise:

◊ This week, spend time each day reading a scripture that reminds you of God's faithfulness.

◊ Write it down and meditate on it, allowing it to light your path and bring certainty to your heart.

Reflective Questions:

» Where in your life do you need the light of God's Word to guide you?

» How can you rely on His faithfulness in uncertain times?

DAY 334: THE PAIN OF PRUNING - GROWING STRONGER

"He cuts off every branch in me that bears no fruit, while every branch that does bear fruit he prunes so that it will be even more fruitful." — John 15:2 (NIV)

Pruning is essential for growth, both in nature and in our lives. It is like a gardener cutting back the branches of a tree. Pruning may seem harsh, but it's necessary for growth. It involves letting go of things that hold us back—bad habits, limiting beliefs, unhealthy relationships, or unproductive ways of thinking. Pruning can be painful, but it's meant to help us grow stronger and more fruitful.

This process pushes us to break old habits and create new, healthier patterns. Our brains naturally prefer what's familiar, so change can feel uncomfortable. But this discomfort is part of growth. Pruning is not easy, but it helps us develop resilience, strengthening us for future challenges.

Imagine a rose bush. If left unpruned, it grows wild and tangled, producing fewer blooms. However, when a gardener trims away the dead and overgrown parts, the bush becomes healthier and produces more beautiful flowers. Similarly, when God allows us to undergo pruning, He's preparing us for a season of growth. It might involve removing things we've become attached to, but it's so that we can reach our full potential.

There were times in my life when I felt like things were being taken away, leaving me feeling exposed and vulnerable. Certain friendships faded, projects stalled, and plans didn't go as expected. Yet, looking back, I see how those experiences created space for new growth. They prepared me for opportunities and fruitfulness beyond what I could have imagined.

Practical Exercise:

◊ This week, think about one area in your life that feels like it's being "pruned."
◊ Write down how letting go of this could lead to new growth.
◊ Offer a prayer for strength and guidance during this process.

Reflective Questions:

» What in your life might God be asking you to let go of right now?
» How can you trust that this process will lead to something better?

Day 335: The Holy Spirit's Power in Shaping our Minds

"But the Advocate, the Holy Spirit, whom the Father will send in my name, will teach you all things and will remind you of everything I have said to you." — John 14:26 (NIV)

Our brains are incredibly adaptable, constantly forming new neural connections based on our experiences and thoughts. But did you know that the Holy Spirit is crucial in this process? John 14:26 tells us that the Holy Spirit teaches and reminds us of God's truth. He guides us to create new ways of thinking and can even help us overcome painful memories, leading to healthier thought patterns.

The Holy Spirit dwells in us and helps us renew and transform our minds. He can "delete" the grip of negative memories and replace them with God's truth, just as we clear out the old and bring in the new within a temple. This divine help influences the physical structure of our brains.

Picture your mind as a beautiful temple. Over time, this temple can accumulate clutter—old memories and negative thoughts that don't belong. The Holy Spirit works as the caretaker, helping you clear away the clutter and create new spaces filled with peace, hope, and truth. By doing this, He creates new brain connections that lead to a transformed life. Unused negative paths fade as new, healthier ones take over.

I have observed the Holy Spirit actively reforming my thoughts in my own life. Some memories tried to dominate my mind and lead me down paths of fear and doubt. Through prayer and surrender, the Holy Spirit helped me replace those old paths with new ones rooted in God's promises.

Practical Exercise:

◊ This week, focus on a negative thought or memory you want to change.
◊ Invite the Holy Spirit into that part of your mind, asking Him to replace it with God's truth.
◊ Write down the new truth and repeat it daily, imagining your transformation.

Reflective Questions:

» What areas of your mind need the Holy Spirit's transforming power?
» How could viewing your body as God's temple impact your mindset?

Day 336: Live Your Life Intentionally

"Your life does not get better by chance; it gets better by change." — Jim Rohn

Living intentionally means making choices that reflect your values and goals. It's about taking control of your life instead of letting things just happen. When you set clear intentions, you activate the prefrontal cortex, the brain's executive centre for decision-making and planning. This focus helps build strong neural pathways, making it easier to turn your intentions into actions and create habits that support the life you want. By living with intention, you become more connected to your values and goals, leading to a more fulfilling life.

Living intentionally also brings emotional stability. When you have a clear understanding of your "why" and take action based on it, you experience a greater sense of control and purpose in your life. Instead of reacting to life's events, you're shaping your experiences. This reduces stress and anxiety because you're not just going through the motions but making thoughtful choices that reflect who you are and what you truly want.

Scripture encourages us to live intentionally. Ephesians 5:15-16 (NIV) says, *"Be very careful, then, how you live—not as unwise but as wise, making the most of every opportunity."* This means being mindful of how you spend your time and energy, ensuring that your actions align with God's purpose for your life. Living intentionally honours God and the gifts He has given you.

Think of life like planting a garden. Without planning, it can look chaotic, quickly become messy, and overrun with weeds. But when you plant with purpose and tend to it regularly, you create a beautiful garden. In the same way, intentional living means sowing seeds of purpose and taking care of them through your actions.

Practical Exercise:

◊ This week, pick one area of your life where you want to be more intentional.
◊ Set a clear goal and take small, deliberate steps toward it.
◊ Notice how this changes your sense of control and purpose.

Reflective Questions:

» Are you shaping your life or letting life shape you?
» What is one area where you can start living more intentionally?

Day 337: Rehearse Your Future Self

"Act the way you'd like to be, and soon you'll be the way you act." — Leonard Cohen

Rehearsing your future self is about seeing who you want to become and starting to live that way right now. This isn't just about imagining your goals—it's about embodying them. Think of it as living in alignment with your future by acting as if it's already happening. Neuroscience shows that you build new neural connections when you envision yourself succeeding and then start behaving in ways that match that vision. Your brain starts to adapt to this new reality, making it easier to adopt the habits and mindset of your future self.

The Bible speaks to this practice of faith in action. Mark 11:24 (NIV) says, *"Therefore I tell you, whatever you ask for in prayer, believe that you have received it, and it will be yours."* This means stepping into the person you wish to become by acting and believing you're already there. When you rehearse your future self, you're not just dreaming—you're living as if it's already true. This changes your behaviours, decisions, and even the way you approach challenges.

Imagine starting each day as if you are already that future version of yourself. Speak, make decisions, and carry yourself with the confidence and purpose of the person you want to become. When you do this, you align your actions with your beliefs, transforming how you approach your daily life. For example, if your future self is a confident leader, start making decisions and speaking with that confidence today. Notice how this shift in mindset reshapes your actions and responses.

Practical Exercise:

◊ This week, practice one action or behaviour of your future self each day.

◊ As you do, remind yourself of Mark 11:24—believe you have received it, and let your actions reflect that belief.

Reflective Questions:

» Who is your future self, and what does that person look like daily?
» How can you start acting and believing in that future today?

Day 338: Jesus Said, "Ask in My Name"

"If you ask me anything in my name, I will do it." — John 14:14 (NIV)

When Jesus said, *"Ask in my name,"* He was giving us a powerful key to unlock heavenly resources. Asking in His name means aligning our requests with His will and believing in His authority. It's not just about adding "in Jesus' name" at the end of our prayers; it's about understanding the weight and power of His name and believing in Him. Neuroscience shows that when we pray with intention and faith, it can change our brain's chemistry, leading to increased feelings of hope, peace, and trust. Asking in Jesus' name taps into a spiritual principle that also influences our minds. When we pray with belief, it activates the brain's reward system, releasing neurotransmitters like dopamine. This gives us a sense of expectation and builds neural pathways that reinforce trust and positivity.

Emotionally, this practice encourages us to approach life with confidence, knowing that we have divine authority in every situation. It's a powerful reminder that we are not navigating life alone; we have the support of our Father - **ABBA**.
In John 14:14 (NIV), Jesus says, *"If you ask me anything in my name, I will do it."* This promise is rooted in a relationship with Him. When you pray in His name, you align your desires with His will, trusting that He hears and acts. It's like having a blank cheque signed by Yeshua, not to fulfil everything we desire but to meet every need that aligns with God's purpose for you.

Imagine having a direct line to the CEO of a company with unlimited resources. Every time you have a need or face a challenge, you have the assurance that the CEO is ready to support you. That's what asking in Jesus' name is like. It's a direct connection to the 'One' who holds all power and authority, assuring you that your requests are heard and will be answered according to His will.

Practical Exercise:

◊ This week, make a habit of asking in Yeshuas' name with faith and confidence.
◊ Choose one specific prayer request and bring it before God in Jesus' name, believing in His power to act.

Reflective Questions:

» Are you asking in Jesus' name with the confidence that He will answer?
» How can you align your prayers more closely with God's will?

DAY 339: TRUSTING GOD THROUGH SEASONS

"Life is about timing. The unreachable becomes reachable, the unavailable becomes available, the unattainable becomes attainable. Have the patience, wait it out. It's all about timing."
— Stacey Charter

We all experience seasons in life—times of growth, waiting, pruning, and harvest. Just as nature moves through spring, summer, autumn, and winter, our lives also cycle through phases. Often, we want to escape difficult times quickly, yet true growth comes from embracing these seasons with trust and patience.

Instead of praying or fasting solely to leave a challenging season, we can invite the Holy Spirit to guide us and reveal the lessons in this phase of our lives. Facing difficulties with a learning mindset reduces stress and anxiety. When we pray out of fear, it activates the amygdala in our brain, triggering a stress response that clouds our thinking. However, praying with trust calms our emotional brain, bringing peace and clarity that empowers us to make wise decisions.

Trusting God through each season means recognising that every phase serves a purpose. Ecclesiastes 3:1 (NIV) reminds us that *"there is a time for everything."* Instead of rushing to escape, we can ask the Holy Spirit to equip us. We can pray for insight into what God wants us to learn and how He is working within us during this time. Staying present in our current season allows us to grow, preparing us for what lies ahead.

Imagine a tree in winter. It appears lifeless, stripped of its leaves and enduring the cold. Yet beneath the surface, its roots are deepening, getting it ready for new growth in spring. The tree isn't rushing to bloom; it is preparing. Likewise, when we embrace our season and trust God's timing, we allow Him to strengthen our foundation and deepen our resilience.

Practical Exercise:

◊ This week, pray for understanding and growth instead of asking God to change your situation.

◊ Ask the Holy Spirit to help you see what He is doing in this season of your life and to equip you for what lies ahead.

Reflective Questions:

» Are you trying to rush out of a difficult season?

» How can you shift your prayers from asking for escape to asking for growth and learning?

Day 340: Radiate His Glory

"The Son is the dazzling radiance of God's splendour, the exact expression of God's true nature—his mirror image!" — Hebrews 1:3 (TPT)

Just as Jesus perfectly reflects the glory of God, we are called to mirror His nature in our lives. This reflection isn't just about words but about living in a way that demonstrates God's character. In 2 Peter 1:5-9 (NKJV), Peter outlines qualities that enable us to reflect God's glory: faith, virtue, knowledge, self-control, perseverance, godliness, brotherly kindness, and love. As we grow in these areas, we become reflections of God's light to those around us.

> **Faith:** Faith is our foundation, anchoring us in trust and confidence in God's promises. It's the basis on which all other qualities build, giving us hope and strength in all circumstances.
> **Virtue:** Virtue, or moral excellence, calls us to live with integrity, aligning our actions with God's standards and reflecting His holiness.
> **Knowledge:** Knowledge of God and His Word equips us to act with wisdom. This knowledge isn't just intellectual; it's a practical understanding that shapes our responses to life's challenges.
> **Self-Control:** Self-control shows that we are guided by the Spirit, not our impulses. It helps us respond to temptations and difficult situations in ways that honour God.
> **Perseverance:** Perseverance allows us to endure with faith. Continuing to trust God during trials displays our commitment to Him and reveals the strength of our relationship.
> **'Godliness':** 'Godliness 'reflects a deep reverence for God, shaping our character and choices. It shows devotion and respect for His presence in our lives.
> **Brotherly Kindness:** Brotherly kindness means showing active compassion and care to others. It reflects the unity and love that God desires among His people.
> **Love (Agape):** Agape love embodies God's unconditional, selfless love. By loving others without expecting anything in return, we reflect God's heart for the world.

These qualities enable us to reflect God's glory more clearly, like a mirror free of distractions. Cultivating them removes the "dust" of self-centeredness and impatience, allowing God's light to shine brightly through us.

Practical Exercise:

◊ This week, choose one quality from 2 Peter 1:5-9 to focus on.

Reflective Questions:

» How can you show God's nature more clearly in your actions?

DAY 341: THE RIPPLE EFFECT OF KINDNESS

"Be kind and compassionate to one another, forgiving each other, just as in Christ God forgave you." – Ephesians 4:32 (NIV)

Kindness involves showing compassion and generosity, whether through small or large acts. Proverbs 11:17 (NIV) says, *"Those who are kind benefit themselves, but the cruel bring ruin on themselves."* Acts of kindness stimulate neurotransmitters like serotonin and dopamine, which increases positive emotions and social bonding

Imagine brightening someone's day with a minor act of kindness, such as a compliment or a helping hand. These acts can create positive connections and foster a sense of community. Make it a point to perform one act of kindness each day. This practice will make others feel valued and enrich your life with joy and satisfaction.

In our busy world, it's easy to overlook opportunities for kindness. However, being kind can improve your mental well-being and positively impact those around you. Acts of kindness release feel-good hormones like oxytocin, serotonin, and dopamine, which can lower stress levels, enhance mood, and improve overall health. Kindness can also strengthen relationships and foster a sense of community, reminding us that we are all interconnected and part of a larger whole.

Practical Exercise:

◊ Perform an act of kindness today. It could be something simple, like holding the door for someone, offering a sincere compliment, or helping a neighbour.
◊ Afterwards, take a moment to reflect on how this act made you feel and how it impacted the other person.
◊ This reflection will help you become more aware and appreciative of the impact your kindness can have.

Reflective Questions:

» How do you feel after performing an act of kindness?
» What are some small ways you can incorporate kindness into your daily routine?
» How have acts of kindness affected your relationships and community?

PART TWELVE

REFLECT, RECHARGE, AND MOVE FORWARD

PART 12 INTRODUCTION

As you reach the final part of this journey, it's time to reflect on how far you've come and look ahead to what's next. This part is about pausing to reflect, learning from your experiences, and recharging your mind and spirit for the path ahead. You've spent the last 341 days rewiring your brain, mastering your emotions, and growing in your faith. Now, you're equipped with the tools to live a truly purposeful limitless life—one grounded in emotional intelligence, shaped by neuroscience, and rooted in scripture.

In these final days, you'll focus on reviewing your personal growth, celebrating your achievements, and setting new goals. This is an opportunity to solidify the powerful habits you've built and step confidently into the future, knowing that you can continue evolving and thriving. This isn't just the end of a book—it's the start of a new chapter in your life.

So take a breath, reflect on the journey, and get ready to soar even higher and boldly, fearlessly live the life God has equipped you to live..

DAY 342: LOOKING BACK TO MOVE FORWARD

"The only real mistake is the one from which we learn nothing." — John Powell

Reflection is like taking a pit stop during a race. It's not slowing down; it's gaining perspective so you can move forward with better clarity and planning. It's like checking your rearview mirror—not to live in the past but to navigate the road ahead more safely. We learn from our experiences to better understand ourselves and the path we're on.

When you pause to reflect, don't waste time overthinking things or dwelling on mistakes. Instead, identify patterns that worked, those that didn't, and why. Imagine an artist who steps back to view their painting from a distance. They might miss the overall picture up close, but stepping back reveals what needs to be adjusted. Scripture echoes this in Lamentations 3:40 (NIV): *"Let us examine our ways and test them."* It's about learning and using that insight to guide future actions.

Emotional intelligence (EQ) helps us reflect on our reactions or responses and understand why we feel the way we do. For example, if you often feel overwhelmed, reflecting might reveal a pattern. Maybe you take on too much because saying "no" feels uncomfortable. By recognising this, you can start making changes that align with your well-being and goals.

Maybe you push through your day without taking breaks, thinking that slowing down means you're not working hard enough. You might believe constant hustle is the only way to show strength, but then you feel burned out and exhausted. By reflecting on this mindset, you may realise it's draining your energy more than helping you. It's time to give yourself permission to take short breaks? These small pauses would refresh your mind and boost your productivity. Sometimes, the most productive step forward starts with a moment to breathe. Could this be the change you need to regain your energy and focus?

Practical Tips:

◊ Spend 5 minutes each evening reflecting on one challenge from your day.

◊ Ask yourself, *"What did this reveal about my approach?"* and *"What one small change can I make tomorrow to guide myself in the direction I want to go?"*

Reflective Questions:

» What recent situation taught you something about your habits?

» How can this insight shape your next step?

Day 343: Celebrating Achievements

"Rejoice in the Lord always. I will say it again: Rejoice!" – Philippians 4:4 (NIV)

Celebrating achievements is like pausing at the top of a staircase you've been climbing for a while. You've put in the effort and felt the burn in your legs, and now you deserve a moment to catch your breath and appreciate how high you've climbed. So often, we rush to the next step, the next challenge, without recognising how far we've come. But when you take the time to celebrate small victories, you tell yourself, "This matters." Your brain responds by releasing feel-good chemicals that boost your motivation and confidence.

Think of it like completing a marathon. When you cross that finish line, you don't just shrug it off and walk away. You celebrate. Maybe you feel a wave of pride, relief, or even tears of joy. This moment of celebration reinforces the hard work you've put in, filling you with the strength to take on future challenges. The Bible reminds us in Psalm 126:3 (NIV), *"The Lord has done great things for us, and we are filled with joy."* Celebrating isn't about pride; it's about recognising the journey and God's faithfulness in every step.

Perhaps you've challenged yourself to finish a difficult project at work, or you've achieved a personal milestone, such as forming a new habit. Instead of rushing past it, take a moment to acknowledge your success. Treat yourself to something you love—a favourite meal, a relaxing evening, or simply sharing your success with someone who supports you.

Practical Tips:

◊ Make celebrating a habit.
◊ After each accomplishment, big or small, pause and acknowledge it.
◊ Give yourself permission to feel joyful.

Reflective Questions:

» What achievements have you overlooked recently?
» How can celebrating these moments fuel your motivation?

Exercise: Write down three things you've accomplished lately, no matter how small. Choose one and celebrate it today—call a friend, enjoy a quiet moment of gratitude, or do something that makes you happy. Notice how this lifts your spirit.

Day 344: Letting Go of Control

"Surrender to what is. Let go of what was. Have faith in what will be." – Sonia Ricotti

The need for control can feel like gripping the wheel of a car on a bumpy road. You try to steer every outcome, not because of an immediate threat, but due to the anxiety about what might go wrong. Your brain's left hemisphere, known for its role in logic and reasoning, often acts like an expert storyteller. It tries to make sense of things, sometimes creating stories to explain uncertainties that don't add up. This tendency can lead to overthinking and the need to control every detail, turning unknowns into sources of anxiety.

Scripture offers a different path. Proverbs 3:5 (NIV) says, *"Trust in the Lord with all your heart and lean not on your own understanding."* This isn't about ignoring responsibilities but learning to release the grip where it's no longer serving you. Think of a gardener planting seeds. You can prepare the soil and water the plants, but you can't control the weather or exactly how each seed will grow. There comes a point where you must trust the process.

When you're anxious and trying to control every aspect of a situation, like planning an event down to the smallest detail, you often miss the joy of the moment. Your left hemisphere keeps spinning stories of what could go wrong, driving you to micromanage and often end up in 'action paralysis'. But letting go of this need doesn't mean you don't care; it means trusting that you've done all you can do, so now it's time to leave the rest in God's hands, trusting He is in control.

Practical Tips:
- ◊ When you feel the need to control everything, pause and ask, *"Is my brain creating a story here that's causing me anxiety?"*
- ◊ What can I influence, and what do I need to let go of?"

Reflective Questions:
- » In which areas of your life do you find yourself caught in overthinking and trying to control every outcome?
- » How might releasing this need for control bring you peace?

Exercise: Identify one situation where you feel the need to control. Notice the stories your mind is creating around it. Today, practice letting go of one small part of this situation. Observe how it feels to release that grip and trust the process.

Day 345: Finding Calm Within

"Calmness is the cradle of power." – Josiah Gilbert Holland

In the busyness of life, our minds can become cluttered, leaving us feeling anxious and overwhelmed. Techniques like deep breathing, muscle relaxation, mindfulness, meditation, and good sleep are some of the essential tools we have discussed to create inner calm. But remember, it's not enough to just know these techniques; it's important to use them. When you engage in deep breathing, for instance, you send signals to your limbic system—your emotional brain—that it's safe to relax, reducing stress and allowing your prefrontal cortex, the thinking brain, to function more effectively. So, it's up to you to take the reins and commit to these practices for your own well-being.

Imagine your mind as a shaken snow globe. Stress stirs up your thoughts and emotions, making it difficult to see clearly. Breathing exercises act like placing the snow globe down, letting the flurry settle so you can see things more clearly. By practising muscle relaxation techniques, you are able to physically release the tension that is stored in your body, effectively signalling to your brain that it relinquishes the "fight or flight" response. Improved coordination between the limbic system and the pre-frontal cortex helps you respond to life's challenges more clearly and calmly.

Scripture often emphasises the power of stillness. Psalm 62:1 (NIV) says, *"Truly my soul finds rest in God."* Taking time to be still—whether through mindful breathing, meditation, or rest—allows you to connect deeply with yourself and with God. The purpose is not to avoid reality but rather to equip yourself with calmness and a balanced mindset to confront it.

Practical Tips:

◊ Start each day with 5 minutes of mindful breathing or meditation.
◊ Close your eyes, take slow, deep breaths, and focus on the present moment.

Reflective Questions:

» How do you currently manage stress and overwhelming emotions?
» Which calming technique can you practice to bring more peace into your daily life?

Exercise: Tonight, try a mindfulness exercise before bed. Sit comfortably, close your eyes, and focus on your breathing. As thoughts arise, gently guide your focus back to your breathing. Notice how this practice helps quiet your mind and prepares you for restful sleep.

Day 346: Escaping Thinking Traps

"You can't cross a sea by merely staring at the water." —R Tagore

Thinking traps are mental pitfalls that distort reality and keep you stuck in negative patterns. Some common traps to watch out for are - **catastrophising** ("If I mess up this presentation, my entire career is over"), **mind reading** ("She didn't say hi, so she must be mad at me"), **all-or-nothing thinking** ("I failed this task, so I'm a total failure"), and **overgeneralising** ("I always mess things up"). These traps activate the brain's stress response, creating a cycle of anxiety and self-doubt. Our brains often take mental shortcuts, which can lead to distorted conclusions. The limbic system, which controls our emotions, can overwhelm the rational prefrontal cortex, making it difficult to see the bigger picture. It's like wearing dark glasses in a room filled with light—you miss the full reality because your view is filtered through these traps.

To break free from these traps, use the 'FACED' technique:

> **Feel it:** Recognise the emotion you're experiencing. Name it to reduce its intensity.

> **Accept it:** Understand that it's okay to feel this way. Accepting the emotion doesn't mean you agree with the thought; it just means acknowledging its presence.

> **Challenge it:** Question the thought. Ask, *"Is this thought a fact or an assumption?"* Is there evidence against it?

> **Examine it:** Look at the situation from different angles. Consider other possibilities or perspectives. For instance, if you're mind reading, think, "What else could explain this person's behaviour?"

> **Do:** Decide on a constructive action based on a more balanced view. What can you do that aligns with a more accurate understanding of the situation?

Practical Tip:

◊ Whenever you are trapped in negative thinking, pause and go through the FACED steps. This process helps you break down negative thoughts and reframe them more realistically.

Reflective Questions:

» What thinking traps do you frequently encounter?
» How can using the FACED technique help you change your perspective and responses?

Exercise: Recall a recent thinking trap, apply each step of FACED to reframe it, and choose one positive action to take forward.

Day 347: Precision in Life: Using Lessons from Microbiology

"Small acts, when multiplied by millions of people, can transform the world." – Howard Zinn

As a medical microbiologist, I learned the importance of precision. In the laboratory, determining the *Minimum Inhibitory Concentration (MIC)* of antibiotics is key to finding the right treatment for infections. This concept of precision is just as vital in life. You need to identify what is holding you back in order to address it effectively.

Consider the challenges in your life as forms of **"resistance."** Fear, self-doubt, and negative habits can be barriers keeping you from moving forward. Just as bacteria develop resistance to antibiotics, your mind can resist change. Yet, thanks to neuroplasticity, your brain can rewire itself and create healthier patterns. The first step is recognising these mental blocks.

Imagine your mind as a vast laboratory where mindfulness and emotional intelligence act as valuable diagnostic tools, helping you understand your inner workings. When faced with a challenge, pause instead of reacting right away. Ask yourself: What's the *"resistance"* here? Is it fear of failure or a habit of negative thinking? By identifying the obstacle, you create an opportunity for change. With neuroplasticity, you can practice building new connections in your brain, like constructing a fresh road that leads to growth and success.

Practical Tips:

◊ Identify the *"resistant"* thought or behaviour when you face a challenge.
◊ Use neuroplasticity by consistently practising a new, positive response.
◊ With time, this will rewire your brain for more positive outcomes.

Reflective Questions:

» What *"resistances"* do you face in your thoughts or habits?
» How can you create new, positive pathways in your brain?

Exercise: Identify one negative thought or habit that often holds you back. Write it down. Now, choose a positive thought or action to replace it. Practice this new response whenever you fall into the old pattern. This is like treating a condition to create lasting change.

Day 348: Adapt with Clarity

"Change is the end result of all true learning." – Leo Buscaglia

In microbiology, adapting to evolving pathogens requires a clear and precise approach. Scientists use various tools to detect, analyse, and respond to these changes effectively. Likewise, the ability to adapt to change is crucial for growth and success. Just as laboratories (lab) employ careful analysis to tackle drug-resistant bacteria, you can use self-reflection, meditation and mindfulness to navigate the changes and challenges that arise in your life.

Data analysis and diagnostics are essential for understanding and managing resistance in the lab. Tools like self-reflection, mindfulness, and emotional intelligence enable us to understand and respond appropriately to change. When facing an unexpected situation, instead of reacting out of fear or habit, take a moment to examine it with clarity. What about this change feels challenging? What part of it can you influence, and what do you need to let go of?

Have you ever felt overwhelmed by a sudden change? Perhaps a sudden change at work or a personal challenge. Instead of diving headfirst into stress and anxiety, in future, try viewing the situation like a scientist studying a sample. Gather the "data" of your thoughts and feelings without judgment. This approach will help you identify what is truly happening rather than getting caught up in emotional reactions. From this place of clarity, you can decide on the best action to take. Microbiology labs use an integrated approach to streamline processes and ensure accurate results. You can do the same by combining practices like deep breathing, journaling, and seeking support. This creates a balanced approach to change, helping you adapt with less stress.

Practical Tip: When faced with change, pause and use your "diagnostic tools." Reflect on what's causing your discomfort. Then, choose one clear action to help you adapt, focusing on what you can control.

Exercise:

> Think of a recent change that challenged you. Write down what made it difficult.
> Using a "scientific" mindset, break down the situation.
> What were your initial reactions? What could you have done differently?

Reflective Questions:

» How do you typically respond to changes in your life?
» What tools can help you adapt to change with more clarity and calmness?

Day 349: Building on Your Successes

"A man is not defeated by his opponents but by himself." – Jan C. Smuts

Think of your journey like climbing a staircase. Each success you achieve is a step that lifts you higher, giving you a better view of what's possible. But many people don't take full advantage of their past successes. Instead of building on them, they start over each time, feeling like they have to prove themselves again. Imagine how much further you could go if you used each success as a foundation for the next one.

When you reflect on your achievements, you trigger a powerful response in your mind. Your brain releases feel-good chemicals like dopamine, boosting your confidence and motivating you to keep moving forward. It's a reminder that you've conquered challenges before, and you can do it again. Philippians 3:13-14 encourages us to press on toward our goals: *"Forgetting what is behind and straining toward what is ahead."* This doesn't mean ignoring your past victories but using them to fuel your next steps.

Remember a time when you achieved a significant achievement. You may have completed a challenging project at work, reached a fitness goal, or overcome a personal struggle. You didn't succeed by chance; you used certain strategies, took specific actions, and stayed committed.

Instead of starting from scratch with each new challenge, why not build on what you've already learned? It's like using a tried-and-tested recipe—you know the ingredients that work so you can create even more beautiful dishes.

Practical Tips:

◊ After each success, take a moment to reflect.

◊ What strategies helped you succeed?

◊ Write them down and think about how you can use these insights for your next goal.

Reflective Questions:

» How can you use your past successes as building blocks for your future?
» What specific actions or mindsets helped you achieve your goals?
» How does remembering your successes help you stay motivated?

Exercise: Reflect on a recent success and write down three key actions or strategies that helped you achieve it. Keep this list handy, and the next time you face a challenge, revisit these steps to remind you that you already have the tools you need to succeed.

Day 350: Preparing for New Challenges

"Challenges are what make life interesting and overcoming them is what makes life meaningful." – Joshua J. Marine

Life is full of challenges, both big and small. But it's not about trying to avoid them; it's about preparing ourselves to face them with confidence. Challenges give life purpose and meaning, pushing us to grow and discover our strengths. Each one is a chance to learn, adapt, and move closer to the person you're meant to become. Preparing for challenges doesn't mean predicting every twist and turn; it means building a mindset that can handle what comes your way. Think of it like preparing for a long hike. You wouldn't set off without water, food, and a map to guide you. In the same way, preparing for life's challenges involves gathering the right tools, resources, and strategies. When we do this, neuroscience shows that the brain's prefrontal cortex—the part responsible for planning and problem-solving—kicks in, making us feel more in control and reducing stress when obstacles arise.

Imagine you're gearing up for a big work project. Instead of diving in unprepared, you take a moment to organise your time, gather the resources you need, and set realistic goals. This planning doesn't make the project any easier, but it makes you feel capable and ready, turning an intimidating task into one you can handle. Preparation helps you build resilience, allowing you to face new challenges with a calm and confident mindset. God encourages us to embrace growth and resilience. As Philippians 1:6 reminds us, He is continually at work within us, preparing us for what lies ahead. Challenges shape us, and each one you overcome is a step toward the purpose He has designed for you.

Practical Tips:

◊ Take a moment to consider any upcoming challenges.

◊ Write down one or two possible obstacles, and brainstorm ways to address them.

◊ Preparing now will make you more adaptable and less stressed when challenges arise.

Exercise:

> Identify an upcoming challenge and list steps you can take to prepare for it.

> What resources, skills, or strategies will you need?

> Planning helps you overcome obstacles and builds confidence.

Reflective Questions:

» What challenges do you see coming in future?

» How can preparation help you approach them with a sense of calm and strength?

Day 351: Embracing Life's Journey

"For I know the plans I have for you, declares the Lord, plans to prosper you and not to harm you, plans to give you hope and a future." – Jeremiah 29:11 (NIV)

Life is not just about reaching the destination; it's about your journey to get there. Embracing life's journey means accepting both the highs and the lows, learning from every experience, and finding joy in the process. It's easy to become fixated on goals, thinking that happiness will come only once you've achieved them. However, real fulfilment comes from appreciating the path you're on right now. Ecclesiastes 3:1 reminds us, *"There is a time for everything, and a season for every activity under the heavens."*

When you embrace the journey, you activate areas of your brain involved in emotional regulation and mindfulness. This helps you navigate life with a sense of peace and resilience. Think of it as a road trip. If you're solely focused on getting to the destination, you'll miss the beautiful scenery, the interesting stops, and the moments of laughter along the way. Being present and grateful for each part of your journey enhances your mental well-being and builds a stronger, more positive mindset.

Consider your personal or professional journey. There have likely been moments of challenge and moments of triumph. Each experience, whether joyful or difficult, has contributed to who you are today. Embracing the journey is about acknowledging this growth, appreciating the lessons learned, and finding joy in the present moment. Many people get caught up in the idea of *"I'll be happy when..."* and miss out on the richness of the here and now.

Practical Tips:

◊ Set aside regular time to reflect on your journey.
◊ Celebrate your growth, express gratitude for your experiences, and appreciate where you are right now.

Reflective Questions:

» How can you appreciate your journey, not just the destination?
» What valuable lessons have you learned from your experiences along the way?

Exercise: Reflect on your journey so far. Write three things you've learned from your experiences and three things you're grateful for in the present moment. This practice will help you find joy and fulfilment in the journey, not just the end goal

DAY 352: LOOKING AHEAD WITH CONFIDENCE

"Optimism provides you with durability and resiliency. You must do that which you think you cannot do." — Eleanor Roosevelt

Looking ahead confidently means having a vision for your future and trusting that you can achieve it. This confidence doesn't come from knowing every detail, but from believing in your ability to overcome obstacles and adapt to challenges. Philippians 4:13 (NKJV) reminds us, *"I can do all things through Christ who strengthens me."* It's about embracing the journey with optimism, knowing that every step you take is towards realising your goals.

When you confidently look to the future, you align your mind with a sense of purpose and clarity. This approach helps you to not just dream about your goals but actively pursue and achieve them. Imagine standing at the start of a marathon. The finish line might seem so far away, but you grow stronger and more determined with each stride. Confidence empowers you to keep moving forward, even when the path is uncertain. This resilience empowers you to turn your vision into reality.

Think of a time when you set an ambitious goal, like going for a promotion, pivoting in your career, starting a new business, or scaling your business. The journey likely involved moments of doubt and challenge. Despite the initial challenges, you witnessed significant progress as you started breaking your goals into manageable steps and addressing them one by one. Eleanor Roosevelt's words remind us that real growth happens when we push beyond our comfort zones and do what we once thought impossible. This is not just about striving; it's about achieving.

Many struggle with self-doubt, but confidence enables you to take the necessary steps toward your goals and achieve them. It's about trusting in your growth and your ability to succeed.

Practical Tips:

◊ Create a vision board or detailed plan for your future goals.
◊ Write down your vision and identify three concrete actions you can take today.
◊ Regularly review and adjust your plan to stay focused on achieving your goals confidently.

Reflective Questions:

» What are your long-term goals, and how can you confidently achieve them?
» How can embracing optimism help you take decisive actions toward these goals?

Day 353: Do You Have Capacity?

"The oak fought the wind and was broken, the willow bent when it must and survived." – Robert Jordan

Having the capacity to achieve your goals involves more than just time or skill; it's about balancing energy, mindset, and continuous growth. We often push ourselves to exhaustion, believing that sheer effort is the key to success. However, true capacity comes from a balanced approach that includes rest, learning, and self-care. Even Jesus recognised the need for renewal, often withdrawing to quiet places to recharge (Luke 5:16). To fulfil your purpose effectively, you must also take time to restore your capacity.

Think of yourself as a tree facing the seasons. The oak tree that stands rigid against the storm may break, while the willow that bends with the wind survives and grows stronger. Your mind and body need similar periods of flexibility and recovery to thrive. Neuroscience shows that chronic stress impairs cognitive function, making it difficult to make sound decisions or think creatively. Building true capacity involves knowing when to push forward and when to step back, empowering yourself through growth and rest.

Consider a demanding project. If you're running on empty, your performance suffers. But if you've taken the time to rest, learn, and reflect, you can tackle challenges with clarity and strength. Capacity isn't about taking on everything at once; it's about prioritising what matters most, ensuring you're prepared to tackle challenges effectively.

Practical Tips:

◊ Integrate rest, learning, and action into your daily routine.
◊ Make space for relaxation, personal growth, and skill-building to ensure you have the capacity to meet challenges head-on.

Reflective Questions:

» Are you giving yourself the freedom to build true capacity?
» How can you create a routine that includes both rest and growth?

Exercise:
Identify one way you can recharge today and one area where you can grow. Whether it's taking a brief break, learning something new, or seeking guidance, use this to build a stronger capacity to overcome obstacles and achieve your goals.

DAY 354: EMBRACING ENDLESS POTENTIAL

"Your potential is endless; go do what you were created to do." – Unknown

You are created with limitless potential. Often, we hold ourselves back because of past experiences, fears, or what others say. But your potential isn't fixed—it's like an open ocean, ready for you to explore. God has planted seeds of greatness within you, and with faith, determination, and action, you can achieve more than you ever thought possible. As Ephesians 3:20 (NIV) says, *"God is able to do immeasurably more than all we ask or imagine, according to his power that is at work within us."*

Your brain is wired to grow and adapt. Through neuroplasticity, your brain can form new connections, learn new skills, and let go of old habits. This means you're not limited by what you know or where you've been. Every day is a chance to stretch your mind, expand your abilities, and step into new possibilities. It's like standing before a blank canvas—you get to decide what to create. The only limit is your imagination.

Think of people who started with little but went on to achieve amazing things. They didn't stay in their comfort zone; they took risks, learned, adapted, and pushed beyond limits. You have that same capacity. Your past is only a stepping stone to your future. When you start believing in the endless possibilities within you, you begin to take actions that align with that belief.

Practical Tips:

◊ Remind yourself daily of the endless potential within you.
◊ Set small, bold goals that challenge you to step outside your comfort zone.
◊ Visualise what you can achieve, and take small steps toward that vision.

Reflective Questions:

» What limits have you placed on yourself that you can let go of?
» How can you start embracing your endless potential?

Exercise: Write down one bold goal that excites and challenges you. Outline a single step you can take today toward achieving it. Remember, the journey to a life of limitless possibilities starts with one intentional step.

DAY 355: THE POWER OF THE SUBCONSCIOUS

"Your subconscious mind works continuously, while you are awake, and while you sleep." – Napoleon Hill

As you reflect on this journey, remember that your subconscious mind is like a tireless gardener, nurturing whatever seeds you plant. It doesn't choose what to grow; it simply nourishes what you feed it—whether seeds of doubt or seeds of hope. Proverbs 23:7 (KJV) reminds us, *"For as he thinks in his heart, so is he."* Your subconscious shapes your reality based on the thoughts and beliefs you give it.

Picture your mind as a garden. When you plant seeds of negativity and fear, your subconscious grows weeds that can choke your confidence and dreams. But when you plant seeds of faith, positivity, and possibility, your subconscious nurtures these into a flourishing garden of growth. It's like a tape recorder, repeating the messages it's given. The more you fill it with affirmations of your potential, the more it supports you in achieving your goals and thriving.

Think back to a time when you faced a challenge and discovered the strength to overcome it. That was your subconscious drawing on the positive seeds you planted earlier. As you continue this journey, focus on reinforcing those positive seeds, allowing them to grow and guide you toward a future filled with confidence and growth.

Practical Tips:

◊ Revisit and reinforce the positive affirmations you've cultivated.

◊ Make it a daily habit to visualise your goals, planting seeds in your subconscious that reflect the limitless possibilities ahead.

◊ This daily practice will keep you focused and motivated on your journey of growth.

Reflective Questions:

» What "seeds" have you planted in your subconscious throughout this journey?

» How can you continue to nurture those seeds to support your future?

Exercise:

> Choose one affirmation that embodies your future aspirations.

> Each day, take a moment to repeat it and visualise it blossoming into reality.

> This simple act nurtures your subconscious garden, ensuring it grows into your desired vibrant future.

Day 356: Sowing Seeds for Success with R.E.A.P.

"Do not be deceived: God cannot be mocked. A man reaps what he sows." – Galatians 6:7 (NIV)

R.E.A.P. represents a robust process called **Reflect, Embrace, Act, and Persist**. This process serves as a guiding tool to help you achieve the desired harvest in your life. Like a farmer who prepares the soil, plants seeds, and nurtures the crops until harvest, R.E.A.P. will help you create a life that reflects your goals and values as you intentionally shape your future.

Reflect: Reflection is like examining the soil of your life. Reflect on your journey, recognising the lessons learned and the growth you've experienced. Proverbs 4:26 says, *"Give careful thought to the paths for your feet."* Reflecting allows you to see what has worked and what hasn't, providing clarity for your next steps.

Embrace: Embrace where you are right now, with all the successes and challenges. It's like nurturing the soil—accepting that every season has a purpose. Embracing your current state allows you to move forward with grace and gratitude, understanding that every part of your journey shapes you for what's ahead.

Act: This is where you sow the seeds. Act with intention, knowing that your actions today will shape your tomorrow. James 2:17 reminds us, *"Faith by itself, if it is not accompanied by action, is dead."* You must plant seeds through consistent and purposeful actions to reap the harvest. It's a call to action that fuels your determination and focuses you on your goals.

Persist: Like crops, your goals require time and care to grow. Keep nurturing your dreams, even when progress seems slow. Galatians 6:9 (NIV) encourages us, *"Let us not become weary in doing good, for at the proper time we will reap a harvest if we do not give up."*

Practical Tips:

◊ Use the R.E.A.P. process daily.
◊ Reflect on your journey, embrace your current state, act purposefully, and persist through challenges.
◊ This approach will lead you to a life of abundance and fulfilment.

Reflective Questions:

» How can you use R.E.A.P. to cultivate the life you desire?
» What steps do you need to take today to sow the seeds for your future?

Day 357: Liberating Yourself from Excuses

"He that is good for making excuses is seldom good for anything else." – Benjamin Franklin

Excuses have a way of disguising themselves as valid reasons. They tell you there isn't enough time, you're incapable, or you're not "the type" to achieve your goals. These excuses can become so ingrained that you believe them wholeheartedly. But every time you cling to these beliefs, you rob yourself of motivation and the chance to pursue your dreams. Proverbs 26:13 (NIV) speaks of the sluggard who says, *"There's a lion in the road,"* using fear as an excuse to avoid action.

Your brain naturally seeks comfort and predictability, making excuses to avoid discomfort. But while excuses may protect you from immediate discomfort, they trap you in a cycle of inaction. It's like staying in a safe harbour; while it feels secure, you're not meant to remain anchored forever. Your true potential lies beyond the harbour, in the open waters where growth and discovery happen. Think about the excuses you've been holding onto. Maybe it's *"I don't have time,"* or *"I'm not good enough."* These are just stories your mind tells to avoid the discomfort of change. Recognise these excuses for what they are—shackles that hold you back from your God-given potential and destiny. You can challenge and break free from them by identifying them and gaining a new sense of empowerment and control over your life.

Practical Tips:

◊ Identify one excuse you've been using to avoid pursuing your goals.
◊ Write it down and challenge its validity.
◊ Replace it with an empowering statement that opens the door to possibilities.

Reflective Questions:

» What excuses have you been telling yourself, and how have they held you back?
» How can you challenge these excuses and replace them with empowering truths?

Exercise:
List three excuses that have been stopping you. For each, write why it's not a true barrier but just a story.
Rewrite each excuse as a positive affirmation that drives you to take action.

Breaking free from excuses is the first step to limitless possibilities, showing your strength and determination with every move.

Day 358: Rooted in the Vine

"Abide in me, and I in you. As the branch cannot bear fruit by itself, unless it abides in the vine, neither can you, unless you abide in me." – John 15:4 (NKJV)

Imagine a vine and its branches. The branches draw all their nourishment, strength, and life from the vine. In the same way, when you abide in Christ, you tap into His endless source of strength, wisdom, and peace. Abiding isn't about doing more; it's about staying connected and letting His presence nurture your spirit, mind, and emotions.

Abiding in Yeshua means trusting Him with your deepest feelings, fears, and hopes. It's like being a tree planted by streams of water (Psalm 1:3), drawing from His presence, especially in difficult seasons. You can engage your brain's calming systems through prayer, reflection, and meditation on God's word. This isn't about suppressing emotions but bringing them into God's presence. Neuroscience shows that practices like mindfulness and prayer can activate the parasympathetic nervous system - reducing stress and promoting emotional balance. When you bring your fears and anxieties to Christ, you invite His peace to guide your emotional responses.

Think about those times when your emotions felt like a storm. Abiding in Christ means inviting Him into that storm, letting His peace calm the turbulence within you. This connection is an anchor, grounding you even when external circumstances are chaotic. Instead of reacting to every emotional wave, you find steadiness in His constant love, wisdom, and presence, providing you with a sense of security and stability.

Practical Tips:

◊ Begin your day by bringing your emotions to Christ.
◊ Be honest about what you feel—joy, fear, anxiety, or hope.
◊ Remember, He is there to listen and support you.
◊ Pray or meditate on Scripture, inviting His peace into your heart to bring clarity and calmness.

Reflective Questions:

» How can you align your emotions with Christ daily?
» What specific feelings or worries can you surrender to Him right now?

Exercise: For five minutes, visualise yourself as a branch, drawing peace and strength from Christ and feeling nourished.

DAY 359: STOP APOLOGISING

"Never apologise for showing feeling. When you do so, you apologise for the truth." – Benjamin Disraeli

Apologising when you're wrong is a sign of humility, but constantly apologising for who you are, your dreams, or taking up space diminishes your worth. Many people fall into the habit of apologising for things that don't warrant an apology—like speaking up, setting boundaries, or pursuing their goals. It's as if they're asking for permission to exist, to take action, or to simply be themselves.

God didn't create you to shrink back; He created you to stand firm in the identity He has given you. When you constantly apologise, you reinforce a mindset of inadequacy. Your brain associates taking action or expressing your true self with a need for approval. This is not what you were designed for. Romans 8:37 (NIV) declares, *"In all these things, we are more than conquerors through him who loved us."* You are meant to live boldly, not to apologise for pursuing the path God has laid before you.

Think about how often you've apologised for saying "no," sharing your thoughts or even celebrating your achievements. Each unnecessary apology erodes your confidence and self-belief. Imagine you're a light meant to shine in a dark room. If you keep dimming yourself and apologising for shining too brightly, you reduce the positive impact you're meant to have. Remember, your worth doesn't depend on how much space you take up or how boldly you follow your calling—it's inherent and unchanging.

Practical Tips:

◊ Replace unnecessary apologies with gratitude or assertiveness.

◊ Instead of saying, *"I'm sorry for taking up your time,"* try saying, *"Thank you for your time."*

◊ This subtle shift empowers you to own your space without feeling the need to apologise.

Exercise:

> Pay attention today to moments when you feel the urge to apologise.

> Pause and ask yourself if an apology is truly needed. If not, replace it with a statement of gratitude or assertiveness.

> Remember, it's not just about avoiding unnecessary apologies; it's about actively practising speaking confidently and assertively.

Reflective Questions:

» In what areas do you apologise unnecessarily?

» How can you shift your mindset to embrace who you are without apology?

DAY 360: OVERCOMING IMPOSTOR SYNDROME

"Our deepest fear is not that we are inadequate. Our deepest fear is that we are powerful beyond measure." – Marianne Williamson

Impostor syndrome is that nagging voice that tells you that you're not truly qualified or deserving of your success. But here's the thing: feeling like an impostor is actually a sign that you're stretching yourself, pushing beyond what's comfortable—and that's a good thing. It means you're growing.

This self-doubt often stems from old memories stored in the brain that trigger feelings of inadequacy. However, those thoughts don't define you. God has equipped you with unique gifts and a purpose. As 2 Timothy 1:7 (NIV) reminds us, *"For God has not given us a spirit of fear, but of power and of love and of a sound mind."*

Impostor feelings are linked to the brain's limbic system, which controls emotions and often triggers fear responses. Past experiences—like criticism or rejection—have created pathways that make self-doubt feel automatic. But because of the brain's neuroplasticity, you can rewire these responses. When you start choosing affirming thoughts, you create new pathways, making it easier to believe in your abilities over time.

Think of a time when you doubted yourself, only to realise later you were capable all along. It's like a pilot who faces turbulence; with training, they learn to trust their skills and navigate with confidence. You can do the same by recognising impostor thoughts, challenging them, and replacing them with affirming truths.

Practical Tips:

◊ Acknowledge impostor thoughts without accepting them as truth.
◊ Replace them with affirmations of God's promises.
◊ Write down three times you felt like an impostor but succeeded.
◊ Review these to remind yourself of your strength.

Reflective Questions:

» How can you use emotional intelligence to spot and challenge impostor feelings?
» What affirmations can help you replace self-doubt with confidence?

Day 361: Live Like Royalty, Not an Orphan

"I will not leave you as orphans; I will come to you." – John 14:18 (NIV)

You are not an orphan in this world; you are a child of the King of Kings. Too often, people live with a mindset of lack and insecurity, as though they need to earn their place or prove their worth. But in Christ, you are already royalty. He has adopted you into His family, granting you access to His love, strength, and resources. Living like royalty means embracing the identity and inheritance you've been given, not out of pride but out of the confidence that you belong.

Think of an orphan, uncertain of their place, often struggling with feelings of abandonment or unworthiness. Now, picture royalty—someone who walks confidently, knowing they have access to the kingdom's wealth. Your mindset can significantly affect how you perceive and respond to the world. When you live with a scarcity mindset, your brain reinforces patterns of fear and doubt. But when you embrace a mindset of abundance, rooted in your identity as God's child, it shifts your emotional state, allowing you to approach life with confidence and peace.

Living like royalty doesn't mean living extravagantly; it means living securely. You are loved, valued, and equipped, not because of what you do but because of who you are in Christ. This royal mindset lets you step out boldly, knowing you are not alone or lacking. It's like a prince or princess who, even in challenging times, knows they have the full support of the King.

Practical Tips:

◊ Start each day by affirming your identity in Christ.

◊ Remind yourself that you are not an orphan; you are royalty.

◊ Speak words of abundance and confidence, knowing you have access to God's limitless resources.

Exercise:

> Write three truths about your identity in Christ.

> Place this list where you can see it daily.

> Whenever feelings of insecurity arise, revisit these truths to remind yourself that you are not an orphan—you are royalty, loved and equipped by the King.

Reflective Questions:

» Do you often live with a mindset of lack or abundance?

» How can embracing your identity as God's child change how you approach challenges?

Day 362: Don't Get Lost in Analysis Paralysis

"If you wait for perfect conditions, you will never get anything done." – Ecclesiastes 11:4 (NLT)

Overthinking can be a trap that keeps you stuck, a state often called "analysis paralysis." It's when you spend so much time analysing options, outcomes, and potential pitfalls that you end up taking no action at all. This can stem from a fear of failure, a desire for perfection, or simply feeling overwhelmed by the choices before you. But God didn't create you to be stuck in endless loops of indecision; He calls you to step out in faith.

Your brain is wired to assess risks and make decisions, but when you over-analyse, you activate the brain's fear centre, the amygdala. This triggers a stress response that can actually make decision-making more difficult. It's like standing at a fork in the road, looking down each path so long that the opportunity to move forward slips away. Proverbs 3:5-6 (NIV) reminds us, *"Trust in the Lord with all your heart and lean not on your own understanding."* Trusting God means sometimes taking the next step, even when the entire path isn't clear.

Think of Peter stepping out of the boat to walk on water. If he had stayed in analysis, thinking of every possible outcome, he would have missed the miraculous experience of walking toward Jesus. The same is true for you. Sometimes, progress means making a decision, even if it's not perfect. It's about trusting that God will guide you as you move forward.

Practical Tips:

◊ Set a time limit for making that decision.
◊ When faced with a choice, gather the required information, pray for wisdom, and then take action.
◊ Trust that God will direct your steps.

Exercise:

> Identify one decision you've been overthinking.
> Set a timer for 10 minutes. During this time, pray, reflect, and then commit to making a choice when the timer ends.
> Take that step in faith, trusting that God will guide you on the journey ahead.

Reflective Questions:

» Where in your life are you experiencing analysis paralysis?
» How can you trust God and take a step forward today?

Day 363: Stop Searching for Yourself Externally

"The most loving person is the person who is self-centred." – Neale Donald Walsch

It may sound counterintuitive, but true love begins with understanding and loving yourself. Often, people search for their identity and worth in external factors—relationships, careers, or the approval of others. This is especially common in romantic relationships, where many enter with a "needy brain," hoping to find their completeness in someone else. But when you seek to find yourself through another, you risk losing the very essence of who you are. Your identity isn't something another person can give you; you must recognise and nurture within yourself.

When you base your self-worth on external sources, you place your sense of identity on shifting sands. Relationships can be a beautiful part of life, but they should enhance who you are, not define you. Constantly looking to others for validation can create a dependency pattern in your brain, causing you to rely on external feedback to feel secure. This can lead to an unhealthy cycle where your sense of self becomes entangled in others' opinions and actions. As a result, when the relationship shifts or ends, you can feel lost and disconnected from yourself.

Think of a relationship like a dance. Each person brings their own rhythm and steps to the floor. If you spend the dance focusing solely on matching the other person's moves, you lose your own rhythm and grace. Healthy relationships are formed when two individuals come together, fully aware of who they are, rather than relying on the other person to fill a void. Remember, Jesus called us to love others as we love ourselves (Mark 12:31). This implies that a deep, genuine love for oneself is foundational to loving others effectively.

Practical Tips:

◊ Spend time daily nurturing your relationship with yourself.
◊ Reflect on your strengths, values, and God-given purpose.
◊ Write down three qualities you love about yourself that are not tied to others' opinions.
◊ Revisit this list whenever you seek external validation to remind yourself that your worth comes from within, rooted in God's love.

Reflective Questions:

» Are you seeking validation or a sense of identity through others?
» How can you cultivate a deeper understanding and love for yourself?

DAY 364: PROVE YOUR NAYSAYERS WRONG

"No eye has seen, no ear has heard, and no mind has imagined what God has prepared for those who love him." – 1 Corinthians 2:9 (NLT)

There will always be people who doubt you, criticise you, or underestimate your potential. They may tell you that you can't achieve your dreams, that you're not capable, or that you're aiming too high. But remember, God's plans for you are greater than what anyone else can see or imagine. Your worth and potential are not defined by others' opinions but by what God has placed within you. You don't have to fight or argue to prove them wrong; your actions and success will speak for you.

When critics voice their doubts, it's easy to internalise their negativity, allowing it to affect your mindset and actions. We know the brain is wired to focus on negative feedback more than positive, which can create a loop of self-doubt if left unchecked. However, you can choose to reframe this feedback. Instead of seeing criticism as a setback, use it as fuel to propel you forward.

Prove naysayers wrong, not out of spite, but out of a desire to fulfil the incredible potential that God has placed within you.
Imagine David facing Goliath. Many doubted his ability to defeat the giant. But David didn't pay attention to their opinions; he was focused on the God who had already prepared him through past challenges. Similarly, when you face criticism, remember that God has been preparing you all along. Naysayers may see your limitations, but God sees your potential—a future beyond what anyone else can imagine (1 Corinthians 2:9). Your life is not limited by other people's words but by how you choose to respond to them.

Practical Tips:

◊ Identify a criticism that has held you back and write it down.
◊ Counter it with a truth about what God says about you and your potential.
◊ Keep this truth visible as a reminder of your purpose.
◊ Then, write one dream you have and take a concrete step toward it today, using criticism as motivation to focus on God's calling rather than others' doubts.

Reflective Questions:

» How have other people's opinions influenced your actions in the past?
» How can you shift your focus from proving others wrong to fulfilling God's purpose for your life?

Day 365: Stand Firm in His Power

"The mountains quake before him and the hills melt away. The earth trembles at his presence, the world and all who live in it." – Nahum 1:5 (NIV)

In the face of life's challenges, it's easy to feel small. Yet, the God who makes mountains quake is the same God who stands with you. His power is unmatched, and His presence is constant. When obstacles seem overwhelming, remember that you are not alone. God has equipped you to face challenges with peace and strength, not with fear.

Life often brings storms that can shake your foundation. Neuroscience shows that when fear takes over, your brain's fight-flight-or-freeze response can paralyse you, making it challenging to take action. But here's the truth: you don't face these storms alone. Just as He commands the natural world, He has designed you to be equipped with His peace and strength. You are not just equipped, you are designed to stand firm, knowing that His power is at work within you.

Think of times when you faced what seemed like an immovable mountain—a setback, a fear, or a doubt. And yet, here you are, having overcome it. That wasn't by accident; it was God's hand at work. Use this guide to help you live boldly, knowing that if God can make mountains quake, He has equipped you to overcome any obstacle.

Practical Tips:

◊ When fear arises, remind yourself of God's power within you.
◊ Speak His promises and trust in His strength.
◊ Let His power strengthen you and embolden you in the face of fear.

Exercise:

> Write one fear or challenge that feels like a mountain.
> Next to it, write Nahum 1:5. Reflect on how God's power equips you to stand firm.
> Keep this with you as a reminder that you are designed to overcome.

Reflective Questions:

» What mountains in your life have caused you to fear?
» How can you embrace the truth that God has equipped you to face them?

Day 366: Living a Limitless Life

"With man this is impossible, but with God all things are possible." – Matthew 19:26 (NIV)

Over these 366 days, you've embarked on a profound journey, delving into the depths of your mind, harnessing the strength of your spirit, and fortifying the resilience of your emotions. You've discovered that you are not confined by the boundaries others impose on you or those you've imposed on yourself. God has designed you for a life without constraints, endowed with the ability to grow, adjust, and soar. Your potential transcends your wildest imagination, and you can lead a life without limits through Him.

Neuroscience teaches us that the brain is not static but flexible, constantly forming new connections. This neuroplasticity means that every step you've taken—practising gratitude, embracing challenges, and developing emotional intelligence—has rewired your brain for a limitless mindset. By transforming your thoughts and behaviours, you've trained your brain to see possibilities instead of barriers. Emotional intelligence has empowered you to navigate life's complexities with wisdom and grace.

Envision your journey as a tree that has grown sturdier with each passing season. Its roots have deepened through the storms, and its branches have reached for the sky, unafraid to aspire for more. You are like that tree—anchored in God's love, stretching beyond what you once deemed feasible. Living a limitless life doesn't imply you won't encounter obstacles; it means that you now possess the tools and mindset to conquer them.

Practical Tips:

◊ As you progress, make it a routine to ponder on your growth.

◊ Celebrate your wins, learn from setbacks, and keep setting goals that challenge your faith and abilities.

◊ Remember, your journey is a continuous evolution.

Exercise:

> Write a letter to your future self, reflecting on your growth, challenges, and successes.

> Share your hopes and dreams for the limitless life you will continue to create.

> Keep this letter as a reminder of how far you've come and the limitless possibilities ahead.

Reflective Questions:

» How has your mindset shifted over the past year?

» What limits will you break next in your limitless life?

CONCLUSION

SUMMARY AND FINAL THOUGHTS

As you conclude this 366-day journey, take a moment to reflect on the growth and transformation you've experienced. You have explored the intricate connections between faith, emotional intelligence, and the power of your mind, uncovering the limitless potential within you. You've learned to overcome obstacles, embrace change, and live with purpose through daily reflections, practical exercises, and a deeper understanding of your emotions and thoughts.

Remember the practices that have empowered you—whether it's cultivating gratitude, mastering your emotions, or setting and pursuing goals with clarity. These tools are now part of your daily life, guiding you to continue living boldly. This journey has not only been about discovering your own potential but also about equipping you to inspire and lead others toward their own limitless lives.

As a special thank-you for purchasing *Rewire Your Brain with Neuroscience and Scripture!*, I've created exclusive bonuses just for readers like you:

◊ A free, downloadable mini workbook to help you apply the principles in this book.
◊ Additional tools and resources to deepen your growth and transformation.
◊ Surprises and updates to keep you inspired along the way.

Visit: https://www.themindsightacademy.com/pages/ryb-book, to claim your free gifts!

Let's continue this journey together—I can't wait to see the amazing changes you'll create!

CONCLUSION

Congratulations on completing this year-long journey of growth and transformation. You've unlocked the power of your mind, anchored in faith, to create a life without limits. You have shown resilience, embraced your true identity, and stepped into the life God has called you to live. But remember, this is not the end—it's the beginning of a lifelong journey. Continue to live purposefully, facing each new day with faith and determination.

Your journey is a testament to what is possible when you align your thoughts, emotions, and actions with God's truth. May your life inspire others, showing them that they, too, can break free from limitations and live their best lives. The path ahead is filled with opportunities and challenges, and you are now equipped to face them all.

Step forward confidently, knowing you are living a limitless life.

Much Blessings,

Maureen

About the Author

Maureen Chiana is a passionate leader, coach, and advocate for transformation. She is driven by a desire to help people unlock their fullest potential through faith, neuroscience, and emotional intelligence. As the founder and CEO of **The Mindsight Academy (TMA)**, Maureen empowers leaders, entrepreneurs, and women to break free from limitations, rewire their thinking, and thrive in every area of life. Maureen's journey is one of resilience and faith. With a background in medical microbiology, she spent years working in pathology before transitioning into lecturing, entrepreneurship and leadership development. Her passion for understanding how the mind works and how it connects to faith inspired her to explore the powerful intersection of neuroscience and scripture. Through this work, she developed strategies that equip others to grow emotionally, think clearly, and achieve success.

Her life, however, has not been without its challenges. In 2006, after closing her business, Maureen faced a season of financial hardship and the devastating loss of her mother. These experiences left her with profound grief and uncertainty about the future. But it was in this season that Maureen began to research how the brain shapes emotions, behaviours, and actions. She discovered the concept of neuroplasticity—the brain's ability to rewire itself through intentional effort—and realised that change was not just possible but within reach. By aligning her faith with practical tools rooted in science, Maureen transformed her life. This transformation sparked her calling to help others do the same. Today, she works with leaders and women from around the world, guiding them to overcome adversity, replace doubt with confidence, and live out their God-given purpose.

Through **Mindsight Women's Network (MWN),** Maureen has created a sisterhood of faith-filled women who are supported with resources, workshops, and encouragement to lead and flourish. Whether through retreats or everyday conversations, Maureen's goal is to see women thrive and embrace their unique journey. When she's not coaching or teaching, Maureen loves travelling because it allows her to experience new cultures and see how others live. She's also passionate about reading, especially nonfiction and educational books, and she finds deep inspiration in studying scripture. These activities fuel her creativity and give her new perspectives to share with her community.

Maureen also hosts the **Lead to Excel Podcast,** where she discusses leadership, emotional intelligence, and the integration of faith and science. Her work inspires listeners to rise above challenges, embrace transformation, and live with intention.

Maureen's story is proof that no matter where you start, transformation is always possible. With faith, intentional action, and the right tools, she believes everyone can create a life of purpose and leave a legacy that honours God.

Email: maureen@themindsightacademy.com
LinkedIn: @maureenchiana

SOURCES

Note:
Some quotes included in this book are widely attributed to their respective authors or figures, reflecting their philosophies and teachings. While every effort has been made to verify their authenticity, certain quotes may be paraphrased or popularly attributed without direct sourcing from original works.

PART 1: THE FOUNDATION OF POSITIVE THINKING

Amen, D. G. (1998). Change your brain, change your life: The breakthrough program for conquering anxiety, depression, obsessiveness, anger, and impulsiveness. Three Rivers Press.

Arden, J. B. (2010). Rewire your brain: Think your way to a better life. John Wiley & Sons.

Brown, B. (2012). Daring greatly: How the courage to be vulnerable transforms the way we live, love, parent, and lead. Avery.

Chopra, D. (2009). The ultimate happiness prescription: 7 keys to joy and enlightenment. Harmony.

Clear, J. (2018). Atomic habits: An easy & proven way to build good habits & break bad ones. Avery.

Dweck, C. S. (2006). Mindset: The new psychology of success. Random House.

Emmons, R. A., & McCullough, M. E. (2003). Counting blessings versus burdens: An experimental investigation of gratitude and subjective well-being in daily life. Journal of Personality and Social Psychology, 84(2), 377–389. https://doi.org/10.1037/0022-3514.84.2.377

Fehr, E., & Fischbacher, U. (2008). Social norms and human cooperation. Trends in Cognitive Sciences, 8(4), 185–190. https://doi.org/10.1016/j.tics.2008.02.009

Fredrickson, B. L. (2004). The broaden-and-build theory of positive emotions. Philosophical Transactions of the Royal Society B: Biological Sciences, 359(1449), 1367–1377. https://doi.org/10.1098/rstb.2004.1512

Garvey, M. (n.d.). With confidence, you have won before you have started. Retrieved from The Collected Works of Marcus Garvey.

Goleman, D. (1995). Emotional intelligence: Why it can matter more than IQ. Bantam Books.

Gordon, E. (2011). Integrative neuroscience and personalized medicine. Oxford University Press.

Hetland, H. (2018). Called to reign: Living and loving from a place of rest. Destiny Image Publishers.

Holtz, L. (n.d.). You cannot control your circumstances, but you can control your responses to those circumstances. Retrieved from Motivational Archives.

Kabat-Zinn, J. (2012). Mindfulness for beginners: Reclaiming the present moment—and your life. Sounds True.

King Jr., M. L. (n.d.). Faith is taking the first step even when you don't see the whole staircase. Retrieved from King Center Archives.

Leaf, C. (2007). Who switched off my brain?: Controlling toxic thoughts and emotions. Thomas Nelson.

Lieberman, M. D. (2013). Social: Why our brains are wired to connect. Crown Publishers.

Maxwell, J. C. (2013). The 15 invaluable laws of growth: Live them and reach your potential. Center Street.

Meyer, J. (2006). Battlefield of the mind: Winning the battle in your mind. FaithWords.

Meyer, J. (2014). The power of simple prayer: How to talk with God about everything. FaithWords.

Newberg, A., & Waldman, M. R. (2012). Words can change your brain: 12 conversation strategies to build trust, resolve conflict, and increase intimacy. Hudson Street Press.

Panksepp, J. (2004). Affective neuroscience: The foundations of human and animal emotions. Oxford University Press.

Sher, B. (n.d.). You can learn new things at any time in your life if you're willing to be a beginner. Retrieved from Barbara Sher's Works.

Seligman, M. E. P. (2011). Flourish: A visionary new understanding of happiness and well-being. Atria Books.

Taylor, S. (2007). All about love: New visions. Harper Perennial.

Tolle, E. (1997). The power of now: A guide to spiritual enlightenment. New World Library.

Walker, T. (n.d.). Affirmations are our mental vitamins, providing the supplementary positive thoughts we need to balance the barrage of negative events and thoughts we experience daily. Retrieved from Motivational Archives.

Walsch, N. D. (1995). Conversations with God: An uncommon dialogue, Book 1. Putnam.

Williamson, M. (1992). A return to love: Reflections on the principles of a course in miracles. HarperCollins.

Part 2: Renew and Rewire – The Path to Mental Mastery

Amen, D. G. (1998). Change your brain, change your life: The breakthrough program for conquering anxiety, depression, obsessiveness, anger, and impulsiveness. Harmony Books.

Amen, D. G. (2017). Memory rescue: Supercharge your brain, reverse memory loss, and remember what matters most. Tyndale Momentum.

Arden, J. B. (2010). Rewire your brain: Think your way to a better life. John Wiley & Sons.

Aristotle. (n.d.). The Nicomachean ethics (W. D. Ross, Trans.). Oxford University Press.

(Original work published ca. 350 B.C.E.)

Bennett, B. (n.d.). Visualization is daydreaming with a purpose. Retrieved from Motivational Archives.

Berkman, E. T., & Lieberman, M. D. (2009). The neuroscience of goal pursuit: Bridging gaps between theory and data. Cognitive, Affective, & Behavioral Neuroscience, 9(3), 367–379. https://doi.org/10.3758/CABN.9.3.367

Brown, B. (2012). Daring greatly: How the courage to be vulnerable transforms the way we live, love, parent, and lead. Gotham Books.

Chopra, D. (2009). The ultimate happiness prescription: 7 keys to joy and enlightenment. Harmony.

Clear, J. (2018). Atomic habits: An easy & proven way to build good habits & break bad ones. Avery.

Collier, R. (1926). The secret of the ages. Robert Collier Publications.

Creswell, J. D., Dutcher, J. M., Klein, W. M. P., Harris, P. R., & Levine, J. M. (2013). Self-affirmation improves problem-solving under stress. Psychological Science, 24(12), 2409–2416. https://doi.org/10.1177/0956797613494852

Dekker, T. (n.d.). Sleep is that golden chain that ties health and our bodies together. Retrieved from Timeless Sleep Quotes.

Donne, J. (1624). Devotions upon emergent occasions. London: Thomas Harper.

Duhigg, C. (2012). The power of habit: Why we do what we do in life and business. Random House.

Dweck, C. S. (2006). Mindset: The new psychology of success. Ballantine Books.

Einstein, A. (1996). The world as I see it. Citadel Press.

Einstein, A. (n.d.). Creativity is intelligence having fun. Retrieved from Einstein's Reflections.

Fogg, B. J. (2019). Tiny habits: The small changes that change everything. Houghton Mifflin Harcourt.

Fuller, T. (1732). Gnomologia: Adages and proverbs. London: B. Barker.

Fotuhi, M. (2003). The memory cure: How to protect your brain against memory loss and Alzheimer's disease.McGraw-Hill.

Ford, H. (n.d.). Whether you think you can, or you think you can't—you're right. Retrieved from Ford's Wisdom Archives.

Goleman, D. (1995). Emotional intelligence: Why it can matter more than IQ. Bantam Books.

Holtz, L. (n.d.). It's not the load that breaks you down; it's the way you carry it. Retrieved from The Wisdom of Lou Holtz.

Huberman, A. (2021). Non-sleep deep rest (NSDR): How to rest deeply and recover fast without sleep. Huberman Lab Podcast.

Jung, C. G. (1953). The collected works of C.G. Jung. Princeton University Press.

Jung, C. G. (n.d.). Until you make the unconscious conscious, it will direct your life and you will call it fate. Retrieved from Jungian Analysis Archives.

Kabat-Zinn, J. (2012). Mindfulness for beginners: Reclaiming the present moment—and your life. Sounds True.

Lally, P., Van Jaarsveld, C. H., Potts, H. W., & Wardle, J. (2010). How are habits formed: Modelling habit formation in the real world. European Journal of Social Psychology, 40(6), 998–1009. https://doi.org/10.1002/ejsp.674

Leaf, C. (2009). Who switched off my brain? Controlling toxic thoughts and emotions. Thomas Nelson.

Mårtensson, J. (n.d.). Feelings are much like waves; we can't stop them from coming, but we can choose which ones to surf. Retrieved from Jonatan Mårtensson Quotes Collection.

Maxwell, J. C. (2013). The 15 invaluable laws of growth: Live them and reach your potential. Center Street.

Meyer, J. (2006). Battlefield of the mind: Winning the battle in your mind. FaithWords.

Murphy, K., Michael, G. A., & Ben-Shakhar, G. (2006). Neuroplasticity: How experience changes the brain. Nature Neuroscience, 9(1), 42–51. https://doi.org/10.1038/nn1721

Newberg, A., & Waldman, M. R. (2009). How God changes your brain: Breakthrough findings from a leading neuroscientist. Random House Publishing Group.

Nin, A. (1976). The diaries of Anaïs Nin. Mariner Books.

Ratey, J. J. (2008). Spark: The revolutionary new science of exercise and the brain. Little, Brown Spark.

Robbins, T. (n.d.). Every problem is a gift—without problems, we would not grow. Retrieved from Tony Robbins Official.

Rock, D. (2009). Your brain at work: Strategies for overcoming distraction, regaining focus, and working smarter all day long. HarperBusiness.

Robson, D. (2022). The expectation effect: How your mindset can change your world. Henry Holt and Co.

Sagan, C. (n.d.). The brain is like a muscle. When it's in use, we feel very good. Understanding is joyous. Retrieved from Cosmos Reflections.

Seligman, M. E. P. (1991). Learned optimism: How to change your mind and your life. Knopf.

Seligman, M. E. P. (2011). Flourish: A visionary new understanding of happiness and well-being. Atria Books.

Swart, T. (2019). The source: The secrets of the universe, the science of the brain. Penguin Life.

Suzuki, W. (2015). Healthy brain, happy life: A personal program to activate your brain and do everything better. HarperCollins.

Tracy, B. (n.d.). Your life is a reflection of your thoughts. If you change your thinking, you change your life. Retrieved from Brian Tracy Archives.

Tracy, B. (2010). The power of self-discipline: No excuses! Vanguard Press.

Watts, A. (2011). The wisdom of insecurity: A message for an age of anxiety. Vintage Books.

Yeats, W. B. (n.d.). Education is not the filling of a pail, but the lighting of a fire. Retrieved from The Collected Poems of W.B. Yeats.

Ziglar, Z. (n.d.). Positive thinking will let you do everything better than negative thinking will. Retrieved from Zig Ziglar's Inspiration Archives.

PART 3: UNLOCKING THE POWER OF YOUR BRAIN

Allen, J. (n.d.). The body is the servant of the mind. Retrieved from As a Man Thinketh. Project Gutenberg.

Amen, D. G. (1998). Change your brain, change your life: The breakthrough program for conquering anxiety, depression, obsessiveness, anger, and impulsiveness. Harmony Books.

Arden, J. B. (2010). Rewire your brain: Think your way to a better life. John Wiley & Sons.

Aurelius, M. (n.d.). Meditations. Penguin Classics. (Original work published ca. 180 C.E.)

Benson, H. (1975). The relaxation response. William Morrow & Company.

Black, M. (n.d.). Sometimes the most productive thing you can do is relax. Retrieved from The Resilience Blog.

Brown, L. (n.d.). The only limits to the possibilities in your life tomorrow are the buts you use today. Retrieved from Les Brown Institute.

Cossman, E. J. (n.d.). The best bridge between despair and hope is a good night's sleep. Retrieved from Wisdom Quotes Archives.

Doidge, N. (2007). The brain that changes itself. Penguin Books.

Dr. Eric Kandel. (n.d.). Neurotransmitters are the brain's chemical messengers, essential for communication within the nervous system. Retrieved from The Brain Prize Laureates.

Dweck, C. S. (2006). Mindset: The new psychology of success. Random House.

Eagleman, D. (2015). The brain: The story of you. Pantheon.

Field, T. (University of Miami). (n.d.). Research findings on the vagus nerve's role in mood regulation. University of Miami Touch Research Institute.

Franklin D. Roosevelt. (1933). First inaugural address. Government Printing Office.

Gage, F. H. (2002). Neurogenesis in the adult brain. Journal of Science, 297(5580), 1020–1023. https://doi.org/10.1126/science.1073103

Gilbert, D. (2006). Stumbling on happiness. Vintage Books.

Goleman, D. (1995). Emotional intelligence: Why it can matter more than IQ. Bantam Books.

Gordon, E. (2011). Brain revolution: Understand, protect and train your brain for life. CreateSpace Independent Publishing Platform.

Haanel, C. F. (1916). The master key system. Kallisti Publishing.

Henley, J. (n.d.). The human brain is the most complex organ in the body and is the seat of intelligence, interpreter of the senses, initiator of body movement, and controller of behavior. Retrieved from Cleveland Clinic Research.

Huberman, A. (2021). Non-sleep deep rest (NSDR): How to rest deeply and recover fast without sleep. Huberman Lab Podcast.

James, W. (1890). The principles of psychology. Dover Publications.

James, A. (n.d.). As a man thinketh. Thomas Y. Crowell Company.

Kabat-Zinn, J. (1994). Wherever you go, there you are: Mindfulness meditation in everyday life. Hyperion.

Kabat-Zinn, J. (2012). Mindfulness for beginners: Reclaiming the present moment—and your life. Sounds True.

Kahneman, D. (2011). Thinking, fast and slow. Farrar, Straus and Giroux.

King, S. (n.d.). The brain is a muscle that can move the world. Retrieved from Stephen King Archives.

LeDoux, J. E. (1996). The emotional brain: The mysterious underpinnings of emotional life. Simon & Schuster.

Leaf, C. (2009). Who switched off my brain? Controlling toxic thoughts and emotions. Thomas Nelson.

Lipton, B. H. (2005). The biology of belief: Unleashing the power of consciousness, matter, & miracles. Hay House, Inc.

Lynch, D. (n.d.). The thing about meditation is you become more and more you. Retrieved from Meditation Archives.

Maxwell, J. C. (2013). The 15 invaluable laws of growth: Live them and reach your potential. Center Street.

Meyer, J. (2006). Battlefield of the mind: Winning the battle in your mind. FaithWords.

Nin, A. (1976). The diaries of Anaïs Nin. Mariner Books.

Norman Vincent Peale. (1952). The power of positive thinking. Prentice Hall.

Ratey, J. J. (2008). Spark: The revolutionary new science of exercise and the brain. Little, Brown Spark.

Robson, D. (2022). The expectation effect: How your mindset can transform your life. Picador.

Roosevelt, F. D. (1933). First inaugural address. Government Printing Office.

Schwartz, J. M., & Begley, S. (2002). The mind and the brain: Neuroplasticity and the power of mental force.HarperCollins.

Selye, H. (1976). The stress of life. McGraw-Hill.

Shakespeare, W. (1623). Julius Caesar. In Mr. William Shakespeares comedies, histories, & tragedies. Printed by Isaac Jaggard and Edward Blount.

Swart, T. (2019). The source: The secrets of the universe, the science of the brain. Penguin Life.

Tolle, E. (1997). The power of now: A guide to spiritual enlightenment. New World Library.

Wigmore, A. (1988). The Hippocrates diet and health program. Avery.

PART 4: BECOME LIMITLESS

Adams, J. Q. (n.d.). Patience and perseverance have a magical effect before which difficulties disappear and obstacles vanish. Retrieved from The Collected Works of John Quincy Adams.

Amen, D. G. (1998). Change your brain, change your life: The breakthrough program for conquering anxiety, depression, obsessiveness, anger, and impulsiveness. Harmony Books.

Amen, D. G. (2018). The end of mental illness. Tyndale Momentum.

Anderson, T. (2018). The science of mindfulness: A research-based path to well-being. Routledge.

Arden, J. B. (2010). Rewire your brain: Think your way to a better life. John Wiley & Sons.

Brown, B. (2010). The gifts of imperfection: Let go of who you think you're supposed to be and embrace who you are.Hazelden Publishing.

Brown, B. (2012). Daring greatly: How the courage to be vulnerable transforms the way we live, love, parent, and lead. Gotham Books.

Brown, B. (2010). The gifts of imperfection. Hazelden Publishing.

Churchill, W. (n.d.). Success is not final, failure is not fatal: It is the courage to continue that counts. Retrieved from The Collected Speeches of Winston Churchill.

Cirillo, F. (2006). The Pomodoro technique. FC Garage.

Clear, J. (2018). Atomic habits: An easy & proven way to build good habits & break bad ones. Avery.

Drucker, P. F. (2006). The effective executive: The definitive guide to getting the right things done. Harper Business.

Dispenza, J. (2012). Breaking the habit of being yourself: How to lose your mind and create a new one. Hay House, Inc.

Doidge, N. (2007). The brain that changes itself. Penguin Books.

Duckworth, A. (2016). Grit: The power of passion and perseverance. Scribner.

Dweck, C. S. (2006). Mindset: The new psychology of success. Random House.

Einstein, A. (1996). The world as I see it. Citadel Press.

Fessler, W. (2009). The resilient mind: Achieve success by building mental resilience. Self-published.

Francis, R. C. (2011). Epigenetics: How environment shapes our genes. W. W. Norton & Company.

Hebb, D. O. (1949). The organization of behavior: A neuropsychological theory. Wiley.

Ho, J. (2019). Stop self-sabotage: Six steps to unlock your true motivation, harness your willpower, and get out of your own way. Harper Wave.

Humes, J. (1991). The art of communication. HarperCollins.

Jemison, M. (1993). Find where the wind goes: Moments from my life. Scholastic Press.

Johnson, S. (1750). The Rambler. Oxford University Press.

Kolb, B., & Whishaw, I. Q. (2015). An introduction to brain and behavior. Worth Publishers.

Leaf, C. (2013). Switch on your brain: The key to peak happiness, thinking, and health. Baker Books..

Lipton, B. H. (2005). The biology of belief: Unleashing the power of consciousness, matter, & miracles. Hay House Inc.

Maraboli, S. (2009). Life, the truth, and being free. Better Today Publishing.

McEwen, B. S. (2007). Physiology and neurobiology of stress and adaptation: Central role of the brain. Physiological Reviews, 87(3), 873–904. https://doi.org/10.1152/physrev.00041.2006

McGonigal, K. (2011). The willpower instinct: How self-control works, why it matters, and what you can do to get more of it. Avery.

Mobbs, D., et al. (2007). The neural substrates of threat processing. Current Opinion in Neurobiology, 17(2), 229–234. https://doi.org/10.1016/j.conb.2007.03.005

Mobbs, D., et al. (2015). The neuroscience of threat: Insights from cognitive neuroscience. Neuroleadership Journal.

Oz, M. (n.d.). Your genes load the gun, but your lifestyle pulls the trigger. Retrieved from Dr. Oz Show.

Pert, C. (1997). Molecules of emotion: Why you feel the way you feel. Scribner.

Rock, D. (2009). Your brain at work: Strategies for overcoming distraction, regaining focus, and working smarter all day long. HarperCollins.

Schunk, D. H. (1984). Self-efficacy and classroom learning. Psychology in the Schools, 21(3), 208–217. https://doi.org/10.1002/pits.2310210303

Socrates. (n.d.). Education is the kindling of a flame, not the filling of a vessel. Retrieved from Plato's The Republic(Oxford University Press).

Tolle, E. (1997). The power of now: A guide to spiritual enlightenment. New World Library.

Wayne, D. (1997). Your erroneous zones: Escape negative thinking and take control of your life. HarperCollins.

Part 5: Self Discovery

Amen, D. G. (1998). Change your brain, change your life: The breakthrough program for conquering anxiety, depression, obsessiveness, anger, and impulsiveness. Three Rivers Press.

Arden, J. B. (2010). Rewire your brain: Think your way to a better life. Wiley.

Beck, A. T. (1970). Cognitive therapy: Nature and relation to behavior therapy. Behavior Therapy, 1(2), 184–200. https://doi.org/10.1016/S0005-7894(70)80030-2

Brown, B. (2010). The gifts of imperfection: Let go of who you think you're supposed to be and embrace who you are.Hazelden Publishing.

Brown, B. (2012). Daring greatly: How the courage to be vulnerable transforms the way we live, love, parent, and lead. Avery.

Carter, C. S., & Porges, S. W. (2013). The biopsychology of positive social bonding and affiliation. Nature Reviews Neuroscience, 14(8), 509–520. https://doi.org/10.1038/nrn3504

Chardin, P. T. (1955). The phenomenon of man. Harper & Brothers.

Clark, F. A. (n.d.). Criticism, like rain, should be gentle enough to nourish a man's growth without destroying his roots. In The cyclopedia of practical quotations. HarperCollins.

Covey, S. R. (1989). The 7 habits of highly effective people: Powerful lessons in personal change. Free Press.

Davidson, R. J., & McEwen, B. S. (2012). Social influences on neuroplasticity: Stress and interventions to promote well-being. Nature Neuroscience, 15(5), 689–695. https://doi.org/10.1038/nn.3093

Disney, R. E. (1995). Lessons from the magic kingdom: How a Disney approach to leadership can make your business better. Hyperion.

Drucker, P. F. (2006). The effective executive: The definitive guide to getting the right things done. Harper Business.

Dweck, C. S. (2006). Mindset: The new psychology of success. Ballantine Books.

Eckhart, T. (2004). The power of now: A guide to spiritual enlightenment. New World Library.

Einstein, A. (1996). The world as I see it. Citadel Press.

Goleman, D. (1995). Emotional intelligence: Why it can matter more than IQ. Bantam Books.

Hill, N. (1937). Think and grow rich. The Ralston Society.

Leaf, C. (2009). Who switched off my brain? Controlling toxic thoughts and emotions. Inprov.

Leaf, C. (2013). Switch on your brain: The key to peak happiness, thinking, and health.

Baker Books.

LeDoux, J. E. (2002). The emotional brain: The mysterious underpinnings of emotional life. Simon & Schuster.

Mandela, N. (1994). Long walk to freedom: The autobiography of Nelson Mandela. Little, Brown and Company.

Maxwell, J. C. (2013). Sometimes you win, sometimes you learn: Life's greatest lessons are gained from our losses.Thomas Nelson.

Outlaw, F. (1995). Life lessons by Frank Outlaw. Collins.

Savelle Foy, T. (2012). Make your dreams bigger than your memories. Terri Savelle Foy Ministries.

Schwartz, J. M., & Begley, S. (2002). The mind and the brain: Neuroplasticity and the power of mental force.HarperCollins.

Seuss, Dr. (1998). Seuss-isms: Wise and witty prescriptions for living. Random House.

Shakespeare, W. (1623). The tempest. In Mr. William Shakespeares comedies, histories, & tragedies (First Folio). Printed by Isaac Jaggard and Edward Blount.

Shaw, G. B. (1913). Man and superman: A comedy and a philosophy. Penguin Classics.

Siegel, D. J. (2010). The mindful brain: Reflection and attunement in the cultivation of well-being. W.W. Norton & Company.

Willard, D. (1997). The divine conspiracy: Rediscovering our hidden life in God. HarperCollins.

Winfrey, O. (2005). What I know for sure. Flatiron Books.

Wommack, A. (2016). The power of imagination: Unlocking your ability to receive from God. Harrison House.

PART 6: DEVELOPING EMOTIONAL INTELLIGENCE

Amen, D. G. (1998). Change your brain, change your life: The breakthrough program for conquering anxiety, depression, obsessiveness, anger, and impulsiveness. Harmony Books.

Amen, D. G. (2023). Change your brain every day. Tyndale House Publishers.

Arden, J. B. (2010). Rewire your brain: Think your way to a better life. Wiley.

Barrett, L. F. (2017). How emotions are made: The secret life of the brain. Houghton Mifflin Harcourt.

Baumeister, R. F., & Tierney, J. (2011). Willpower: Rediscovering the greatest human strength. Penguin Press.

Brown, B. (2012). Daring greatly: How the courage to be vulnerable transforms the way we live, love, parent, and lead. Gotham Books.

Carnegie, D. (1936). How to win friends and influence people. Simon and Schuster.

Carver, C. S., & Scheier, M. F. (1998). On the self-regulation of behavior. Cambridge

University Press.

Chödrön, P. (2002). Comfortable with uncertainty: 108 teachings on cultivating fearlessness and compassion.Shambhala Publications.

Chopra, D. (2009). The ultimate happiness prescription: 7 keys to joy and enlightenment. Harmony.

Cialdini, R. B. (2006). Influence: The psychology of persuasion. Harper Business.

Collins, E. (2021). We don't need permission: How Black business can change our world. Transworld Publishers.

Covey, S. R. (1989). The 7 habits of highly effective people: Powerful lessons in personal change. Free Press.

Decety, J., & Ickes, W. (Eds.). (2011). The social neuroscience of empathy. MIT Press.

Duckworth, A. (2016). Grit: The power of passion and perseverance. Scribner.

Dweck, C. S. (2006). Mindset: The new psychology of success. Random House.

Eurich, T. (2017). Insight: Why we're not as self-aware as we think, and how seeing ourselves clearly helps us succeed at work and in life. Crown Business.

Frankl, V. E. (1946). Man's search for meaning. Beacon Press.

Goleman, D. (1995). Emotional intelligence: Why it can matter more than IQ. Bantam Books.

Goleman, D. (2006). Social intelligence: The new science of human relationships. Bantam Books.

Goman, C. K. (2011). The silent language of leaders: How body language can help—or hurt—how you lead. Jossey-Bass.

James, W. (1890). The principles of psychology. Dover Publications.

Jung, C. G. (1960). The structure and dynamics of the psyche. Princeton University Press.

Kabat-Zinn, J. (1994). Wherever you go, there you are: Mindfulness meditation in everyday life. Hyperion.

Kabat-Zinn, J. (2012). Mindfulness for beginners: Reclaiming the present moment—and your life. Sounds True.

Keltner, D. (2009). Born to be good: The science of a meaningful life. W.W. Norton & Company.

Leaf, C. (2009). Who switched off my brain? Controlling toxic thoughts and emotions. Inprov.

Milton, J. (1667). Paradise lost. Penguin Classics.

Nichols, L. (2016). Abundance now: Amplify your life and achieve prosperity today. HarperCollins.

Roosevelt, T. (n.d.). Comparison is the thief of joy. Retrieved from Theodore Roosevelt Association.

Roosevelt, T. (n.d.). The most important single ingredient in the formula of success is knowing how to get along with people. Retrieved from Theodore Roosevelt Association.

Schweitzer, A. (1933). Out of my life and thought. Macmillan.

Siegel, D. J. (2010). Mindsight: The new science of personal transformation. Bantam Books.

Sinek, S. (2009). Start with why: How great leaders inspire everyone to take action. Portfolio.

Toffler, A. (1970). Future shock. Random House.

Tolle, E. (1997). The power of now: A guide to spiritual enlightenment. New World Library.

Winters, M.-F. (2020). Inclusive conversations: Fostering equity, empathy, and belonging across differences. Berrett-Koehler Publishers.

Wilde, O. (1891). The picture of Dorian Gray. Ward, Lock & Co.

PART 7: LETTING GO OF THE PAST

Amen, D. G. (1998). Change your brain, change your life: The breakthrough program for conquering anxiety, depression, obsessiveness, anger, and impulsiveness. Harmony Books.

Amen, D. G. (2010). Rewire your brain: Think your way to a better life. Wiley.

Arden, J. B. (2010). Rewire your brain: How to think your way to a better life. Wiley.

Baumeister, R. F., & Leary, M. R. (1995). The need to belong: Desire for interpersonal attachments as a fundamental human motivation. Psychological Bulletin, 117(3), 497–529.

Beck, A. T. (1976). Cognitive therapy and the emotional disorders. International Universities Press.

Bennett, R. T. (n.d.). If you want to fly, you have to give up what weighs you down. This quote was retrieved from Goodreads.

Brown, B. (2012). Daring greatly: How the courage to be vulnerable transforms the way we live, love, parent, and lead. Avery.

Burns, D. D. (1999). The feeling good handbook. Plume.

Covey, S. R. (1989). The 7 habits of highly effective people: Powerful lessons in personal change. Free Press.

Davidson, R. J., & Kabat-Zinn, J. (2003). Alterations in brain and immune function produced by mindfulness meditation. Psychosomatic Medicine, 65(4), 564–570. https://doi.org/10.1097/01.PSY.0000077505.67574.E3

Dweck, C. S. (2006). Mindset: The new psychology of success. Random House.

Eliot, T. S. (n.d.). Every moment is a fresh beginning. Retrieved from T.S. Eliot Quotes Archives.

Einstein, A. (2009). The world as I see it. Philosophical Library.

Ford, H. (1922). My life and work. Doubleday, Page & Company.

Gale, P. (2013). Your network is your net worth. Atria Books.

Gibran, K. (1923). The prophet. Alfred A. Knopf.

Hayes, S. C., Strosahl, K. D., & Wilson, K. G. (1999). Acceptance and commitment therapy: An experiential approach to behavior change. The Guilford Press.

Hanh, T. N. (1999). The heart of the Buddha's teaching: Transforming suffering into peace, joy, and liberation.Broadway Books.

Holzel, B. K., & Lazar, S. W. (2011). Mindfulness practice leads to increases in regional brain gray matter density. Psychiatry Research: Neuroimaging, 191(1), 36–43. https://doi.org/10.1016/j.pscychresns.2010.08.006

Isaacs, D. (2007). Learning from the feet of Jesus: Lessons for discipleship. New Leaf Publishing Group.

James, W. (1890). The principles of psychology. Henry Holt and Company.

Kabat-Zinn, J. (1990). Full catastrophe living: Using the wisdom of your body and mind to face stress, pain, and illness. Delacorte Press.

Kabat-Zinn, J. (1994). Wherever you go, there you are: Mindfulness meditation in everyday life. Hyperion.

Koenig, H. G. (2012). Religion, spirituality, and health: The research and clinical implications. ISRN Psychiatry, 2012(278730). https://doi.org/10.5402/2012/278730

Leaf, C. (2009). Who switched off my brain? Controlling toxic thoughts and emotions. Thomas Nelson.

Lewis, C. S. (n.d.). You can't go back and change the beginning, but you can start where you are and change the ending. Retrieved from C.S. Lewis Foundation.

Linehan, M. M. (1993). Cognitive-behavioral treatment of borderline personality disorder. The Guilford Press.

Mandela, N. (1994). Long walk to freedom: The autobiography of Nelson Mandela. Little, Brown and Company.

Meyer, J. (2006). Battlefield of the mind: Winning the battle in your mind. FaithWords.

Millman, D. (1980). Way of the peaceful warrior: A book that changes lives. H.J. Kramer/New World Library.

Morgan, J. P. (n.d.). The first step toward getting somewhere is to decide that you are not going to stay where you are. Retrieved from The JP Morgan Archives.

Neff, K. D. (2011). Self-compassion: The proven power of being kind to yourself. William Morrow.

Oz, M. (n.d.). Your genetics load the gun. Your lifestyle pulls the trigger. Retrieved from Health and Wellness Archives.

Pargament, K. I., Tarakeshwar, N., Ellison, C. G., & Wulff, K. M. (2001). Religious coping among the religious: The relationships between religious coping and well-being in a national sample of Presbyterian clergy, elders, and members. Journal of Religion and Health, 40(4), 409–422.

434

Robson, D. (2022). The expectation effect: How your mindset can change your world. Henry Holt and Co.

Sapolsky, R. M. (2004). Why zebras don't get ulcers. Holt Paperbacks.

Schwartz, J. M., & Begley, S. (2002). The mind and the brain: Neuroplasticity and the power of mental force. Harper Perennial.

Shapiro, F. (2012). Getting past your past: Take control of your life with self-help techniques from EMDR therapy.Rodale Books.

Shaw, G. B. (1903). Man and superman. Penguin Books.

Tew, R. (n.d.). The struggle you're in today is developing the strength you need for tomorrow. Retrieved from Robert Tew Motivational Resources.

Tolle, E. (1997). The power of now: A guide to spiritual enlightenment. New World Library.

Walton, S. (1992). Made in America: My story. Doubleday.

Walsch, N. D. (1995). Conversations with God: An uncommon dialogue, Book 1. Putnam.

PART 8: TURN YOUR DREAMS INTO REALITY

Amen, D. G. (1998). Change your brain, change your life: The breakthrough program for conquering anxiety, depression, obsessiveness, lack of focus, anger, and memory problems. Harmony Books.

Arden, J. B. (2010). Rewire your brain: Think your way to a better life. Wiley.

Barrett, L. F. (2017). How emotions are made: The secret life of the brain. Houghton Mifflin Harcourt.

Barker, J. A. (1992). Paradigms: The business of discovering the future. HarperBusiness.

Bennett, B. (2003). Year to success. Archieboy Holdings LLC.

Blanchard, K. H., & Johnson, S. (1982). The one minute manager. William Morrow & Co.

Brown, B. (2012). Daring greatly: How the courage to be vulnerable transforms the way we live, love, parent, and lead. Avery.

Clear, J. (2018). Atomic habits: An easy & proven way to build good habits & break bad ones. Avery.

Collins, E. (2021). We don't need permission: How Black business can change our world. Yellow Jersey.

Confucius. (n.d.). It does not matter how slowly you go, as long as you do not stop. Retrieved from Confucius Institute Archives.

Covey, S. R. (1989). The 7 habits of highly effective people: Powerful lessons in personal change. Free Press.

Damasio, A. R. (1999). The feeling of what happens: Body and emotion in the making of consciousness. Harcourt Brace.

DeVito, F. (n.d.). If it doesn't challenge you, it doesn't change you. Retrieved from Fitness Motivational Archives.

Drucker, P. F. (1954). The practice of management. HarperBusiness.

Duhigg, C. (2012). The power of habit: Why we do what we do in life and business. Random House.

Duckworth, A. (2016). Grit: The power of passion and perseverance. Scribner.

Dyer, W. (2004). The power of intention: Learning to co-create your world your way. Hay House.

Franklin, B. (n.d.). You may delay, but time will not. Retrieved from The Franklin Papers.

Goleman, D. (1995). Emotional intelligence: Why it can matter more than IQ. Bantam Books.

Hill, N. (1937). Think and grow rich. The Ralston Society.

Jobs, S. (n.d.). The only way to do great work is to love what you do. Retrieved from Jobs Biographical Archives.

Kahneman, D. (2011). Thinking, fast and slow. Farrar, Straus and Giroux.

Kandel, E. R. (2007). In search of memory: The emergence of a new science of mind. W. W. Norton & Company.

Kassem, S. (2011). Rise up and salute the sun: The writings of Suzy Kassem. CreateSpace Independent Publishing.

Lao Tzu. (n.d.). The journey of a thousand miles begins with one step. Retrieved from The Tao Te Ching.

Mandela, N. (1994). Long walk to freedom: The autobiography of Nelson Mandela. Little, Brown and Company.

Mandela, N. (2010). Conversations with myself. Farrar, Straus and Giroux.

Maxwell, J. C. (2013). The 15 invaluable laws of growth: Live them and reach your potential. Center Street.

Newberg, A., & Waldman, M. R. (2012). Words can change your brain: 12 conversation strategies to build trust, resolve conflict, and increase intimacy. Hudson Street Press.

Nietzsche, F. (1974). Thus spoke Zarathustra. Penguin Classics.

Ogunlaru, R. (n.d.). The only way to change someone's mind is to connect with them from the heart. Retrieved from Rasheed Ogunlaru Quotes.

Robbins, T. (1991). Awaken the giant within: How to take immediate control of your mental, emotional, physical and financial destiny! Free Press.

Robson, D. (2022). The expectation effect: How your mindset can transform your life. Henry Holt and Co.

Saint-Exupéry, A. de. (1943). The little prince. Reynal & Hitchcock.

Sandberg, S. (2013). Lean in: Women, work, and the will to lead. Alfred A. Knopf.

Schuller, R. H. (1982). Tough times never last, but tough people do! Thomas Nelson.

Sharma, R. (1997). The monk who sold his Ferrari. HarperCollins.

Siegel, D. J. (2012). The developing mind: How relationships and the brain interact to shape who we are. Guilford Press.

Swindoll, C. (n.d.). Life is 10% what happens to us and 90% how we react to it. Retrieved from Motivational Archives.

Tolle, E. (1997). The power of now: A guide to spiritual enlightenment. New World Library.

Twain, M. (n.d.). The secret of success is making your vocation your vacation. Retrieved from Mark Twain Papers & Project.

Ziglar, Z. (1975). See you at the top. Pelican Publishing.

PART 9: ELEVATING YOUR RELATIONSHIPS

Amen, D. G. (1998). Change your brain, change your life: The breakthrough program for conquering anxiety, depression, obsessiveness, lack of focus, anger, and memory problems. Harmony Books.

Arden, J. B. (2010). Rewire your brain: Think your way to a better life. Wiley.

Barrett, L. F. (2017). How emotions are made: The secret life of the brain. Houghton Mifflin Harcourt.

Brown, B. (2012). Daring greatly: How the courage to be vulnerable transforms the way we live, love, parent, and lead. Avery.

Branson, R. (n.d.). Respect is how to treat everyone, not just those you want to impress. Retrieved from Virgin.com.

Carnegie, A. (n.d.). Listening is not hearing; it is taking a vigorous human interest in what is being told to us. Retrieved from Carnegie Legacy Archives.

Chiana, M. (n.d.). What we see in others is a reflection of what we cultivate within ourselves. Retrieved from The Mindsight Academy.

Covey, S. R. (1989). The 7 habits of highly effective people: Powerful lessons in personal change. Free Press.

Damasio, A. R. (1994). Descartes' error: Emotion, reason, and the human brain. Penguin Books.

Dweck, C. S. (2006). Mindset: The new psychology of success. Random House.

Goleman, D. (1995). Emotional intelligence: Why it can matter more than IQ. Bantam Books.

Henry, B. (n.d.). Family is the compass that guides us; it is the source of strength and comfort. Retrieved from Public Addresses Archive.

Hubbard, E. (n.d.). A friend is someone who knows all about you and still loves you. Retrieved from The American Almanac.

Jones, N. (2019). Success from the inside out: Power to rise from the past to a fulfilling future. Zondervan.

Kabat-Zinn, J. (1994). Wherever you go, there you are: Mindfulness meditation in everyday life. Hyperion.

Karrass, C. L. (1986). The negotiating game: How to get what you want. Harper & Row.

Kolenda, N. (2013). Methods of persuasion: How to use psychology to influence human behavior. Kolenda Entertainment, LLC.

Leaf, C. (2007). He said/she said: Discover your secret brain differences in how men and women relate. Thomas Nelson.

Mayo Clinic Staff. (2020). Emotional intelligence: Why it matters. Mayo Clinic. Retrieved from https://www.mayoclinic.org.

Newberg, A., & Waldman, M. R. (2012). Words can change your brain: 12 conversation strategies to build trust, resolve conflict, and increase intimacy. Hudson Street Press.

Plato. (n.d.). Wise men speak because they have something to say; fools because they have to say something. Retrieved from Classical Philosophy Archives.

Robbins, T. (2001). Awaken the giant within: How to take immediate control of your mental, emotional, physical, and financial destiny! Free Press.

Rohn, J. (n.d.). The greatest gift you can give someone is your full attention. Retrieved from Rohn Leadership Materials.

Roosevelt, E. (1948). You learn by living: Eleven keys for a more fulfilling life. Harper & Brothers.

Roosevelt, E. (n.d.). Great minds discuss ideas. Average minds discuss events. Small minds discuss people. Retrieved from Eleanor Roosevelt Papers Project.

Sparks, N. (1996). The notebook. Warner Books.

Young, L. (n.d.). Love is not something you look for. Love is something you become. Retrieved from Loretta Young Legacy Collection.

PART 10: NEUROLEADERSHIP – UNLOCKING CAREER AND BUSINESS SUCCESS

Amen, D. G. (2015). Change your brain, change your life: The breakthrough program for conquering anxiety, depression, obsessiveness, lack of focus, anger, and memory problems. Harmony Books.

Arden, J. B. (2010). Rewire your brain: Think your way to a better life. Wiley.

Barrett, L. F. (2017). How emotions are made: The secret life of the brain. Mariner Books.

Bennett, N., & Lemoine, G. J. (2014). What VUCA really means for you. Harvard Business Review, 92(1/2).

Brown, B. (2012). Daring greatly: How the courage to be vulnerable transforms the way we live, love, parent, and lead. Avery.

Clear, J. (2018). Atomic habits: An easy & proven way to build good habits & break bad ones. Avery.

Covey, S. R. (1989). The 7 habits of highly effective people: Powerful lessons in personal change. Free Press.

Damasio, A. R. (1994). Descartes' error: Emotion, reason, and the human brain. Penguin Books.

Darwin, C. (1859). On the origin of species by means of natural selection. John Murray.

Doidge, N. (2007). The brain that changes itself: Stories of personal triumph from the frontiers of brain science.Viking.

Dweck, C. S. (2006). Mindset: The new psychology of success. Random House.

Einstein, A. (1931). Strive not to be a success, but rather to be of value. Retrieved from public domain sources.

Ford, M. (2014). Neuroleadership: A journey through the brain for business leaders. Springer.

Goleman, D. (1995). Emotional intelligence: Why it can matter more than IQ. Bantam Books.

Grosser, C. (n.d.). Opportunities don't happen; you create them. Retrieved from public domain sources.

Jacobson, B. (2012). Managing multiple priorities: Leading a balanced life. Leadership Press.

Keller, H. (1903). Optimism: An essay. Crowell.

Kahneman, D. (2011). Thinking, fast and slow. Farrar, Straus and Giroux.

LeDoux, J. E. (2002). Synaptic self: How our brains become who we are. Viking.

Maxwell, J. C. (2013). The 15 invaluable laws of growth: Live them and reach your potential. Center Street.

Newberg, A., & Waldman, M. R. (2012). Words can change your brain: 12 conversation strategies to build trust, resolve conflict, and increase intimacy. Hudson Street Press.

Penn, W. (1693). Some fruits of solitude in reflections and maxims relating to the conduct of human life. Public domain.

Pert, C. (1999). Molecules of emotion: The science behind mind-body medicine. Scribner.

Roosevelt, F. D. (1933). First inaugural address. Retrieved from National Archives.

Stevenson, R. L. (1881). Virginibus Puerisque and other papers. Chatto and Windus.

Swindoll, C. R. (1982). Strengthening your grip: How to be grounded in a chaotic world. W Publishing Group.

Thoreau, H. D. (1854). Walden; or, Life in the woods. Ticknor and Fields.

Twain, M. (n.d.). The secret of getting ahead is getting started. Retrieved from public domain sources.

Tyger, F. (n.d.). Ambition is enthusiasm with a purpose. Retrieved from public domain sources.

Ziglar, Z. (2009). Born to win: Find your success code. Thomas Nelson.

PART 11: LIVING A FULFILLED AND PURPOSEFUL LIFE

Arden, J. B. (2010). Rewire your brain: Think your way to a better life. Wiley.

Broadwell, M. M. (1969). Teaching for learning. The Gospel Guardian, 20(39), 1–3.

Clear, J. (2018). Atomic habits: An easy & proven way to build good habits & break bad ones. Penguin Books.

Covey, S. R. (1989). The 7 habits of highly effective people: Powerful lessons in personal change. Free Press.

Doidge, N. (2007). The brain that changes itself: Stories of personal triumph from the frontiers of brain science.Penguin Books.

Dweck, C. S. (2006). Mindset: The new psychology of success. Random House.

Einstein, A. (n.d.). Try not to become a person of success, but rather a person of value. Retrieved from public domain sources.

Feather, W. (n.d.). Plenty of people miss their share of happiness, not because they never found it, but because they didn't stop to enjoy it. Retrieved from public domain sources.

Goleman, D. (1995). Emotional intelligence: Why it can matter more than IQ. Bantam Books.

Gordon, E. (2015). The brain revolution. Self-published.

Howard, M. (2020). Mindfield. Self-published.

Jones, N. (2020). Success from the inside out: Power to rise from the past to a fulfilling future. Zondervan.

Kübler-Ross, E. (1969). On death and dying: What the dying have to teach doctors, nurses, clergy, and their own families. Scribner.

Maraboli, S. (2014). Life, the truth, and being free. Better Today Publishing.

Newberg, A., & Waldman, M. R. (2012). Words can change your brain: 12 conversation strategies to build trust, resolve conflict, and increase intimacy. Hudson Street Press.

Rankin, L. (2013). Mind over medicine: Scientific proof that you can heal yourself. Hay House, Inc.

Robson, D. (2022). The expectation effect: How your mindset can transform your life. Henry Holt & Company.

Rohn, J. (1995). Your life does not get better by chance; it gets better by change. Retrieved from public domain sources.

Siegel, D. J. (2012). The developing mind: How relationships and the brain interact to shape who we are. The Guilford Press.

Tagore, R. (1913). Gitanjali. Macmillan.

Tracy, B. (2010). The power of self-discipline: No excuses! Vanguard Press.

Aesop. (n.d.). No act of kindness, no matter how small, is ever wasted. Retrieved from public domain sources.

Camus, A. (1951). The rebel: An essay on man in revolt. Knopf.

Cohen, L. (1990). Act the way you'd like to be, and soon you'll be the way you act. Retrieved from public domain sources.

Charter, S. (n.d.). Life is about timing. The unreachable becomes reachable, the unavailable becomes available, the unattainable becomes attainable. Retrieved from public domain sources.

PART 12: REFLECT, RECHARGE, AND MOVE FORWARD

Arden, J. B. (2010). Rewire your brain: Think your way to a better life. Wiley.

Buscaglia, L. (1987). Living, loving, and learning. Ballantine Books.

Covey, S. R. (1989). The 7 habits of highly effective people: Powerful lessons in personal change. Simon & Schuster.

Disraeli, B. (n.d.). Never apologize for showing feeling. When you do so, you apologize for the truth. Retrieved from public domain sources.

Dweck, C. S. (2006). Mindset: The new psychology of success. Ballantine Books.

Franklin, B. (n.d.). He that is good for making excuses is seldom good for anything else. Retrieved from public domain sources.

Goleman, D. (1995). Emotional intelligence: Why it can matter more than IQ. Bantam Books.

Hill, N. (1937). Think and grow rich. The Ralston Society.

Holland, J. G. (n.d.). Calmness is the cradle of power. Retrieved from public domain sources.

Jordan, R. (1990). The eye of the world. Tor Books.

Marine, J. J. (n.d.). Challenges are what make life interesting and overcoming them is what makes life meaningful. Retrieved from public domain sources.

Newberg, A., & Waldman, M. R. (2012). Words can change your brain: 12 conversation strategies to build trust, resolve conflict, and increase intimacy. Hudson Street Press.

Ortberg, J. (2001). If you want to walk on water, you've got to get out of the boat. Zondervan.

Ricotti, S. (2011). Unsinkable: How to bounce back quickly when life knocks you down. Penguin Random House.

Roosevelt, E. (1960). You learn by living: Eleven keys for a more fulfilling life. Harper & Brothers.

Smuts, J. C. (1926). Holism and evolution. Macmillan.

Tagore, R. (1916). Stray birds. Macmillan and Co.

Walsch, N. D. (1995). Conversations with God: An uncommon dialogue, Book 1. G.P. Putnam's Sons.

Williamson, M. (1992). A return to love: Reflections on the principles of "A course in miracles". HarperOne.

Zinn, H. (1980). A people's history of the United States. Harper & Row.

FURTHER READING OR RESOURCES

IF-THEN Statements Examples

IF-THEN Statements for Corporate Professionals

- **If** I Feel Undervalued at Work

Then: "I will remind myself of my achievements and strengths and schedule a meeting with my supervisor to discuss my contributions and career goals."

- **If** I Am Overwhelmed with My Workload

Then: "I will take a 5-minute break to breathe deeply, prioritise my tasks, and delegate or ask for support if needed."

- **If** I Am Anxious About a Presentation or Meeting

Then: "I will practice power poses, recite a scripture for confidence (e.g., Philippians 4:13), and visualise a successful outcome."

IF-THEN Statements for Entrepreneurs

- **If** I Face a Business Setback or Failure

Then: "I will take a moment to acknowledge my feelings, reflect on the lesson learned, and refocus on my vision with a specific next step to move forward."

- **If** I Feel Overwhelmed by Business Decisions

Then: "I will pause, pray for wisdom (James 1:5), and break the decision into smaller, manageable steps to tackle one at a time."

- **If** I Feel Like I'm Not Making Progress

Then: "I will review my goals, celebrate small wins, and adjust my strategy if necessary, seeking mentorship or support if needed."

IF-THEN Statements for Those Balancing Multiple Roles

- **If** I Am Feeling Burned Out or Exhausted

Then: "I will schedule 'me time' for self-care, even if it's just 15 minutes, and remind myself that rest is essential for sustained success."

- **If** I Am Struggling to Balance Work and Family Life

Then: "I will set clear boundaries, communicate my needs to family and colleagues, and allow myself to ask for help without guilt."

- **If** I Start Comparing Myself to Others

Then: "I will redirect my focus to my unique journey and recite affirmations reminding me of my purpose and the specific path God has for me."

444

If-Then Statements for Personal Growth and Leadership

- **If** I Feel Insecure About My Leadership Abilities
Then: "I will remind myself of a past success where I led effectively, seek constructive feedback, and commit to learning and growing as a leader."

- **If** I Am Criticised or Receive Negative Feedback
Then: "I will take a deep breath, listen without defensiveness, and use this as an opportunity to grow, reflecting on how I can improve constructively."

- **If** I Doubt My Ability to Achieve My Goals
Then: "I will revisit my action plan, break down my goals into smaller, actionable steps, and remind myself of God's promise to guide me (Proverbs 3:5-6)."

FREE EBook: Divine & Brain Insights: A Christian Female Leader's Guide

Unlock the secrets to peak performance with our new eBook, "Divine & Brain Insights: A Christian Female Leader's Guide"

Achieve Extraordinary Results with "Divine & Brain Insights" 

Inside, You'll Discover:

> **Master Decision-Making:** Strategies to make swift, confident choices that lead to extraordinary results.

> **Manage Stress & Anxiety:** Biblically aligned and neuroscience-backed techniques to keep your mind clear and focused under pressure.

> **Boost Emotional Resilience:** Balance emotional intelligence with critical thinking for impactful leadership.

> **Navigate Career Progression:** Use scriptural wisdom and scientific insights to advance your career or business strategically.

> **Overcome Cognitive Biases:** Identify and mitigate biases to ensure rational, balanced decisions.

Transform your leadership and business approach with insights that drive high performance.

Get your copy today at - https://www.maureenchiana.uk/christianfemaleguide

MINDSIGHT WOMEN'S NETWORK (MWN)
A Space to Grow and Thrive

The Mindsight Women's Network (MWN) is more than just a community—it's a movement for faith-filled women who are ready to grow, lead, and live with purpose. Designed to empower and equip women, MWN offers a unique space where science and scripture meet to inspire transformation.

Why Join MWN?

MWN is for women who are ready to:

- Deepen their faith while growing emotionally and intellectually.

- Build meaningful connections with like-minded women who uplift and inspire.

- Learn practical tools for navigating life's challenges and thriving in every season.

- Pursue their calling with boldness and confidence.

What You'll Gain:

- Access to enriching resources like workshops, devotionals, and the Self-Discovery Toolkit.

- Insightful teachings that blend neuroscience, emotional intelligence, and scripture.

- Opportunities to connect, learn, and grow alongside a supportive community.

- Encouragement to step into the fullness of your God-given potential.

At MWN, we believe every woman is uniquely called to impact her world. This network is a place to be equipped, inspired, and supported as you live out your faith and purpose.

Take the next step in your journey. Join the Mindsight Women's Network (MWN) and discover a community that will empower you to thrive.

Learn more at The Mindsight Academy. ⊕ www.themindsightacademy.com

The Mindsight Academy (TMA) is where neuroscience and emotional intelligence (EQ) come together to drive growth, leadership, and transformation. We believe that lasting success begins with understanding how your brain works and using that knowledge to align your actions with your goals and values. Our mission is to empower individuals with tools rooted in brain science and EQ to create meaningful, impactful lives.

What We Offer

At TMA, we are dedicated to helping you rewire your thinking, grow your emotional intelligence, and unlock your potential. *Our programs include:*

- **NeuroCoaching:** Personalized sessions designed to help you break through mental barriers, build resilience, and rewire your brain for success. Learn how to shift limiting beliefs and create a mindset that supports your dreams.

- **Leadership Training:** Tailored programs for leaders, entrepreneurs, and professionals. These trainings focus on building EQ-driven leadership skills, fostering strong relationships, and navigating challenges with confidence.

- **Personal Development Resources:** From interactive workshops to transformative workbooks and courses, we provide practical tools to help you thrive in every area of your life.

- **Faith-Integrated Growth:** TMA combines the science of the mind with faith-based insights, guiding you to live a life of purpose and balance that reflects your core values.

Why Choose TMA?

At TMA, transformation is more than just a destination—it's an ongoing journey. Through the principles of neuroscience and neuroplasticity, we teach you how to rewire your brain to adapt, grow, and overcome obstacles. Combined with the power of EQ, these tools help you build stronger relationships, make better decisions, and lead with empathy.

We believe that true transformation happens when the mind, body, and spirit are aligned. Our approach merges cutting-edge science with emotional awareness to equip you with the strategies needed to excel in life, work, and leadership.

Your journey starts here. Explore our programs and begin your transformation at The Mindsight Academy.

Visit The Mindsight Academy to learn more.

🌐 www.themindsightacademy.com

www.ingramcontent.com/pod-product-compliance
Lightning Source LLC
Chambersburg PA
CBHW021219060726
47590CB00005B/1566